48198

A 'Favourit' Game

The grand match at Neath in 1868 when the United South of England XI, including Dr W. G. Grace, played a XXII of Cadoxton and District. Note the large attendance and the marquees with their sundry attractions.

A 'Favourit' Game

Cricket in south Wales before 1914

ANDREW HIGNELL

UNIVERSITY OF WALES PRESS
CARDIFF
1992

British Library Cataloguing in Publication Data

A catalogue record for this book is available from the British Library

Jacket design by Design Principle, Cardiff
Typeset in Wales by Megaron, Cardiff
Printed and bound in England by Biddles Ltd, Guildford

Preface

THE SEEDS of this history of cricket in south Wales were sown whilst I was compiling the Centenary History of Glamorgan during the autumn and winter of 1987/88. It soon became clear that nothing had been written tracing the development of the game in the region. Many individual club histories were available, but nothing existed on a collective level, despite the fact that many Welsh newspapers from the second half of the nineteenth century contained a multitude of reports on games, both in and outside the region.

Cricket was well established by the time that Glamorgan CCC was established in 1888, and many club sides had been flourishing for a number of decades. There had even been talk of forming a county side back in 1854. Yet the events of these early years of Welsh cricket have not attracted serious attention and have never been analysed outside the confines of club histories. This is in marked contrast to the later development of rugby during the 1870s and 1880s, with a wealth of books and articles devoted to the growth of the winter game. Ironically, many rugby clubs grew from cricket clubs whose members wanted to play something during the winter.

From a purely historical point of view, the development of cricket in south Wales deserves attention and this book will help to fill the void. However, the chapters which follow do not concentrate solely on a historical framework, but include a geographical dimension in the analysis of the game's development. There are many benefits to be gained from using concepts from the social, economic and industrial spheres of geography, and it is hoped that the ideas which follow will also add to the growing discipline of sports geography. With this in mind, the book includes maps showing the spatial dimension of the changes which took place. Figures 8, 9 and 20, with the place-names annotated on the illustrations, will assist those readers not familiar with south Wales, and provide an even clearer picture of the developments which occurred.

My aim has been to focus attention on the important people, places and events in cricket's development in south Wales during the late eighteenth and the nineteenth century, and to set them briefly against the more recent developments of the twentieth century. During the time period of this study, 1783–1914, society and life in south Wales underwent phenomenal changes, and the area changed from a rural, agrarian one to one with an urban, industrial character. Indeed, it is impossible to divorce the development of the game from the wider changes in society, and it is this intriguing interrelationship between sport and society which provides the backdrop on which the history of the game has been painted. The evidence is at times rather fragmentary or tucked away in peculiar or obscure corners, but hopefully a clear picture emerges.

Andrew Hignell   Post Hill, Tiverton
                                                     September 1992

Contents

Illustrations and Figures

Acknowledgements

QUITE NATURALLY, a book of this nature would not have been possible without the help of many people and what follows is as much the culmination of their research as it is my own. In particular, David Smith has been a mine of information about the South Wales CC and many other aspects of the game, especially at school level during the last century. Bob Harragan provided a mass of detail on the matches before 1860 and allowed me to delve through his copious notes on the game's development in the Llanelli area and south-west Wales. Similarly, Bob Mole gave me a wealth of information on early cricket in the Newport area and pointed me in the right direction through the many references in the *Monmouthshire Merlin* and *The Star of Gwent*. Duncan Pierce also provided details of Newport Athletic Club and matches in the Monmouthshire area, whilst Brian Lile helped with information on cricket in the Swansea area, especially at Killay House. A number of archivists and librarians gave me help during my many visits to south Wales. In particular, Bryn Jones and the staff in the Local Studies Department at Cardiff Central Library never failed to track down a dusty newspaper file in the bowels of the new library, whilst John Vivian Hughes of Swansea Library kindly allowed use of their computerized catalogue of *The Cambrian*. John Davies of Dyfed Record Office helped with the Cwmgwili and Carmarthenshire CCC records, whilst Mrs M. E. Richards of the Badminton Estate provided access to the Duke of Beaufort's records. Mrs Joyce Havard of Neath Borough Council and Neath Antiquarian Society gave me details of early matches at The Gnoll and kind permission to use the excellent print of the 1868 match against the United South of England as a frontispiece. Mike Glenn, the curator of the South Wales Police Museum provided information on Charles Napier, and Frank Olding, the curator of Abergavenny Museum, helped locate many early records in the Abergavenny area. Edward Pinsent of Church House provided biographical details on the many vicars and cricketing clerics, whilst Anthony Bosanquet, Keith Kissack and Mrs Jean Hancock of the Raglan Local History Group provided information on the gentry of Monmouthshire. In addition, I am grateful for the information provided by the archivists at the Glamorgan, Gloucestershire and Gwent Record Offices, and the librarians at Monmouth Museum, Brecknock Museum, Jesus College, Oxford, Brasenose College, Oxford, Eton College, Sherborne School, Rugby School, Westminster School, Shrewsbury School, and the Royal Military Academy at

Woolwich and Sandhurst. Stephen Green, the curator of the MCC Library, and Peter Wynne-Thomas of the Association of Cricket Statisticians, confirmed a number of facts and important dates connected with English cricket, whilst the following officials of Welsh cricket clubs also gave details on the history of their clubs – Stuart Challenger of Abertillery CC; David Williams of Pembroke CC; John Davies of Dafen CC; Steve Lewis of Cimla CC; John Bounds of Barry Athletic CC; Richard Baxter of Cardiff YMCA; Dil Volk of Pontypridd CC; Eric Lewis of Llangennech CC; Gwyn Gratton of Neath CC; and Hugh Morgan of Morriston CC. This work never aimed at an encyclopaedic coverage, so several clubs have not been included in detail. My apologies for excluding those individuals or events which the clubs concerned feel worthy of deserving a mention, and I sincerely hope those whom I have omitted will receive due attention in any follow-up surveys.

I am grateful to Dr David Painting, the curator of the photographs in the possession of the Royal Institute of South Wales, for permission to use the excellent pictures of the Bancrofts (Plates 12 and 25). Dr A. Lloyd-Hughes of the Welsh Folk Museum also provided the photograph of the St Fagan's team in 1900 used as a cover illustration, as well as some splendid shots of late Victorian and early Edwardian matches which fully capture the evocative nature of the 'Golden Era' (Plates 15, 17, 19 and 20). My thanks also to Dyfed Record Office (Plate 1), Gwent Record Office (Plate 2), Keith Kissack (Plate 3), Mike Glenn of the South Wales Police Museum (Plate 4), Bob Mole (Plate 5), David Smith (Plates 6, 10 and 11), John Vivian Hughes (Plate 7), Gareth Hughes (Plate 8), Frank Olding (Plate 9), T. J. Witts (Plate 13), Clive Jones-Davies (Plate 14), Edward Parry (Plate 16), Dr K. A. Moseley of Monmouth School (Plate 18), Gwyn Gratton (Plates 21 and 24), and Mike Fatkin of Glamorgan CCC (Plates 22, 23 and 26). Hugh Morgan, Chris Brain and Howard Evans gave access to other photographs and illustrations which helped to bring the events and personalities back to life.

Finally, I am most grateful to Professor R. A. Griffiths of the Glamorgan County History Trust for generously providing a grant to help cover the research expenses and to John Jenkins and David Smith for reading the early drafts. Both made constructive comments and provided invaluable help throughout the compilation of this book. John Bale also made useful suggestions about the historical-geographical framework of this study and gave advice on other articles connected with sports geography. Susan Jenkins of the University of Wales Press was a constant source of advice and encouragement and, last, but by no means least, my thanks to my wife Debra for her support and tolerant understanding of my regular treks to south Wales.

1 / *Introduction*

'I have frequently heard you talk of cricket as a favourit game and that you would willingly make one of a sett at any time. The following gentlemen are prepared upon to enter into my list and are willing to meet any sett you can produce.'[1]

S
O WROTE a gentleman called Richard Jones to John Philipps of Cwmgwili in the summer of 1783. But whilst his letter is the first record of a cricket match in south Wales, it has, like so many artefacts of early cricket, lain collecting dust, so that many people, quite mistakenly, consider the formation of Glamorgan County Cricket Club in 1888 and its entry into the minor county championship in 1897 and the first-class game in 1921 as the first important set of dates in the history of cricket in south Wales. This is not the case, however; a host of important fixtures and cricketing events took place in the hundred years before the creation of a county side.

It is true though that an air of mystery has surrounded the early days of cricket in Wales, leading one writer to comment in 1877 that 'so little has been heard of cricket in the Principality that few believed it had ever had an existence there'.[2] More recently, Jack Williams has written how 'the shortage of localized studies makes it difficult to estimate when cricket playing reached its highest point in Wales, although newspaper reports of cricket, admittedly a far from infallible guide indicate that in Swansea, probably more than 20 sides were playing regularly in 1900'.[3] Such statements, together with the apparent absence of reliable data, have brought about the popular misconception that south Wales was a cricketing desert before and during the nineteenth century. Even one of the leading broadcasters on the game recently stated that 'with an almost total absence of Welsh cricket literature . . . any history of Welsh club cricket must of necessity lack the colour of early events and personalities'.[4]

It is surprising on two counts that the early days of Welsh cricket have never been examined in detail by either sporting or academic historians. Firstly, despite Williams's comments above, a wealth of information does exist. There are, in fact, extensive primary data sources, including newspaper reports of games and important matches, estate records, letters outlining how early matches were arranged, and even diaries kept by leading personalities. In addition, there are extremely useful secondary sources with many club histories compiled during the past thirty years shedding light on cricket during the nineteenth century. A few problems occur with some of this data (see Appendix A), but these should not detract from their analysis, and providing one moves carefully through all the primary and secondary sources, a clear picture emerges of the extent of cricket and its organization in the region long before Glamorgan CCC was formed. Secondly, this neglect is surprising because cricket played a fundamental role in both the social and recreational history of south Wales. This has already been highlighted by Gareth Williams who stated that 'the history of Glamorgan cricket as a recreation and a spectator sport predates the industrial changes which so transformed football and boxing. Rugby clubs like Cardiff and Swansea came into existence to perpetuate the companionship of a summer recreation into the winter months'.[5]

The purpose of this book is quite simply to fill this void and to analyse the game's evolution in south Wales during the eighteenth and nineteenth centuries. But it is not going to be a mere assemblage of scores and reports. The statistical approach has several pitfalls. W. F. Mandle has observed how 'the history of sport has for too long consisted of the collection of results, anecdotes and reminiscences. Sports, and those who played them and organised them, are part of society and deserve the historians attention'.[6] Christopher Brookes extended Mandle's argument and applied it to cricket, criticizing the futility of assembling a mere chronological order of cricket's origins in the absence of detailed facts. He believed:

> The questions posed by cricket's evolution from a folk-game to a modern sport cannot be brought nearer solution until a fresh approach to the subject is adopted. If the study of the game is to embody more than a collection of dates, hearsay, and a few witty anecdotes, its history has to be related to the history of the society in which it was nurtured. Cricket's evolution was not an isolated phenomenon, but part of a complex process in the course of which a whole range of games and pastimes emerged and which was in itself closely related to basic changes in the structure of English society.[7]

Likewise the game's development in south Wales must be considered in the context of the important economic and social changes which occurred in the region. In fact, it would be very difficult to ignore the socio-economic context as cricket like other sports, grew hand in hand with the economy of the region.

I have chosen a geographically-based conceptual framework in order to piece together the growth of cricket in terms of these socio-economic changes. A geographical focus provides a number of benefits to an analysis of the way sports develop. As John Bale has pointed out 'by using the tools of analysis and the conceptual framework of a geographer, new and hitherto unperceived insights on sports may be obtained and new patterns exhumed which besides being of intrinsic interest, are highly relevant to an understanding of the significance of sport in society'.[8]

It was R. J. Rooney who pioneered the geographical study of sports history, arguing that there is a sports geography of every region which, if analysed through a topical approach, reveals both a temporal evolution and spatial spread.[9] His framework in Figure 1 embraces the concept of diffusion which has itself received much attention from mainstream geographers, besides those interested in sports geography. The leading worker in this field is Torsten Hagerstrand, who analysed the diffusion of new ideas and methods in Swedish agriculture.[10] Hagerstrand defined an innovation as the successful introduction of ideas or artefacts, which are perceived as new, into the existing social system. He believed that innovations show distinctive patterns of adoption over both time and space, rather than a random or haphazard distribution. When plotted as a frequency curve, the cumulative number of adopters over time approximates to a S-shaped function, as shown in Figure 2.

At first, the number of adopters is small, but over time, there is a steady increase, before reaching a ceiling level as the majority of the population accept the innovation. Using his data on Swedish agriculture in the 1920s and 1930s, Hagerstrand concluded that this pattern was the result of the following three effects:

1. A *neighbourhood effect*, with contagious diffusion so that the greater the distance from an area of adoption the smaller the amount of spread. People close to the area of adoption were more likely to know about the innovation because the spread of information took place by private rather than public means, that is word of mouth.

2. A *barrier effect*, restricting the spread of ideas, especially in the early stages of diffusion. Although people may have heard about an innovation, they may be reluctant to adopt it because of economic restraints such as the lack of capital or the means to introduce new ideas. Other barriers may also restrict diffusion including psychological ones such as not trusting the informant, or topographical ones including hills or marshes so that

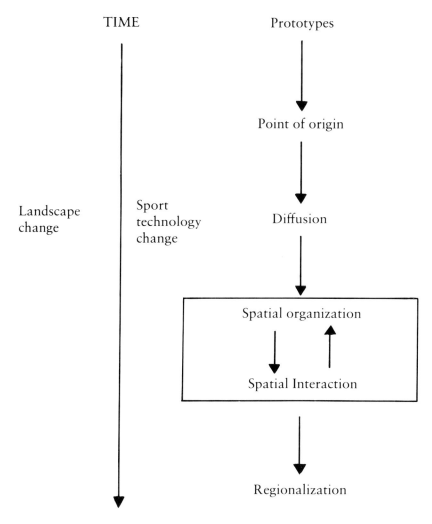

TIME

Prototypes

Landscape change

Sport technology change

Point of origin

Diffusion

Spatial organization

Spatial Interaction

Regionalization

Figure 1. Rooney's conceptual framework for the study of sports geography

areas are isolated and an integrated transport network cannot develop.

3. *A hierarchical effect*, with diffusion spreading from the top of the hierarchy (most important or largest) to the bottom (least important or smallest). In Hagerstrand's fieldwork, it was the rich farmers who introduced new ideas or methods, simply because they could afford to take the risks, leaving the poorest farmers to be the last adopters.

In terms of a spatial process, the most appealing aspects of Hagerstrand's work for this survey of the spread of cricket are firstly that

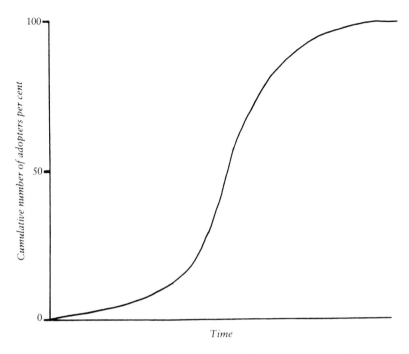

Figure 2. Hagerstrand's cumulative frequency curve for
innovation diffusion over time

diffusion occurs from a specific point, or culture hearth, which itself has
certain benefits or advantages.[11] Secondly, the concept of hierarchical
diffusion suggests that innovations trickle down from the richest people
at the top of the social ladder to those lower down with less money.
Diffusion might also take place down the urban hierarchy with larger
settlements much more likely than smaller ones to adopt innovations or
new sports. Using the formation of clubs (see Appendix C) and the
playing of fixtures as indicators of diffusion, one aim of this study is to see
whether the pattern of adoption of cricket in south Wales is in keeping
with Hagerstrand's three concepts, thus enabling the identification of the
game's growth points.

Another basic aim of this analysis is to investigate whether or not
south Wales followed the same evolutionary pattern in cricketing terms
to that proposed by Brookes.[12] He identified five distinctive stages in the
growth of the game in England. Some cricket historians may quibble
with his dates, but few would argue with the following sequential stages:

1. The age of the folk-game (pre-1660).
2. The era of the aristocracy and gentry (*c*.1660–1830).

3. The end of patronage and the era of the professional elevens (*c*.1830–70).

4. The apogee of amateurism (*c*.1870–1945).

5. The business years (post 1945).

Comparisons with the English pattern are important, because as Hugh Morgan succinctly observed in his history of the Morriston club 'in many ways the introduction of cricket into Wales may be viewed as but one of the aspects of the gradual process of Anglicization of the Principality that took place in the eighteenth and nineteenth centuries. The Welsh establishment has never been slow to ape its English counterparts. If cricket in England was the sport to indulge in then the Welsh gentry were quick to follow in their English cousins' footsteps'.[13] If south Wales did indeed follow this pattern, then it is clear that this study must also identify the leading agents of diffusion and the channels through which the game expanded after its first appearance in the region. It is therefore time to look back and attempt to discover the origins of the game in south Wales.

Despite such positive aims, one has no option but to start in a rather negative way, because there is no known date of when the game was first played. As Desmond Eager has stated 'cricket historians since the early nineteenth century have sought in vain to date the birth of cricket, but it will remain for ever shrouded in mystery'.[14] Indeed, there is a firm belief that no one actually invented cricket, but that it simply evolved from other ball games. This point of view was expressed by Harry Altham and Jim Swanton who wrote 'cricket was not born, it just grew'.[15] An investigation into the early days of cricket therefore requires consideration of other games which may have shown little, if any, linkage to cricket. One of these early ball games from which writers believe English cricket may have evolved is club-ball. According to F. S. Ashley-Cooper this involved striking a ball with a curved club, with the ball bowled along the ground at a wooden gate or wicket with two uprights, and is the predecessor of other games including lacrosse, golf, hockey and shinty.[16]

Other writers refer back to wardrobe accounts, written in Latin, belonging to Edward I, dated 1299–1300 when an entry mentions Prince Edward, the King's son 'playing creag'. In his *Cricket: A History of its Growth and Development Throughout the World*, Rowland Bowen considered this to be short for 'creaget', an alternative spelling of cricket.[17] His assertions have though been queried, and we have to wait until 1611 for the earliest precise reference to both cricket and the nature of the game. It appeared in Randle Cotgrave's *Dictionarie of the French and English Tongues*, with the word 'crosse' being defined as 'a cricket staff or the crooked staff wherewith boyes play at cricket', and 'crosser' meaning 'to play at cricket'.[18] Without becoming diverted into an etymological wrangle, Cotgrave's definition alluded to how the word cricket may have evolved, with the description of 'a cricket staff or the crooked staff' suggesting that it was derived from 'crooked' or the shape of the implements used for club-ball.

In 1622 we find the first reference to a cricket bat, in 1658 a cricket ball, and in 1695 the earliest mention of a wicket.[19] Yet despite the presence of these three basic implements, other aspects of the early form of cricket are rather hazy. For instance, there was no accepted number for a team, with single-wicket games and matches involving only four players on a side. This might not be too surprising because, as Eric Midwinter shows, there was likely to have been an infinite variety in the rules governing these early games and 'what we might have found across Britain was not several discrete games, but, more probably, thousands of games, each slightly different from the one in the next valley or village. It might be more truthful to say there was one amorphous game, multifarious in its infinite variety'.[20]

Regardless of which theory one accepts as the ancestor of cricket, or even which is the earliest reference to the English game, historians have shown how the earliest centres, or culture hearth, of the game in England was south-east of a line from The Wash to The Isle of Wight, with major games being played in The Weald of Kent and Sussex in the late seventeenth century. This was the time when the game, according to Harry Altham, 'developed from the pastime of boys, or at best, of the yeomen of the exclusive Weald into one of the favourite recreations of the fashionable world'.[21] Other writers believe the game was even more widespread – C. J. Robb suggested that cricket was played in Ireland at the time of Oliver Cromwell,[22] whilst Rowland Bowen argued that the game originated in areas with a Celtic population and that this blood-group was widely distributed. Doubt has been placed on both Robb's and Bowen's theories, and most cricket historians agree that south-east England was the game's 'culture hearth' in the seventeenth century.[23]

The eighteenth century saw many fundamental changes in the location and organization of the game. There is a reference in 1709 to what many consider to be the first county match on record in England between Kent and Surrey at Dartford.[24] By 1729 the game had spread west to Gloucestershire, but the new growth areas were Hampshire and Sussex, especially Hambledon and Broadhalfpenny Down, where between 1750 and 1787 a host of changes took place, with the introduction of a third stump and the refinement of batting and bowling techniques.[25] As a result of this, cricket acquired a more recognizable and 'modern' form by the time the Marylebone Cricket Club was established in 1787.

This brief review of Christopher Brookes's first two stages in the development of English cricket assists this study of the game's origin in south Wales because there are many similarities in the game's evolution. If club-ball was the ancestor of cricket in England, its Celtic form, *bando*, may well have assumed the same role in south Wales. *Bando* involved a ball being hit along the ground by teams of players with curved clubs, and bore a close resemblance to shinty. Gareth Williams showed that *bando* was the first mass spectator sport of not only Glamorgan, but also Wales, during the late eighteenth and early nineteenth century. The centres of the game were the settlements on the coastal plain of south Wales, including Baglan, Aberavon, Margam and Pyle, with matches taking place on the sandy beaches. There was intense rivalry between the competing teams, and their spectators, many of whom found *bando* a popular medium for gambling. This had an important consequence because the laying of wagers demanded an agreed format, and *bando* was a typical pre-Industrial game in that it was at times apparently haphazard with quite flexible rules.[26]

A game of *bando* normally involved between twenty and thirty players over a playing area of about 200 yards, with goals ten yards wide. This format means that one cannot base an argument on *bando* being the sole origin of cricket in south Wales, because there are important cricketing skills missing. To find these we have to consider other early Welsh ball games, including *cnapan*, a popular recreation in west Wales in the seventeenth century.[27] *Cnapan* was played on Sundays or Holy Days, and took a variety of forms. One quite violent type involved teams on foot, and on horses, fighting with cudgels, up to three feet long, for the possession of a small wooden ball. A more placid variant involved throwing the ball the furthest distance, and the physical skills which people learnt from this game would have been extremely useful in early cricket.

There might be generic links with the game of trap-cat, which innkeeper John Taylor wrote about during his travels through Wales in 1652. Trap-cat, or tip-cat, was played elsewhere in Britain and took several forms, but the basic method, and the one which Taylor saw, involved a large ring being marked out on the ground, at the centre of which was a striker with a club, possibly a curved weapon from club-ball, surrounded by an opposition team. The striker had to hit a small piece of wood, known as a 'cat' out of the ring. If he failed he was out and, like American baseball, another striker took his place. A variant involved four, six or eight holes, marked out inside the ring and, similar to baseball again, strikers ran between these 'popping holes' after hitting the 'cat'. But the striker could be caught by the opposition or run out as he dashed between these popping holes; in short, it was a game with a ball and bat, and involved catches, boundaries and run outs, which are fundamental elements of cricket.[28]

During his seventeenth-century travels, Taylor observed this game of tip-cat being actively played in several churchyards, and to his horror on Sundays as well. But as Hilarie Waddington showed, a variety of games were played in Welsh churchyards because they provided ample space and were not surrounded by walls, or other buildings, which could hamper play.[29] Early forms of cricket could therefore have begun in Welsh churchyards by the mid-eighteenth century. But if this was the case, a few barriers, albeit not in the physical sense, started to appear during the late eighteenth and early nineteenth century, with a change in public attitude towards these games in churchyards and playing on Sundays, following the Methodist Revival and the spread of Nonconformity.

The growth of Nonconformity strengthened the belief that the playing of any games, even on weekdays, was vain and inconsistent with the seriousness of life. Many rural games suffered because they had previously taken place on Saints' Days or Sundays, but with Non-conformity, the playing on the former was considered to bring ill fortune, whilst the latter was a day of rest, and it was therefore sinful to play games on God's Day. Consequently, the playing of games in churchyards was frowned upon, especially on Sundays, and at Crickhowell in 1744 four young men were each fined twenty shillings 'for playing ball on the Lord's Day'.[30] Many believed that there would be a greater penance to be served after death and on the walls of the church at Llanfair Discoed in Caer-went, the following inscription was discovered:

> Whoever hear on Sunday
> will practis playing at ball.
> It may be before Monday
> The Devil will have you all.[32]

But this religious disapproval was not constant across south Wales and Nonconformity failed to gain even a foothold in some areas. This meant that 'playing at ball' continued to occur in the churchyards of the region during the eighteenth and nineteenth centuries. Hilarie Waddington showed how a form of fives became the most popular churchyard game, in which the ball was struck by hand, or with a club, up against the wall of the church.[32] Yet the following story dating back to the 1820s by a woman from Llanelli shows that these games were increasingly acquiring a cricketing format. Her recollections included one:

when they used to play ball in the parish churchyard. One day when Mr Skewen, Mr Goring Thomas and others were at the Old Llanelly House, the game of ball was proceeding and Capt Griffiths struck it right through one of the windows, and it fell on the very table where the gentlemen were seated.[33]

She continued to reminisce that the horror-stricken Capt. Griffiths was summoned to Llanelly House, and fearing a telling off, was surprised to be rewarded with a half-crown for his athletic efforts. What is certainly more interesting is to consider the direction of this mighty blow. Llanelly House was situated opposite the church, so he was hitting with great force away from the church, rather than towards it as in fives. The power of his stroke could hardly have been by hand alone, so Capt. Griffiths must have been using a bat or club, making it even more likely that he was playing a form of cricket rather than fives.

Therefore, the first stage of the game's evolution was reached by the eighteenth century with early forms of cricket being played in the churchyards and the open spaces close to these communities. We do not know whether the game Capt. Griffiths was playing evolved from club-ball, *bando* or tip-cat, or a combination of all three, but we do know that in seventeenth- and eighteenth-century England, many early games of cricket also took place in churchyards. T. J. McCann and P. M. Wilkinson have even shown how six parishioners at Boxgrove, Sussex were prosecuted for playing the game in the churchyard in 1622.[34] These folk-games – club-ball, *bando*, tip-cat and 'playing at ball' – all formed part of the traditional cultural and recreational heritage of south Wales, and their form and rules were passed between generations by word of mouth, rather than being written down. The net result is an absence of written evidence, making it impossible to prove beyond any shadow of doubt that these games evolved into cricket and were staged in churchyards, but there were too many parallels with the game's development in south-east England for them to be purely coincidental.

Even if one accepts the hypothesis that the game developed from such rustic sports or churchyard ball games, there is still one major problem to be overcome to allow a smooth transition into the next stage in the game's evolution and its emergence as a popular team game. The difficulties revolve around the fact that the population of the region during the eighteenth and nineteenth centuries was still predominantly rural, rather than urban, and displayed the same dispersed characteristics as those described by twelfth-century writers such as Giraldus Cambrensis. The chief stumbling block was that cricket in its competitive, or team, form requires at least half a dozen people, or two or more teams. Therefore, participation in these early forms of cricket would have been somewhat limited to either practice with a few friends, or single-wicket matches in these isolated rural communities. But what happened when there were gatherings of the district community, such as at fairs, regular festivals or on market days at the nearby town or large village? To answer this question we have to briefly cross Offa's Dyke, where Gerald Howat also came to a similar conclusion about the importance of fairs, and found cricket in seventeenth-century Kent at fairs and on traditional holidays or meetings of hop farmers.[35] So if English cricket developed into a mass participation sport at these gatherings, then the same may well have happened in south Wales.

Gareth Williams has clearly illustrated the importance of fairs in the agrarian society of south Wales in the seventeenth and eighteenth centuries with a variety of games staged at these communal gatherings. 'The major recreational events of the year were the *mabsantau*, the wakes or revels, whose original purpose of celebrating the local saint had become the pretext for boisterous festivity of all kinds. They varied in length from a day to a week ... The *mabsant* and the *taplas haf* (summer dances) ... were the occasions of athletic contests that provided for all sorts of ball games, races and animal sports'.[36] If cricket, or whichever primitive form it took, was one of the churchyard ball games that were increasing in popularity, then it seems likely that during the eighteenth century organized contests or even team events were held at these festive gatherings and were one of the 'sort of ball games' mentioned by Williams.

However, the eighteenth century was the time when the Noncon-formists were frowning upon any form of organized games and even casual recreations. The spread of their ideas would have resulted in the decline of sports on feast days and the *mabsantau*. But it did not result in the complete decline of recreational pursuits, because the date and venue for these ball games, races and animals sports simply switched to the nearest regular gatherings, which in many cases were the market days in the neighbouring towns. They also survived because the games were increasingly being patronized by the landed gentry, and leaders of local society, who by the mid-nineteenth century in England had given cricket a popular image. The Llanelli example above, and the involvement of Capt. Griffiths shows this was also the case in south Wales. So if one moves away from the churchyards of south Wales to the region's market towns and locations where regular gatherings took place and also focuses attention on the leading figures in the social and political world, one finds the next stage in the evolution of the game, and competitive forms of cricket, with the first written record of the game in Wales, near the county town of Carmarthen in 1783.[37]

2 / *Cwmgwili and the Early Clubs*

C HRISTOPHER Brookes[1] showed how the main feature of English cricket's development during the eighteenth century was the increasing participation of the social élite. He traced how they played an influential role in the game's subsequent evolution both on and off the field, with the devising of rules and the establishment of clubs such as the Marylebone Cricket Club, which has become cricket's governing body. The same process of gentry involvement happened in south Wales, albeit at a slightly later time, with the organization of grand challenges and, later, the participation in the affairs of cricket clubs. But this second stage in the game's evolution in Wales was different from the English 'pattern' in the sense that there was no Welsh MCC, although several teams laid claim to being the premier side of south Wales.

The involvement of the landed gentlemen in Welsh cricket began in the eighteenth century, and included the earliest recorded match in Wales. It was announced as follows in the *Hereford Journal* in July 1783:

> A match to be played for 50 guineas a side on Monday, August 4th, on Court Henry Down near Cross Inn in the county of Carmarthen, between the Gentlemen of the East side of the Cothy and those of the West : to play 11 a side. To be on the ground at 10 o'clock in the forenoon. An ordinary upon the Down, near Black Moors Inn at 2 o'clock.[2]

The person responsible for organizing one of these teams of gentlemen was John George Philipps, a member of one of the leading families in west Wales. He lived at Cwmgwili, two miles to the north-east of Carmarthen, although he spent much of his life outside south Wales. Like so many of the Welsh gentry, Philipps had been educated in England, and it was at Westminster School, and subsequently Brasenose College, Oxford where he learnt the role of a gentleman and involvement with cricket. He also found his movement in high circles up in 'town' highly compatible with his legal and political career. The year 1783 was an important one for the 22-year-old J. G. Philipps, because he was appointed Carmarthen's mayor and was elected as MP for Carmarthen Borough, succeeding John Vaughan of Golden Grove, the other major 'house' in west Wales, some two miles from Llandeilo.[3] Vaughan's home at Golden Grove was a popular meeting place for the gentlemen, both young and old, of Carmarthenshire during the second half of the eighteenth century and it is likely that he also organized suitable recreation for his guests, including cricket, during their summer visits along the lines of what he had witnessed in London. There are no surviving records to prove Vaughan's involvement, but fortunately one of Philipps's letterbooks has survived to give remarkably clear evidence of the nature of the fixtures involving the gentlemen of the area. It contains the following letter from Richard Jones concerning the match in July 1783 near his home, Pantglas, at Cross Inn alongside the road between Carmarthen and Llandeilo:

> There is a very good place on the little common between me and Court Henry. We may fix the tent near and dine in it. Batts, balls, etc. shall be provided by me. If you accept the challenge it should be soon as the ground and weather are favourable. The dress, if you approve it, may be a swan-skin jacket with sleeves, edged with coloured ribband, which will not stand each person above 2s. 6d. or 3s. 6d. at the utmost, and be of use afterwards. If you should not be able to make up a sett we may meet and toss up for choice of partners, as I am sure there will be number sufficient to make up a double wicket.
> With my best compliments to Mrs Philipps.
> Yours sincerely,
> Richard Jones.[4]

Jones's terminology proves that Philipps was keen on the game, whilst 'a very good place' shows that this was not the first ever challenge in the area, because other games must have taken place both at Court Henry Down and other locations, possibly even Golden Grove or Cwmgwili, for Jones to know the wicket on the Down was 'very good'. So this 1783 challenge may have been just one of a number of encounters which Philipps organized and participated in whilst he was down from London, and he may even have had a return match with Jones's side at Cwmgwili. He could hardly have found a better way to spend his time and money by playing cricket with his social and political acquaintances, and mixing with them at the luncheons or dinners afterwards. In fact, Philipps certainly enjoyed the entertaining side of his lofty social position as he spent over £15,000 on 'entertainment' during his election campaign in 1803![5] It could be argued that Philipps was copying the patterns he had witnessed at first hand growing up in the London area, where the social leaders were actively involved in grand matches, and it is debatable whether the Welsh gentry, such as Philipps, would have organized lavish challenges without knowledge of what was happening in the south-east of England. What is known for certain was that many of the prominent members of west Wales society were keen to participate in cricket, because attached to Jones's letter was a list of his side for the fixture:

> 1st William Philipps, Court Henry; 2nd Rev Richard Lewis, Ynyswen; 3 Rev Thomas Williams, Llanegwad; 4 T. Evans, Aberlash; 5 William Evans, Aberlash; 6 John Evans of Aberlash; 7 Thos Howell of Kincoed; 8 Rd Ll Davies, Pibor; 9 Mr William Anthony; 10 David Stephenson; 11 Richard Jones.[6]

William Philipps was a leading barrister who may have been an acquaintance of both his namesake and Vaughan in London, whilst numbers 2 and 3 in the order were prominent clergymen. The rest of the side were local landowners and members of the squirearchy who found cricket enjoyable, and believed that it was in keeping with their social aspirations and position as members of the gentry to participate in these challenges during the summer and hunt or shoot in the winter. Indeed, Philip Jenkins noted that 'the basic division in society concerned leisure, for the "gentle" were those wealthy enough to have no need to perform manual labour'.[7]

However, the gentry were not the only ones to be playing cricket during the 1780s, because the young townsfolk of Swansea had formed a recreation club to partake in a variety of games on the sandbanks and beaches along the foreshore of Swansea Bay. Once again, the *Hereford Journal* contained a direct reference to the cricketing activities of the young men of Swansea, with the following notice appearing in the issue for May 1785:

> Swansea Cricket Meeting. Notice is hereby given that according to the last years resolutions, the sixth day of May next was fixed upon for the first meeting of the season. The gentlemen subscribers are desired to meet at the bathing house early to appoint a steward for that day and a treasurer for the season. Wickets as usual, to be pitched at 11 o'clock.[8]

Like Jones's letter, this notice clearly indicates that cricket was already in existence and popular in the town prior to 1785. The reference to the 'bathing house' suggests that games took place on the beach, similar to those in the Caribbean today, and lends further credence to a generic link with *bando* and other seashore games.

Further inland, games took place on common land and a letter in 1787 to Roger Jones, an attorney in Talgarth, refers to a match taking place 'on the common by Glasbury Bridge'. It also mentions the first dispute between players on record: 'the first meeting proved a peaceable one, but the second proved a bloody one. Capt. Walbeoff and Mr Aythene Lewis fought and there was a great effusion of blood on both sides.'[9] So although they involved a collection of gentlemen, these contests certainly aroused deep passions amongst the participants and provoked some rather ungentlemanly conduct.

These early matches also mixed recreation with socializing, as is clearly evident in the arrangements for the next match on record in 1792 between the Gentlemen of Monmouth and the Gentlemen of Grosmont. The challenge was for 'four casks of ale and a quantity of punch to be paid for by the losers and to be drunk on the ground after the game'.[10] There is no record of the outcome or what happened afterwards, but presumably everyone had a jolly time![11]

The early nineteenth century saw a steady rise in the number of clubs being formed and although records of their activities are sparse, the newspapers contained several clues to the growing popularity of cricket. For example, when a club was formed in the then small market town of Cardiff, with its population of a couple of thousand, a report stated that 'such is the rapid proficiency of the members that they bid fair to rival in a very short time any similar club in Glamorganshire'.[12]

The reputation of some clubs had grown sufficiently by the second decade of the nineteenth century for them to be able to accept challenges from other clubs and special fixtures were arranged. The *Bristol Gazette* for September 1815 recorded home and away contests between Usk and Pontypool, whilst in July 1820 *The Cambrian* reported a match between 'eleven select of the Pontypool club against eleven select of the Newport club'.[13] The same newspaper also covered an interesting match in 1819 between two teams near Crickhowell, and commented how:

> the lawn adjoining the hospitable mansion of Cwrt-y-gollen, the seat of Col Davies near Crickhowell, was rendered a scene of much festivity and attracted a numerous assemblage of beauty and fashion to witness a cricket-match played by the following gentlemen, viz the Rev C. Vaughan, Mr D. Williams, Col Darling, Mr Goldsmid, Mr Ormond, Capt Baillie, Mr Rane, the Rev G. Bevan and Mr Ousley against Lord W. Somerset, Capt Clifton, Capt Cator, Mr West, Mr G. Davies, Mr B. Davies, Mr Bury, Mr W. Bevan and Master Gabell. The contest terminated about four o'clock greatly in favour of the former party – particular praise is due to G. Davies and G. Ormond Esq for their indefatigable exertions.[14]

This match took place at the home of the Davies family. The Revd Richard Davies had recently inherited the estate on the death of Colonel Richard Davies in 1818, and he set about improving the house and grounds.[15] Revd Davies was educated at Worcester College, Oxford, and in keeping with his position as a gentleman, he keenly arranged games amongst his friends from the clerical and social world. This explained the participation of two local vicars and Lord William Somerset, alias the seventh son of the Fifth Duke of Beaufort, who was a key figure in the game's development during the 1820s and the emergence of a club at Raglan.

Lord William Somerset was vicar of Stoke Gifford, near Bristol, and also rector of several parishes in Monmouthshire, including Llangattwg and Crickhowell. He was also a keen cricketer, having learnt the game at Westminster School and Jesus College, Cambridge. The matches at Cwrt-y-Gollen probably coincided with his visits to see his Welsh estates, and included several of his clergymen friends and contacts from the West Country. It was probably as a result of these gatherings of gentlemen at Cwrt-y-Gollen and his visits to south Wales that his father, the Duke of Beaufort, established the Monmouthshire club at Raglan, on land behind the Beaufort Arms, which was part of the Duke's extensive estate in south Wales.[16]

Raglan was a convenient assembly point for the young gentlemen, lying at the junctions of the Chepstow to Abergavenny road, and the route from Gloucester and Monmouth to Usk and Caerleon. The market town's nodal position in the local transport network meant that the club had excellent accessibility and a wide catchment area, making it easy for gentlemen to assemble in the town and to practise and play on a regular basis. This wide sphere of influence was reflected in both the choice of the name 'Monmouthshire' and the large number of members, which by 1836 had topped the hundred mark.[17] As a result, the Monmouthshire club was able to stage a number of fixtures, with games in 1825 against Brecon at Raglan and Cwrt-y-Gollen, indicating its close links with the cricket-playing gentry assembled by the Davies family.[18] The Raglan club diversified its fixture list during the 1820s and, in August 1829, met the Barristers of the Oxford Circuit at Widemarsh Common near Hereford. These matches were the highlights of the season for the members of the Raglan club in both cricketing and social terms, with *The Cambrian* reporting after the 1829 match that 'after the amusements of the day were over, both parties partook of an elegant dinner given by those members of the Bar who played in the match'.[19]

These early fixtures were, however, the exception rather than the rule in the early nineteenth century, a time when travel over any distance was difficult, and sometimes hazardous. It took over two days to travel from London to Swansea, whilst a journey on *The Diligence* from Swansea to Bristol was also lengthy. The coach ran every Sunday, Wednesday and Friday from The Mackworth Arms in Swansea, leaving at 4 a.m. to head for Chepstow, where a ferry took passengers across the Severn to arrive in Bristol at eight the next morning.[20] Not only was it expensive in time, but a fare cost thirty shillings, and so most clubs contented themselves with matches amongst their members or devised single-wicket competitions. These challenges, such as the one held by Swansea CC in June 1831 between the married and single members, were the highlights of the season if no inter-club fixtures could be arranged, and often coincided with grand dinners.[21] Another example was the contest in August 1835 between the members of Abergavenny CC, with the losing side paying for dinner and wine afterwards at the Angel Inn. The Blues beat the Reds in a two-innings match by forty runs, and the *Monmouthshire Merlin* commented how the challenge 'excited a general interest in the town and was consequently attended by a numerous assemblage of respectable persons, who appeared to be highly gratified and interested by the success of their respective friends'.[22]

The contemporary newspapers therefore show that a number of clubs were in existence by the 1830s, although they were not like modernday cricket clubs with an extensive fixture list, and were more akin to golf or squash clubs where members came together on weekends or weekday evenings to play amongst themselves. Indeed, the newspapers contained more records of these practice sessions than actual matches.[23] Such sessions attracted large numbers of spectators, with a report on a gathering by members of Newport CC commenting that 'there was a good muster and the batting and bowling were first rate. The unrivalled band of the 75th was on the ground, and played several delightful pieces of music. A vast number of the elite of the neighbourhood honoured the club with their presence'.[24]

These early clubs represented a small, yet significant, step forward in the game's evolution in south Wales, yet in terms of the type of cricket being played, these practice sessions and single-wicket contests were only modified versions of the 'playing at ball' in the churchyards of the eighteenth century. Nevertheless, there were a number of subtle differences:

1. *The venue* – no longer in churchyards, but at a variety of sites including the lawns of mansions, land next to public houses, in farmer's fields, on common land and at fairgrounds or racecourses.
2. *The scale of organization* – clubs had a secretary and annual fees. For instance, a notice in 1824 stated that the Raglan club would meet 'subject to the rules and regulations entered into the previous year', whilst another in 1832 stated that any member of the club 'wishing to practice on any day will find two men ready to attend him by applying at the Beaufort Arms'.[25]

3. The level of support – this has already been highlighted above in the report on Newport's practice session in 1845. Few people would have gathered to watch the churchyard games and the attendance of a military band would have been unheard of!

The major move forward came when these teams started to play regular fixtures with other clubs and scratch elevens raised by local dignitaries. The actual date for this progress varied across the region. The teams in Monmouthshire played regular contests from the 1830s, taking the lead from the Raglan club. The *Monmouthshire Merlin* in June 1838 was in no doubt about the way the Monmouthshire club acted as a catalyst and stated that 'stimulated by the support of the Monmouthshire club (the father of cricket in this district), other cricket clubs have been embodied in the neighbourhood and several spectacular and well contested matches between them have been played'.[26] During the 1830s the Monmouthshire club held regular home and away fixtures with Brecon, Newport and Chepstow,[27] and because so many residents of the county thought of themselves as 'English gentlemen' rather than 'Welsh', the Raglan club arranged games with Hay-on-Wye and Ross.[28] They even ventured further afield and challenged both the Clifton club from Bristol and the Lansdown side from Bath,[29] whilst in July 1836 they travelled to Widemarsh Common for a game with Hereford. Edwin Anthony stated that it was a red letter day for the Hereford club, and so important was this fixture considered by the Herefordians that a trial match was organized during the previous week.[30] It also gave an indication of the Monmouthshire club's standing in the neighbouring counties, and how the Raglan side boosted cricket in areas outside south Wales.

It was not just the Monmouthshire area where inter-club fixtures gradually became more frequent and widespread during the 1830s, because this decade also saw a growth in the number of matches in south-west Wales. In 1830 there were contests between Cardigan and Lampeter, whilst Tenby challenged Pembroke as well as considering a match with Swansea.[31] By the middle of the decade, the Haverfordwest club was using a wicket in the centre of the racecourse on Portfield Common, although the game's spread in the locality met an unusual barrier during 1837 as the town's elections meant that the club could only organize a limited number of fixtures. Its members were leading local figures and did not have the time to practise or play until all the excitement was over, by which time they were keen to get back onto the field and soon forgot their political rivalries. The local press reported that 'it was a gratifying spectacle to see persons so largely pitted against each other in the arena of political contest, forgiving and forgetting their former fierce contest and good humouredly contending with another for gymnastic honours'.[32]

Inter-club matches in Glamorgan were quite rare in the 1830s. Swansea challenged Merthyr to home and away fixtures in 1831,[33] but for the most part, their members played matches amongst themselves. Extra opposition came when the young gentlemen of the town returned home for the summer from their schools or colleges in England. Having caught the cricket bug, they were eager to continue playing and a letter in 1830 to the nine-year-old H. H. Vivian from an older friend in Mount Pleasant related how 'a cricket match took place last Thursday between eleven of our boys against the Swansea club. They beat us by seven wickets . . . I hope we shall make up a club between us next holidays and beat them in return'.[34]

In the 1840s the Swansea club extended its fixture list to include annual matches with Llanelly and Neath.[35] Similarly, Bridgend and Cowbridge started playing fixtures during the 1840s,[36] whilst this decade also saw dramatic developments with Cardiff CC. By 1847 the Cardiff club found 'it is barely possible to muster in sufficient strength for a game of single wicket, and the proceedings seem to droop and decline'.[37] But support rapidly improved and the club was soon able to diversify from practice games or matches amongst friends[38] to regular fixtures with Newport, Merthyr, Tredegar and Aberdare. By June 1848 they were still unbeaten and felt they had enough expertise to challenge Clifton or Lansdown.[39] A fixture was eventually agreed with Clifton, and it was when playing the top Gloucestershire side that the Cardiff team was finally defeated.[40]

Therefore, by 1850 a host of cricket clubs were firmly established throughout south Wales, catering chiefly for the upper classes, and playing a number of annual fixtures against neighbouring teams and sides in England. The season ran from early May into late September, although some matches were even played in October, much later than today, with Cowbridge meeting Bridgend on 2 October 1840.[41] There were many other differences compared with modern cricket, starting with the number on each side. Whilst eleven was the accepted number, sides varied from seven to thirteen,[42] with some contests taking place between eleven and sixteen, eighteen or twenty-two opponents. Even the dress and headgear were vastly different, with tall white or black beaver hats being worn, and the players sporting coloured jackets with a variety of colours and patterns similar to jockey's silks. However, there was one similarity with today in that trousers were mostly white though secured by ornate belts or colourful sashes.[43]

These contests frequently did not take place on specially prepared surfaces, with some being staged on ridge and furrow fields, whilst others were held on marshes or river meadows.[44] The wicket would often be the only mown or rolled area, with the outfield having a thick cover of lush grass, although some even took place where no preparations had been made, and the captain who won the toss decided where to pitch the two stumps or have choice of innings.[45] This lack of preparation meant that cricket was rather dangerous on a rough and uneven surface. There are several references to batsmen being hit, and in the 1850s there was a fatal accident to a fielder about six feet from the bat during one of Pontypool's practices, as 18-year-old Edwin Sanders had a brain haemorrhage after being hit on the temple the previous evening.[46]

Other major differences were that sight-screens had yet to be invented, and there were only boundaries when the ball was hit out of the ground. Hits had to be fully run out, with the possibility of all run sixes or even seven or eight from one stroke. Batting on the rough wickets was both mentally exhausting and physically dangerous, so it was not surprising that totals below fifty were commonplace, and half centuries by individual players, never mind hundreds, were notable exceptions. A solid and firm defence was highly admired, rather than dashing strokeplay, and despite the absence of boundaries, the rate of run scoring was very slow in meadows with lush grass. Llanelly took over three hours to score seventy-five against Carmarthen in 1853, whilst T. Conway Lloyd won favourable comments for occupying the crease for eighty minutes for 0* in a match in 1850.[47]

During the 1830s and 1840s, the best batting performances came at Raglan, and it was no coincidence that this was one of the few specially prepared wickets, with the publican of the Beaufort Arms and his staff spending time looking after the ground, besides being prepared to roll up their sleeves to bowl to club members.[48] Needham was one of the leading batsmen, and whilst playing for Pontypool against Newport in 1836, he made thirty-three of Pontypool's first innings score of seventy-two, followed by an unbeaten eighty-two in their second innings total of 157.[49] Had he received more support from his colleagues, he might have had the distinction of making the first century on record in south Wales. Instead, this honour fell to Edward Brewer, from Newport, who scored 118 for the town club against the Officers of the 73rd Regiment in 1844.[50]

There were four deliveries to an over, with the bowling being chiefly underarm, although some roundarm bowling took place, with the bowler raising his hand level with the elbow. Roundarm bowlers could be quite fast at times, with long stops required if the wicket-keeper missed the ball.[51] However, this style met with a hostile reception and queries were sometimes raised over bowlers' actions and if their hands were too high. This happened in Newport's game with Merthyr in 1846 with debates over the legality of the Newport bowling – one correspondent wrote that 'the manner in which the ball was delivered by Messrs Attfield and Prothero, we consider, not strictly within the prescribed manner somewhat recently defined by the Marylebone club to be fair bowling'.[52] The modern form of overarm bowling started to appear in the early 1860s, and was legalized by the MCC in 1864.

The decision to arrange and play fixtures was not always based on purely cricketing criteria. Dates for matches would often coincide with market days, such as the game Haverfordwest played at Pembroke in 1846 though their choice of market day brought a peculiar distraction and danger with a rare case of 'cow stopped play', described as follows by the *Carmarthen Journal*:

> a cow when in transit to the shambles, considering her personal freedom in danger, rushed from her conductor, seeking safety in flight. The line of country which she took led directly over the cricket ground, which she attempted to cross, but the players were determined to dispute her passage, and a veritable volley of bats, balls and wickets were hurled at her devoted head. Still she fought her way, overturning every object that obstructed her path ... She finally left the field after gloriously making a rent in the unmentionables of a chaw bacon who had joined the pursuit.[53]

It was advisable to avoid clashes with local races which would attract many people. Cardiff and Aberdare found this to their cost by arranging a game on the same day as the 1854 Newport Races. The clash meant that the match finished up as an eight-a-side contest.[54] There was a throwback as well to the days of the *mabsant*, as cricket formed part of a variety of sporting contests. Other athletic pursuits occurred at the end of games, with the 1855 encounter between Llandeilo and Cwmamman being followed by a 120-yard race between Mr Samuel Lloyd of Cwmamman and Mr Jonathan Wade of Llandeilo.[55]

Another motive behind the organization of games was gambling. Gerald Howat has shown how close links occurred between cricket and horse-racing in England, with a match in June 1785 in Essex during the morning, followed by racing in the afternoon and a dinner in the evening.[56] This link may explain why Haverfordwest played at the Portfield racecourse, whilst Swansea arranged games on Crumlin Burrows where horse-racing took place. Many matches were struck as part of bets; Swansea played the Rifle Brigade in August 1841 for ten shillings a side,[57] whilst a contest between a Monmouthshire XXII and a Herefordshire XII at Monmouth in 1840 was for 100 guineas.[58] Other incentives were also available, with Abergavenny's members having a bottle of wine hanging in the entrance of their tent as a reward for any batsman who hit the ball out of the ground during a match.[59]

It was not just the players who could lay wagers on the outcome of games, as gambling was actively encouraged amongst the spectators who turned up. This may have been one of the reasons why games attracted large crowds, with a match in 1843 at Haverfordwest attracting enough people to fill the racecourse grandstand.[60] In 1837 when Abergavenny challenged Pontypool, spectators could get odds on Abergavenny of 5 to 1 against.[61] The odds were normally much closer, with the 1838 encounter between Monmouthshire and Newport having the latter at '3 to 2 and we learn, even 2 to 1 were offered'.[62]

As in the early nineteenth century, there were social factors behind the arranging of fixtures, simply because they promoted comradeship and gave the participants an excuse to relax and enjoy themselves before departing. In the case of a match in Swansea in 1845, the revelries went into the small hours, with the diary of L. W. Dillwyn recording that 'at two I drove with Miss Mary to a great cricket match at Singleton where we remained for a Dinner and a Ball, and we reached home at quarter past three in the morning'.[63] Similarly, in August 1836 the fixture between Pontypool and Newport was followed by a dinner at a local pub, and the players enjoyed themselves so much that they needed hangover cures the following morning – a fact eloquently reported by the *Monmouthshire Merlin* which described how the dinner 'brought the rival clubs harmoniously together and a delightful evening was passed causing some of the party next morning to seek a pleasure worthy of Xerxes the Great King, some hock and soda water'.[64] In fact, some games even finished early so that the participants could socialize before returning home, with the match between Neath and Swansea in 1854 ending at 5p.m. so that the Neath players could go to the nearby tavern before heading home.[65]

The socializing was not confined to post-match celebrations, with the Monmouthshire club having lavish luncheons between innings. The early rules of the club stated that no wine should be consumed at these luncheons to ensure that the players remained in a state which enabled them to finish the match,[66] but this regulation was relaxed a few years later and the *Monmouthshire Merlin* reported that between the innings of a match in 1840 'a capital dinner was served at the Beaufort Arms; the viands and wines were of the finest description and did much credit to the worthy hostess'.[67]

Fixtures were often secured at these social gatherings, and sometimes the wine flowed so much that rivals got carried away and struck challenges in similar vein to ancient duels. An example came during the sumptuous dinner in the Beaufort Arms following Raglan's match with Herefordshire in July 1840. The *Cardiff and Merthyr Guardian* reported how 'a gallant officer threw down the gauntlet on behalf of the new Abergavenny club, and challenged the Hereford, Monmouth, Newport or any other cricket club. But the glove was not taken up by the Hereford gentlemen, to whom it was offered. The Newport club were understood to accept the challenge, but the day is not yet fixed'.[68] In fact, within a fortnight Hereford subsequently agreed to play Abergavenny, whilst Newport met them two months later.[69]

Sometimes, the challenges were made with strict clauses, especially regarding who was eligible to play. For instance, Monmouth accepted a challenge from the Forest of Dean club in July 1839 on the understanding that only their subscribing members played, rather than introducing two or three talented guests in order to boost their chances.[70] But in some cases the wagers were waived, possibly because the challenger had sobered up and realized his mistake! This was the case in the encounter between Merthyr and Dowlais in August 1842. The local paper reported how 'it was understood from a previous arrangement that the match was to have been for a dinner and wine for twenty-six gentlemen, the losing party to pay the whole of the expenses, but on coming to the scratch, the Merthyr gentlemen declined playing for a wager, but would play for the honour of the game'.[71]

Some clubs arranged social visits to neighbouring towns or resorts to coincide with fixtures. In September 1849 the members of Cardiff CC spent the day at Penarth,[72] whilst Llanelly CC arranged fixtures and outings to Tenby during the 1850s. For their first visit, they hired the steam-tug *Samson* to convey over sixty members to the resort, and *The Cambrian* reported how 'the weather in the morning was most unpromising, heavy rain falling both before and for a few hours after starting; however, before they reached their destination the sun shone joyously out, and the rest of the day was beautiful and fine. On arriving at Tenby, the Llanelly "team" at once repaired to the ground and the game commenced'.[73] So successful was this outing that it was repeated in mid-September and in the following years, special trains were hired for this highlight in the club's calendar.

Despite the growing public interest in the game and its rising popularity, many of the clubs in the early nineteenth century had teething problems and found it difficult to arrange and honour their fixtures. Cardiff CC was one of the clubs to receive variable support and in August 1846 the club had to combine with players from the Tredegar side so that a match with Newport could be staged.[74] Its secretary, Edward Harte, was forced to place a notice in the *Cardiff and Merthyr Guardian* in an attempt to drum up support and the paper 'often regretted to observe a very thinly attended field. From assurances made to the officers of the club, we believe we may infer that during the ensuing season the game will be carried on with spirit – that members will be regular and punctual in their attendance'.[75]

The Cardiff club had only just been created, so it was no surprise that it should have a few early problems. Yet the more established clubs were also having difficulties, including Newport where a club had been formed in 1834, and the game had been played since 1820.[76] A variety of difficulties faced them, the most severe being financial. This was possibly the result of overexpenditure on lavish dinners, or travel to Hereford and Bristol, and in 1845 grass from their ground on the Newport Marshes had to be sold to raise money.[77] There were other headaches caused by disputes and friction between members resulting in the creation of a second side called Uskside.[78] Several reconciliations were attempted, but it was not until 1855 that a united club with new financial resources was formed, by which time the Newport and Pontypool Railway viaduct had been constructed across the Marshes.[79] Even Swansea, one of the earliest clubs, faced problems in the early nineteenth century, especially when their leading players and administrators left the town to work elsewhere. The club temporarily lapsed, before being re-established in 1845 to the delight of *The Cambrian* which was 'happy to see this manly sport revived among our fellow townsmen'.[80] However, the reformed club met an unusual obstacle in 1849 when there was an outbreak of cholera in the surrounding area during the summer months. Members were reluctant to travel for fixtures in case they contracted this virulent disease, but when the epidemic was over, they quickly renewed their links with Neath, Merthyr and Llanelly. By the start of 1852, the flourishing club had 105 members and *The Cambrian* reported that 'too much praise cannot be awarded to the committee and indefatigable secretary who have re-established the club which now appears fixed on a solid basis'.[81] There was enough support by 1852 for a second team to be established, called Swansea Union CC plus a side representing Kilvey.[82]

The financial reserves of some clubs were strong enough to allow the hiring of a professional. This was chiefly the case with the clubs in the flourishing industrial towns, with Cardiff hiring a professional in 1850 called William Selby who had made two appearances for Nottinghamshire. The fact that Selby was referred to as 'their professional advisor' and 'a professional instructor' shows that he took on more than just a playing role, and assisted with the coaching and preparations of the wicket.[83] This would have meant that Selby received a weekly fee for his efforts, and other less wealthy clubs would not have been able to afford this. Their solution was to hire professionals on a casual basis to boost their chances in major fixtures, or to attract the support of leading players from elsewhere – this explains why two famous players in Henry Grace and Alfred Pocock appeared for Swansea against Cardiff in 1854.[84]

Another major benefit to be gained by having a paid player amongst their ranks was that it allowed the gentry and affluent classes to maintain their involvement in what was a mentally and physically tough game. The rough wickets and outfields with long grass were just two of the factors making batting a tiring business, so the last thing that was needed after a long innings was a lengthy bowling spell. But it was a different matter if a professional was available, as the gentry only had to devote their energy to batting, as the professional earned his fee by undertaking the brunt of the bowling.

The active participation of the gentry was a major feature of the game's evolution during the first half of the nineteenth century. English cricket reached the same stage some 100 years earlier and, as Christopher Brookes has shown, the involvement of these higher status groups was the result of 'a growing realization that the game offered an opportunity to re-enact vestiges of an earlier life-style in a setting which combined the maximum excitement with the minimum of danger'.[85] Overall, the gentry and the people with ample time and money to play the game, saw cricket as both a pleasant diversion and a means to escape from the rigours of urban life and the claustrophobia of the social world, a way of acting out their rivalries without having to resort to duelling pistols or swords, and a means of gambling by betting on the outcome of games.

These factors prompted grand fixtures such as the Cwmgwili match in 1783 and those held by gentlemen's teams such as the Monmouthshire club. Their matches at Raglan bore certain similarities to a presentday Royal Ascot or Henley Regatta, with the leading members of the social world travelling to the Beaufort Arms to play or spectate. A report in 1834 gave evidence of this by reporting how 'numerous carriages of the leading families of the county, and many ladies and gentlemen from more distant quarters were on the ground at an early hour'.[86] Similarly, the club held annual balls at the Beaufort Arms at which 'all the beauty and fashion of the neighbourhood assembled. Quadrilles, waltzes and gallops were kept up with great spirit . . . an assemblage of fashionables were present and seemed thoroughly to enjoy the sport'.[87] One of the leading cricketers in the higher echelons of the Monmouthshire social world during the 1830s and 1840s was Capt. W. R. Stretton of Dan-y-Park, near Abergavenny. He was actively involved in several socially acceptable forms of recreation. Stretton hunted during the winter months and was steward of the Breconshire Races,[88] whilst in the summer he played for the Monmouthshire club and acted as president of Abergavenny CC.[89] He took a keen interest in the promotion of the game and allowed sides to use the grounds of Dan-y-Park – an example was the fixture between Monmouthshire and Hereford in August 1837. The sides had met twice earlier in the season, with one victory apiece, so Stretton's mansion was the neutral venue for the decider. Much to his joy, the Raglan club bowled Hereford out for 23 and 21, and won by ten wickets.[90]

The gentry were also promoting the game in the west, with the

Grenfells of Kilvey being leading players with Swansea. They owned one of the copper-smelting businesses in the town and the newspapers were full of glowing reports of the prowess with bat and ball of St Leger and Arthur Grenfell, which gave Swansea the reputation of being the leading club in west Glamorgan. The Grenfells also encouraged their work-force to play and in 1850 St Leger Grenfell raised a side from the Kilvey works, plus his three sons, to play two fixtures against an eleven from the Swansea club.[91]

However, the leading figure in the social and cricketing world of the Swansea area in the mid-nineteenth century was John Henry Vivian, the town's MP. Vivian was a native of Cornwall and arrived in south Wales at the age of twenty-one in 1806 to manage the family's copper-smelting works at Hafod, and in the next fifty years he transformed both the works and the former village into 'a fine seaport and the copper capital of the country'.[92] Like Capt. Stretton, Vivian actively encouraged games in the grounds of his lavish home at Singleton, and in August 1847 the estate staged the local derby between Swansea and Neath. The latter won a close match by fifteen runs and afterwards Vivian entertained both teams to a dinner in his house.[93] After its earlier difficulties, the Swansea club was grateful for Vivian's patronage and the matches at Singleton became the annual highlight of both the cricket club's and the town's social calendar.[93] *The Cambrian* noted in its match report of the 1852 game with Neath that 'amongst the ladies and gentlemen assembled to witness the play were J. H. Vivian Esq MP; Mrs Vivian and family, H. H. Vivian Esq MP, Howel Gwyn Esq MP and Mrs Gwyn, Captain and Mrs Lindsey, the Messrs Eden, L. L. Dillwyn Esq, Rev Samuel Davies, Mr Davies, T. Grove Esq, H. S. Coke Esq and many others'.[94]

A number of motives accounted for J. H. Vivian's active involvement with the town's cricket club. Firstly, he was the leader of the industrial, political and social world in the Swansea area. Like Philipps of Cwmgwili, Vivian moved in high circles both in London and south Wales, and knew many leading figures of the court and political world.[95] After having played such a fundamental role in the town's growth, it was understandable that he should see it as his job to provide a special venue for, and boost, the game in which Vivian's acquaintances were avidly involved.

Vivian became Swansea's first MP following the Reform Act of 1832, and until his death in 1855, he was a kindly benefactor to Swansea, seeing 'the place and people in the truest sense his own'.[96] He took a close interest in the life and problems of Swansea's residents, and made sure it had adequate services and modern facilities.[97] Vivian also displayed his social standing and position as a leader of Swansea society by acting as steward for the Swansea and Neath Races, and in 1835 he entertained 150 ladies and gents at the Assembly Rooms after the races.[98] So the provision of a venue and first-class hospitality for Swansea CC was in keeping with his role as a benefactor and father figure to the growing industrial town. It was also consistent with his views on living a good and healthy life as he was a supporter of the Temperance Movement, never allowing a public house to be built on his land, and his patronage of the town's cricket club ensured that some of the young gents did not get sidetracked by the demon drink which was so prevalent in the pubs and unlicensed beerhouses. A final reason why Vivian became so involved was simply that he enjoyed cricket and learnt the rudiments of the game whilst in London. He spent a lot of his early life studying and travelling on the Continent, and he was introduced to the game when he became Swansea's MP and lived with his wife at St James' Place in London. He had a reasonable ability, although in 1847 he was struck in the face whilst batting against Neath and was unable to continue his innings.[99] Overall, his involvement as a player, as well as a promoter of a game which was patronized by the gentry, allowed him to maintain contact with other people of a high social standing and a similar political outlook.

This case study of J. H. Vivian highlights how, for a variety of reasons, the leading members of society were actively involved in the playing and promoting of the game. In particular, it became an acceptable and popular form of recreation among the social élite, and membership of a local club was a symbol of social status. The members' lists for many of these early clubs read like a Who's Who, with the members of the Brecon Town and Garrison CC for 1850 including Col. Lloyd Watkins and James Bailey who were the two local MPs, John Lloyd the High Sheriff of the county, and Lord Alexander George Russell who was the son of the Sixth Duke of Bedford.[100]

The *nouveaux riches* were keen to establish their newly acquired social importance and rub shoulders with the gentry by playing on a regular basis or being involved with the administration of the club. For example, the leading members of the Abergavenny side in the mid-nineteenth century were Mr Williamson, an articled clerk to a lawyer, and Mr Charles Davies, the son of the parish clerk,[101] whilst Llanelly's secretary for 1852 was Edward Douglas, an auctioneer, their treasurer was a colliery agent called John Griffiths, whilst their leading batsman, Bernard Rees, was an accountant.[102] Their rising social aspirations were fuelled by the chance to play alongside the gentry and leading members of local society. In the case of Llanelly, Douglas, Griffiths and Rees played alongside Apsley Smith whose family were partners in the Dafen Steelworks, Henry Howell, a local politician, and a gentleman called Mr Hopkins who ran an iron foundry in the town.

However, it was not just the social élite or *nouveaux riches* who were playing and promoting the game during the first half of the nineteenth century. In 1837, eleven tradesmen from the Pontypool area were assembled for a game against the town club,[103] whilst in 1838 the tradesmen of Haverfordwest met the gentlemen of the town.[104] Nevertheless, the opportunities for workingmen to become involved with these early clubs were limited by a number of constraints. Firstly, there were restrictions on time, as many working people could not get time off to participate in practices or matches, or any form of recreation. Secondly, it was expensive, and beyond their means, to join the clubs, with annual subscriptions of at least half a guinea, and fines for bad conduct. For example, any member of Chepstow CC disputing an umpiring decision would pay five shillings, anyone leaving a game before it was over would pay 2s. 6d. and the same amount would be paid by anyone guilty of 'throwing his bat on the ground on leaving the wickets'.[105] A final barrier was that some clubs, such as Newport, imposed a limit on the number of members, whilst others had clauses whereby members had to be proposed and admitted by the committee at the Annual General Meeting.[106]

These financial and social restrictions all prevented many of the less wealthy or influential people from joining clubs, and made it well nigh impossible for the workingmen. Yet cricket originated at grass roots level and some of the lower classes took matters into their own hands and created their own sides, but without the social trappings of the gentlemen's clubs. An example was the formation of a Mechanics cricket club in Llandovery, and by July 1845 it had sufficient support for a fixture between married and single members.[107] To overcome the problem of a shortage of spare time, an Early Risers' club was formed in Merthyr in June 1848. Their practices were held 'on Mondays, Wednesdays and Fridays, commencing at half-past five in the morning'.[108] This ingenious solution was copied in Neath, and by 1853 the town had a Tradesman's club, an Evening Association, an Early Risers' team and a Gentlemen's club. The latter two even met in August 1853 as *The Cambrian* announced a match where the Early Risers 'composed of many of the young men of the town played the town club, comprising the elite of the residents'.[109]

Simply because of their limited means, most of these early workingmen's clubs were based on practice sessions or games between members. By the mid-nineteenth century there were occasional games with other sides in the neighbourhood, but they rarely travelled any distance, and unlike the other clubs at that time, had a restricted fixture list. This absence of inter-club games, plus their lower social standing, accounted for the limited coverage they received in the contemporary newspapers. They had a significance in that they were a response to the exclusiveness of the gentlemen's clubs, yet in the context of the game's evolution, their format in mid-century was not a significant step forward, and they were only modified, as opposed to totally different, versions of the eighteenth-century churchyard and common games.

So it was predominantly the landed gentlemen and the *nouveaux riches* who were involved with the cricket clubs in the first half of the nineteenth century. Yet some of the behaviour and events both on and off the field at times could hardly be described as gentlemanly, as the fixtures aroused intensely partisan feelings and local rivalries, none more so than between Llanelly and Swansea in the early 1850s. Their first dispute came in June 1852 when Swansea were the visitors at Llanelly House. The game was evenly matched, but events swung in Llanelly's favour when one of their batsman, after being caught off a deflection, was adjudged not out by the umpires, because they could not determine whether the ball had struck him on his arm or glove. Llanelly won by three runs, yet the reporter from *The Cambrian* wrote that 'morally and fairly the Swansea side were the victors . . . the player afterwards acknowledged that he was out and that the ball struck his fingers, but that he was not obliged to give himself out'.[110]

This pro-Swansea stance ruffled many feathers to the west of the Lougher, and the following week the newspaper carried some strong comments submitted by officials of the Llanelly club:

> Let your correspondent, whoever he may be, that shouts that the Swansea cricketers were not beaten on the day referred to, consult any authority as to whether it is the duty of the batsman to act as referee in case the umpires do not happen to be looking on; he will then perceive, by the answer he obtains, how little he knows of this splendid and noble game. I have only to add that the gentleman who kindly acted as umpire for the Swansea side seemed much more competent to judge the merits of the particular case referred to than your correspondent, if we are to take his remarks as any criterion of his knowledge of the game.[111]

Llanelly won again in 1853, though the Swansea club felt that Llanelly had acted unfairly once more by hiring a guest player. The following year Swansea travelled to Llanelly without four of their regulars and in a tit-for-tat gesture they obtained three decent replacements from outside the town. Llanelly still managed to win, and their correspondent to *The Cambrian* gloated at their success, writing that:

> Swansea, having a population of three times the number of Llanelly, act unfairly and uncreditably in doing so, and that such a course is not at all calculated to advance cricket or foster that good feeling which it brings about

. . . It is but right to state that Llanelly was impersonated in its own real members resident in Llanelly or neighbourhood.[112]

The hiring of guests for local derbies was a major source of worry in the early 1850s, and many felt it was leading to quite unnecessary tension between clubs such as Swansea and Llanelly. For some, it tainted the image of the game, so *The Cambrian* pleaded that they would like to see the end of:

> soliciting the aid of strange players proficient in cricket in matches and thus making up a good eleven. We do not accuse any particular club of this not very honourable practice, knowing that most are alike participating in it, but hope to see in the future, each club arrayed in its own real men, manfully contesting in good spirit with its opponents for a friendly game at the athletic and healthful sport of cricket.[113]

This vexed topic of guest players was also brought about by the rather lax membership criteria of some clubs, and gradually they started to tighten up their rules, so that both the image of their club, and the game itself, could be improved. This was the next important move forward in the game's evolution and its conversion from an unruly folk-game. The initiative for these changes came from the gentry and wealthier club members in the same way that these people led local society and were agents of social reform. Once again, their involvement ran parallel with events in the development of English cricket, and Christopher Brookes stated that it was 'not until members of the aristocracy and gentry began to patronise and play cricket that it acquired a degree of organisation unknown in folk-games'.[114]

The Raglan club once again led the way in the formulation of rules, and their members' list for 1838 contained their thorough regulations, which subsequently became the model for other clubs, including Newport. Five of the county's MPs were members of Raglan, and almost all of the Monmouthshire gentry, from Sir Charles Morgan of Tredegar Park to Hanbury Leigh of Pontypool Park, belonged to the club so it was no surprise that Raglan should have such strict rules. One of the patrons of the Raglan club was Lord Granville Somerset, the second son of the Sixth Duke of Beaufort. He became Conservative MP for Monmouthshire in 1816 and held this position until his death in 1848.[115] During this time, he persuaded many of his political and cricketing friends in the county to join the Raglan club, including Joseph Bailey, an ironmaster of Glanusk Park near Crickhowell who represented the county of Hereford and Benjamin Hall, alias Lord Llanover, who became MP for Monmouth.[116]

The patronage of these MPs and the landed gentry assisted the game's spread during the first half of the nineteenth century from the high and influential circles of London society into the quieter and more rural atmosphere of Monmouthshire. It resulted in the transformation of the game, which in the late eighteenth century had been a disorganized folk-game played on commons and in churchyards, into the more modern, formalized recreation which by the 1850s had seen the creation of many sides following the pattern established by the early clubs such as Raglan.

3 / *Raglan, Riots and Railways*

THE FIRST half of the nineteenth century was therefore an important era in the evolution of cricket in south Wales, with the patronage of the landed gentry and society leaders acting as a catalyst for many of the changes which took place. However, many other factors played a role in this transformation from a folk-game, and these need to be examined if the events of these years are to be fully understood.

The previous chapter identified the playing of inter-club fixtures as one of the fundamental changes, and Figure 3 shows the number of these contests involving clubs in south Wales (excluding practice games amongst members or single wicket matches) which were reported by the newspapers between 1815 and 1855.[1] As Appendix A outlines, these newspapers did not include all of the inter-club games that were played in the early nineteenth century, so Figure 3 is not an actual measure of the total number of fixtures. Yet in the absence of any other written records, these difficulties must be tolerated as an unfortunate hindrance and we must accept that the true total will never be known. Even so, Figure 3 shows an overall upward trend in the number of fixtures, especially from the 1830s onwards, and a rise in the newsworthiness of cricket which was not too surprising given the involvement of society leaders. Another illustration of its increasing popularity and diffusion is shown in Figure 4 which graphs, on a cumulative scale, the number of clubs mentioned in these newspaper reports. Back in 1820 a mere five clubs were known to be in existence, yet by 1850 over fifty were included in the press reports.

Three distinctive phases stand out on these graphs, namely 1815–36, 1837–48 and 1849–55. Figures 5, 6 and 7 show the geographical location of fixtures in each of these phases, and some extremely interesting spatial patterns emerge which provide important clues to the other factors which influenced the game's diffusion and evolution in the early nineteenth century.

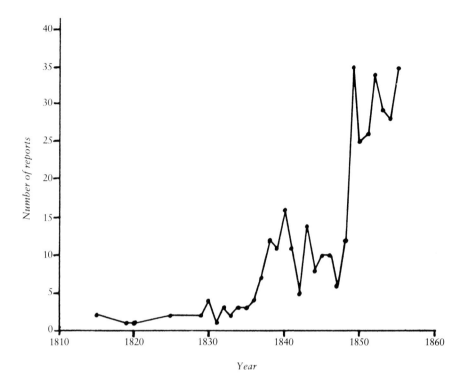

Figure 3. Number of matches reported in newspapers 1815–1855

Figure 5 shows the location of games reported between 1815 and 1836, and it clearly illustrates the dominance of south-east Wales, particularly the Monmouthshire club at Raglan. To the west of Newport and Usk there was a fairly barren area in terms of fixtures, even though clubs were in existence by 1836 in Maesteg, Carmarthen, Cardigan, Lampeter, Merthyr and, for a short time, in Cardiff. Pembroke managed to play their neighbours Tenby in 1830, but it was impossible for many of the other clubs to consider playing each other, because of their wide geographical spread and the poor transport facilities on the rutted tracks or turnpike roads. It is worth remembering that a journey from Carmarthen to Swansea on the Picton stage-coach would take over five hours. This meant that clubs in the far west were restricted to games amongst their members and occasional fixtures with another club. If challenges were made, they were sometimes held at a convenient location midway between the two clubs. This explains why the 1831 fixture between Merthyr and Swansea was held at Pontneathvaughan in the Neath Valley,[2] whilst another popular location was the field alongside the Lamb and Flag Inn at Glynneath which was a major stopping point

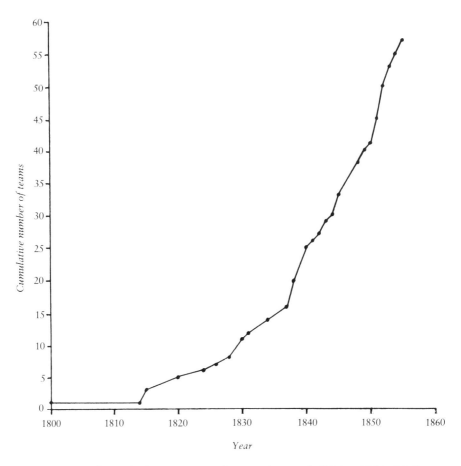

Figure 4. Cumulative number of teams in south Wales 1800–1855

for the mail coaches which went to and from west Wales. Transport facilities were much better for the Monmouthshire club adjacent to the English border and close to well-established and good routes into Herefordshire and Gloucestershire. The superiority of the transport in this area, plus the patronage by the Monmouthshire gentlemen, were highly instrumental factors behind the establishment of Raglan as a cricketing 'culture hearth' in south Wales. It was assisted by the fact that the club and its members thought of themselves as being English, and had a lot of contact with sides and top class players in England. Their contacts were not merely confined to the neighbouring sides in Hereford, Usk, Hay-on-Wye, Clifton or Lansdown, because the members of the Monmouthshire side were frequent visitors to London. Some were even members of the MCC, as testified by a report of a match which stated

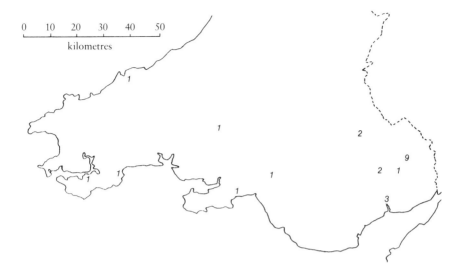

Figure 5. The location of inter-club fixtures in south Wales 1783–1836

that 'play is spoken of by some of the best judges who are not strangers at Lord's Cricket Ground, as admirable'.[3] So the emergence of the Monmouthshire club is another example of cricket's spatial diffusion across the geographical boundary between England and Wales.

Two other types of movement into Wales were responsible for the next phase of the game's evolution between 1837 and 1848. Figure 6 shows the location of fixtures in this next period, and illustrates how the Monmouthshire area was still dominant and clearly benefiting from its establishment as a 'culture hearth'. But several new 'growth poles' were evident in the rapidly industrializing valleys of the south-east, as well as in the more peaceful and rural areas of west Wales in Haverfordwest and Carmarthen.

The economic boom in the valleys attracted vast numbers of people to south Wales from other parts of Wales and neighbouring English counties. The 1830s and 1840s saw the population of Glamorgan and Monmouthshire dramatically rise. In 1801 it had only been 116,447, but by 1851 it was 389,267. The most marked increases occurred in the valley settlements of the two counties, and the 'Black Gold Rush' saw their transformation from small villages into booming industrial towns. For example, Aberdare's population rose from 1,486 in 1801 to 14,999 by 1851. The migration flows from England brought in people who had learnt and played the game, and were keen to continue their involvement with cricket. Many people also arrived from rural parts of Wales and as David Egan stated they 'brought not only their language, but their

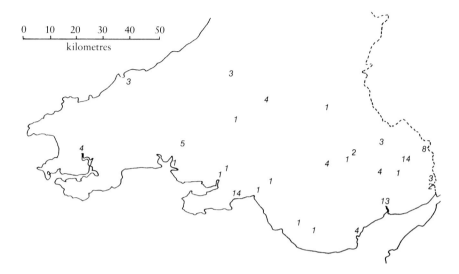

Figure 6. The location of inter-club fixtures in south Wales 1837–1848

customs, traditions and religious beliefs. Sports such as foot-racing and fist-fighting, festivals such as the Cwrw Bach where people drank, sang and generally entertained themselves, and local eisteddfodau all flourished in the growing town'.[4] They would also have brought the tradition of playing the churchyard and *mabsant* ball games, and when combined with the experience and money of the arrivals from England, it appeared to be a potent mixture for the spread of cricket.

Merthyr Tydfil was the largest settlement in south Wales during this period, and owed its importance at the top of the urban and industrial hierarchy to the four ironworks of Dowlais, Cyfarthfa, Penydarren and Plymouth. By 1823 the town was producing 43 per cent of Britain's iron and the area was attracting a flood of migrants. Yet despite this rapid industrial growth and rising population, Merthyr only had one cricket club, and there are few reports of fixtures taking place, despite the abundance of decent routes to the industrial centre. There are a number of reasons for this. Many of the immigrants from rural parts of Wales were strict Nonconformists and their strong views against recreation outweighed those with an English or Anglican background, who were in favour of ball games such as cricket. In fact, research has shown that at this time there were eight times the number of Nonconformist or chapel members in Merthyr than members of the local Church of England, whilst G. O. Pierce estimated that in 1851 Nonconformity was the religious persuasion of around 80 per cent of the population.[5]

Another salient factor was that there was only a small ruling élite in

Merthyr who might have had the wealth and spare time to devote to playing or supporting cricket. Harold Carter and Sandra Wheatley used data from the 1851 Census to show that only 1.3 per cent of the town's population were in socio-economic group I, and just 4.9 per cent in group II, compared with 63.9 per cent in group III.[6] The absence of an affluent and aspiring middle-class has also been noted by Kenneth Morgan who has described the town as 'a rough, raw frontier settlement, consisting largely of uneducated colliers and ironworkers'.[7] In short, Merthyr lacked the personnel for a cricket boom.

Those people who joined the town's club were more likely to have been from the minority with both an English background and plenty of spare time. Whilst the lucky few were playing cricket, the labourers in the ironworks worked a twelve or thirteen-hour shift, seven days a week, with just two official holidays a year, on Christmas Day and Good Friday. As David Egan has stated 'it was work which had created Merthyr Tydfil and work certainly dominated the life of its people',[8] so they hardly had time to devote to either cricket or any other recreation in the early nineteenth century. Life was harsh in the industrial centre, with appalling living conditions, a lack of sanitary provision, overcrowding and periodic epidemics. The slump in the iron trade and wage cuts in the late 1820s and early 1830s did not help matters, and ultimately the workers revolted against the ironmasters in the Merthyr Rising of 1831. Therefore, industrial expansion and immigration did not lead to the expansion of cricket in Merthyr during the early nineteenth century, which explains why it does not feature as an early centre on Figures 5 or 6.

It was, however, a different story elsewhere in south Wales during the late 1830s and 1840s. This was the period when the impact of the Industrial Revolution was being felt in the coastal belt of the region, and major ports and commercial centres developed at Swansea, Cardiff and Newport. Rapid rates of population growth were also recorded in these settlements with Swansea's population rising from 6,831 in 1801 to 24,902 in 1851. The chief difference compared with the valley towns was that these settlements attracted businessmen, traders and office workers from the neighbouring counties of England, and unlike the manual labourers from rural Wales who moved to Merthyr, these were the people with both the time and money, as well as the instincts and inclinations, to establish cricket clubs in these towns.

A club was established in the thriving port of Cardiff during the early 1840s,[9] and as both the number of migrants from England and the trade from the Bute Docks increased during the decade, the game rose in popularity. A second club called Taff Vale, was formed in 1847, followed in 1849 by a Juveniles side so that the youngsters of the growing town could follow in their fathers' footsteps.[10] The local paper was delighted by the cricket boom, and in 1849 their editor wrote that he was able:

> to take the greatest satisfaction to witness the growing interest which the young men of this town take in the game of cricket. Youngsters generally contrive to have periods of relaxation from business, and if they do not habituate themselves to employ their leisure hours usefully, or at least harmlessly, it is rather more than probable that the taproom, or even worse places, will be frequented and a confirmed habit of smoking and tippling be induced.[11]

His report also reflected the growing concern about the lack of recreational facilities in the squalid industrial centres such as Merthyr as well as the lure of the demon drink. Industrialists were steadily learning the lessons of the Merthyr Rising and did not want another 'Dic Penderyn' on their hands. The outcome was that many entrepreneurs in the 1830s and 1840s followed the example of J. H. Vivian in Swansea and took an active interest in the social and living conditions of their workers. Creating a cricket club was one of the ways they could help their employees to spend a more healthy life, and an early example of industrial patronage was the creation of Taibach CC in 1843 by Capt. Robert Lindsay for the workers of the local copperworks and colliery. His generous actions had the desired effect because the *Swansea Journal* soon afterwards was able to report that 'the establishment of the Taibach cricket club has had a most beneficial effect upon the habits and morals of the young men, withdrawing many of them from the neighbouring tap-rooms and other places of disreputable resort'.[12]

Therefore, the patronage of industrialists and the influx of migrants were important agents in cricket's development during the 1830s and the 1840s. The arrival of money and people from England led to the creation of thriving clubs, and in some cases there were so many English members that matches were held between the migrant and native elements.[13] But there were other important factors assisting the game's growth in the years leading up to 1850, as the towns of Newport, Swansea and those in the far west saw the arrival of troops *en route* for Ireland and to quell civil unrest in south Wales.

The arrival of the military in the south-east of the region was caused by the Chartist disturbances which culminated in a People's March to Newport from the surrounding valleys of Monmouthshire in the autumn of 1839.[14] A riot occurred in Newport during November and, to quell the rebellion, large numbers of soldiers were moved into the town and the coalfield areas from the garrisons at Newport and Brecon. The three leaders of the Monmouthshire Chartists were captured, convicted and transported to Australia, but the movement continued to receive support. There was a Chartist strike in Merthyr in 1842 and even in 1858 when the last Chartist Conference was held, delegates attended from Merthyr and Aberdare. Ric Sissons noted an association between cricket and Chartism, with the All-England XI being formed in the Chartist stronghold of Nottingham. He stated that 'although there is no direct connection, Chartism did inspire self-confidence amongst skilled workers and artisans, and created an innovative political climate. For a group of professional cricketers to take the initiative and launch their own touring eleven, similar self-confidence and innovative thinking was required'.[15] These factors would have also given a boost to south Wales clubs although, overall, Chartist unrest boosted the wealthy rather than the poor cricketers.

In the west, the arrival of troops from Brecon in July 1839 followed attacks on tollgates and tollhouses. Three years later, further attacks took place in Pembrokeshire, Cardiganshire and Carmarthenshire, which led to the Rebecca Riots. By June 1843 Infantry from the 73rd and 75th Foot Regiment and Cavalry of the 4th Light Dragoons were stationed in west Wales, as well as Marines at Pembroke Dock.[16] The presence of such large numbers of troops in south Wales resulted in the construction of new garrisons and, in 1841, the military authorities decreed that all barracks should be provided with a cricket ground for the entertainment of their officers and soldiers. This was important for the development of the game because it meant that there were now proper wickets and improved facilities in settlements where only a rough field or common had previously been available. The military presence presented a host of other benefits to cricket. Both the Rebecca Riots and the Chartist unrest were in essence workingmen's protests against the gentry and the Establishment, so it was in the gentlemen's best interest to build up good relations with the troops who had been sent to protect both them and their symbols of wealth and power. The upshot was that clubs arranged fixtures with the military teams and, once again, the Monmouthshire club took the lead by staging a game in August 1840 against a Military XI.[17] The following year, Newport staged four matches with the Rifle Brigade who were in the town until September when the Chartist disruption started to die down,[18] whilst in Usk there was a special contest between the Civilians and the Military.[19]

In 1843 the 73rd Regiment travelled throughout south Wales to play fixtures with Pontypool, Newport and Swansea. The person responsible for these matches was none other than the Chief Constable of Glamorgan, Capt. Charles Napier who had himself been violently attacked during unrest near Pontarddulais in July 1843.[20] Napier was an useful player in his own right and played for the Rifle Brigade against Newport.[21] Whilst in south Wales he became friendly with the Morgan family of Ruperra and the Bosanquets of Dingestow Court who were both members of the Raglan club. His military rank and social contacts therefore allowed him to spend much of his spare time during the summer in gentlemanly pursuits. In August 1843 Napier led a combined side from the 73rd and 75th Regiment against Starling Benson's Swansea team on Crumlin Burrows as a goodwill gesture to boost morale in the west. As the *Monmouthshire Merlin* reported these games were 'well calculated to relieve body and mind from the severe toil and anxiety now felt by all classes during these eventful times'.[22] However, these games were also a social vehicle for Napier, for he had a deep desire for recognition by the gentry, as he was considered by some to be a 'foreigner in Wales' and had a rather genteel background. What better way to highlight his new position as chief constable than selecting his own cricket team which toured the region and allowed him to mix with the local gentry into whose social circle he was trying to break.[23]

Members of the military also joined local clubs and helped raise the standard of play. Indeed, in June 1839, a report on the practices of the Raglan club noted the presence of 'the officers at present quartered at Newport, Monmouth and Abergavenny amongst whom are several adepts in the noble game'.[24] The Abergavenny club also benefited greatly from the presence of the Scots Greys whose officers joined the town club. One of these was Capt. Barnett whose batting boosted not only Abergavenny, but also the Monmouthshire club for which he was invited to play. He repaid their kindness with two matchwinning innings in 1840 against Herefordshire. He firstly topscored with forty-two as the Welsh club won by three wickets at Widemarsh Common, and later struck sixty-two in the return game at Raglan as the Hereford team were defeated by nine runs.[25] The Hereford team usually won these encounters, but the presence of Barnett tipped the balance for once in Raglan's favour. Not surprisingly, the Hereford newspapers wryly commented 'that but for the casual aid of a first-rate player in the person of an officer of the Scotch [sic] Greys now quartered at Abergavenny, the players of this county would still have retained their laurels'.[26]

As well as these positive side-effects, the civil unrest in south Wales in the early 1840s also had a few negative ones. The Rebecca Riots and attacks on the turnpikes and tollroads meant that travel was dangerous, especially by the gentry and affluent figures in local society, against whom the protesters were venting their anger. Naturally, many of the clubs in the west were wary of going any distance to play games, and this explains why Figure 3 shows a drop in the number of inter-club fixtures in 1842 and 1843. The wealthy club members had far weightier matters on their minds than cricket, and could hardly spend any time either to practise or play in games, whilst friction between the upper-class and middle-class, pro-Rebecca members would have made it difficult to organize both teams and practices.

These negative aspects of the Rebecca Riots were highlighted by Bob Harragan who stated that the Llanelly club 'nearly died in the ashes of the Sandy toll-gate, smashed by Rebecca rioters and the ill feeling which split the cricket playing establishment from their tradesmen team-mates'.[27] The people who came together in 1839 to establish the town's cricket club found themselves in the early 1840s pitched against each other, with the bad feeling and squabbling caused by the Rebecca Riots. The man leading the protests in the Llanelli area was Francis McKiernon, a publican who owned the field which the club used for its matches, whilst the chairman of the local magistrates, where the rioters were tried after the attack at Sandy, was William Chambers of Llanelly House, who had been the driving force behind the club's creation and had secured the use of McKiernon's field. The morning after the attack at Sandy in 1843, McKiernon was named by the gatekeeper as the ringleader behind the disturbances, and the publican ended up in the Assizes facing Chambers. McKiernon was highly regarded by the Llanelli community, for he was also the owner of several local businesses as well as the mail coach which ran to Carmarthen. His good character and cricketing contacts with Chambers secured bail, before the episode took another strange twist, as the locals vented their anger on the gatekeeper for squealing to the authorities. As the local paper commented, 'the town was full of excitement, for Mr McKiernon's amenity of manners upon all occasions had rendered him very generally beloved, and most people heard of his position with regret'.[28] A few nights later the gatekeeper received a 'visitation', and it prompted him to return to court and say that he had lied on oath and had never seen McKiernon. A furious Chambers charged the gatekeeper with perjury before delightedly dropping all charges on his cricketing friend!

Therefore, the disturbances in south-west Wales temporarily halted the development of cricket, whilst in the south-east the game was given a boost during the 1840s by the arrival of English troops. But the latter was nothing like the impetus which the arrival of a railway line from England gave the game later in the 1840s and the early 1850s. Figure 7 shows the location of fixtures between 1849 and 1855, and highlights the new importance of the coastal belt where the South Wales Railway had opened in 1850. It is also clear that the focus of the game had shifted west away from the Monmouthshire club. The Raglan wicket was no longer the best in the region, and the club was geographically distant from the railway line and the booming centres of commerce and industry on the coast, to which the wealthy and innovative migrants from England were being attracted. It was in these towns, rather than Raglan, that they

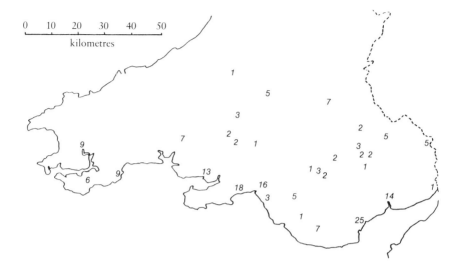

Figure 7. The location of inter-club fixtures in south Wales 1849–1855

invested their time and money in cricket, and it was hardly worth while travelling for an hour or more inland to Raglan when these other towns, especially after the military involvement had perfectly good wickets of their own.[29]

The new growth points were the coastal towns of Cardiff, Newport, Neath, Swansea and Llanelli, which were all strategic points on the newly created rail network, and from which lines ran inland to the industrial valleys. It was no coincidence that the number of inter-club fixtures in these nodal points dramatically increased following the construction of this new network. There were only four matches in Cardiff between 1837 and 1848, yet between 1849 and 1855 there were twenty-five. Neath saw an increase from one to sixteen, whilst Llanelli recovered from the traumas of the Rebecca Riots to stage thirteen fixtures. The primitive and slow transport by road had hindered the arrangement of fixtures in the earlier two phases, and even in the 1840s teams frequently met at a midway location, as is shown by the match played between Llanelly and Carmarthen at Ferryside in 1841.[30] It also presented a barrier to the ambitious clubs in the east, who were contemplating fixtures with English sides. If Newport or Cardiff challenged Clifton, there was the prospect of a long road journey via Gloucester, so the more feasible alternative was to use the Bristol Packet across the Severn. Even this however had its drawbacks, with the boat bringing the Clifton team over in July 1844 arriving late, causing the two innings match to be reduced to a single innings contest, with the Bristol

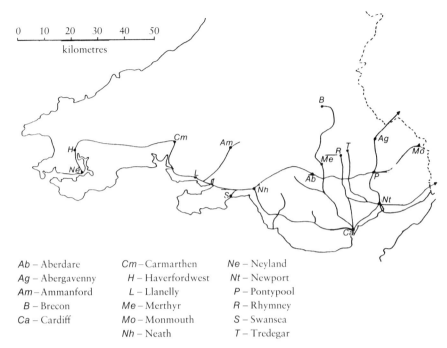

Ab – Aberdare   Cm – Carmarthen   Ne – Neyland
Ag – Abergavenny   H – Haverfordwest   Nt – Newport
Am – Ammanford   L – Llanelly   P – Pontypool
B – Brecon   Me – Merthyr   R – Rhymney
Ca – Cardiff   Mo – Monmouth   S – Swansea
                   Nh – Neath   T – Tredegar

Figure 8. The railway network in south Wales before 1860 [Adapted from W. Rees, *A Historical Atlas of Wales* (London, Faber and Faber, 1951)]

players more than a little weary after their rough journey.[31] However, they had a smile on their faces when they visited Newport in June 1845. They only made 105 but, when the home team was on the verge of winning at 100–6, the ring of the Packet bell came to the rescue and the match was hastily terminated to allow the Clifton players to catch the boat back and avoid a rare defeat.[32]

Most teams had to use the stage-coaches or travel by their own horse and carriage. Indeed, some of the match reports for the 1820s and 1830s spent as much time commenting on the grand carriages the players arrived in, as they did describing the game, and it seemed that a means of private transport, plus one's own coachman, was as important a playing requirement as proficiency with bat and ball.[33]

These barriers which had restricted travel disappeared with the opening of the new railway lines during the late 1840s and early 1850s. Figures 8 and 9 show the abundance of new routes compared with the earlier hazards of the rutted tracks and roads. Teams which had previously been too far away in terms of either time or distance now entered the 'catchment area' of the new centres on the railway network,

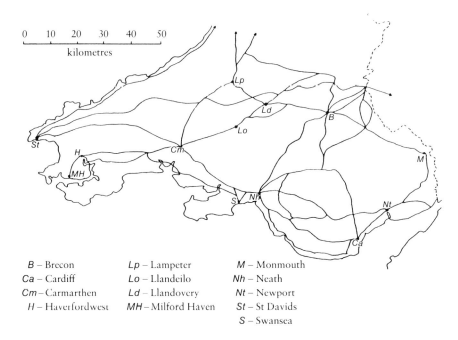

B – Brecon   *Lp* – Lampeter   *M* – Monmouth
Ca – Cardiff   *Lo* – Llandeilo   *Nh* – Neath
Cm – Carmarthen *Ld* – Llandovery *Nt* – Newport
H – Haverfordwest *MH* – Milford Haven *St* – St Davids
                S – Swansea

Figure 9. The road network of nineteenth–century south Wales [Adapted from W. Rees, *A Historical Atlas of Wales* (London, Faber and Faber, 1951)]

and regular fixtures could be arranged following this shrinkage of distance. Chepstow CC was just one of many clubs to benefit from the opening of new lines to Gloucester in 1851 and Hereford in 1853. They had previously relied on travelling in the horse-drawn brake belonging to Mr Curre, the squire of Itton Court, and only had a fairly localized fixture list. But the new lines allowed them to expand their list in the 1850s to include home and away contests in Gloucester, Bristol and Cheltenham.[34]

The flow-line maps in Figures 10 and 11 illustrate the way the teams were able to travel further for away fixtures during the 1850s compared with the 1840s.[35] In the pre-railway age, Cardiff travelled a mean distance of 30.5 km for away matches, and when they accepted a challenge from Tredegar in 1847 they had to meet half way at Merthyr.[36] However, they were more mobile than Swansea and Llanelly whose mean away distances were 13.2km and 16.3km respectively, and the two clubs frequently met on neutral soil at Pontarddulais or Llangennech.[37] Everything changed following the opening of the railway line and by the 1850s the Cardiff team was travelling a mean away distance of 47.2km following the construction of routes into the valleys – Taff Vale 1840,

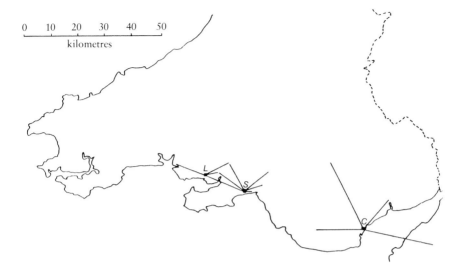

Figure 10. The sphere of influence of Cardiff, Llanelly and Swansea in the 1840s

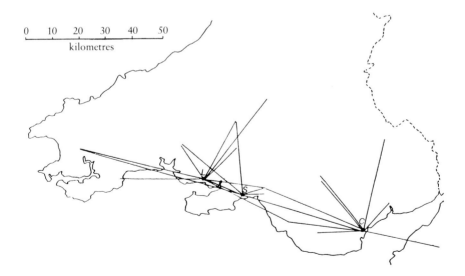

Figure 11. The sphere of influence of Cardiff, Llanelly and Swansea in the 1850s

Aberdare 1846, Vale of Neath 1851 and Rhymney 1854 – as well as tracks to Gloucester and Hereford. The changes however were more dramatic in the west, as Swansea's mean away distance rose to 41.4km and Llanelly's to 44.7km. They could now travel to each other's ground, rather than finding a midway location, whilst the lines into Carmarthen-shire and Pembrokeshire allowed both clubs to play Haverfordwest and Carmarthen. Previously the journey from Llanelli to Carmarthen in one of McKiernon's coaches had taken three hours on narrow, rutted roads, but now the market town was just fifty minutes down the line!

This shrinkage of distance allowed regular contact with sides in south-west Wales which had previously survived on practice games amongst their members, plus occasional matches with garrison sides or local villages. This was a great step forward even if the timing of fixtures was reliant on the train timetable; the 1854 encounter between Llanelly and Haverfordwest had to be finished early so that the Haverfordwest team could catch the 6 p.m. train back home.[38] Not only did the opening of Brunel's great new line reduce travel times, it also reduced the costs which the members and the clubs had to pay for these away ventures. In some cases, the railway companies even provided special trains and Llanelly CC was fortunate to be provided with them at a cheap rate for its outings to Tenby and annual visit to Gwauncaegurwen to play Cwmamman. It also allowed more spectators to travel and, in 1853, *The Cambrian* was able to report that 'a special train, per Llanelly and Llandeilo Railway, conveyed a large number of excursionists from Llanelly and other places to witness the rather novel game . . . which shows a love for the renovating and healthful pastime. Cricket is becoming more and more appreciated'.[39]

The provision of this new form of public transport had three other important consequences. Firstly, it allowed more people to travel and play in away matches. A cheap day return fare was within the scope of more working people compared with the rather exclusive days of coach and horse. The only stumbling block now that travel costs were lower was getting time off to play, but after the passing of the 1847 Factory Act and Early Closing Movement, workers had more spare time and found that they were able to travel if away games were arranged on their free afternoons.

Secondly, the improved transport network allowed better commun-ication between clubs and news about cricket could be disseminated throughout the region. Derek West believed that cricket historians should not underestimate the role of the newly inaugurated postal system in 1840, because the Penny Post provided 'a cheap, rapid means of forwarding match reports to the Press and at the same time, facilitate the arrangement of fixtures between clubs'.[40] More people were able to read

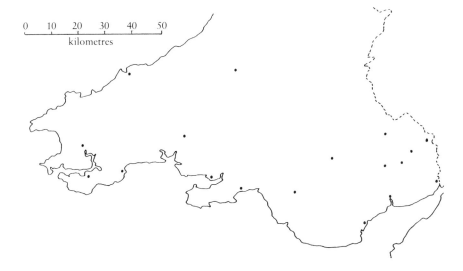

Figure 12. Location of teams in south Wales formed 1785–1839

about games that took place in south Wales, and a growing number of national papers and journals were available following the removal of stamp duty. The cricket lovers and players of the area were therefore able to read about the performances of top English players, as well as reports of leading clubs in the Welsh papers.

A third factor was that the railway lines united the entire region and meant that diffusion no longer occurred by the neighbourhood effect. It also meant that the early 'culture hearths' in the Carmarthen and Raglan areas were not isolated growth points and allowed easier travel into England. More aspiring clubs could contemplate fixtures with the 'crack' sides in the West country and could challenge a wider choice rather than just those in the Hereford or Bristol area. In short, the opening of these lines meant that south Wales was no longer isolated from England or reliant on a few roads over the hills for occasional contact. Some of the barriers had been broken down and new channels of diffusion were available along which the game could quickly spread.

Even so, there were still a few obstacles to be overcome in mid-century, especially Nonconformist opposition. In some areas it was prompted by the drinking and after-match convivialities, whilst in others it was the result of workingmen playing sport on Sundays, which was their only spare day due to the long demands of the six-day week. Keith Kissack has shown that there was religious disapproval of games in the Monmouth and Forest of Dean area, with a pamphlet issued in 1851 by the Revd

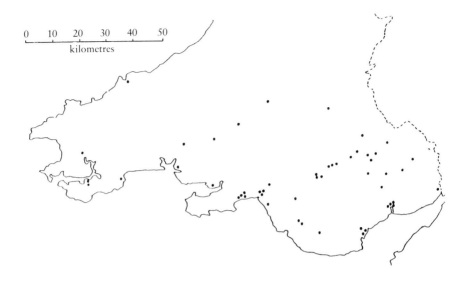

Figure 13. Location of teams in south Wales formed 1840–1855

P. M. Procter describing how a miner called Thomas Morgan, who was normally first on the ground yet the last to return home, decided one Sunday to refrain from his heathen tendencies and drinking habits by going to church instead. He was 'immediately converted and never went near a cricket ground again. He died deeply penitent and Heaven gained a very good batsman'.[41]

Nevertheless, cricket had clearly established a strong foothold by the middle of the nineteenth century. Figures 12 and 13 show the location and proliferation of clubs which were in existence by 1855, compared with the period before 1840. The agents responsible for the game's rapid growth between these two dates were the gentry, MPs and affluent industrialists. They had the social standing, entrepreneurial skills and money to ensure that the game took a firm hold in both the expanding industrial towns and ports of Glamorgan, as well as the more rural areas of Carmarthenshire and Monmouthshire. But the mid-nineteenth century did not mark the end of their involvement and it was wealthy individuals such as George Homfray of Newport who continued to play a leading role in the next stage of the game's development.

4 / *The Wandering Welshmen and the Rise of Cadoxton*

T HE FORMATION in 1846 by William Clarke of Nottingham of an All England XI to tour the country playing exhibition games was a key date in the history of the game in England during the days before regular country cricket. As A.A. Thomson wrote 'the part played by the touring sides in cricket's progress cannot be overvalued . . . their effect in entertainment and emulation over the remoter parts of England was enormous. Indeed, they spread and delighted in spreading the whole art and true spirit of the game'.[1] This itinerant eleven and its offshoot, the United All England XI both played important roles in the further development of the game in south Wales.

By the early 1850s Cardiff and Newport were able to hold their own against English teams. Their officials were looking for fresh and exciting challenges, and they fancied contests with some of the top players whose deeds they had read about in the English newspapers that were now freely circulating in the region. The leading players in south Wales were well aware of the All-England Eleven's activities and the financial boost they gave several clubs, because in 1850 the Eleven had challenged a XXII of Hereford and District. Colonel T. Conway Lloyd of Brecon donated £30 to the subscription fund which was created for this match, and the Hereford side included the best four players of the Brecon Town and Garrison Club.[2] The match on Widemarsh Common attracted a crowd in excess of 2,000, including people from Monmouthshire and Brecon, and to their delight, the All-England team was defeated. The victory gave Herefordshire a cricketing and a financial boost, with the *Carmarthen Journal* noting that 'very large sums of money changed hands'.[3] This intensified the rivalry between the clubs in south Wales and their neighbours over the border, making the Welsh teams even more eager to meet and hopefully beat the All-England players.

A contest had been out of the question before the early 1850s, but with the improved transport network, south Wales was more accessible and William Clarke was approached about a grand three-day match in the region during June 1855. No records survive about who made the initial approach to Clarke's team, but it would appear that a consortium of leading figures in the Neath area were prominent in the discussions, including Alex Cuthbertson, a local solicitor and former mayor of the town. Using his political contacts, Cuthbertson gained the support of several local MPs and a fund was set up to raise cash to allow the arrangements to go ahead and meet Clarke's requests.[4] He also obtained the use of a large field owned jointly by the Earl of Jersey and the Bute Estate, opposite Court Herbert near the road leading to Neath Abbey. By selecting this location, Cuthbertson believed that considerable support would be attracted from the surrounding valleys. R. T. Crawshay agreed for the Cyfarthfa Band to travel from Merthyr to entertain the crowd, whilst the local railways agreed to run special excursion trains to the match.[5]

The team that challenged the All-England side was chiefly composed of players from Neath, Swansea and Cardiff, and the contest was billed as 'Eleven of All-England versus Twenty-Two of Neath and South Wales'. Even so, Cuthbertson secured the services of Henry Grace and Alfred Pocock, the Graces' famous coach, plus Selby, the professional assisting Cardiff, whilst on the day 'Ducky' Diver was given to Cuthbertson's team from the England squad, to make the XXII rather more cosmopolitan than Welsh. The Neath club clearly saw the fixture as a lucrative financial venture, as well as a cricketing one, and hoped that the attraction of the leading names in the region against some of the top names in English cricket, would lead to a bumper crowd, and help cover the expenditure they incurred in staging the match, as well as a concert in the town hall and a grand ball at the Castle Hotel. A measure of their sizeable outlay was the rather steep charge of a shilling into the ground, plus an extra sixpence for a seat in one of the special grandstands erected around the ground.

Heavy rain soaked the outfield in the days leading up to the match, before restricting play on all three days. In between the showers, the All-England side made a modest 66, and the XXII still had six wickets to fall in their first innings when the match was prematurely ended. Yet despite the rather soggy outcome and the financial loss which Neath incurred, the game helped put cricket in south Wales on the map, and one newspaper proudly claimed that 'the event will prove an epoch from which we shall hereafter have to date the progress of south Wales to a higher elevation in the noble art of cricketing'.[6]

The match certainly fired the imagination of the cricket lovers in the Neath and Swansea area, and the officials of clubs in the south-east were eager not to miss out on the opportunities. Soon after his visit to Neath, William Clarke met the officials of Cardiff CC,[7] and the outcome was a three-day match in August with a XXII of Cardiff and District in the field behind the Cardiff Arms Hotel. Once again, Henry Grace and his uncle and coach, Alfred Pocock, appeared as guests, plus the Hon. Wingfield and Cecil Twisleton-Wykeham-Fiennes who played for Winchester School, I Zingari and Hereford. The weather for this match was more favourable and a large crowd attended expecting a good showing from the local players. The *Cardiff and Merthyr Guardian* reported how they had practised hard for the game by 'assiduously testing sinew and muscle, by throwing the ball, plying the bat and practising the various rapid manoeuvres requisite for this vigorous and healthful game'. But on the day, these grand words were not enough and the Cardiff team struggled against the bowling of Clarke and Edgar Willsher, as the All-England side comfortably won.[8]

The year of 1855 set the pattern for the next few years, with annual visits by the All-England teams to the Principality. They returned in 1856 to Neath for a contest billed as a challenge between 'England and Wales'[9] on a field below Gnoll House. The outfield was surrounded by a number of refreshment stalls, 'together with a grandstand for the ladies, a roulette table and a target for rifle shooting'.[10] Despite these sundry attractions and the presence of leading players, the game drew only a sparse attendance. Once again, the high entrance fee limited the crowd to just the affluent gentlemen and political figures of the Neath area, and the lack of mass public support caused the Neath officials, who were more cautious after their excesses the previous year, to cancel the ball at the Castle Hotel. Later in the season, the United All England XI travelled further west to play a XXII of Llanelly and District. Llanelly were keen to show their rivals in Neath that they could also organize grand challenge matches, and they secured the use of Llanelly House for their match with the English side. They also had the services of leading players from Cardiff and Yorkshireman Ned Stephenson, and they put up a good fight, before losing by four wickets.[11]

The United All England side played a XXII from Cardiff and District in 1857 and proved yet again far too strong for the local team. Half of the forty-four innings of the Cardiff players ended in ducks, but what was of major significance was the presence of Captain Samuel George Homfray of Newport in the home team. He was a member of the influential Homfray family of Glenusk, who were closely associated with the flourishing industrial centres of the south Wales valleys. His father's uncle, Jeremiah Homfray had opened the Penydarren Ironworks in Merthyr in 1805 as well as others in Ebbw Vale and Tredegar. The family were also major landowners in the region following the purchase by

Jeremiah Homfray of Penlline Castle near Wenvoe in 1847, and the acquisition of vast areas of land in the Cardiff and Newport area. Although not an outstanding player, George Homfray was an enthusiastic supporter of cricket and his efforts on and off the field helped establish Newport as a leading club after the earlier difficulties of the 1840s and early 1850s. He was also closely involved with the club at Tredegar, where his father acted as a managing partner of the town's ironworks, and ensured recreation was provided for the employees at the works. Indeed, in 1849 the *Monmouthshire Merlin* noted how 'Tredegar C.C. have, under the fostering care of Mr. George Homfray, been doing well',[12] and to boost their funds and reputation, he arranged a single-wicket contest at Tredegar which drew a crowd of over a thousand.[13]

Homfray had therefore been an innovative force at club level, and by arranging a game in 1858 between Monmouthshire and All England he saw an opportunity to use his obvious organizational flair at a higher level. A further testament to his abilities was that the fixture in September 1858 proved to be the best organized of these exhibition games during the 1850s. He also opted for a much lower admission charge – just sixpence – compared with the games at Neath and he was rewarded with a lot of local support, as shown by the following press report:

> The Marshes Road was densely crowded, fruit and ginger beer stalls were pitched along the sidewalks, and the upper windows in most of the houses displayed numerous smiling faces, while stands were erected for the accommodation of the public. The taverns and beer houses did a thriving business along the road during the match.[14]

Homfray also assembled a decent side from the Newport and Cardiff clubs, plus Francis Tinley of Nottinghamshire and a pair of professionals from Lancashire who held engagements with local clubs. The Monmouthshire and South Wales XXII made ninety in their first innings, and then bowled out the England team for sixty-three. The *Monmouthshire Merlin* reported that 'the twenty-two began to think that all was well and went in for their second innings in good spirits. Their opponents however, now showed that they meant to win, and Jackson dropped his men one after the other in brilliant style'.[15] Fast bowler John Jackson took fifteen wickets as the Welsh side were dismissed for eighty-four, and then George Parr hit forty-eight to see the All-England team to a four-wicket win.

Despite the defeat, the match showed that the cricketers of south Wales could hold their own with the top English players, and the rematch in 1859 was eagerly awaited. Once again, Homfray selected from his own Newport team, but this time he added players from Cardiff,

Abergavenny, Brecon and Llandovery reflecting the range of his influence. The South Wales XXII also included professionals Grundy and Brampton from Nottinghamshire, Samuel Belcher who later played for New South Wales and two cricketing clergymen from Hampshire. The All-England team were without several regulars and they struggled against Homfray's team. All of his diverse guests made useful contributions, none more so than Grundy who took six wickets as the Englishmen were dismissed for ninety-six chasing 158 to win on the final day. The long awaited victory was celebrated by Homfray and his team for many hours after the visitors and spectators had left the ground.[16]

This victory in 1859 proved to be a turning-point in the history of cricket in south Wales, as Homfray was keen to maintain and consolidate upon the impetus this victory, and the other exhibition matches, had given Welsh cricket. When coupled with the further construction of rail lines and the continuing influx of talented players from England, Homfray realized that the time was right for the formation of a side to represent south Wales. He was the ideal man to take this action because he had already arranged his own elevens to play the top clubs and the exhibition games showed that he had a wealth of contacts. In July 1859 he secured fixtures with Clifton and the South Wales Cricket Club was born.[17]

The South Wales CC, however, began rather shakily in its opening game at Clifton on 28 and 29 July. Homfray only managed to raise the help of nine other players and he had to obtain a substitute from the home club. Despite the fact that Clifton included an eleven-year-old lad called W. G. Grace, they proved far too strong from Homfray's side. E. M. Grace made seventy-two in Clifton's second innings and the south Wales CC lost by 114 runs.[18] In spite of this reverse, Homfray did not lose heart and flushed with the success over the All-England team was confident enough to wager £50 on his team winning the return game at Newport at the end of August. But with so much at stake, the contest was marred by a furious row over an umpiring decision, and after the visitors had scored 147–9 the match was abandoned, leaving the bemused correspondent of the *Newport Gazette* to report that 'the game for some reason was not concluded'.[19]

This game at Newport was also the only one that the club actually played on Welsh soil during their first seven seasons.[20] The result was that between 1860 and 1865 the South Wales CC led a nomadic existence travelling to fixtures in the West of England and undertaking an annual tour of London. Through Homfray's contacts, these tours consisted of a week- or ten-day period during which games over two or three days were held with top sides including the MCC, I Zingari, Prince's, Surrey Club and Ground, Knickerbockers and the Gentlemen of Sussex and Kent.[20] In

1864 their tour lasted for three weeks beginning on 11 July at The Oval and finishing on 29 July after visits to Brighton, Gravesend, Islington and Southgate.

To a large extent, the South Wales CC was a throwback to the days of Philipps of Cwmgwili and the Raglan club, in the sense that it was a gentlemen's club rather than a representative side. As David Smith has observed, 'the composition of the early South Wales teams revealed the blend familiar in regional sides of that period: predominantly gentlemen who had been coached at English public schools, some talented local cricketers and the hard toiling professionals who were especially welcome for lengthy bowling stints'.[21] There were many reasons for this, – for a start, the gentlemen were the only ones who could afford to spend such a large amount of both time and money playing cricket outside south Wales. The annual visits to the London area also satisfied their social and political aspirations, whilst the fixtures fulfilled the desires of Homfray and his friends from the local gentry to play a good standard of cricket.

The exploits of the South Wales CC also allowed the participants to believe that they were maintaining the gentry's position at the forefront of the game's development in south Wales. At times, this was a false belief as the South Wales CC was heavily beaten by crack English opponents, but they did manage a number of notable victories in their early years. In August 1860, they won at Clifton by eight wickets and, in July 1861, the MCC was defeated by seven wickets in the first Welsh victory at Lord's. But it was an Englishman who steered them to victory as E. M. Grace returned match figures of 15–111 with his roundarm and underarm deliveries as the MCC was dismissed for 103 and 140.[22]'The Coroner' produced another matchwinning performance the following year at Lord's, hitting 118 as the South Wales CC amassed the large total of 259. He then took six wickets in the MCC's second innings as they subsided to a 232-run defeat.[23]

In 1863 E.M. scored 129 at Cranbrook as the Gentlemen of Kent were beaten by fifty-three runs, followed by a score of eighty at Lord's in the victory over I Zingari. Then, in 1865, E.M. hit eighty-nine and took 12–129 as I Zingari were beaten again. Homfray was most fortunate to have one of the most talented young players in the country at his disposal. Grace had an immense appetite for the game and travelled widely to play for a host of teams. He was in huge demand and one can only speculate on the sums Homfray had to offer him to secure his services.[24] But Homfray felt it was well worth it as Grace's efforts with bat and ball boosted the name of the South Wales CC and helped cover up the inadequacies of many of the native players. Homfray himself took only fourteen wickets in nineteen matches, and scored just ninety-two runs in his twenty-seven innings, and without E.M.'s presence, the club could easily have ended up as a fanciful pipe-dream. As well as overseeing the operations of the South Wales CC, Homfray organized his own eleven which held two-day games against clubs and scratch teams in south Wales.[25] Several famous players turned out for Homfray's side including some of his South Wales CC 'guests' such as Belcher. As Jim Coldham once observed, 'Captain Homfray could not possibly pass a season over unless he had some cricketers to entertain'.[26] In 1861/2 Homfray's business commitments enforced a move west from Newport to Swansea, whose cricket club welcomed him with open arms. He soon became their president and continued to play a leading role on the field. One of Swansea's annual fixtures in the 1860s was a two-day match at home to the Pembroke Dock Garrison, for whom several MCC members played including William McCanlis who also appeared for Kent. The Garrison's visit to Swansea was the highlight of their season, and no doubt by mixing with them, Homfray realized the potential for a wandering eleven in west Wales to further assist the spread of the game. Homfray's missionary-like zeal resulted in the creation of another nomadic team called the Welsh Wanderers, who played fixtures in the 1860s and 1870s against sides such as Pembroke Garrison, Newcastle Emlyn, Haverfordwest and even Brecon further north, as well as playing host to touring sides ranging from the students of Jesus College, Oxford to the employees of the Great Western Railway Locomotive Depot. They also occasionally ventured outside the area, playing at Swindon in 1867 and Cheltenham College in 1870.[27]

The Welsh Wanderers were yet another example of a gentlemen's club, but there were important differences compared with the South Wales CC in the sense that there was a greater native element, and the Wanderers included players such as Hore and William Bancroft senior of Swansea, Whittington, Lovering and Moore of Neath, plus Rees and Arthur of Llanelly. Yet as in the early days of the South Wales CC Homfray sometimes had problems raising an eleven. Only eight turned out against Brecon in 1863 leaving *The Cambrian* to hope that 'in future this little band will respond to their captain's call and rally round him in full numbers'.[28] Homfray occasionally hired professionals for the Wanderers,[29] but he relied chiefly on top amateurs and leading personalities from Welsh clubs, attracted more often by the opportunities for socializing than by the cricket. For instance, *The Cambrian* reported in 1863 how 'the Wanderers were most liberally entertained by their Tivyside friends at the Salvation Hotel and the harmony was protracted to a late hour'.[30]

While Homfray wined and dined his way around west Wales, the South Wales CC continued its annual visits to England and the London tour. John Lloyd of the Brecon Town and Garrison club took over the reins of the club in 1862 following Homfray's move west and served as secretary and match manager. The 29-year-old was an established member of the Breconshire gentry and was the third son of John Lloyd senior of Dinas and Llangattock Court who had attended Eton and Oxford and served as a JP for the county. John Lloyd junior also aspired to the world of law, so after studying at St John's, Oxford, he became a practising barrister, and all in all, possessed the right social credentials for leading the South Wales CC.[31]

Despite the change of personnel, Lloyd continued the framework established by Homfray and, most importantly, secured the support of E. M. Grace and other members of the Grace family. In fact, it was during Lloyd's managerial period that W. G. Grace made his famous debut in 1864 for the South Wales club. Lloyd had drawn up a shortlist of players for the London tour and the match at Brighton against the Gentlemen of Sussex, and he contacted Thornbury to see if E.M. and Henry Grace were available. Henry was, but E.M. was still travelling back from a winter tour of Australia, so Henry suggested that his 15-year-old brother should play. W.G. was duly booked by Lloyd to appear in the game against Surrey at The Oval followed by the match at Brighton as he knew the youngster was one of the most promising performers with the West Gloucestershire team. Even so, Lloyd still wondered if the opposition at Brighton would be too strong for the young lad and soon after arriving in London he was offered the services of a MCC member for the Sussex match. Lloyd approached Henry Grace on the morning of the Surrey match about W.G. standing down at Brighton, but Henry strongly objected and said 'the boy was asked to play in both matches and he shall play in both matches or none, and I hope every member of the team will do as I expect him to do'.[32] The fifteen-year-old repaid his brother's faith by scoring five and thirty-eight at The Oval, followed by 170 and fifty-six not out at Brighton to dispel Lloyd's fears that he was not good enough. In 1891 the famous Doctor published some of his recollections and he clearly remembered the events of 14 July 1864 by writing:

> I had scored 170 – made up of 19 fours, 9 threes, 17 twos and singles – without giving a chance. I was out in attempting to cut a wide ball, getting over it too much and cutting it into my wicket. We had news the same afternoon that E. M. had stepped on English soil, and was wired to turn up the next morning. He did not, possibly satisfied that there was no need for him after our large score. They gave me a bat, which I have today, and am very proud of . . . I value it for the reason that it marks the date of the beginning of my long scores. I was not quite sixteen years of age, and had gained my first experience in playing steadily and consistently through a long innings.[33]

W.G. also turned in some useful bowling performances for the South Wales CC taking 5–59 as the I Zingari were beaten at Lord's in 1865 and in the following match 8–72 against Surrey at The Oval. But the youngster was playing more and more first-class cricket by this time, and his appearance against Surrey was his last for the South Wales CC. At the end of the 1865 season, the Graces withdrew their patronage of the Welsh club, partly because of W.G.'s involvment elsewhere, and also as a result of the club no longer being able to afford large sums to pay their expenses. The loss of their support was just one factor to explain why little was heard of the South Wales CC in the rest of the 1860s. W.G.'s recollections also show the rather haphazard way the team was selected, with preference often being given to the wealthy stalwarts rather than young and upcoming talent. By the mid 1860s many of these veterans were past their best, so a decline in playing standards may have also have caused the club's demise. A further factor was that John Lloyd was starting to lose interest in the club, and spent more time with his Breconshire club after handing over the duties of secretary in 1865. The decline of the South Wales CC in the mid-1860s ironically occurred at the time of the rise of Cadoxton CC near Neath and left the way clear for J. T. D. Llewelyn to assume the mantle of cricket's leading promoter in south Wales during the second half of the nineteenth century. John Talbot Dillwyn Llewelyn was the son of J. D. Llewelyn of Penllergaer, who besides being a wealthy industrialist and Mayor of Swansea, holds the distinction of being the first photographer in Wales.[34] J.T.D. was educated at Eton and Oxford, and it was in these august surroundings that the young Llewelyn improved on the cricket skills he had learnt on the lawns of Penllergaer House. He read law at Christ Church, and entered himself as a student of the Inner Temple in 1859, but he then changed his mind about a legal career and opted to follow the example of his father and J. H. Vivian by going into business and politics in south Wales.[35] After coming down from Oxford in 1856, J.T.D. established himself as a leading all-rounder with Swansea, and several other clubs for whom he guested.[36] He was an unorthodox, but hard-hitting batsman and a lively right-arm bowler, considered by contemporary writers to be the first person to bowl a consistent length in south Wales with roundarm deliveries. One commented that:

> he was a better bowler than we realised in those days, for while we others depended largely on the eccentricities of the pitch, he could keep his end going on a hard true wicket, on which we were innocuous, bowling with an easy action, a good length ball and with a certain amount of spin. He was a shocking bat, it is true, but then he never pretended to be anything else. He had a way of scooping at a half-volley with his nose pointed heavenwards.[37]

Shocking or not, he once hit a ball out of the Corporation Field in Neath into an adjoining garden,[38] and made an unbeaten seventy-one batting at number eight for Cadoxton against a strong Cardiff side in 1865.[39] With his wealthy and comfortable background, it was fitting that Homfray and Lloyd frequently called upon Llewelyn's services for the South Wales CC and the Welsh Wanderers.

In 1861 J.T.D. married Caroline Hicks-Beach the daughter of Disraeli's Colonial Secretary and sister of a former Chancellor of the Exchequer, and the 25-year-old settled down to launch his own career in south Wales. He had enjoyed his cricket with Swansea and the wandering sides and, in keeping with his social aspirations, the young gentleman was eager to improve cricket at club level. In the same year he became President of Swansea CC, giving them a sizeable donation to help them through after the club incurred a loss due to bad weather.[40] However, the area on which he focused his time, energy and capital over the next half century was further east near Neath, and in March 1863 he founded Cadoxton CC which became the MCC of Wales. Neath had previously been one of the flourishing young clubs in south Wales, but following the visits of the All-England Eleven in the 1850s and the financial failure of these exhibition games, the club had mounting debts, forcing it out of existence. They re-formed in 1863, but were still weak and lacked the services of good players.[41] Even so, there were many reasonable players in the locality and there was a demand for recreation which Llewelyn in his role as patron of the local school and church, was only too well aware. He knew as well that residents of the area moved to play elsewhere, and so to relieve these problems and help the parishioners, he re-formed Neath under the name Cadoxton CC.[42]

Llewelyn obtained both the use of the grounds of Court Herbert House, owned by the Dynevor Coal Company, and the services of a professional called Deacon, and he used his contacts throughout south Wales to build up an impressive fixture list. As *The Cambrian* reported in mid-May, 'Cadoxton CC was only established about six weeks ago but as the matter has been taken in hand by so great a cricketer and influential and active a gentleman as J. T. D. Llewelyn, great results may be expected from it.'[43] Cadoxton's inaugural match was fittingly against J. T. D.'s old club Swansea, at Court Herbert on 13 May, and was followed by games against Cowbridge Grammar School, Llanelly and Briton Ferry. An indication of the quick progress Cadoxton made in their first season was that they won against the powerful Llanelly XI and also ran a second eleven, which was quite rare for any club at that time.[44]

By 1864 the club had enough support to open the season with a match between the 1st XI and the Next XXII,[45] which like the rest of their home games in 1864, was staged on the Neath recreation ground. The club ventured even further for their away matches in 1864, visiting Brecon, Carmarthen and Cardiff and, in July, J.T.D. arranged a fixture with the Welsh Wanderers, which led to a social gathering of the top gentlemen cricketers in the area. He also arranged a cricket week in September along the lines of the Canterbury Festival which was a social highlight of the English season.[46]

By 1865 Cadoxton had 120 members and held an annual dinner and presentation evening hosted by J.T.D. himself.[47] It was attended by their prominent members, who included several members of the social and political scene, such as Howel Gwyn, the locally-born MP and friend of the Vivians, and William Mackworth, a member of the family which owned the Gnoll House and ran the town's copperworks, as well as having other commercial interests in London.[48] Through the influence of Mackworth and J.T.D., Cadoxton acquired a new home in the grounds of Gnoll House, which was being sold off for housing development as Neath rapidly expanded. J.T.D. realized how important it was for the club to have a permanent base and a good wicket of its own, so he paid the rent to ensure the use of the Gnoll.[49]

With such a lavish ground and respectable members, Cadoxton's fixture list rapidly expanded to include contests with premier English clubs.[50] Llewelyn often used his cricketing contacts to strengthen the Cadoxton side for their major fixtures and amongst the regular 'guests' were Llanelly's Ben Arthur and Swansea's William Bancroft senior. His close relationship with the Swansea side was important because in July 1866 a number of the Cadoxton players guested for the St Helen's club when a Swansea XXII challenged the United All England Eleven. In fact, J.T.D. himself opened the batting and top scored in Swansea's first innings. After the financial failure of Neath's exhibition fixtures, there were a few worries over Swansea's monetary commitments when arranging this fixture. A donations fund was opened to ease the fears, but the organizers also worried about whether the match would attract a decent crowd. Once again, J.T.D. came to their aid, in his capacity as a Director of both the Vale of Neath and Great Western Railway, as the companies agreed to run special excursions at low fares from Carmarthen, Bridgend, Merthyr and Aberdare.

J.T.D.'s support and assistance on and off the field helped ensure the success of the United England fixture, and a sizeable crowd attended on each day, paying a total of almost £131 in admission fees which more than covered the £66 paid to the England side for the game. The Swansea club finished with a profit of £13, allowing them to make a generous donation to the town's new General Hospital.[51] In addition, J.T.D.'s influence made Cadoxton the strongest club side in south Wales, and in May 1868, he was able to arrange a match between the Cadoxton club and the United South of England XI who included W. G. Grace for their visit to Neath. Llewelyn strengthened his Cadoxton XXII with Arthur and Bancroft, plus Middleton from Bridgend, Capt. Fyfe of Newport and a professional left-arm fast bowler called George Howitt who had played for Middlesex and Nottinghamshire. Once again, Llewelyn turned out against the illustrious opposition, and he showed his ability as a bowler by taking seven wickets, but it was Howitt who took the laurels by dismissing Grace for a duck in both innings.[52]

The United South of England match drew a decent crowd and there was also good support later in the season when Charles Lawrence's Australian Aborigines played at Swansea, and became the first overseas touring team to play in Wales.[53] Yet again J.T.D. played an influential role on and off the field by assembling a team called the Gentlemen of Swansea to challenge the tourists. He took 6–64 as the Aborigines made 193, but their bowling was far too strong for Llewelyn's side and they won by an innings. However, J.T.D.'s efforts were rewarded with another decent crowd, who were entertained by a display of boomerang throwing and other athletic sports by the tourists.[54]

Swansea's officials took another financial gamble by arranging this fixture. They could not meet the Aborigines' request, in the region of £200, for their appearance at St Helen's, so instead they agreed that the tourists should collect all the gate money, pay the expenses and give Swansea £20 for the time and effort spent in arranging the fixture. Their fears proved groundless once again, as the gate money amounted to £142, and despite having to cover the cost of a train journey from Rochdale, the Australians profited by £44. The Australians met a few financial problems during their tour, with eight of the forty-eight fixtures resulting in a loss, whilst the profit from eighteen others were below the Swansea level. This reflected the rising interest in cricket in south Wales, and Llewelyn's influence both in cricketing and railway circles in assembling a decent side and securing cheap excursion trains to Swansea.[55] Llewelyn also assisted the Welsh Wanderers and appeared in their annual visits to west Wales and Cheltenham College. It was fitting that when the Wanderers disbanded in 1868, Cadoxton took over their fixtures with Cardigan and ensured that the cricketers of the west were not left isolated. The following year J.T.D. also arranged two-day fixtures with Clifton,[56] as Cadoxton by the late 1860s had become the nearest team in south Wales, in terms of importance and 'missionary work', to the MCC. No doubt, comparisons were drawn at these social gatherings of the game's élite in south Wales, and Llewelyn must have been delighted in 1869 to secure a fixture with the MCC and in August he took a team of twelve up to Lord's. Once again, Llewelyn called upon his friends Ben Arthur and William Bancroft senior for the journey up to London, but this time J.T.D. opted to sit in the pavilion, rather than play, no doubt giving one of his gentlemen friends the opportunity to appear on the hallowed turf at Lord's. The Welshmen rose to the occasion with Joseph Lovering, the 33-year-old Cadoxton professional, taking fifteen wickets, all bar one clean bowled with his fast roundarm deliveries, as the Cadoxton team beat the MCC by twenty-four runs.[57] The victory proved that club cricket had come of age in south Wales, and was the result of Llewelyn's wholehearted and enthusiastic endeavours with Swansea and Cadoxton. It was no surprise that the squire of Penllergaer did not rest there, and became one of the people responsible for the establishment of county sides in the region.

5 / *The Formation of County Clubs*

A SERIES of regular fixtures between county elevens increasingly became the highlight of the summer sporting calendar in south Wales during the 1860s although there had been sides purporting to represent the various counties a long time before this decade.[1] The first 'county' team to establish itself was the Monmouthshire side at Raglan, and as far back as August 1825 its members were playing home and away games with a team representing Breconshire. But as Chapters 2 and 3 showed, the Monmouthshire side was more of a gentlemen's club than a truly representative county team playing other similar elevens. (see Appendix B). Nevertheless, the Raglan club was important in that it established both the important contacts with England and a membership structure with rules and annual subscriptions, and over time it became a model for the true county teams that followed in the second half of the nineteenth century.

Other embryonic county teams appeared during the 1850s in both the west and east of the region. From 1850, Sir William Style of Ruperra Castle assembled a team of gentlemen and soldiers from Monmouthshire which played home and away games with Cardiff and held home fixtures on the lawns in front of his mansion.[2] In 1853 Style's Monmouthshire and Military XI extended its fixture list to include contests with Abergavenny and Major Rolls's team at Monmouth. Two years later Style and Rolls pooled their resources and organized a Monmouthshire XI to play Herefordshire at Ross.[3] This pattern of assembling 'county' sides for one-off, or annual, games was repeated in the west. As early as July 1830 a 'county' team based at Pembroke held annual games against Tenby. By the 1840s the Pembrokeshire team regularly travelled to Carmarthen, and like the Raglan side was composed of members of the local gentry who met at Haverfordwest.[4] In August 1851 the Pembrokeshire side played home and away games with the Royal Artillery based at

Pembroke Dock and included the local MP, J. H. Philipps of Picton Castle, who was a relation of the Philipps of Cwmgwili.

Another gentlemen's side assisted by the military was established in Carmarthenshire and, in August 1852, staged a match between those people who lived in the county town and those who resided elsewhere. Later in the season the gentlemen, plus Captains Rush and Herbert, travelled to Haverfordwest to play a two-day fixture against the Pembrokeshire team, whilst in August a side called the Carmarthen Zingari journeyed to Tenby.[5]

By 1853 transport improvements allowed the Carmarthen club to challenge Llanelly, Swansea and Llandovery (see Figure 18 on p. 89). Much to their delight, the Carmarthenshire gentlemen managed to defeat the highly regarded Swansea club by eight wickets, and they twice travelled to Llanelly and on both occasions returned home victorious.[6] Flushed with success, arrangements were set in hand during 1854 for a county match between Carmarthenshire and Glamorgan. In July the *Western Telegraph* announced that 'arrangments are in progress for the playing of a match between the counties of Carmarthen and Glamorgan, which if carried out cannot fail, we think, to prove advantageous to the advancement of this noble recreation'.[7] But nothing came of the fixture – Capt. Rush, their top batsman, was soon posted elsewhere, whilst their talented young opener Trevor Alcock died tragically in September 1854 at the age of just twenty-seven.[8] Without its star performers, the team failed to maintain the standards set in 1853 and without an influential promoter such as Llewelyn or Homfray, the idea of a Carmarthenshire side was temporarily dispelled.

Yet within five years a new Carmarthenshire XI had been created and during the 1860s the team was staging annual fixtures against other county sides. Two factors were responsible for the creation, and success, of this new side – the first operated on a local scale, whilst the other applied at a regional or national scale. Firstly, the Carmarthenshire club acquired the support of Charles Bishop, the son of a country judge in Gloucestershire, who lived at Dolgarreg, on the road from Llangadog to Llandovery. Bishop was the clerk to the Carmarthenshire Justices and chief steward to the Earl of Ashburnham's Estate. If his social credentials were impressive, so were his cricketing ones, with an English public school background and membership of the MCC. The second factor lay outside the cricketing world and was related to the expanding economy of the region, and a growing sense of national pride. The latter has been analysed by Kenneth Morgan who wrote that:

> it gained new momentum in the early and middle decades of the nineteenth century. The expansion of industry and the growth of new towns, the internal

colonization of the industrialised areas of their own land by Welsh-speaking migrants gave new urban and institutional direction to the native culture. It was the industrial towns of south Wales and the expanding smaller towns of the rural north and west – Merthyr, Pontypridd and Swansea; Caernarvon, Aberystwyth and Carmarthen – that provided the main agencies by which Welsh national consciousness was to flourish.[9]

When added to the fact that Carmarthenshire was one of the game's original growth points, it was no surprise that the seeds were sown in the market town for the formation of a county side to challenge other representative teams, both inside and outside Wales.

In September 1859, Bishop convened a meeting to discuss the formation of a Carmarthenshire team,[10] and as a result a trial match to assess the strength of the potential players took place in July 1860 between Upper and Lower Carmarthenshire at Bishop's country mansion.[11] Two days later, a fixture took place at Carmarthen against a Pembrokeshire side, although it was predominantly a match between the members of Carmarthen and Haverfordwest CC.[12] A return match took place in mid-August at Haverfordwest, but Bishop was unable to take part because he was on tour with the South Wales CC at Bath. However, his contacts with the South Wales CC came in handy for the next phase of the early county matches, because it was through his appearances for Homfray's wandering side and acquaintance with other leading players in south Wales that the seeds were sown for the first inter-county match between Carmarthenshire and Glamorgan at Llanelly Park on 5 and 6 August 1861.

The Glamorgan side was assembled by J. W. T. O'Donoghue, the Swansea captain and a stalwart of the South Wales team. His eleven contained two other South Wales regulars, Cardiff's Wallis and Worthington, plus Palanet, an Oxford student, whilst the rest of his side contained O'Donoghue's gentlemen friends from the Swansea side and their professionals Spencer and William Bancroft senior. However, on the morning of the match, one of the Swansea gentlemen was unable to travel to Llanelli and O'Donoghue had to ask C. W. Coombs, a member of Llanelly's committee and a partner in the town's pottery to act as a late substitute. Six of Coombs's Llanelly club mates appeared for Carmarthenshire, including his trading partner Teddy Holland. The rest of the XI was made up by two players from Carmarthen, the Arthur brothers of Llanelly, Duntze of Haverfordwest and John Lloyd of Brecon who was one of Bishop's team mates from the South Wales CC.

The Cambrian stated that this, 'the first game that had ever been played between the two counties, was looked forward to with some interest'. Unfortunately, the weather intervened and the report continued to say that 'the ground, through the late incessant rains, was from the commencement in a truly pitiable condition; wherever the ball alighted, there it remained, almost motionless, as if checked or detained by some magnetic force'.[13] Consequently, none of the batsmen on either side played with any degree of authority, and although Palanet made thirty-seven and twenty, the bowling of the Arthur brothers proved too much for his Glamorgan colleagues and Carmarthenshire won by twelve runs.

Despite being inter-county in name, the two teams were clearly not representative of all the leading clubs within the two counties, and were simply composed of colleagues and acquaintances of the two captains – in fact, *The Cambrian* called the sides 'Mr C. Bishop's Eleven' and 'Mr O'Donoghue's Eleven' – rather than using either of the county's names. Nevertheless, it was a starting point and, for the next couple of years, the Glamorgan and Carmarthenshire teams met on an annual basis, with gentlemen and leading figures from the social and business world taking part.[14]

The Carmarthenshire club dramatically expanded its operations after a meeting on 14 February 1864 at the Ivy Bush Hotel in Carmarthen. The stimulus for the change was Bishop gaining the support of Capt. D. E. Jones of Velindre, plus Lord Cawdor, the Lord Lieutenant of the county, who owned extensive areas of land in the area and organized summer gatherings of gentlemen at his home, Golden Grove. The meeting began with the election of Lord Cawdor as the club's president, followed by the appointment of Bishop as the honorary secretary of the new organization. A set of rules was agreed and a management committee was formed, including Capt. Jones, J. H. Barker of Carmarthen, H. W. T. Howells of Glaspant, and E. W. Mansel Lewis, the owner of the Stradey Park Estate in Llanelli. There was considerable support for the new club and over sixty members were enrolled at half a guinea each, although the new club remained exclusive stipulating that 'no tradesmen, or any of the working class being admitted',[15] whilst the annual meetings were held during the week of Carmarthen Races when there would be a gathering of the county's élite. Seven two-day fixtures were arranged with Clifton, Glamorganshire, the Gentlemen of Breconshire, the Hon. F. C. Morgan's XI, the Gentlemen of Tivyside and Cardiganshire and a team composed of the Gentlemen of Pembrokeshire plus the officers of the Pembroke Garrison. Bishop agreed for home matches to be held at Dolgarreg, and they were given a further boost when the Llanelly and Vale of Towy Railways agreed to provide cheap excursion fares on their services to Llandovery, so that spectators could easily travel to Bishop's ground to watch the Carmarthenshire fixtures.[16] All that was needed was a decent eleven, so in April 1864 Bishop sent out the following letter to the seventy people who had enrolled as playing members:

I beg to forward you below a list of County matches as arranged for the coming season, and request the favour of your informing me, before the 18th of next month, in which of those matches you would wish to play, should there be a vacancy for you. Your subscription of half a guinea, due 1st of May, should be remitted to me at your earliest convenience.[17]

His requests yielded the desired result and Carmarthenshire was able to field strong sides, whilst on occasions, Bishop's contacts with the West Country and the South Wales CC meant that E. M. Grace's services were secured. Their first season with an expanded fixture list was successful, and one of their best performances came at The Gnoll, with Grace making thirty-four and forty-one, and taking 6–46 in Glamorgan's first innings. Unfortunately, Grace was unable to bowl in Glamorgan's second innings, allowing them to hang on for a draw. E. M.'s involvement with Carmarthenshire was perfectly within the club's regulations, despite the fact that he lived near Bristol. This was simply because rule one stated 'The Carmarthenshire Cricket Club should comprise Resident and Non-Resident members of the county.'[18] This also allowed a number of Bishop's friends from the South Wales CC including Llewelyn and Cuthbertson from Cadoxton, Homfray of Newport and Swansea, and Worthington of Cardiff to appear for Carmarthenshire alongside the county's gentry, including Lord Cawdor's son, Frederick Vaughan-Campbell of Eton and Oxford University.

The new Carmarthenshire side was therefore a more indigenous and localized version of the South Wales CC, organizing games for gentlemen within the region rather than chiefly outside. There was considerable overlap in terms of membership and their 1864 list included all of the leading patrons of cricket and gentry of south Wales, from Llewelyn and Howel Gwyn MP in the west to the Crawshays and Baskervilles of Clyro Court in the east. With such an impressive array of support, the Carmarthenshire club could easily have developed into a national, rather than a regional team, and all of the county sides which were subsequently established were created by patrons or members of this embryonic county club.

These may well have been Bishop's long-term aspirations, and he gave a hint of these grand ideas for the club by organizing a tour to Ireland in 1865. It began on 23 August with a fixture against Pembrokeshire and after the match the team sailed across the Irish Sea to become the first Welsh team to travel overseas. The next day they met the Phoenix Park CC in Dublin, followed by fixtures with the Vice Regal Club, and the Officers stationed at the Curragh Camp. The party then returned home and on 4 September played another match with Pembrokeshire at Tenby.

However, it seems that the tour severely drained the club's funds, because in 1866 they arranged a less extravagant and more limited fixture list. Support also began to drop with just seven players turning up to play Glamorgan during June.[19] The mid-1860s and the tour to Ireland were, therefore, the heydays of the Carmarthenshire club and little was heard of the club in the newspapers after 1866.

Despite the failure of Bishops's bold, and slightly too grand, efforts, he was a pioneering influence, showing that a county side could be created. His actions were copied in the east, and in 1863 a team from Monmouthshire was organized to play Breconshire after a trial game a few days before at Chepstow. The Ruperra Castle estate was once again connected with this side and the Hon. Frederick Courtenay Morgan assembled the gentlemen for the games. There were similarities as well to the 'good old days' of the Monmouthshire club, as the new county side held its annual meetings at Raglan on the day of the hunt dinner when many gentlemen of the area would be present.[20] But there were important differences from the former Raglan side as the club strove to become more representative of the entire county and included gentlemen from many of the teams throughout Monmouthshire. Even so, it still drew heavily on support from the squirearchy with Major Edward Curre, of Itton Court, Chepstow, and J. A. Rolls of The Hendre, Monmouth representing the club. Monmouthshire did not have as extensive a fixture list as the Carmarthenshire club but, nevertheless, in 1866 they secured a match with the powerful West Gloucestershire side for whom the Grace family were the leading players. Through their influence and contacts in south Wales, they arranged a tour of Wales and the Marches, during which they defeated the XXII assembled by the Monmouthshire club.[21]

In the mean time, the Breconshire Cricket Club which had been formed in 1847 went from strength to strength.[22] During the 1850s they only played club teams such as Crickhowell, but by the 1860s they were able to challenge other 'county' sides. Their leading players in the 1850s were members of the de Winton family, including Henry de Winton of Maesderwen, who later became Archdeacon of Brecon, as well as William and John Jeffreys de Winton,[23] the two sons of John Parry de Winton, a former Mayor of Brecon, who lived at Llanfrynach.

However, the leading personalities in the Breconshire club were the members of the Lloyd family of Dinas. The founder of the club was Old Etonian John Lloyd, the father of the South Wales CC's secretary. He was prominent in political circles and served as a local councillor,[24] but he was a country gentleman at heart, with a love of hunting, shooting, coursing and fishing as well as other gentlemanly pursuits such as cricket. These passions were passed on to his three sons, Thomas Conway, Penry and John junior. Together with his two brothers, John Lloyd junior helped establish their father's club as one of the top sides in the region, with fixtures against the likes of Abergavenny, Newport and the Welsh Wanderers. As well as promoting the Brecon club, the Lloyds also helped to spread the game with Penry Lloyd organizing a wandering gentlemen's eleven which played fixtures against premier clubs such as Cardiff.[25]

Through his contacts with the South Wales CC, John Lloyd junior realized the scope for expanding Breconshire's fixture list along the same lines as the Carmarthenshire club, to include games with other county elevens. In August 1863 the Breconshire team met the Monmouthshire XI raised by the Hon. F. C. Morgan, with John and Penry Lloyd opening the batting as the Brecon team notched up a comfortable victory. In June 1864 a two-day fixture was held at Brecon with Cadoxton, followed by an away match at Dolgarreg against Carmarthenshire. The Lloyds selected a strong team for these fixtures and included Levick and Rosher from Abergavenny, Baskerville of Clyro Court and the top players from the Crickhowell club.[26] In 1865 Breconshire added Radnorshire to its fixture list, and as a result of their friendship with the Baskervilles, home and away contests were secured with Herefordshire in 1866.

By 1868 Breconshire's fixture list included matches with Shropshire, Monmouthshire, the Royal Welch Fusiliers and also Glamorgan. The latter had previously only played Carmarthenshire and this fixture in 1868 with Breconshire was the outcome of growing calls for the creation of a county side to represent Glamorgan. Back in 1855 a team formed of the gentlemen of the county met the Neath club,[27] whilst during the early 1860s O'Donoghue and Llewelyn arranged elevens for the matches with the Carmarthenshire side. But these were only one-off teams rather than formal clubs and, by the 1860s, as other county clubs were created, there was a feeling that a Glamorgan club could, and should, be formed.

The first person actively to support these ideas for a Glamorgan team was another Old Etonian, John Cole Nicholl, the son of Sir John Illtyd Nicholl, the MP for Cardiff between 1832 and 1852. J. C. Nicholl inherited the Merthyr Mawr estate, near Bridgend, after his father's death in 1852, and spent a great deal of money improving the house and laying a wicket in the grounds. He had learnt the game whilst at Eton, and in the 1850s he began playing for Bridgend. After inheriting Merthyr Mawr, he allowed his club to play in the estate's grounds, and it soon became one of the best wickets in the county. In August 1862 the *Cardiff and Merthyr Guardian* paid Nicholl the following compliment – 'knowing the expense and trouble Mr. Nicholl has been at to bring into the present state of perfection, let it suffice by saying that it is the finest piece of ground for cricket in south Wales'.[28] Not surprisingly, his private ground was soon in huge demand and Nicholl let other clubs use the first-class wicket, including Cardiff who twice met Cadoxton at Merthyr

Mawr in 1865, finding it a most suitable and convenient neutral venue.[29] Nicholl's efforts to promote cricket were also assisted by a close friendship with the Llewelyns, and in 1860 he married Mary Dillwyn, whose father Lewis Dillwyn was a patron of Swansea CC and an uncle of J.T.D.

Merthyr Mawr was also the venue for an early form of country house cricket. In 1859 Nicholl raised a Merthyr Mawr XI to play his Bridgend colleagues [30] and during the 1860s this eleven played regular matches, with many of the leading names in south Wales cricket taking part. Nicholl also used his family contacts to arrange matches at Merthyr Mawr. In 1866 his XI met a side made up of the Volunteers of the 3rd Glamorgan Rifles, selected by his father-in-law Major Dillwyn,[31] whilst his brother, Revd Edward Powell Nicholl, also brought over a team from his parish at Lacock in Wiltshire.[32] Their sisters also got involved and handwrote a spoof newspaper called *The Tiddle-Taddle* with reports on their brothers' cricketing exploits which were distributed amongst friends and family who stayed at the house when the cricket was taking place.[33] The grounds and house at Merthyr Mawr therefore saw the regular meeting of Nicholl's cricketing friends from all parts of the county, and it was at these gatherings that ideas for a Glamorgan side were given their first airing. J. C. Nicholl soon added his support, and in 1866 he raised a county eleven to challenge Charles Bishop's Carmarthenshire club. The Glamorgan side consisted of top players from both the west and the east, with the Bancrofts of Swansea, Llewelyn and Lovering of Cadoxton, plus Nicholl's team-mates from Bridgend. He also chose his close friend and fellow Old Etonian F. E. Stacey of Cardiff, whose father, the Revd Thomas Stacey, was the chaplain to the Nicholl's neighbour the Earl of Dunraven. Stacey was a fine batsman, and in 1859 scored eighty-nine for the Gentlemen of England against the Gentlemen of Kent, and his presence strengthened the Glamorgan line-up. However, heavy rain put the match in some doubt, and only seven of the Carmarthenshire side were present when play eventually began at 4 p.m. on the first day, presenting Nicholl's team with an easy victory.[34] In June 1868 Nicholl gave a further test to the idea of a Glamorgan side by organizing a two-day match between sides chosen from the eastern and western sides of the River Ogmore. Although the East Glamorgan XI, formed of Cardiff and Bridgend players, had a comfortable win by six wickets, it was a keenly fought contest and confirmed the potential for a county eleven.[35] Nicholl attempted to further these claims by contacting the All-England Eleven for a fixture in 1868 against a Glamorgan XXII which would also raise cash to help start a county club. But negotiations broke down over a suitable date as well as payments to the England team, and Nicholl's valiant efforts to form a county side were thwarted.

J. C. Nicholl was not the only person banging the drum for the creation of a Glamorgan side, however. His friend J. T. D. Llewelyn had for many years believed a county club could be established. He had captained the West XI in their fixture at Merthyr Mawr in 1868 and, after the defeat by the East, he knew only too well of the emerging talent in the Cardiff area. He felt the time was therefore right to start forming a county side, and if anyone was going to achieve this task, J.T.D. was the man to do it, for not only was he amongst the top social and cricketing figures, he also had a wealth of contacts by virtue of his associations with South Wales CC, Cadoxton, Carmarthenshire and the Glamorgan elevens which had played at Merthyr Mawr. Moreover, with his heart in the Neath and Swansea area, he did not want the rising stars in the east to seize the initiative and take the glory after all he had done to promote and boost cricket in the region.

In 1868 Llewelyn stepped into Nicholl's shoes and organized a Glamorgan side for home and away games with Breconshire. J.T.D. used his contacts to assemble a strong eleven from the clubs in the west and the east for the match at Brecon. Much to his delight, Glamorgan won by 149 runs with William Bancroft junior making fifty-one, Westwood of Swansea hitting eighty eight and J.T.D. himself taking six wickets. The victory boosted his resolve and during the winter of 1868/9 he contacted officials and patrons from clubs throughout the area regarding the formation of a county club to represent Glamorgan. The responses were favourable, no doubt prompted by the emergence of similar teams elsewhere, and the rising feelings of regional and national identity in the county's flourishing industrial centres.

Economic growth gave south Wales, and Glamorgan in particular, a huge boost, so that it now had an industrial identity and position of rising importance. It must have hurt the pride of businessmen, and gentry alike, still to see rather condescending comments about south Wales, such as the one below in an English gentleman's magazine of 1868:

> As for the Principality, a Welsh cricketer is as scarce an article as a Welsh cricket ground. Probably the Welsh are too much employed in providing the needful flannel for more enlightened districts.[36]

A meeting of the leading cricket officials in the county was convened during the following March at The Castle Hotel, Neath and as a result Glamorganshire CCC was created. The correspondent of *The Cambrian* was delighted with the news and wrote how:

> Other counties in south Wales have set the example and while we have so good a patron as J. T. D. Llewelyn, there can be no doubt that there will be a large enrolment. The formation of the above club will have no connection

with the Cadoxton one already in existence and which has always stood A1, but in all probability many of the gentlemen being members of the Cadoxton club will enrol their names for the county.[37]

To the contrary, Llewelyn was anxious to see the new club not solely restricted to the gentlemen of the larger clubs, such as Cadoxton. He felt that there was scope for a side which would not merely be used as a social stepping-stone as the South Wales CC had become, but which would instead develop stronger ties with the area than many of the other so-called county sides in south Wales. With this in mind, a game was organized on 12 and 13 May between the full county side and a Colts XXII drawn from Cadoxton, Swansea, Merthyr, Bridgend, Kilvey and Morriston 'with a view of testing the ability of the Eleven and also showing the talent in the rising generation of cricketers'.[38]

Five county matches were also organized in 1869 against Radnorshire, Breconshire and Monmouthshire. Glamorganshire's first county fixture was held at the Arms Park in mid-June against the Monmouthshire side which had been resurrected the year before by Capt. Hugo Pearson, a Royal Naval officer who resided near Ross. The match aroused considerable interest, chiefly because it was the first ever county contest on the Cardiff ground.[39] Llewelyn's Glamorganshire side was formed chiefly of players from the Cardiff club, plus Whittington and J.T.D. himself from Cadoxton, and the almost ubiquitous Homfray. During the season, many of the other gentlemen who appeared in the Merthyr Mawr gatherings were chosen, including J. C. Nicholl, whilst Joseph Lovering acted as the county's professional bowler. Also in the side on a regular basis were two Army officers, Captains Maxwell and Dangerfield, who were stationed in the area.[40]

Few of the Colts who played in the trial match back in May actually made it into the Glamorganshire side, and it was still predominantly a gentlemen's club. Even so, the team was a proper county side in the sense that the players lived in the locality and played for local clubs. Llewelyn was not tempted to introduce talent from outside the county boundaries in the way that Carmarthenshire allowed talented players who did not live in the county to bolster its batting line-up, which also included the not so-talented members of the local gentry.

It was this reliance on native talent which subsequently became the strength of the Glamorganshire side. Other county sides launched ambitious programmes and hired outside help and, to a large extent, they paid for this lack of local identity by going into decline later in the nineteenth century. But this was not the case with Glamorganshire and the present first-class club was created in 1888 out of the fledgling organization formed in 1869 by J. T. D. Llewelyn. Indeed, the cricket-loving squire of Penllergaer more than anyone else deserves the title 'the father of Glamorgan'.

6 / *Growth at the Grass Roots*

T HE PERIOD from 1850 until 1870 saw the county sides, the South Wales CC and the Cadoxton club become fixed at the top of the cricket hierarchy in south Wales. These years also saw a phenomenal rise at grass roots level, as shown by Figure 14 which charts the number of new clubs being formed or re-formed. During the 1830s and 1840s a total of thirty-eight clubs came into being, yet in the 1850s a total of fifty-one were created, followed by 105 in the 1860s. This was matched by an increase in newspaper coverage as shown in Table 1. During the 1830s an annual average of 4.9 matches was reported. By the 1850s this had risen to 37.2 and 70.2 by the 1860s. Figure 15 also shows the rise in the number of fixtures reported during the 1850s and 1860s as the game spread and became more newsworthy. These two decades saw the reporting of more than 1,000 fixtures, compared with a mere 176 during the previous twenty years.

TABLE 1 – MATCHES INVOLVING SOUTH WALES CLUBS REPORTED IN NEWSPAPERS, BY DECADE, 1830–1869

	1830–9	1840–9	1850–9	1860–9
Total reported	49	127	372	702

The geographical nature of this cricket boom of the 1850s and 1860s is illustrated in Figure 16 which plots the location of settlements with teams by 1870. In particular, it shows the location of the new clubs established in the booming industrial valleys of Glamorgan and Monmouthshire, as well as the continued expansion of the commercial settlements which had flourishing clubs in the 1840s and saw the creation of many new teams during the 1850s and 1860s. For instance, there were eighteen teams in the Cardiff area, twelve in Newport, eight in Neath, seven in Swansea and five in Llanelli.[1] There were also five clubs in Haverfordwest, which

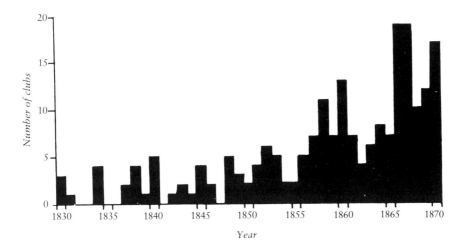

Figure 14. Number of clubs formed 1830–1870

Figure 16 shows was one of the towns in west Wales where new teams were created.

Several of the new sides in the industrial settlements of the south-east were tradesmen's teams. In Cardiff there were sides of drapers and ironmongers, whilst in June 1868 a schoolmasters team challenged Penarth.[2] In Newport the clubs included commercials, engineers and tradesmen, whilst Neath had a Drapers Assistants Club. One of the most bizarre teams however, was the eleven formed by employees and patients of Carmarthen Asylum, which challenged the local clubs and schools.[3] The participation of people in commercial occupations was increasingly encouraged during the 1860s as a healthy escape from the humdrum life in the Victorian cities. A report, based on the Cardiff area, in *The Cambrian* in May 1866 summed up their motives:

> Every exertion is being used by the influential residents . . . to provide the numerous clerks and other gentlemen engaged in sedentary occupations at the docks, telegraph stations etc. amusement of a healthy and invigorating tendency for both mind and body. In the winter months, there were readings, pleasant evenings, chess clubs etc. and now there are two cricket clubs in action – the Prince of Wales and the Windsor.[4]

Even so, the formation of tradesmen's teams was not a major new direction in the game's development in the second half of the nineteenth century, because the teams were chiefly concerned with organizing practices and the clubs themselves had a somewhat limited

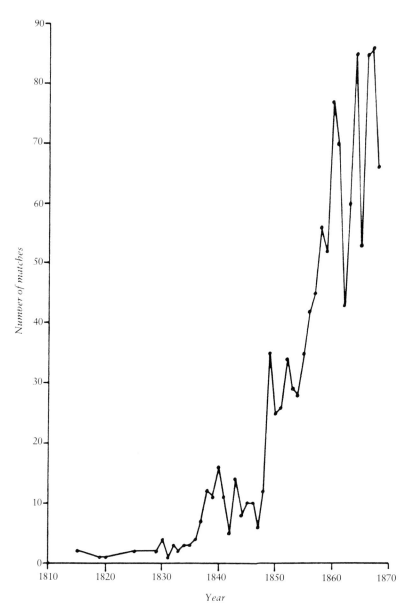

Figure 15. Number of matches reported in the newspapers 1815–1868

fixture list. So although tradesmen were playing the game, their involvement was similar to that of the gentlemen's clubs of the late eighteenth and early nineteenth centuries, with annual challenge

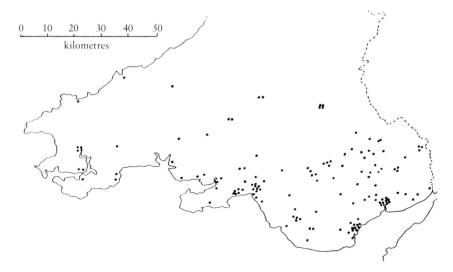

Figure 16. Location of teams in south Wales formed before 1870

matches, such as the game at the Arms Park in August 1867 between the Shop Assistants of Cross Brothers and Mr Evans's Temple of Fashion.[5]

These shopowners and tradesmen still faced many barriers to their cricketing or other sporting activities. They might have been extremely eager to play, or had rising social aspirations, but a major handicap still existed in that their spare time was limited by the demands of office work or long hours at shops or businesses. The premier clubs in the towns were chiefly interested in all-day games rather than late afternoon fixtures whilst games on Sundays were unheard of. Consequently, the traders and office workers were left on their half days to become involved in practices or to challenge assistants from other shops or employees in rival businesses. Even so, getting away from work during the afternoon was often quite difficult, with the start of the match in June 1860 at Pontymoile against the Usk Juveniles having to be delayed – 'considerable time elapsed before play commenced, owing to the Pontymoileans not mustering their eleven, several of them being unable to leave their employ. One o'clock came and only seven were on the ground'.[6] So once again, ingenious ways were sought of overcoming the lack of spare time, with the creation of Morning Clubs, allowing people to play before going to work. By 1858, there was a Morning Club in Brecon, followed in 1861 by a similar club in Abergavenny.[7]

Figure 16 also illustrates how the game filtered down the settlement hierarchy from the larger places to smaller towns and villages. Even Llantilio Crossenny and Magor with around 750 residents and Penmaen with only 161 could boast their own cricket clubs by the 1860s. Many of these larger villages held regular matches, with Llantilio Crossenny challenging Abergavenny, but often the clubs from these smaller places had to join together to undertake fixtures, with Ystalyfera and Ynyscedwyn combining to challenge Pontardawe in 1867 and 1868.[8]

Once again, these games aroused great feelings of local pride, and fixtures between neighbouring sides were often interrupted by disputes. For instance, when Magor met Usk in 1865, the former strengthened their side with talented non-residents and much to the displeasure of Usk, secured a victory. The townsmen of Usk did not like losing to the villagers and the *Monmouthshire Merlin* reported how 'the Usk side having adhered to the conditions laid down were consequently taken at a disadvantage'.[9] In the fixtures between larger settlements, it was often the umpiring decisions which triggered disputes, and the 1861 contest between Bridgend and Maesteg ended abruptly when one of Bridgend's best batsmen was given out leg before by the Maesteg umpire. According to the report in *The Cambrian*, the Bridgend team refused to continue 'unless the umpire was sent off the field. With this modest request, the Maesteg party declined to comply, having no reason to doubt the judgement of their umpire and bowler', and the game finished abruptly.[10] The following year, the Bridgend team was involved in another rumpus when Cadoxton's William Whittington was dismissed for handling the ball. His team refused to take the field when Bridgend batted for a second time but, after discussions over the laws and the standard of umpiring, the game continued.[11]

A further indication of the game's rising popularity was that many clubs had enough playing members to organize a second eleven which also staged regular fixtures. In many cases, the second teams of the leading clubs challenged the first teams of the newly formed organizations.[12] This surfeit of members was not confined to the long-established clubs or those in the largest settlements, as many valley clubs and village teams could now raise two sides.[13] As membership levels rose, it meant a theoretical increase in the financial assets of the clubs but, with more members, the clubs were obliged to stage more games and the increased fixture list meant a higher expenditure.

This was the case with Swansea, who by the end of 1860 had eighty playing members. With subscriptions at 12s. 6d. their treasurer estimated an income of around £55, but at the AGM he announced the club's expenditure in 1860 was £50. With a surplus of just £5 he gloomily stated that:

> should the club decide on securing the services of a professional bowler, the necessary amount must be raised by additional subscriptions. Towards this

object, over £20 has been promised and it is hoped that the members and friends of the club will unite in raising the small sum, say £15 now required for this object.[14]

He need not have worried as more people joined the club to boost its subscriptions, and together with other donations, enough cash was raised to pay for a bowler called Best in 1861.[15]

The most significant trend during the 1850s and 1860s was undoubtedly the growth of cricket at schoolboy level. In 1855 the Neath correspondent of *The Cambrian* alarmingly reported that anyone walking near the cricket ground at weekends 'will be shocked to perceive a host of boys playing cricket and other sorts of games'.[16] Several of the foremost clubs took steps to harness this growing interest by establishing juvenile sides which were coached by their professionals. The clubs hoped that these youngsters, having acquired the rudiments of the game, would later become the lifeblood of their respective clubs. Several clubs were also able to arrange fixtures with local clubs and trades teams, with Swansea Juveniles playing a Penllergaer XI in 1857 arranged by Llewelyn, who was always willing to promote the game.[17] The growth of juvenile sides was not confined to just the oldest clubs in the largest settlements. The presence of decent professionals in the valleys during the 1860s allowed clubs such as Pontymoile, Aberdare and Aberamman to run junior teams,[18] whilst, in the south-west, the flourishing club at Haverfordwest welcomed and actively coached junior members, and in July 1867 a contest was held between the club's second eleven and a side called 'The Young Beginners'.[19]

It was not just the clubs who were promoting the game at junior level, as the 1850s onwards witnessed the introduction of the game at schools and colleges in south Wales. In terms of the game's later development, this was to have far-reaching consequences in the diffusion process throughout the region. Previously young members of the Welsh gentry were sent to public schools in England to acquire both a correct accent and a proper education. Philipps of Cwmgwili went to Westminster, the de Wintons of Brecon attended Shrewsbury, whilst John Lloyd senior, J. C. Nicholl and J. T. D. Llewelyn were all Old Etonians. Neither of the latter made the Eton XI, but one of the Welsh boys who did was F. E. Stacey of Cardiff and the early Glamorganshire side. Indeed, there was a strong element of Old Etonians in south Wales during the 1850s and 1860s, and their old boy network must have assisted the expansion of both the gentlemen's and county sides, as well as the arranging of fixtures.

In contrast, the rest of the population in the early nineteenth century had to make do with a rudimentary education in the comparatively backward schools in Wales, whilst many had no formal schooling whatsoever. Those fortunate enough to attend school had few opportunities for recreation simply because it had no place in the timetable or curriculum. This was highlighted by the Commission of Inquiry into the Welsh education system set up in the aftermath of the civil unrest and riots of the 1830s and 1840s. The Commission's three-volume report in 1847 made only a handful of references to any form of physical exercise, as most Welsh schools believed it had nothing to do with the life of working men in the industrial centres. In some cases, the absence of any recreation was out of necessity, because the schools were run by people with a disability or without an arm or leg![20]

The situation improved dramatically during the second half of the century as private schools were established in south Wales for the sons of the gentry, thus helping to prevent their parents from having either to send them away or to employ private tutors. There were fundamental improvements to education at grass roots level as well, and in both the public and humbler new schools, cricket was introduced and actively encouraged. Such schools were following the model of English public schools where the introduction of team games had proved beneficial in both educational and recreational terms, with the channelling of athletic energies into organized games helping to instill self-control, respect for legality and authority, breeding unselfishness and reinforcing the discipline which the school was seeking to impose. This coincided with the spread of the ethic of Muscular Christianity and the writings of Charles Kingsley, who advocated recreation as a means of bodily purification and practical Christianity:

> Through sport boys acquire virtues which no books can give them; not merely daring and endurance, but better still, temper, self-restraint, fairness, honour, unenvious approbation of another's success, and all that 'give and take' of life which stands a man in good stead when he goes forth into the world and without which indeed his success is always maimed and partial.[21]

There was a straightforward belief that brute strength and power were good and godly characteristics, whilst physical weakness or a lack of exercise were synonymous with moral and spiritual inadequacy. These views were illustrated in novels such as *Tom Brown's Schooldays* where Thomas Hughes drew a clear parallel between manliness and sporting prowess. Cricket was one of these manly and virtuous games which Kingsley and his followers encouraged because it taught respect and adherence to regulations and conventions, such as walking when the umpire gave a batsman out. There were other healthy spin-offs through playing cricket because it strengthened the physique and helped people build up an immunity to the range of ailments, including typhoid, pneumonia and cholera, which plagued Victorian society and caused it to be in mortal fear of illness and disease. The introduction of rugby football epitomized this outlook and many writers have chronicled how the game developed and thrived during the winter months at English schools.[22] Cricket was also encouraged during the summer because it too had many beneficial effects on the pupils. As Christopher Brookes has shown, 'the sons of the upper classes acquired those qualities of self-discipline and loyalty which were fundamental to Victorian gentility', whilst a contemporary gentleman's magazine pointed out that 'it encourages obedience, discipline, tact; it engenders health and strength, and it leads to no possible ill results except the spending of a summer's day in the summer air rather than over an inky desk'.[23] Not surprisingly, an official report in 1864 concluded that 'the cricket and (rugby) football fields are not merely places of exercise and amusement, they help to form some of the most valuable social qualities and manly virtues'.[24]

The first improvement in the Welsh education system came through the involvement of the Anglican National Society and the non-denominational British Society which established 'Normal' schools or 'British' schools, where gymnastic recreation or military training was encouraged. Cricket was one of the games to be introduced following the example in England, but with a smaller number of pupils these early games took the form of single-wicket competitions, and when fixtures were considered, masters or old boys had to help out to make up the numbers.[25] Numbers were boosted as a result of educational reform in the 1850s as the Normal School Movement took a firm hold and, in 1856, Swansea Normal College started regular fixtures on Crumlin Burrows.[26]

This decade also saw the introduction of cricket to the school routine in the Valleys, as the Victorian reformers believed that the game was a healthy diversion to life in the industrial settlements. Indeed, in 1850 *The Cambrian* was 'glad to see the efforts in Merthyr latterly by the schoolmasters in improving the physical structure of their scholars by cricket matches'.[27] It also assisted the Anglicization of these valley areas, with the 1847 Commission of Inquiry into Education in Wales having reported that large numbers of people in Wales spoke their native language and were ignorant of English. The Commission believed this to be synonymous with ignorance in general and, as a result, the encouragement of English habits and pastimes was seen as highly desirable. Inter-school fixtures were arranged as cricket grew in popularity and in Llanelli the pupils from the British School played the apprentices of the town's copperworks.[28]

However, it was at the new Welsh public and grammar schools created under the 1840 Grammar Schools Act that the game took a firm hold.

The Welsh grammar schools were intended to be centres of Angli-cization, so it was not surprising that it was from these new centres that cricket diffused during the second half of the nineteenth century. The earliest centre of schoolboy cricket was Cowbridge Grammar, the oldest school in Glamorgan, which was bequeathed to the Warden of Jesus College, Oxford in the will of Sir Leoline Jenkins in 1685.[29] Close links existed between Jesus and Cowbridge. The school's earliest masters were graduates of the College, and Oxford strove to establish the best academic and sporting traditions at Cowbridge, with all matters of entry and appointment having to be approved by Jesus College. It was also one of the schools in Wales from which the College accepted pupils on scholarships and, over the years, the influence of old boys of Cowbridge and graduates from Jesus College was highly instrumental in the spread of cricket as people put into practice what they had enjoyed at these two seats of learning.

Cricket took off at Cowbridge Grammar during the 1850s, although there are references to recreation taking place much earlier than this, some of which could be early forms of cricket. These are contained in the diary of Daniel Walters who, on 17 April 1777, wrote 'went to school, played ball, came home, and that's all'.[30] There are further references to playing ball during May and August, which Iolo Davies considered as examples of *bando* or tally.[31] Walters, however, uses the word '*bandy*', rather than playing ball, later in the autumn,[32] and when considering the time of year, the entries for May and August hint that the young scholars of Cowbridge were playing an early form of cricket during the summer afternoons.[33]

Cowbridge Grammar declined in the early nineteenth century, but it was rebuilt with money from the Jesus College following the appoint-ment of the Revd Hugo D. Harper as headmaster in February 1847, and it was after this that cricket took off.[24] Harper was keen to improve all aspects of the school and, under his paternal guidance, the number of pupils increased from thirty-one at Christmas to eighty in Midsummer 1849.[35] The increase in pupils allowed Harper to introduce team games, and organized games of cricket were soon taking place. By 1849 the boys had reached a standard that enabled Harper to organize fixtures. The absence of other cricket-playing schools in the locality meant that in September 1849 an eleven from the school, plus a couple of masters challenged the Cardiff club, and the following year played the town side in Cowbridge.[36] The year 1850 was Harper's final year at Cowbridge and he left in midsummer to take the headship at Sherborne.[37] He was replaced by another fellow of Jesus College, Revd W. Holt Beever who ensured that the good work of Harper was continued, and that two annual 'town versus gown' matches were arranged with the Cowbridge club. The grammar school's fixture list diversified during Beever's headship and, by 1857, included games with the St Mary's club of Cardiff,[38] home and away fixtures with Maesteg and, during September, the School entertained J. C. Nicholl's Merthyr Mawr team.[39] Nicholl's XI included his brother Edward and the Staceys of Cardiff. Yet despite this strong opposition, the Cowbridge scholars recorded a comfortable victory. Other indications of the game's rising popularity were the house matches between the boarders in the Revd Beever's house and the rest of the school, and the fact that the school could muster a second eleven against the town's Morning Club.[40] They also had their own colours of dark green shirts and caps,[41] whilst in August 1860 the first Past and Present match was held. The school's aspirations rose over the next few years to include games with Cadoxton, Bridgend and the Golden Mile club.[42] Contact with these prestigious clubs, plus an annual Old Boys fixture, allowed the scholars to make the right contacts and mix in a suitable atmosphere, whilst reinforcing the school's position as the leading cricket school in the region.

Cricket diffused from this early centre at Cowbridge through the actions of the school's Old Boys. Many followed in the footsteps of Harper and Beever and entered the clergy after studying at Jesus College, and helped spread cricket after taking up posts in south Wales. An example was Thomas Llewellyn Lister, who had been in the Cowbridge XI during the mid-1850s. After graduating in 1861, he became curate of St Woolo's and rector of St Mark's, Newport, where he actively encouraged his parishioners to play the healthy and manly game he had learnt at Cowbridge. Lister even assembled his own eleven to play teams in the Newport area.[43]

Watkin Price Whittington, another Old Boy of Cowbridge and Jesus College, helped promote cricket at Llandovery College, which had been founded in 1847 by Thomas Phillips as the Welsh Collegiate Institution.[44] In its early years, Llandovery concentrated on providing an education for potential young clergymen, and its first warden was Archdeacon John Williams.[45] At first, the curriculum was strictly clerical and classical, with little time for recreation, and it was only when the Revd E. O. Phillips became warden in May 1854 that consideration was given to any form of recreation. Phillips believed that 'we must never forget that man consists of mind, soul and body, and we must not neglect the cultivation of all these parts'.[46] In 1858 a covered fives court was erected, and an area for cricket practice laid out. By the early 1860s Llandovery was playing the students of St David's College Lampeter[47] and, in 1864, matches were played against an Old Boys XI and the Llandovery Town side, whose ground they used until 1878 for their home fixtures.[48]

Recreation at Llandovery was given an impetus by the appointment of

W. P. Whittington as second master in 1868. He taught previously at Merchiston College in Edinburgh, and the former Cowbridge pupil wholeheartedly set about promoting cricket and rugby on his move back to Wales. The playing standards rose as Whittington took a leading role with the coaching of the young Llandovcrians, and the fixture list dramatically expanded. By 1872 the match against Christ College, Brecon was 'one of the events of the year',[49] and through Whittington's actions, Llandovery became the leading rugby playing school in south Wales.[50]

Annual matches between Llandovery College and Christ College began in 1865, and the growth of cricket at the Brecon school was due to the actions of the Revd M. A. Farrar, who had been second master at Cowbridge Grammar. In 1857 Farrar took up the same position at Christ College, under the headship of Revd J. D. Williams, who himself had moved to Brecon the previous year from Sherborne at the age of twenty-seven.[51] Williams must have welcomed the arrival of the experienced 43-year-old from Cowbridge, and he was delighted when Farrar introduced cricket as the first team sport at the Brecon school, knowing full well of its beneficial effect at Sherborne, following Harper's encouragement of the summer game. In 1857, the school rented a field in the town for cricket and as the number of pupils rose from thirty in 1857 to forty-six by 1860, Farrar was able to organize fixtures as well as regular practices. On 31 August 1858 the first recorded school contest took place at Christ College between the boarders of Farrar's House and the rest of the school,[52] which served to prepare the boys for their two games in September with the Brecon United Morning Club.

The following year the pupils and members of the Morning Club challenged John Lloyd's Brecon Town side, but the development of the game at Christ College met a temporary setback as Farrar left in 1860 and his replacement W. H. Parry was more of a cleric than a sportsman. Without the dynamic influence of Farrar, cricket at the Brecon school temporarily declined, with only sporadic fixtures and, when an annual series of fixtures with Landovery commenced in 1865, Christ College went down to a heavy ten-wicket defeat in the inaugural contest.

Farrar left Christ College in 1860 to become head of Swansea Grammar School. The Swansea school was established in 1682 for the free education of twenty sons of the town's less wealthy burgesses by the Right Revd Hugh Gore, a former Rector of Oxwich, who was the Lord Bishop of Waterford and Lismore. By the early nineteenth century, the premises had fallen into disrepair and, some years after the 1840 Grammar School Act, a scheme was drawn up for the improvement of the school, with its proposers believing there was 'every prospect that the school will . . . be reinstated with vigour and in a manner suited to the progressive wants of the age'.[53] A Board of Trustees was appointed in the late 1840s, including L. L. Dillwyn, J. H. Vivian and Starling Benson, the captain of Swansea CC. Through their presence and the 'progressive' aims of the school, cricket was encouraged and a field for practice laid out on the lawn in front of the school. These practices were well attended and, as the playing standards rose, Swansea Grammar was able to challenge other schools, and the first recorded match took place on Crumlin Burrows in September 1856 against Swansea Normal College.[54]

In theory, the arrival of Farrar from Christ College Brecon should have boosted the development of the game, but he was at the school during a period of internal wranglings and disputes, and the number of pupils fell from seventy-one in 1857 to just forty in 1862 when Farrar resigned over a financial disagreement.[55] Farrar left Swansea without having made much of a mark on the school or its cricket, and he was replaced by Revd C. T. Heartley. It was during Heartley's headship from 1862 until 1868 that the game took off at the school. Heartley knew of the benefits of encouraging recreation, and in a report in 1863 on the future develop-ment of the school, he wrote 'a good playing field, thoroughly drained and easily accessible is almost as important to a well-educated school as the school room itself'.[56]

To a large extent, Heartley based these plans for the grammar school along the lines of an English public school, and soon after the publication of the Report, the school acquired a new cricket and rugby field to replace the heavily used lawn in front of the school. The head also obtained the services of Swansea's professional William Bancroft senior to help coach the pupils. Bancroft assisted other clubs including Gorseinon, Kilvey and the Swansea Colts and, in September 1863, he raised an eleven from these clubs to play the grammar school.[57] Bancroft's presence, the new ground and the headmaster's encourage-ment saw the fixture list expand to include games with clubs such as Cadoxton and, in 1868, the school team challenged Llandovery College.[58] As one old boy remembered 'cricket became practically compulsory to the great benefit of those who like myself used to avoid public games. In a very short time, the whole tone of the school was changed by the energy and enthusiasm of the new Head'.[59]

Cricket flourished at several other grammar schools during the 1850s and 1860s, despite their small number of pupils. A more pressing problem was the lack of a suitable playing area in some of the smaller settlements. This was the case at Carmarthen Grammar, whose first ever match in September 1857 led the correspondent of *The Welshman* to write that 'the ground was in a very bad condition and we hope this will be remedied by next season, if the game is to be encouraged especially among the lads who may become members of clubs with any high pretensions'.[60]

Gradually these schools in the west acquired suitable premises, and during the 1860s Ystrad Meurig in Cardiganshire and Llandysul Grammar School held regular fixtures with local clubs,[61] whilst Haverfordwest Grammar staged an annual contest against a scratch eleven drawn from the local clubs and members of the local gentry.[62] In the east the problem was often finding enough suitable opponents because of the abundance of trades' teams and fewer gentlemen's sides. Abergavenny Grammar School was able to overcome these worries by holding matches with the doctors and employees at the Joint Counties Asylum,[63] and through the efforts of their headmaster, Mr Peake, became the leading grammar school side in Monmouthshire. Indeed, when a new cricket club was created at Pontypool in 1861, the new side opted to measure its strength by challenging the pupils of Abergavenny Grammar.[64]

Cricket also increased rapidly at college level and by the 1860s regular matches were played by the students at St David's College, Lampeter. It became another outpost of Muscular Christianity following the introduction of a rule in 1850 that students should spend their spare time in 'healthful exercise rather than in clownish lounging about the shops or market place'.[65] However, there were few facilities at the College to allow the students to comply with this regulation. This lack of sporting facilities struck the College's new vice-principal, the Revd Rowland Williams, who was a fellow of King's College, Cambridge and a follower of Charles Kingsley's writings. Williams quickly rectified matters after his appointment in 1850, introducing cricket and other sports to the college. Despite the fact that the annual student intake was only around fifteen, Williams was able to organize regular practices and, in June 1852, the students challenged the town club. It was a brave move given the small intake – not surprisingly, the students lost by thirty-four runs, and *The Welshman* added that 'they rather over-rate their strength as yet to compete with the veteran town club'.[66]

There was a similar story of quiet beginnings at Trinity Training College at Carmarthen. Established in 1848, it too had a link with St David's College because its first vice-principal was the Revd William Edmunds, who was an old boy of the college and Lampeter Grammar School. Edmunds was a typical Victorian cleric in that he ensured the students had a sound classical upbringing as well as participating in healthy recreation. He encouraged several sports, although fixtures were restricted, like at Lampeter, by the small numbers, and the students were left to play games amongst themselves. Another factor prompting Edmunds to introduce the game was a keen interest in cricket; his diary for 1849 refers to attending and enjoying a match between the Carmarthen club and the military.[67] In 1854 Edmunds moved on to become headmaster of Lampeter Grammar, but cricket at Trinity College continued to be encouraged, and as student numbers rose, they were able to challenge the town club in September 1856 and, much to the students' joy, they won by sixty-nine runs.[68] Cricket at Trinity College continued to develop during the 1860s as the game, in general, took a firm hold in west Wales, and the Carmarthenshire county club became well established. An indication of this progress was the hiring by the college of a professional called Campbell in 1860, and during the next decade, their fixture list expanded to include matches with local schools, clubs and the doctors at Carmarthen Asylum.[69] The overriding impact of this growth of cricket at school and college level was the establishment of a host of new centres from which the game could spread and the creation of new diffusion channels involving schools and colleges in south Wales, as well as more traditional and august centres in England. By the 1850s and 1860s many young Welshmen were learning to play the game at grammar and public schools in Wales before going up to Oxbridge or theological college and returning home to spread the game from their pulpit or schoolroom.

A perfect example of these new agents of diffusion was the Revd William David of St Fagan's. He attended Cowbridge Grammar between 1837 and 1842, before gaining a scholarship to Jesus College, and becoming ordained in the Church of England. After spells in Shropshire and Canada, he took over the parish of St Fagan's in December 1856.[70] He was a man of immense energy and soon set about improving both the buildings and life of the people in the parish. Through his influence, the rectory and parish church were rebuilt, and in 1862 he formed St Fagan's CC to encourage the healthy recreation of the villagers.[71] During the 1870s, the St Fagan's side became one of the leading clubs in the Cardiff area and the David family maintained a high profile in Welsh cricket throughout the Victorian era, as the Revd David's sons followed in their father's footsteps and helped spread the game at both club and county level. Bearing in mind the impact of Muscular Christianity on the game's diffusion at grass roots level, it was most appropriate that William David's second son, Edmund Ussher, should lead Glamorgan in their inaugural contest in 1889.

7 / *Gentlemen and Prayers*

C LERGYMEN such as the Revds Farrar, Harper and David were the leading promoters of cricket at school and college level from the 1850s onwards, and their encouragement was in marked contrast to the first half of the nineteenth century when the game's spread faced opposition from local vicars and Nonconformist leaders. However, there was a change in attitude during the middle of the century, with the waves of immigrants from large industrial centres in England fuelling a decline in Nonconformist antipathy towards sport of all kinds. The urbane arrivals lacked the conservatism of the rural Welsh, and recreation was undertaken and actively encouraged. These views spread to the close communities of the valleys, and as Hilarie Waddington observed 'even the attitude of the Nonconformists amongst them could not but be affected by their living side by side with people who had no inhibitions about games'.[1]

The most important factor, however, in the diffusion process was the spread of Muscular Christianity. These virtues were easily introduced at school level because many clergymen served as headmasters or second masters in the grammar and public schools, and from these lofty positions they were able to construct a curriculum which dovetailed with their staunch beliefs about Muscular Christianity. This also boosted the further spread of Kingsley's views because many of these schools were established to provide an education for potential clergymen. In fact, the 1861 Past and Present match at Cowbridge Grammar saw no less than nine clergymen in the Old Boys side.[2]

The common practice for young gentlemen after attending such schools as Cowbridge or Llandovery was to attend Jesus College, Oxford or theological colleges such as St David's, Lampeter where Kingsley's writings also held sway. St David's was an Anglican institution, established in 1828, and cricket was played there from 1845 when the college's students challenged the Llandovery club.[3] As mentioned in Chapter 6, the game took off following the appointment of Revd Rowland Williams as vice-principal and professor of Hebrew. Williams was a staunch supporter of Kingsley's beliefs, and felt that recreation had an important role to play in the life of the College students. Cricket, rugby, fives, athletics and croquet were introduced as Revd Williams stated that 'whatever time a student may require for relaxation should be spent in healthy exercise'.[4] In 1855 an annual series of games between St David's and the town side began[5] and from 1863 matches were staged with Llandovery College following the construction of a railway line which meant there was a physical link as well as a spiritual one between these two seats of learning.[6]

Once they had passed their exams and had been ordained the young clergymen, from institutions such as St David's, continued to act as perfect examples of Muscular Christians, and spread cricket either by returning to schools as teachers or going out into their parishes, and like Revd David, formed cricket teams amongst their parishioners. The latter course of action also assisted their paternal control over the parishioners by bringing together diverse social groups and encouraging temperance and abstinence from the demon drink.

To a large extent, even the formation of Cadoxton CC fitted this category of sides formed by religious leaders; J. T. D. Llewelyn held strong Christian views and assisted the rebuilding of Cadoxton parish church. When the club was created in 1863 the incumbent was the Revd David Hanmer Griffith, a native of Brecon and another graduate of Jesus College, Oxford.[7] He was a typical Muscular Christian in the sense that he enjoyed sports, especially cricket, and it was no surprise that together with his close friend J.T.D., he helped establish the Cadoxton club.[8]

The Young Men's Christian Association also helped spread the gospel of cricket, with the provision of outdoor recreation for young people being seen as a healthy and normal alternative to the immoral and physically harmful attractions of the public houses. Besides acting as an agency for moral and social reform, the YMCA aimed to shape the values and influence the behaviour of the next generation, so cricket was a perfect vehicle for the YMCA to spread its beliefs. In 1858 the members of the Cardiff branch played Roath CC, and matches continued during the 1860s on the Arms Park, before the branch acquired a ground of its own in 1867 to the east of the town, allowing them to expand its activities.[9]

Clergymen and religious organizations were, therefore, prominent in the game's development during the 1850s and 1860s. With Noncon-formist opposition declining, the ethic of Muscular Christianity took hold and cricket was positively encouraged. Vicars did not confine their influence to a purely passive, off-field role or preaching from the pulpit, as

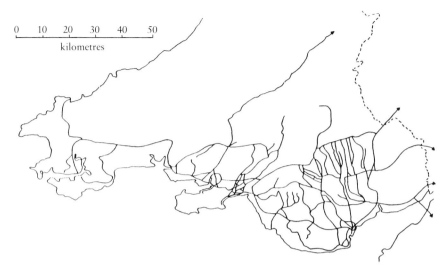

Figure 17. The railway network in south Wales around 1890

many actively played the game, and there were enough taking part by the late 1860s for J. C. Nicholl to organize two-day matches at Merthyr Mawr between the clergy, led by his brother, and the laity.[10]

Judging by the correspondence in many of the contemporary newspapers, their actions proved successful and the ethic of Muscular Christianity took a firm hold amongst the gentlemen, middle classes and working people of south Wales in the late 1860s. An example was a long letter published in the *Swansea and Glamorgan Herald* for August 1866 by 'A Lover of Manly Exercise, by the Church, Morriston'. It appealed for support for the recently formed club in Morriston, with the author writing at length about cricket's virtues. He concluded that playing the game was 'very suitable for schoolboys and young gentlemen who have plenty of means at command and no business prospects in view. Those whose pursuits in life are of a sedentary character may derive much benefit from a few hours by way of a change'.[11]

The patronage of religious leaders at club and school level was just one of the factors responsible for the rapid rise in cricket's popularity at all levels during the 1850s and 1860s. As in the first half of the century, there were a variety of other agents who assisted the spread of the game, including the landed gentry and migrants from England, whilst once again, improvements and extensions to the public transport network played a crucial role in the diffusion of cricket throughout the region. Figure 17 illustrates how the railway network continued to improve and diversify by the 1870s, with a myriad of lines extending across the coastal

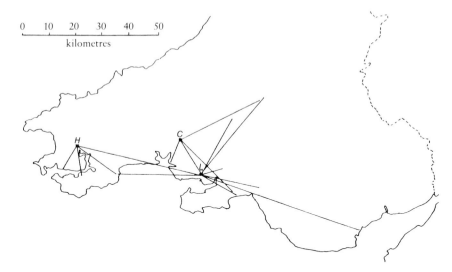

Figure 18. The sphere of influence of Carmarthen, Haverfordwest and
Llanelly in the 1850s

plains from west to east, as well as northwards into many of the
previously isolated valleys. Almost every major settlement now had its
own railway station, and services ran to all parts of the region. The
impact of these new routes was considerable, and allowed fixture lists to
expand and incorporate games with hitherto distant clubs, especially in
the far west where several new routes were opened. One of the clubs to
benefit from improved accessibility was Tenby which, from 1866, was
served by a line from Whitland which branched off the main Fishguard to
Swansea route. No longer was the seaside town isolated and, at the AGM
of Tenby CC in 1866, its members were overjoyed by the opening of the
new lines – 'there is little doubt that the cricket season of 1867 will be
such a one as Tenby has never seen'.[12]

Figures 18 and 19 show the distances that Haverfordwest, Carmarthen
and Llanelly travelled for away fixtures during the 1850s compared with
the 1860s, and clearly illustrate that the distances travelled by the three
clubs were increased over time (as measured in straight line distances).
During the 1850s Carmarthen went a total of 87km, while Haverfordwest travelled 84km for their away matches. But by the 1860s, they were
both journeying a total of 237km, with Haverfordwest able to arrange
games with Swansea, which previously had been almost a day away. The
improved communications network also permitted the Carmarthenshire
county side to travel to Clifton, whilst in July 1869 Llanelly hired a
special excursion train to play the Ceredigion club at Aberystwyth.[13]

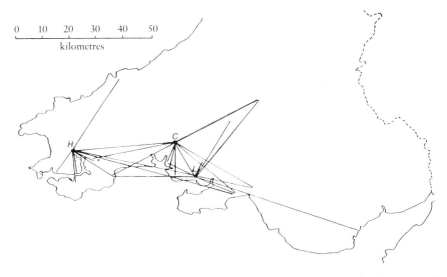

Figure 19. The sphere of influence of Carmarthen, Haverfordwest and Llanelly in the 1860s

These improvements also allowed regular trips into England by a greater number of club sides. Back in the 1840s and 1850s, it was only the top clubs in the south-east, such as Cardiff and Newport, that were able to challenge teams in south-west England. By the 1860s, clubs further west could undertake regular ventures into England, with Cadoxton holding away matches at Clifton and Swindon, after securing special excursion fares.[14] The availability of cheap tickets allowed smaller clubs, without rich members or patrons, to travel further and even sides such as Abercarn and Crumlin could hold games with English clubs as far afield as Swindon, although it meant the players from Swindon having to leave home at 6 a.m. and arriving at their Monmouthshire destination at midday.[15]

The opening of the Mid-Wales line in 1864 also meant that teams such as Brecon could quite easily travel into Herefordshire and Worcestershire. It also boosted county fixtures, with Breconshire playing Herefordshire from 1866 onwards, and Worcestershire in 1869. Another fixture facilitated by improved long-distance transport was the visit by a South Wales XI to Denbigh to challenge a side representing north Wales, drawn chiefly of players from the Wrexham club. The South Wales team was assembled by C. C. Bishop and John Lloyd junior, and included Penry Lloyd, Ben Arthur, Joe Lovering and other leading players from the Cadoxton and Brecon clubs.[16] It was a pity that, after the long journey made by the gentlemen from the south, the contest was marred by disputed umpiring decisions and when the home batsmen went out for their second innings, the South Wales fielders refused to continue the game.[17] A return match was planned at Brecon later in the month as part of an annual north–south challenge, but after the dispute this was cancelled, and nothing more was said about the idea.

As well as an improved rail network, the presence of employees of several rail companies also gave the game a boost because many were talented players. An example was H. H. 'Bertie' Young, an engineer from Swindon, who moved to work on the Vale of Neath Railway and, whilst based in south Wales, he joined the Cadoxton club, helping them to become one of the top sides in the region. Indeed, it was through Young's influence that Cadoxton, and the Welsh Wanderers were able to secure fixtures with the Great Western Railway's employees at Swindon.[18] The leading railway company in south Wales, and the most prosperous in Britain by 1870, was the Taff Vale Railway, and its leading engineers, Charles Hurry Riches, and his son Tom, were both useful cricketers. Charles Riches helped form the Taff Vale CC, so that many of the company's staff could partake in recreation, including the clerks and apprentices in the Taff Vale workshops as well as the company's well-educated engineers.[19] The club was encouraged by the company's directors, who included the almost ubiquitous F. E. Stacey of Cardiff and Glamorgan, but one stumbling block facing the club was securing a decent ground. The best wicket in Cardiff was the Arms Park, owned by the Marquess of Bute, but the relationship between the Bute estate and the Taff Vale Railway was not always harmonious, especially over the use of the Bute-owned docks at Cardiff. However, the Riches had close working contacts and friends with the Bute estate, and they were able to secure the regular use of the Arms Park for the Taff Vale club.[20]

A further hindrance facing the Taff Vale cricketers was the lack of spare time for matches. To solve this, games were often spread over several days, with a match against the Bute Docks in September 1859 spanning three evenings,[21] and in 1864 the fixture between eleven of the Taff Vale fitters and eleven of their clerks was played on their two half-day afternoons, Thursday and Saturday.[22] This lack of spare time meant that the Taff Vale club concentrated on practices amongst members or games between various departments, or other sides in the Cardiff district. However, in August 1864 their engineers were able to travel to Newport to challenge their counterparts working in the western valleys of Monmouthshire.[23] The presence of these railway employees from an English background was also an example of the continued benefits produced by immigration to south Wales. Brinley Thomas used census data to estimate that between 1861 and 1871 around 21,000 people migrated into Glamorgan, but found that 70 per cent of these came from neighbouring Welsh counties, with only 400 or so people moving from London and the south-east.[24] Although they were less significant in numerical terms, these English migrants had an important impact in cricketing terms.

The previous chapter has already highlighted the arrival of Oxbridge-educated graduates and theology students at the schools and colleges of south Wales. The benefits occurred at club level as well, with many sides taking advantage of the arrival of decent cricketers who had played for a good club, county gentlemen's team or in the case of R. T. King of Monmouth, the Cambridge XI. By the late 1850s, some clubs had enough English members to stage games between their Welsh and English members, such as the challenge at Swansea in August 1859.[25] The native members batted first and were restricted to ninety-seven runs, with six wickets falling to club captain D. A. Onslow, whose relatives played for Hampshire and Kent.[26] However, the English were then dismissed for just forty-seven runs, with J. T. D. Llewelyn claiming six victims.

A positive effect was also caused by people migrating into the area on a temporary basis, to resorts such as Tenby and Mumbles. They attracted many respectable gentlemen from England who were keen to play cricket whilst on holiday in a peaceful haven away from life in the industrial and commercial centres. These Welsh resorts gained in popularity following the opening of railway lines into the west, and in 1855 Llanelly travelled to Tenby to play a team who apart from one man were summer visitors to the resort and were students or old boys of colleges at Oxford and Cambridge.[27] The volume of students, clerics and affluent gentlemen into Tenby was so great each July and August that a Visitors cricket club was formed in the mid-1860s, and annual challenges were staged with Haverfordwest.[28] The number of visitors from Oxbridge was also sufficient in 1860 for Tenby to stage their own version of the Varsity Match, with a fixture between gentlemen from Oxford and Cambridge.[29]

The Mumbles also developed into a popular summer watering hole for the gentry during the mid-nineteenth century, attracting a host of visitors from England. A Mumbles Visitors cricket club was formed in the late 1860s, and held annual fixtures against Swansea. However, the cricketing standard of the migrants to the Mumbles was inferior to those visiting Tenby and, in August 1871, the Visitors XI were dismissed by Capt. Treffey's Swansea team for two. The first ten of the Mumbles batsmen failed to score and it was just number eleven C. Lewis who scored, and then only when a nudge to square-leg was badly fielded, and the poor return resulted in overthrows.[30]

Any analysis of the influential actors in the diffusion process during the 1850s and 1860s must also consider the continued involvement of the landed gentry, as they were still keen to support the game in which leaders of local society and politics were involved. As the middle and lower status groups became increasingly involved, the landed gentry became even more eager to reinforce their position at the top of cricket's hierarchy. The way in which J. C. Nicholl formed his own eleven, laying a good wicket and then encouraging games at Merthyr Mawr, typified their actions and was repeated by other landowners with a similar outlook. His neighbour, the Countess Dowager of Dunraven, also formed her own side in the 1860s which played annual games with Cowbridge in the gounds of Dunraven Castle near Southerndown. The cosmopolitan Dunraven XI included workers on the Dowager's Estate, friends from their homes in Ireland, plus leading members and professionals from Cadoxton and Bridgend. The fact that they attracted gatherings of the local gentry and were accompanied by dinners in the castle meant that they were early examples of the country house games which were to become very popular during the closing years of the nineteenth century.[31]

Many of the landed families who promoted the game during the early nineteenth century continued to support cricket in the 1850s and 1860s. The Duke of Beaufort still encouraged the game on his land in south Wales and also in Gloucestershire, where a side called the Gentlemen of Gloucestershire played at Badminton from the late 1850s.[32] The main centres of Beaufort involvement in south Wales continued to be Raglan and Monmouth, whilst the duke encouraged cricket on his estate at Llangattock Park. A Crickhowell XI played there from the late 1850s against local clubs, scratch elevens and annual fixtures with Abergavenny Grammar. As in the past, these games on Beaufort land were accompanied by gatherings of the leading names in the county, and a match report in 1861 commented how 'the Duke and Duchess of Beaufort seemed to take great interest as did the young Marquis of Somerset. Major Rolls of the Hendre, and other noted gentlemen were also present'.[33] In the west, William Chambers continued to promote the game and freely allowed the use of his grounds at Llanelly House and Hafod House at Pontrhydfendigaid for matches. In July 1860 the Chambers family assembled a Hafod XI which challenged Ystrad Meurig at cricket and a variety of other athletic pursuits. After the match, there were races on the lawns in front of the house and a cricket-ball throwing competition, before the two teams sat down to a grand supper provided by Chambers.[34] Many local MPs also continued to support and promote cricket during this period, with the most active in the south-west being J. H. Phillips, the member for Haverfordwest, who appeared regularly for various teams in the district and staged games in the grounds of his home at Williamston.[35] In the east, Col. Henry Morgan Clifford, an Old Etonian and MP for Hereford, organized matches at his country retreat in Wales and encouraged the Llantilio Crossenny club.[36]

The actions and involvement of the gentry therefore took the same form as in the pre-1850 era, with games acquiring a social significance and attended by leading members of local society. But the 1850s and 1860s saw the emergence of a new type of wealthy patron, as industrial philanthropists played an increasingly prominent role in the promotion of the cricket following the example of the Grenfells and J. H. Vivian in the pre-1850 period. The industrial development of the region boosted the local economy and with many industrialists having a large work-force, they were in a position to act as moral and social reformers, and could take positive steps to improve the life of their employees. Many industrialists took this philanthropic action in the hope that it would prevent a repetition of Chartist unrest or the Merthyr Rising, whilst for others, promoting cricket was a tangible way to display their newly acquired wealth and social position.

One of the earliest industrial patrons in the Glamorgan valleys were the Guests, who owned the huge ironworks at Dowlais. In July 1852 the *Cardiff and Merthyr Guardian* applauded their actions by reporting that:

> through the liberality of Lady Charlotte Guest, a large field has been given to the players and her ladyship paid the expense of draining and turfing the ground. This, together with the kindess of the Manager of the Works, and Mr White, surgeon, in procuring a tent for the members and in contenancing the game, has enabled the young men of the Works and of the town of Dowlais to spend many happy evenings in healthful recreation.[37]

Cricket in Merthyr increased in popularity following Lady Guest's support, and a second club was formed in 1857 and promoted by Captain Robert Thompson Crawshay, the son of William Crawshay who owned the Cyfarthfa Works. Crawshay provided a ground for the new club and a local newspaper commented how the club promised 'to be a very effective one, through the kindness of R. T. Crawshay, who is an encourager of the manly and noble game . . . we hope with all these advantages to see them victorious in many matches'.[38] Captain Crawshay also played for some of the gentlemen's teams, including the Crickhowell side at Llangattock Park, and it may well have been as a result of his playing activities and contacts with the Beaufort estate that he decided to help some of his family's 7,000 employees. Nevertheless, there was some opposition in various quarters to this industrial patronage of cricket and the encouragement of daytime matches. Some people felt that the money could be invested more profitably elsewhere, as in the case of the Morriston area, where a correspondent to one newspaper in 1866 appealed:

> to the employers of labour not to give their patronage and encouragement to the cricket clubs of Morriston unless for evening practice, and for that no

expense worth mentioning is required. The great want of Morriston is schools for educating the rising generation and to that object should the best energies of all be directed.[39]

A few weeks later the same correspondent warned against 'subscribing to cricket clubs which could only have a tendency to make more idlers in the place and to cause the minds of workpeople to become unsettled',[40] observing that:

> a simple game cannot be played for a few hours without a drinking booth being considered necessary, afterwards wound up by halfcrown and five shilling dinners with occasional trips at 3 or 4 shillings a head, making an expenditure of about 10 shillings a day by working men with wives and children . . . Can such things be carried on by men of humble means and satisfaction given to their families, me thinks not.[41]

His protests met with a wave of protests, especially from the Muscular Christians who wholeheartedly supported Morriston CC, and who replied that:

> he cannot be aware of the many advantages derived from a regular and systematic kind of exercise such as cricketing. He would also use the money that is now being paid as subscriptions for its support to educate the rising generation, forgetting that all work and no play makes Jack a dull boy. A healthy body and a healthy mind are the two great essentials of human nature.[42]

The leading ironmasters in the Monmouthshire valleys also supported cricket, especially the Hanbury-Leighs who owned the Pontymoile Ironworks to the south-east of Pontypool.[43] In 1804, Capel Hanbury-Leigh acquired the works at the age of twenty-eight, a few years after his marriage to Molly Miers of Cadoxton, the widow of Sir Humphrey Mackworth. As output from the ironworks increased, Hanbury-Leigh was able to enlarge Pontypool Park House and improve its grounds.[44] Pontypool CC had played their matches in the grounds of the house from the 1830s and, during the 1850s, the Hanbury-Leigh family became increasingly involved in the affairs of the club. Capel Hanbury-Leigh acted as the club's patron,[45] whilst his son John Capel Hanbury-Leigh became one of its regular playing members.[46]

An indication of the rising popularity of cricket in the Monmouthshire valleys was that the Pontypool club had a membership of 110 by 1856. This prompted Hanbury-Leigh to establish a team at his Pontymoile Works and allow its members to use the grounds at Pontypool House.[47] The game certainly flourished under Hanbury-Leigh's patronage, with the working classes increasingly involved after learning the rudiments of cricket at school, and seeking to play it as a release from the arduous and physical demands of their jobs. There had previously been religious opposition towards their participation in recreation, but the influence of Nonconformity had declined as Muscular Christianity took a firm hold during the 1850s and 1860s.

In contrast to earlier years, the local vicars now encouraged their parishioners to participate in healthy recreation. One of the most vociferous was the Revd David James, the rector of Panteg. He acted as warden of Llandovery College in 1853/4 and was aware of the many spiritual and physical benefits provided by recreation.[48] His encouragement was another example of the way in which the game diffused from academic circles down to the grass roots. It also encouraged participation in other sports as the workers enjoyed their summer recreation so much that they looked for other suitable pastimes. At the end of the 1868 season, the members of the Pontypool club held a meeting at the Hanbury Arms to discuss 'taking up physical activities during the winter months to keep fit'.[49] The Revd James's two sons were leading members of the cricket club, and through their involvement and knowledge of rugby football at school and university, it was introduced as the winter game and the world-famous Pontypool RFC was born.[50]

A final factor in the growth of cricket in both the valleys and the industrial settlements on the coast was the rise of the *nouveaux riches* including shopkeepers, solicitors and small businessmen as well as the many clerks who were employed in the new commercial centres.[51] This group expressed its newly acquired wealth and elevated social position through the establishment of cricket clubs, following the example of the landed gentry on the coastal plain and the industrialists in the valleys. The clubs also fostered and promoted the new community spirit of the valley settlements, whilst in the case of the larger towns on the coast, the aspiring middle classes could play alongside the established society leaders. An example was the Newport XI which contained several mayors and local politicians as well as two warehouse-owners, Edmund Cairns and David Harrhy.

Garndiffaith CC was one of the new clubs formed by the middle classes in the valleys. The man behind its formation was Thomas P. Davis, who ran the town's post office. In May 1865 he wrote to the *Pontypool Free Press* saying:

> Some few years ago, there was a cricket club at Abersychan and the members met in the field opposite Talywain church, but the field is now used for other purposes. The club comprised several good players, and it is my humble opinion it did no harm to the young men of the neighbourhood who were

connected with it, and I think if a few young men were to take it in hand again, a field might be had at no great distance and without much cost and that in a few weeks they would be able to form a good club. I cannot see why the members might not if they pulled together and practised regularly, obtain the honour of being the Eleven of All Wales, and become as competent at the game as the Eleven of All England.[52]

Grand aims and bold words, yet within a few weeks, Garndiffaith had its own club as local supporters rallied around their postmaster; within a month it had thirty members.

The 1850s and 1860s were therefore highly important decades in the evolution of the game, witnessing the emergence of cricket at grass roots level. New channels of diffusion were established by the Muscular Christians and schoolmasters, and these supplemented the existing structure, so that by 1870 there were a host of flourishing clubs in the valleys and coastal plain, which were incorporated into an integrated railway network. The twenty years also saw the game take off at school and college level, and the net result was that the game was supported by an ever widening cross-section of south Walian society from the landed gentry, industrial philanthropists and the *nouveaux riches* to clergymen and headmasters.

8 / *The Re-formation of the South Wales Cricket Club*

B Y THE 1870s the game in south Wales appeared to be in a healthy state, with clubs ranging from the gentlemen's teams in the largest settlements to the elevens at the thriving schools and more humble village sides. The county sides were at the top of this hierarchy, and their fixture lists of two-day matches were attractive in both cricketing and social terms to the gentlemen who aspired to play cricket at 'county' level. For example, in 1870, the Breconshire club, led by Penry Lloyd, played matches against a Colts XXII, a Past and Present XI of Christ College, Glamorganshire, Monmouthshire and Herefordshire.[1]

During the 1870s several of the Welsh counties increasingly sought fixtures with representative sides from England, with Monmouthshire having regular encounters with the Cotswold Magpies and Herefordshire.[2] Once again, it was J. T. D. Llewelyn who took the lead when it came to arranging matches with sides across the border, and in 1870 he secured two games for his Glamorganshire side against the crack West Gloucestershire team patronized by the Grace family. Given the rising standard of play by the Welsh gentlemen, Llewelyn was optimistic of his side's chances against the top West Country team, but these high hopes quickly evaporated in the first match in mid-May at Bristol.

Neither J. T. D. nor Lovering were able to play, and Glamorganshire travelled to Bristol without their two best bowlers. To make matters worse, they were dismissed for just 104, before West Gloucestershire rattled up the small matter of 418, as W. G. Grace scored a magnificent 197 and Frank Townsend of Clifton College made 105. The correspondent of the *Western Daily Press* reported 'the bowling was severely punished and the fielders had a very long course of leather hunting; the big hits which the batsmen continued to make sending them all over the field. For one tremendous drive, W. G. Grace scored nine (including three for an overthrow) and no less than 17 runs were scored in the over'.[3] Things went from bad to worse on the second day as Best and Young had to return home, and Glamorganshire with only nine batsmen were dismissed in only an hour for forty-six to leave the Gloucestershire team victors by the emphatic margin of an innings and 267 runs. The 'Doctor' produced a matchwinning performance with the ball in the return game at the Arms Park. He took 6–51 in Glamorganshire's first innings, whilst his younger brother George Frederick claimed 6–37 in the second innings. For once W.G. failed with the bat and was smartly caught at the wicket by F. E. Stacey off Edwin Bennett's bowling for just twenty-four. Had he stayed at the crease for much longer it could have been a repeat of the Bristol match, but even so, the Grace family's bowling dashed the hopes of Llewelyn's team and West Gloucestershire comfortably won by eight wickets.[4]

These fixtures were a brave attempt by Llewelyn to boost Glamorganshire cricket, but they only served as a gloomy notice that the game in south Wales had a long way to go before the gentlemen of the county could compete with the leading representative elevens across the border. There was one brief ray of hope midway through the 1870 season when Breconshire travelled to Hereford and defeated the home side by an innings and 120 runs. But as one contemporary source commented, the Herefordshire XI contained 'the names of but few, if any, cricketers of note',[5] and were certainly not in the same league as the West Gloucestershire side. It also suggested that the encounter with the Breconshire gentlemen did not generate as much excitement in Hereford as it aroused on the Welsh side of Offa's Dyke. The defeat, however, rankled their pride and a much stronger Herefordshire side travelled to Breconshire for the return game and duly restored its honour with a victory by an innings and forty-one runs.

Neither Llewelyn nor Lloyd became too disillusioned by these heavy reversals and persevered with promoting cricket in south Wales. No doubt, they were mindful of the rising interest in the game amongst the working classes and were keen to maintain the gentry's position at the forefront of the game's development, but they were faced with several difficulties. Firstly, the defeats by the West Gloucestershire side meant that Llewelyn was unable to secure further fixtures with Grace's team, who were seeking more testing challenges and were capable of holding their own with first-class opposition.[6] The only English teams who subsequently became regular visitors in the early 1870s were Herefordshire and the Cotswold Magpies, and although they may have been a social success, on several occasions both sides went down to crushing defeats at the hands of the Welsh teams.[7] During 1872 the Clown Cricketers, led by Harry Croueste, Queen Victoria's jester and one of the country's leading pantomime artists, made a tour of south Wales and played against Monmouthshire at Newport and Glamorganshire at

Merthyr Mawr.[8] A band and various circus acts entertained the crowd whilst Croueste's team was a mix of acrobats, clowns and professionals. They drew a fair attendance, but these games were a novelty rather than a test of cricketing skill.

A second stumbling block was that the committee created antagonism with local clubs over the use of the Arms Park for county matches. These matches generated considerable support from a wide social spectrum, yet the county officials were keen to maintain an exclusive air about proceedings and thus exclude the average workingman who had started to become interested in the game. With the blessing of Cardiff CC, they charged an admission fee of sixpence for their matches on the Arms Park and persuaded the Bute estate to bar the use of the Arms Park by any other team during the duration of the county fixtures. They also wanted to prevent the more raucous element, especially those who flocked to the beer tent, from entering the Park, and the *Western Mail* in June 1870 noted how the charging of a high admission fee 'was very effective in excluding the rabble, whose expressions of strong partizanship were tempered by the distance from which they witnessed the progress of the game and mingled their not very judicious comments and not over complimentary remarks'.[9]

This quite naturally failed to foster good relations with local sides who were normally given free access to the Park for their matches, and between the Cardiff committee and its members, who wanted to use the pavilion which had recently been erected for them by the Bute estate. It meant that whenever Glamorgan played at the Arms Park, Cardiff's members had to pay for the use of what Lord Bute had given them free of charge! But this was only the thin end of the wedge, as many of Cardiff's members felt that a drive towards a somewhat old-fashioned exclusive attendance was not how the game should be promoted, especially when it was gaining in popularity at junior club and school level. Protest letters appeared in the local papers, and one claimed that a restricted admission policy was:

> scarcely consistent with the dignity of the premier cricket club of so important a town as Cardiff . . . surely it would only be magnanimous for the Cardiff CC which possesses such great and exceptional advantages to permit the general public to enter the field during its matches and share in the pleasure which good cricket always affords.[10]

The smaller and less prestigious clubs in Cardiff enjoyed using the spacious Arms Park for their practices and matches. When this was added to the fact that the Bute estate had given the land free of charge for the recreation of the town's inhabitants, they were justifiably angered by the high-handed action of the county officials and the Cardiff club to obtain the exclusive use of the entire area. Then to rub salt into the wound admittance was limited to the wealthy, thereby depriving the less affluent supporter of cricket a chance to either watch or play.[11]

Matters took a sinister turn during the 1871 season as a letter, apparently from Edward Jones, the Cardiff secretary, appeared in the *Western Mail* during July claiming that 'no charge will be made for admission to any of our matches in the future'.[12] Sadly this was a hoax and the following day the paper carried an irate statement from Jones that 'the letter is a wilful mis-statement and that the writer has been guilty of an imprudent attempt to deceive the public'.[13] The fake indicated the depth of feeling over the issue and clearly showed that something had to be done to resolve the matter. The solution came the following week when a letter from a representative of the Bute estate announced that 'no charge of admission will be made to the ground',[14] thereby allowing both the rich and less wealthy cricket lovers in the Cardiff area to watch the county games.

This solved a local difficulty for the Glamorganshire officials, but there was still another much more pressing problem, namely the nature of the opposition. Rather than playing regular games against the leading West Country cricketers, the Glamorganshire side had to make do with fixtures against Penry Lloyd's Breconshire team and the Monmouthshire XI raised by Hugo Pearson, a former captain in the Royal Artillery, who lived at Craig-yr-Haul, near Castleton.[15] This paucity of strong opposition contrasted with the days of the earlier South Wales CC when gentlemen cricketers could rub shoulders with some of the top names in the London area and West Country. By the early 1870s they were left with only internal county matches within south Wales, plus games for scratch sides against schools such as Monmouth or Cheltenham.[16]

Ironically, the economic and industrial boom meant there was an increasing number of sides and well-to-do players who aspired to greater things than that offered by the weekly inter-club friendlies. It was an ironic situation that the demise of a club which had been chiefly concerned with matches outside Wales and had done little for many of the clubs in south Wales itself, had left such a large hole. Since the demise of the South Wales CC in 1865, the game inside the region had become far stronger and healthier but, without the flagship of the South Wales side, the emerging county sides were left to organize their own fixture lists, whilst the individual clubs were left to fend for themselves in the absence of a ruling body to oversee their activities.

This was in stark contrast with England where the Marylebone Cricket Club, after its formation in 1787, developed into the administrative centre for the English game and, during the 1870s, oversaw an embryonic county championship. In 1873 representatives of the leading nine counties met in London and drafted up basic rules for a county championship. These included regulations that a cricketer should not play for more than one county in the same season, that a qualifying period of two years residence be imposed on anyone wishing to play for another county and, in the case of any disputes, the MCC would arbitrate and resolve matters.[17] In south Wales, it was not uncommon for gentlemen to appear for several counties during one season, with a Mr Pierce playing for Breconshire, Monmouthshire and Radnorshire, whilst any disputes were normally fought and settled in the correspondence columns of the local newspapers, rather than at any headquarters in front of a ruling committee. The county game in England had therefore moved forward by the 1870s, whereas in south Wales the game at the top level was stationary, despite the improvements at grass roots level.

Quite naturally, the leading figures in south Walian cricket were worried by the lack of organization and means to promote the game in their domestic affairs. Nobody had put more into Welsh cricket than J. T. D. Llewelyn, and no one was more committed than the squire of Penllergaer to gaining due recognition for south Wales cricket. In order to move out of this stalemate, he decided to re-form the South Wales CC during the spring of 1874 and resurrect the London tours. He secured fixtures with the MCC, Prince's, and Surrey Club and Ground, and during July he led a team up to town containing several of the aspiring gentlemen, plus some of the old guard such as Penry Lloyd and Ben Arthur, and William Bancroft senior as the professional. Two of the games ended in defeat, but Llewelyn's team were honoured to have H.R.H. Prince of Wales and two dozen lords, earls and their ladies as interested spectators at Prince's.[18]

J.T.D. wanted the new South Wales CC to have more than just a social function, and hoped that it would undertake the same role as the MCC by co-ordinating the county programme in south Wales and provide an administrative structure for the clubs. During 1874 Llewelyn held a number of meetings to discuss these aims, with the first taking place in the pavilion at Prince's during the London tour.[19] He received a favourable response and a committee chaired by J.T.D., with Penry Lloyd as secretary, was appointed to debate the ideas in more detail and implement any suggestions. The first committee meeting was held at Brecon on 4 August and a number of important resolutions were passed, as the committee agreed to act as a co-ordinating body. They agreed that each of the six Welsh counties – Glamorganshire, Breconshire, Carmarthenshire, Cardiganshire, Radnorshire and Pembrokeshire – would be represented by a sub-committee consisting of three members. The sub-committees would organize the county games into a structured format, and give more of the gentlemen of the area a chance to represent south Wales. In an attempt to appeal to a wider audience and boost financial support, they took the bold step of reducing membership fees from a guinea to 10s. 6d., and asking each of the county sub-committees to 'solicit the support and patronage of the county and borough members and other persons of position in their respective counties'.[20] Several members of the new committee remembered the good old days of the South Wales CC, so it was not surprising that they wanted the club to remain firmly on an amateur basis. They felt that there were few professionals attached to clubs in south Wales who could boost their side. There were also the financial aspects to be considered, so with a wary eye on the slim accounts they resolved that 'until professional cricket in south Wales reaches a higher standard, that the eleven selected to represent the club continue to be amateur'.[21] This did not meet with unanimous approval amongst the rank and file cricketers of the area, and in August 'An Old Cricketer' wrote in the *Western Mail* that professionals should be selected if the strongest possible eleven was going to represent south Wales, and added that 'by judging from the performance of the eleven in London, I think we must not play an inferior team and exclude three of the best men for any reason of economy or to make room for gentlemen players to distinguish themselves on Lord's or The Oval'.[22]

The composition and representatives of the sub-committees were also questioned, as shown by another letter in the *South Wales Daily News* which raised doubts over C. H. Lascelles, Picton Evans and W. North representing Pembrokeshire. The author, again called 'An Old Pembrokeshire Cricketer' asked three questions:

> First, whether either of the three gentlemen named resides in the county he represents? Second, has either Mr North or Mr Lascelles ever played for any Pembrokeshire club or taken any interest in Pembrokeshire cricket? Third – is it not a fact that all three 'representatives of Pembrokeshire' reside in the county of Cardigan.[23]

The re-formation of the South Wales CC and the establishment of county sub-committees was a move in the right direction, and overall, the new South Wales CC was met with guarded optimism. Nevertheless, it was still felt in some quarters that 1874 had only seen a resurrection of old amateur ideals. In an attempt to refute these suggestions and hunt for new talent, a two-day match was organized at St Helen's during August 1875 between the eleven who were invited on the London tour, and the next best eighteen players in south Wales, including some from the smaller and less illustrious clubs, such as Llandaff, Cardigan and Ystalyfera. The contest attracted a decent crowd, many of whom turned up to see if the up-and-coming talent could turn the tables on the London eleven. It proved to be a close run thing, but the touring gentlemen managed to hold on by eight runs, and the *Western Mail* astutely concluded that 'from the interest taken in the match throughout the whole of south Wales, a great stimulus has been given to the manly game'.[24]

Attempts were made to secure a fixture with Oxford University in 1875, but no dates were agreed, and once again, the London tour formed the club's playing calendar. They were defeated at Lord's, and at Brighton against the Gentlemen of Sussex, but they defeated Surrey Club and Ground by sixty-five runs. The architects of the Welsh victory were the two bright young hopes of south Wales cricket, with C. P. Lewis scoring sixty-four and T. B. Jones taking 15–132 with his fast-medium bowling. They were also the first two cricketing blues at Oxford from Welsh schools – Jones from Christ College and Lewis from Llandovery – and, as David Smith [25] suggested in his study of the club, their cricketing prowess may have been another factor encouraging Llewelyn to reform the club. Certainly, their feats at Oxford gave clear proof that there were many talented young Welsh cricketers, who if nothing else, deserved higher exposure.

Charles Prytherch Lewis was only twenty-one at the time of the South Wales victory at The Oval and was the babe of the team. He received his early education at Llandovery School, before moving to the Cathedral School, Gloucester[26] in January 1870 and gaining an exhibition at Jesus College, Oxford. He was not in the Oxford XI in 1875, but after a lot of hard toil and sweat, plus the small matter of 206 for Jesus against Queen's College, he won a place in the side for 1876.[27] Twenty-four-year-old Thomas Babington Jones spent three years in the Christ College XI and played in their inaugural contest with Llandovery in 1865.[28] After starting study for a BA degree at Trinity College, Dublin, Jones left and went up to Jesus College and, in 1874, he secured a regular place in the Oxford side after hitting forty against the Gentlemen of England and taking 10–59 against Middlesex.[29] The youthful prowess and athleticism of Lewis and Jones must have been a delight and blessed relief for the aged amateurs in the South Wales XI.

The emergence of these two Welsh lads at Oxford, plus the higher exposure of the London tours and the victory at The Oval, gave South Wales cricket the sort of boost it needed after several lean years. It also encouraged Llewelyn to arrange a three-day exhibition match in May 1876 between a XXII of Swansea and District against a United South of England XI which included both W. G. and G. F. Grace. Their presence gave a grim reminder to J.T.D. of how his ploy of fixtures with West Gloucestershire had backfired, but he was typically confident that his team would give a good account of themselves. Swansea batted first and made a reasonable 160, with J.T.D. leading from the front with a characteristically aggressive thirty. The 'Doctor' made a brisk start in reply, and as the ball disappeared to all parts of the St Helen's ground, it looked ominously like being a sombre repeat of the West Gloucestershire encounters, but to the relief of the Welsh side, he was caught by the professional Parnham off Platts's bowling, and the South collapsed for 125 with their batsmen playing some rash strokes. A first-innings lead was more than J.T.D. could have wished for, and it was just the sort of fillip his side needed. But it also spurred on the English side, and W.G. took fifteen wickets as the Swansea side were bowled out for forty, with none of their batsmen reaching double figures.

The South were set seventy-six to win, and after his first innings display, many expected the 'Doctor' to singlehandedly see his team to victory. But Parnham and Platts combined with great effect to send the master batsman back to the pavilion for just nine runs, and as wickets continued to fall, the pendulum swung back in Swansea's favour. The 'Doctor' was disappointed by getting out for such a low score against the Swansea bowlers and, as more of his colleagues returned at regular intervals, he got changed and walked around the boundary rope. He was even heard to shout 'Here's a joke' as the Swansea attack made further inroads, but the collapse and Grace's comments were halted by the stubborn batting of James Lillywhite and gradually the English side edged closer to the target. A handful of runs was needed as the last pair came together, and the reporter from the *Western Mail* observed W.G. standing on the boundary rope 'looking rather excitedly on, having no doubt long made up his mind as to the result'.[30] The tension mounted as the scores became level, but then Platts bowled Bramhall to earn a tie, and a standing ovation from the crowd and many of the England team.

This nail-biting match and the other events of 1875 were ample rewards for the efforts of J.T.D. and the committee of the South Wales CC. After the celebrations died down, they started planning their fixtures for 1876 and how they could build upon the progress already achieved by re-forming the club. It had not escaped J.T.D.'s attention that it was still felt that the club was elitist and, despite the presence of C. P. Lewis and T. B. Jones, relied on the old guard and ignored many of the emerging players who had performed so well in the 1875 trial game at Swansea. Another headache was the far from healthy balance sheet, and to a large extent, the various sub-committees had failed to elicit further support.

On 4 July, 1876 Llewelyn called a general meeting of the club to discuss two ways of overcoming these stumbling blocks. The first suggestion was that all recognized cricket clubs in south Wales should be invited to register as subscribers of the South Wales CC and that a representative of each club be admitted to the AGM, normally held at The Royal Hotel in Cardiff on the first day of the town's races. Secondly, he advocated reviewing the standard of professional play in the region and even went as far as suggesting that if the meeting decided not to select professionals, that the name of the eleven representing the club should be changed to 'The Gentlemen of South Wales'.[31]

His first proposal met with unanimous support and Penry Lloyd stated that the 'object was to get all clubs in south Wales to take an interest in the central club which was intended to promote cricket in south Wales and the more clubs associated with it, the more likely it was to prosper'.[32] The members wholeheartedly agreed with these sentiments and decided that each county sub-committee would choose which of the clubs in their districts would be registered as members. However, the question of professionals was more contentious and struck at the whole ethos of the club.

There were two contrasting lobbies, with one rather conservative group, made up of the older players, feeling that the club had always been predominantly a gentleman's side and wanted it to remain so, without more than a token, if any, professional. The other more liberal group felt that more professionals were needed if the team was going to achieve progress, and their arguments were supported by the performance of Platts against the South of England. Moreover, they showed that many of the so-called gentlemen's sides in the London area had been fielding several professionals for many years, so if the South Wales CC stuck to these old-fashioned principles, they would be playing at a disadvantage. The quest for more members was going to raise more money which could pay for the services of the professionals whom they felt would be beneficial to the club.

The voting was close, and the traditional lobby was defeated by two votes, allowing the committee to draft up a new resolution relating to the selection of professionals. After some lengthy discussions, they agreed with C. C. Chambers of Swansea that professionals would be selected provided they were Welsh by birth, or if not, provided they had two years consecutive residence in the region, or had played for a bonafide club for at least two seasons. It marked the dawn of a new era for the South Wales club, and met with widespread approval from the clubs in the region. The local papers, for so long critical of the club, applauded J.T.D. for his initiative in seeking changes, and one letter claimed that the new resolutions 'will make the club more popular than at present. Good players will not be so frequently overlooked and the whole strength of the district will have a chance of being thoroughly canvassed and the best men selected. Above all, the suspicion of cliquism which has hitherto attached to the club will be eliminated'.[33]

A squad of thirteen was chosen for the London tour in July, including some new faces, and J.T.D. could not have wished for a better start to this new phase in the club's history, as the South Wales CC enjoyed its most successful ever tour. It began however with a nine-wicket defeat against the MCC, but was followed by three successive victories. Prince's were defeated by seven wickets, Surrey Club and Ground were beaten by an innings and 111 runs, and the Gentlemen of Sussex lost by five wickets. C. P. Lewis was the undisputed hero of the tour and these wins owed much to his all-round abilities. He celebrated his recent Blue by scoring half centuries at Brighton and Prince's, 120 at The Oval and then returned figures of 12–111 against the Gentlemen of Sussex with his fast roundarm bowling.

The 1877 season began with two trials at Swansea. The first was between two elevens composed of gentlemen who had not been on the London tour,[34] whilst in the second the pick of the rising talent challenged the club's regular eleven.[35] Consequently, more of the young gentlemen were included in the party for the London tour, and hopes were high of a repeat of the previous year's success. But the 1877 tour ended with two heavy defeats, as the Welshmen were beaten by nine wickets at Brighton and then went down to an innings defeat at The Oval. The final match at Lord's was a 12-a-side contest, but even with an extra man, Llewelyn's team once again found the MCC a difficult proposition and ended up hanging on for a draw.

Despite these defeats, the omens for the South Wales CC were still promising, with several young players emerging to supplement the established talent. Now that they were fielding more professionals and had more support from the clubs, they were altogether a stronger and more representative side rather than a collection of talented and not-so-talented gentlemen. South Walian cricket at the top level seemed to be on the move again, and a further boost came when the Australian tourists provisionally agreed to a two-day fixture at Swansea in July 1878.[36]

During the spring and early summer, the South Wales CC worked closely with Swansea to make the necessary preparations for this most prestigious fixture. Once again, J.T.D. used his influence with the railway companies, and in June the Swansea club was able to announce that 'special arrangements have been made with the various companies to issue tickets at reduced fares for the two days. Excursion trains will also be run'.[37] At the same time, the committee of the South Wales CC drafted up a squad for the game. The Australians were going to be the most talented opposition the club had ever faced, so they wanted to ensure a strong side was chosen. Even so, after some discussion over professionals, a squad of fifteen amateurs was announced.[38] It was led by J.T.D. himself and included many of the promising youngsters including

T. B. Jones, C. P. Lewis, R. L. Knight of Oxford University and Bridgend, and G. B. Elkington of Burry Port and Carmarthenshire. Nevertheless, the squad raised a few eyebrows, chiefly because the South Wales CC proposed the game to be on equal terms. As one letter in the *Western Mail* said:

> If ever there were an instance of pluck superseding judgement, it is surely revealed at present when the South Wales eleven, with eyes wide open are rushing not only to certain defeat, but probably to certain ridicule. I do not blame them for trying conclusions with the doughty Australians; far from it, I am only too glad to find that they have had the energy to bring them among us . . . but to play it as an eleven a side match seems to be to remove from it every element of interest and leave it an absurdity . . . What the cricketers of south Wales wish to see is a match not a walkover. I hope therefore an alteration may even now be made, trusting the south Wales executive may see their way to arrange for at least eighteen representatives.[39]

Other similar pleas appeared in the local press, bringing the committee's attention to the fact that they were being over ambitious by fielding only eleven.[40] Llewelyn certainly did not want a repeat of the West Gloucestershire matches, so in early July, another four gentlemen were added to the squad, and it was agreed that the Aussies would challenge eighteen opponents.

There was much excitement in Swansea at the presence of the famous cricketers, including many of the Australian team who played in the inaugural Test match against England in March 1877. A grand banquet was held at the Mackworth Hotel to celebrate their presence, during which brave words were exchanged about the Welshmen's chances.[41] Morale was boosted when Llewelyn won the toss, and he valiantly invited the tourists to bat, hoping that the fact that they had spent the night travelling from Twickenham, and had only arrived in Swansea at 4.30 a.m. would be in his favour.[42] Thoughts of an even contest were quickly dispelled as the Bannerman brothers began confidently, and to make matters worse, soon after the start Edward Davies, the talented Breconshire wicket-keeper and batsman, split the webbing between his thumb and forefinger and was unable to take any further part in the match.

C. P. Lewis and T. B. Jones tried their best, and were ably supported by Frank Cobden from Radnorshire, who had earned fame in the 1870 Varsity match by taking a hat-trick in the final over to secure a Cambridge victory. Although he took 5–41, Cobden was not the tearaway fast bowler he had been in his youth at Harrow and Cambridge, and the Australians rattled up a formidable 219. The fast bowling of 'The Demon' Spofforth and the steady seam of Boyle then proved too much for the Welsh batsmen. Lewis stubbornly defended for a brave eleven, but Spofforth took 10– 35 to enforce a follow-on. Second time around, it was Boyle who caused the damage, taking 9–33 and despite a valiant fifteen from 31-year-old Lewis Jenkins of Cadoxton, the tourists won by an innings and thirty-seven runs. Nevertheless, Llewelyn's team had done far better than many anticipated, and by scoring ninety-four and eighty-eight with one of their best batsmen indisposed, they had proved they could mount a reasonable challenge against the Test players. Their collective performance also showed that the South Wales CC had achieved its first goal – to restore the name of south Wales cricket at the highest level, and to give prominence to the emerging youngsters. But the match also proved to Llewelyn and his enthusiastic committee that a lot of hard work still had to be done. Even so, they had learnt a lot by challenging the Australians and, together with the matches in London, the youngsters had become better players. Evidence of this came on the 1878 London tour where they drew with the MCC and Prince's, but defeated the Gentlemen of Sussex by the handsome margin of 143 runs, thanks to half centuries from Lewis Jenkins and the fully fit Edward Davies. Llewelyn felt they could share this experience by playing more matches in south Wales and that, by flying the flag, more talent and support could also be gained. So in 1879 he resurrected the west Wales tours undertaken by Homfray's Welsh Wanderers, and arranged a four-match itinerary in July, with games at Pembroke, Cardigan and Carmarthen.

Judging by the reports in the newspapers, the missionary work of Llewelyn's team was not confined to the playing area and, besides spreading the name of cricket, a good time was had by all. The tour started with matches at Pembroke Dock against the 37th Regiment and a Pembrokeshire XIII. Thanks to J.T.D.'s contacts, for the most part, the party were able to travel in comfort by train, but they had to use a horse-drawn vehicle from Crymych to Cardigan to play the Cardiganshire side. During this journey they met the only mishap of the tour when a wheel broke on the wagonette and the tourists had to walk, with their kit and clothing, for two miles through the Cardiganshire countryside before they met a blacksmith, who repaired the wheel and allowed the team to reach its destination. Despite these problems, the touring party fully enjoyed themselves in Cardigan, where they were entertained to a lavish dinner at the town's Guildhall at the end of the game. Many of the leading gentlemen and ladies of the county attended, and as the tour correspondent wrote in the *Western Mail*:

> The fair sex, whose smiles are an excellent substitute for the absent sun, gladdened us with their presence, for it need hardly be said that the

Wanderers love the ladies. We will pass over the speeches with the sole remark that it was the unanimous opinion that the captain would have made an A1 bishop. Singing soon became the order of the day, and altogether we had a real good time in Cardigan, and hooray for Abertivy for so say all of we.[43]

The dinner ended well after midnight and Llewelyn's team wearily climbed into their beds. Yet they were up soon after six the next morning to catch the first train to Carmarthen. 'The yawns all round would have put to shame the hippopotamus at the Zoo',[44] and the team took the chance to catch up on some sleep. They arrived at the Carmarthen ground at 10 a.m. and gleefully tucked into bacon, eggs, salmon cutlets, tea and coffee and, despite their exertions on and off the field, then went out and dismissed the Carmarthenshire XVI for just thirty-eight runs! Llewelyn's men fully enjoyed themselves on this goodwill tour, and after their successful visit to London in 1878 they looked forward to another good time up in town. However, they were brought down to earth with a bump and were comprehensively outplayed by both the MCC and Surrey Club and Ground. Lord Anson hit 144 as the South Wales CC lost at Lord's by 256 runs, and then went down to a nine-wicket defeat at The Oval.

Judging by their activities in 1879 it looked as if some of the South Wales gentlemen spent too much time socializing and not enough practising their skills. A lot of emphasis was still placed on the entertaining and peripheral aspects of cricket. The attitudes in many club matches were still very relaxed and casual and, only in local derbies, did any deep competitive instincts come to the fore. For many people, cricket was still a form of social entertainment, yet the game at the higher levels in England was changing, with Test matches and a county championship adding an element of rivalry and competition. The social factors had been the strength of the club game in south Wales during the early and mid nineteenth century, but now they were becoming a growing weakness as the game in general became more professional and competitive.

So far, there had been little stimulus for change, as aspiring gentlemen and the *nouveaux riches* were quite content to perpetuate the traditional sporting philosophies established by the gentry in the first half of the nineteenth century. If the young players were going to challenge the top English teams, a less cavalier and tougher element needed to be introduced at club level to supplement and enhance the existing framework of friendly games. In other words, it was back to the argument that too many old-fashioned, amateur principles still permeated south Walian cricket at a time when the game was moving rapidly forward elsewhere. Indeed, many felt that this was another factor explaining why the region lagged behind and had not made as much progress at the higher level.

Despite their fondness for wining and dining, several prominent members of the South Wales CC recognized this paradox, and believed it was time for change. Once again it was the club's officials who took the initiative, based on their experience of the rapidly emerging game of rugby football where a cup competition amongst the newly established clubs boosted participation, raised standards and generated public interest. In September 1875 the South Wales Football Club had been formed in Brecon and amongst their leading officials were T. Conway Lloyd, T. P. Whittington and C. C. Chambers, who were all closely involved with cricket in south Wales. There were many similarities with the philosophy of the South Wales CC as the new club had 'the intention of playing matches with the principal clubs in the West of England and the neighbourhood'.[45] To boost the game, they introduced a competition called the South Wales Challenge Cup in October 1877, and as David Smith and Gareth Williams observed:

> for the next ten years, the South Wales Challenge Cup was keenly, sometimes literally fought for, to become the pivot around which early Welsh rugby revolved . . . It played a formative role in the emergence of Welsh rugby and in its growth as a spectator sport . . . It generated intense local rivalry and brought excitement and spectacle into the routine lives of congested, industrial towns.[46]

One of the finals for the Challenge Cup attracted a crowd of 6,000 and as one newspaper commented on the eve of the 1881 final:

> the question is not one merely of beating fifteen picked men from each of the other towns . . . It means much more. It means vindicating the honour of Llanelly against her many detractors . . . It means raising her name and her fame amongst the towns. It tends to bring more trade, a more vigorous public spirit and a healthier social life.[47]

Rugby took a firm hold and by 1880 at least thirty clubs had been formally established, leading to the creation of a new body called the South Wales Football Union to co-ordinate matches and select representative teams. Having lost some of their influence in rugby circles, the sporting gents such as Lloyd, Whittington and Chambers were keen to hold onto the cricketing reins, yet their grip was becoming weaker as the treasurer at the 1879 AGM announced a balance of a mere £3. 16s., and a membership of only 106.[48] The time had come for a drastic change, and the value of a cup competition had been clearly proved by the rugby clubs. Consequently, on the motion of J. E. Moore of Neath, and seconded by J.T.D., they instituted The South Wales Cricket Challenge

Cup. Rules for the new competition were drawn up, and an entry fee was agreed upon to cover the costs of having a silver cup from Elkington and Company of Birmingham. It was also agreed that the South Wales CC would take a share of the gate money and, by the start of the 1879 season, acceptances had been received from Cadoxton, Llandovery, Brecon, Llanelly, Newport, Cardiff, Carmarthen, Canton, Swansea and Llandovery College. A draw took place and in mid-June the first round of matches took place, all on neutral territory.[49]

The format of the new competition was a series of one-day contests, with both sides having two innings, although it was agreed that if time ran out, a decision would be made on the first innings scores. It immediately raised interest amongst the participating clubs, with keen competition for places. In the case of Llanelly, it prompted some of the talented players to put in a more regular appearance. Llanelly's first round match was against Brecon, and their local newspaper commented how:

> there was more importance attached to these matches in cricketing circles than to the ordinary home and away matches. This may be seen by the names indicated in the Llanelly team, some of whom rarely ever play in an ordinary match, but are ready to assist when their own club has to make a supreme effort to maintain its prestige.[50]

Llanelly won by sixty-nine runs, but lost in the quarter-final to Cadoxton who proceeded to the final to play Cardiff at the end of August at St Helen's. Quite fittingly, after Llewelyn's efforts, his Cadoxton side became the first winners of the new competition, and as an illustration of the benefits of playing for the South Wales CC, Lewis Jenkins was the top scorer in the match, making thirty-two runs in Cadoxton's second innings.[51] Once again, J.T.D.'s pioneering efforts had yielded positive results, as testified by the now improving bank balance of the South Wales club,[52] and he had material proof of the competition's success in the shape of the silver cup which took pride of place on the mantelpiece of his mansion at Penllergaer over the winter months.

9 / *The Rise of the Workingmen*

T HE PRESENCE of Llandovery College in the inaugural year of the South Wales Cricket Challenge Cup indicated the game's rapid progress at school level during the 1870s, allowing challenges to be made with the best adult clubs. Their participation was also the result of the influence of C. P. Lewis, who had returned to his old school in 1877 to become master of the junior school and assistant master-in-charge of athletics, as the Revd A. G. Edwards attempted to make Llandovery a top public school to rank with the best in England. Edwards leased a large field and laid out rugby and cricket pitches, besides adding a spacious sports pavilion for the young Welsh sportsmen.[1]

The presence of C. P. Lewis, the Oxford double Blue and Welsh rugby international, gave another huge boost to sport at the school, and he spent many hours in the winter and summer coaching the boys. Indeed, one of them later reminisced how Lewis's influence was marvellous – 'I have seen him transform, without a word, the lackadaisical efforts of a set of rabbits into irreproachable activity.'[2]

His wholehearted efforts were rewarded in the opening cup game of 1879 as Llandovery College challenged Newport at St Helen's. To everyone's sheer disbelief, the premier club was routed for just six, with Lewis taking 6–4. He had earlier carried his bat for forty-two as the schoolboys earned a healthy first-innings lead, but he was bowled for a duck in the second innings and the College was dismissed for twenty-four. Newport's batsmen showed more respect for the Llandovery bowling and batted with greater discipline a second time around. They warily defended against Lewis's bowling and were content to gather runs from the boys at the other end. Their respect for Lewis was rewarded with a seven-wicket win, but the clatter of first-innings wickets was a chastening reminder of the improvements at schoolboy level.[3]

Further evidence came the following year as Lewis's pupils gained revenge over Newport, but they owed much to their coach for an unbeaten seventy prevented the College from being bowled out in their first-round tie with the Monmouthshire club.[4] Under the competition's regulations, a replay had to be held because Llandovery's first innings was not complete, so a fortnight later, the students turned the tables on the club side, dismissing them for fifty-five, before compiling under Lewis's guidance a massive 233.[5] The following week they caused a further upset by defeating Cadoxton by an innings and sixty-five runs, thanks to another half century from their mentor.[6]

This victory gave Llandovery a place in the final against Cardiff, and Lewis top scored yet again with forty, giving Llandovery a first-innings lead over the Arms Park side. Lewis then took 5–19 and the Llandovery pupils were left with a target of just thirty-three to win the competition. It seemed a formality, but Lewis was clean bowled for nought by Edward Jones, his South Wales CC colleague, who then proceeded to work his way through the rest of the school's batting, taking match figures of 9–15 as Cardiff won by eighteen runs.[7]

The following year Llandovery had more luck and recorded some overwhelming victories in the early rounds. Firstly, they defeated Aberdare by an innings before recording a 120-run victory over Morriston, with Lewis scoring eighty-six and taking 7–14.[8] Their semi-final opponents withdrew and, in the final, Llandovery faced Swansea Workingmen's club who received byes in the quarter- and semi-finals. The Llandovery scholars dismissed the Swansea workingmen for thirty-one, with Lewis taking five wickets. Bill Gwynn scored fifty-eight in the Workingmen's second innings, but the boys reached their target with six wickets down to win the Challenge Cup, and confirm the progress which had taken place at school level.[9]

Nobody had done more for either the school, or indeed the knock-out competition itself, than C. P. Lewis and it was a pity that the relationship between him and Llandovery took a turn for the worse soon after the school's famous victory in the 1881 competition. Three years before, Lewis was reputed to have received an invitation to join Lord Harris's English eleven on their tour to Australia, New Zealand and the United States, but was unable to get time off from his scholastic duties and therefore had to decline the invitation.[10] He was naturally disgruntled at missing out and returned to Llandovery, but the question of his loyalties and duties at the school rose to the surface again during the early 1880s. In 1882 and 1883 Lewis won a place as full-back in the Welsh rugby team and it was around this time that the relationship between this Corinthian sportsman and his employers took a turn for the worse. Despite the publicity his efforts produced, the warden of the College did not like Lewis's absences, especially when he had responsibilities towards the school's boarding pupils. The dispute was resolved when Lewis resigned from the school in 1883 and left to train as a solicitor and enter the legal practice of his cricketing chum Charles Bishop in 1886, where he could more easily mix business with pleasure.[11] The loss of Lewis's services was a blow to the school but, from 1884, they acquired the services of a professional and this combined with the efforts of Revd F. E. Chapman to ensure that cricket continued to flourish at the school during the 1880s and into the 1890s.[12]

There was a similar story of growth and expansion at a number of grammar schools building on the good work of the 1860s and 1870s. Annual fixtures with nearby rivals became the highlight of the summer term, and in the case of the schools at Llandysul and Newcastle Emlyn, cricket was only part of a wider athletic challenge. A cricket match was held in the morning and, after lunch, the pupils took part in a series of running races.[13] The encouragement of cricket during the headships of the Revds M. P. Williams and J. C. F. Morson allowed Cowbridge Grammar to maintain its position as the leading sporting academy in the south-east. Their fixture list was extended to include matches with top club sides, plus home and away fixtures with Gloucester College, but they declined the chance to follow Llandovery and did not enter the Challenge Cup.[14]

The Cowbridge school continued to be a diffusion centre with A. F. Laloe moving to become head of Queen Elizabeth Grammar in Carmarthen in 1874, where he introduced both rugby and cricket. In 1875 he arranged a Past versus Present match and at lunchtime entertained both teams to a grand meal to celebrate heartily the dawn of a new era at the school.[15] By the late 1870s, the Carmarthen school held regular fixtures plus an annual sports day, including running races, a tug of war and a throwing the cricket ball competition. A sports day was also the highlight of the Lent term at St David's College, Lampeter where cricket continued to be encouraged under the Principal Revd Francis Jayne. He had been educated at Rugby and Jesus, Oxford and was not afraid to fly the flag of Muscular Christianity in the face of certain Welsh theological groups who still disapproved of sport.[16]

The one seat of learning to make dramatic headway during the 1870s and 1880s was Christ College, Brecon. In 1880 it followed in the footsteps of its great rivals Llandovery by taking part in the Challenge Cup, managing to reach the semi-finals before losing by just one run to Cardiff in a nailbiting encounter.[17] The following year the two sides met in the first round, and the Brecon school gained revenge thanks to a fine all-round display from 17-year-old James Gifford who took four wickets and made an unbeaten thirty-three. The youngster had previously been at school in north Wales, but he moved to Christ College when the Revd D. L. Lloyd of Friars School, Bangor was appointed to the headship at

Brecon in 1879.[18] Lloyd was an enthusiastic supporter of cricket and he and his staff gave every encouragement to the talented young players in their charge. Also prominent in the raising of standards during the 1880s were two Oxford graduates – A. J. Tuckwell, a forceful opening bat, and W. S. Rawson, a soccer Blue and English footballer, who played Minor County cricket for Herefordshire.[19] An early indication of their positive efforts came in the quarter-final of the 1881 cup, when the Brecon school initially tied with the illustrious gentlemen of the Cadoxton club, and then defeated them in the replay at Newport by seventeen runs, thanks to some fine strokeplay by Tuckwell.[20]

However, it was not just the premier sides and leading public schools who took part in the South Wales Challenge Cup, because Swansea Workingmen's Club were regular participants during the 1880s. In fact, one of the most important social trends in the game's evolution during the 1870s and 1880s was the rise of working-men's sides, and the inclusion of the Swansea team in the competition in 1880 marked their acceptance by cricket's hierarchy in south Wales, which for so long had been dominated by the gentlemen's sides. It also showed that the South Wales CC were not solely interested with the jollies and niceties that accompanied their London tour, and considered the game at grass roots level in south Wales.

Swansea Workingmen's Club was formed in the 1870s, and with Pascoe St Leger Grenfell, the leading cricketer and entrepreneur from Kilvey, as their president, it did not take long for a cricket club to form. They played their first fixture in 1876 and, within a few years, claimed some notable scalps. Their leading performers were the Gwynn brothers, William and David, who also shone at rugby and won Welsh rugby caps in the 1880s.[21] Bill Gwynn taught at Swansea Parochial School and led by example for the club, opening the batting and bowling cunning off-spin. His efforts acted as a flagship for the Workingmen's Club as a whole and, by 1879, they had 131 members. At the club's annual meeting its treasurer paid tribute to the cricket team by stating that 'many gentlemen have enrolled themselves in the institution during the past year through its instrumentality'.[22]

It was also because of the Gwynn brothers that the cricket side gained a chance to prove itself in the highest company. Appropriately enough, Bill Gwynn shone with bat as the club scored 215–8 in its initial cup match against Rhymney, but the dream ended in the second round as the team lost to Christ College Brecon by fifty-four runs. Despite this defeat, actual participation in the competition generated interest in the game and swelled membership, allowing further improvements to be made to the club's wicket. The hard work and modest investment paid off handsomely, as the first team defeated the Swansea side and was able to

1   Detail from an Ordnance Survey map for 1830 of Carmarthenshire, showing
     Court Henry Down, north of Cross Inn, where the first cricket match on
     record in south Wales took place in 1783.

MONMOUTHSHIRE CRICKET CLUB,
1838.

LIST OF MEMBERS.

1 Duke of Beaufort.
2 Lord Granville Somerset, M. P.
3 Sir Charles Morgan, Bart.
4 Sir Samuel Fludyer, Bart.

5 Alfrey, John, Newport
6 Alfrey, Edward, ditto
7 Bailey, Joseph, M. P. Glanusk
8 Bailey, Joseph, Jun. M. P. Nant-y-glo
9 Baldwin, John, St. Pierre
10 Baldwin, Edward, ditto
11 Batt, William, Abergavenny
12 Batt, Frederick, Abergavenny
13 Blewitt, R. J. M. P. Llantarnam Abbey
14 Bosanquet, Samuel, Dingestow
15 Bosanquet, James, ditto
16 Court, Charles, St. Briavels.
17 Cairns, Edward, Newport
18 Coke, R. Newland
19 Croft, C. H. Pontypool
20 Davies, Touchet, Crickhowell.
21 Dilwyn,—Glamorganshire
22 Davies, Henry, Monmouth
23 Edwards, Thomas, Bryngwyn
24 Edwards, Alexander, Pontypool
25 Edwards, Edmund, ditto
26 Gisbourne,—Brynderry
27 Hall, Benjamin, M. P. Llanover
28 Hunt, James, Snatchwood
29 Hawkins, H. M.
30 Hill, Stephens, Blaenavon
31 Hutchings, Edward, Dowlais
32 Ives, William, Brecknock
33 Jones, Philip, Llanarth
34 Jones, William, Clytha
35 Jones, Edward, Llanarth
36 Jones, Wybourne, ditto
37 Jones, William, Monmouth
38 Johnson, Richard, Bute Iron Works
39 Kenrick, G. S. the Varteg
40 Leigh, C. Hanbury, Pontypool Park
41 Lawrence, George, Blue Broom

42 Lewis, Thomas, Newport
43 Lewis, J. Glaslyn
44 Little, H. Panty Goitre (upper)
45 Livett, Andrew, Newport
46 Marriott, Major, Newport
47 Miers, John, Bridgend
48 Morgan, William, Panty Goitre
49 Moggridge, Matthew
50 Nares, Captain, R. N. Clifton
51 Needham, W. the Varteg
52 Nixon, John, Ditto
53 Payne, D. R. Newport
54 Partridge, William, Bishopswood, Ross
55 Phillips, William, Whitsun
56 Pocock, Henry, Beech Hill
57 Powell, Charles, Abergavenny
58 Powell, Captain, Monmouth
59 Powell, Rev. T. Cantriff
90 Pritchard, J. W. Caerleon
61 Price, Rev. T. Monmouth
62 Prothero, T. Jun. Newport
63 Prothero, Charles, ditto
64 Prothero, Edward, ditto
65 Prothero, George, ditto
66 Rickman, Richard, St. Briavels
67 Rolls, J. E. W. the Hendre
68 Secretan, W. W. Abergavenny
69 Stretton, W. R. Dany Park,
70 Stretton, Charles
71 Wilkins, Walter, M. P. Woodlands
72 Wilkins, J. Jeffries, Maes Derwin
73 Waters, Richard, Newport
74 Williams, F. Hanbury, Coldbrook Park
75 Williams, Rev. A. Usk
76 Williams, Thomas, Newport
77 Wright, W. C. Clytha Cottage
78 Wyatt, Thomas H.

COMMITTEE.

1 PHILIP JONES, Esq.
2 JOSEPH BAILEY, Jun., Esq. M. P.
3 W. R. STRETTON, Esq.
4 R. J. BLEWITT, Esq., M. P.
5 WILLIAM JONES, Esq.

6 J. E. W. ROLLS, Esq.
7 EDWARD JONES, Esq.
8 F. H. WILLIAMS, Esq.
WILLIAM NEEDHAM,
Treasurer and Secretary.

2 The members for 1838 of the Monmouthshire club at Raglan, dubbed 'the father of cricket' in the region. It reads almost like a Who's Who of the landed gentry in south Wales.

1. THAT the season shall commence on the first Tuesday in May, and conclude on the last Tuesday in August.

2. That a committee of management, consisting of five members (any three of whom shall be empowered to act), shall be appointed, at a meeting duly convened, in every season, by a majority of the members present.

3. That every person desirous of becoming a member must be proposed and seconded by members, at some meeting of the club, and ballotted for at the next succeeding meeting, when three black balls shall exclude him.

4. That every member, on being elected, shall pay seven shillings and sixpence to the treasurer, as his subscription for the season; and shall afterwards be called upon for an annual subscription of the same sum, to be paid on or before the first day of meeting in every year.

5. That the days of playing during the season shall be every Tuesday. The wickets to be pitched at two o'clock in the afternoon on the first day and on every alternate Tuesday during the season; and on the other Tuesdays at four o'clock.

6. That any member disputing the decision of an umpire, shall pay a fine of two shillings and sixpence.

7. That any member leaving a game unfinished (unless he shall, previous to his being chosen in, state a probability of his being obliged to do so), shall pay a fine of two shillings and sixpence.

8. That upon any impropriety of conduct in any member, the members present shall, at the request of any one member, form themselves into a special committee to inquire into such conduct, and the majority shall expel such member if they think fit.

9. That no challenge to play another club shall be given or accepted, without the consent of the majority of members who shall be present on the day on which such challenge shall be received, or proposed to be given.

10. That if any member shall incur any expense whatever to the club, without the concurrence of the committee, such expense shall be paid by such member.

11. That the members dine together, on the 28th day of July, at the Beaufort Arms: tickets not to exceed ten shillings.

12. That any member shall be at liberty to bring any friends with him, on condition of their being subject to the rules 6 and 7.

13. That the subscriptions and fines be applied (under the direction of the committee) in the purchase of bats and bails, and for other purposes of the club; and if any surplus remain in the treasurer's hands on the last day of meeting in the season, that the same be then applied as the majority of the members present shall direct.

14. That the Marylebone rules, as far as regards play, be the rules of this club.

15. That every member shall remain subject to these rules, until he shall express, in writing to the secretary, his desire to withdraw his name.

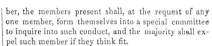

3   The set of rules for the Monmouth club in 1840. These were subsequently copied by other teams formed in the middle of the nineteenth century.

4   Charles Napier, a keen cricketer and the Chief Constable of Glamorgan at the time of the Rebecca Riots. Following the unrest, he organized special games between the military and the top sides in the district.

GRAND CRICKET MATCH.

A PUBLIC BALL

WILL BE HELD

AT THE KING'S HEAD HOTEL, NEWPORT,

On Wednesday, the 15th September,

AFTER THE

CRICKET MATCH BETWEEN THE ALL ENGLAND ELEVEN

AND

TWENTY-TWO OF MONMOUTHSHIRE.

STEWARDS:

COLONEL BELL, C.B.,

23rd Royal Welsh Fusiliers;

SAMUEL HOMFRAY, ESQ.,

Glen Usk.

Lady's Ticket ... ... **7s. 6d.**

Gentleman's Ditto ... ...**10s. 6d.**

——oo——

DANCING TO COMMENCE AT HALF-PAST NINE O'CLOCK.

——oo——

Tickets to be had of the Hon. Sec. CAPT. HOMFRAY, King's
Head Hotel, Newport.

5 A poster advertising a grand exhibition match at Newport in 1858. It contains a reference to Captain Homfray, who founded the South Wales Cricket Club during the following year.

6 The South Wales Cricket Club for 1861, including the leading personalities of south Wales cricket. The following team defeated the MCC that year. *Back row*: Pullen (umpire), J. N. O. Lloyd, H. Grace, C. W. Fryer, P. Lloyd, E. M. Grace, S. H. Belcher, Capt. Lloyd. *Front row*: G. C. Williams, Capt. Homfray, G. Worthington.

7 Swansea Grammar School. The lawn in front of the school was where the headmaster encouraged the playing of healthy ball games including cricket.

8 A postcard of Trinity College, Carmarthen, one of the western outposts of Muscular Christianity, where cricket was encouraged by the principal from the 1850s onwards.

9 The Abergavenny side of 1864, showing the early forms of dress and headwear, plus the equipment used in mid-nineteenth century.

10   Sir John Talbot Dillwyn Llewelyn, the squire of Penllergaer, was truly the
      father of cricket in south Wales; overseeing the game's development and
      helping form Glamorgan CCC.

Photograph by H. A. CHAPMAN.　　　　　　　*High Street, Swansea*

Yours faithfully

Charles P. Lewis

11　C. P. Lewis, the Corinthian sportsman, Oxford cricket blue and Welsh rugby international, who helped to establish high standards of schoolboy cricket at Llandovery College.

12 William Bancroft (junior), one of the earliest and most successful professionals in south Wales. He was also employed by J. T. D. Llewelyn as his family's private coach.

13 Llanharan CC leaving the Vale of Glamorgan village to play a fixture in 1892. Despite the arrival of the railways in mid-century, many teams travelled by horse-drawn wagonette until the early 1900s.

14 Workingmen playing cricket at Pontyberem in 1913. Few could afford whites, and the bats and other equipment were presumably shared.

15 The Riverside club around the turn of the century. The club was one of the many workingmen's sides in Cardiff, and it was out of its summer activities that Cardiff City FC was formed in 1899, allowing the members of the cricket side to stay fit during the winter.

16 The boys of Christ College, Brecon celebrate their win in 1905 over their arch rivals Llandovery College. Their annual encounters were the Welsh version of the Eton–Harrow games at Lord's.

17 The boys' cricket club at St Fagan's in 1900, created by the Earl of Plymouth. His estate agent, H. A. Pettigrew (standing top left) helped to coach the village boys and the earl's two sons (fourth and fifth from left on top row of boys).

18 The boys of Monmouth School at a net practice around the turn of the century. Judging by the attendance, it was a popular way of spending late afternoons and early evenings before tackling prep.

19 Canton Baptist CC in 1900. Canton was one of the sides established in Cardiff following religious approval for cricket as a healthy recreation in the polluted urban centres. Note the more ornate dress, compared with Abergavenny in plate 9 and those of the workingmen in plates 14 and 15.

20 The beautiful grounds of St Fagan's Castle, one of the tranquil venues for country house cricket during the Golden Age.

21   Action from one of the early 'county' matches, between the Gentlemen of Glamorgan and the Gentlemen of Essex at Neath in 1906.

22   Vernon Hill of Oxford University, Somerset and Cardiff. One of the English migrants who appeared for Glamorgan and helped to boost the game in south Wales.

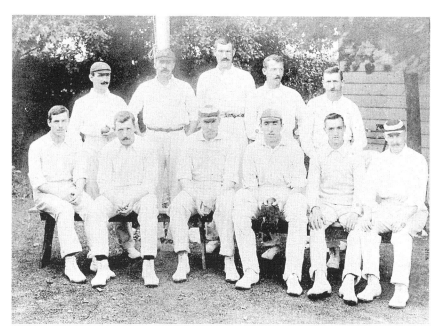

23 The Glamorgan side of 1901, which the previous year were Minor County champions. *Back row*: (left to right) Harry Creber, Richard Lowe, Sam Lowe, William Russell and Billy Bancroft. *Front row*: Norman Riches, Herbie Morgan, Joseph Brain, William Brain, Arthur Osborne and Alec Cameron.

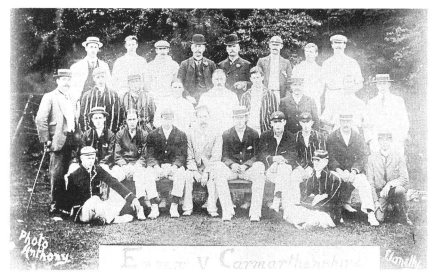

24 The Carmarthenshire cricketers with the Gentlemen of Essex, who met at Llanelli in 1906. There were few smiles on the faces of the Welsh amateurs as they slumped to a crushing defeat by an innings and 276 runs.

25 The four generations of the Ban-
    croft family, who acted as pro-
    fessionals and groundsmen for
    the Swansea club. On the far left
    is William (senior), in the middle
    William (Junior) and on the right
    his son Billy. On the ground is
    Billy's younger brother John,
    who like his elder brother also
    played cricket for Glamorgan and
    rugby for Wales.

26 Edmund Ussher David, – the
    captain of the first Glamorgan
    side in 1889. He was the son of
    Revd William David of St
    Fagan's, one of the Muscular
    Christians who actively oversaw
    the game's development.

field a second team against the town seconds.[23] They received a further boost when the club reached the 1881 final, beating Penarth in the first round, and being fortunate to receive byes in both the quarter- and semi-finals. There were high expectations of a famous victory for the Workingmen's Club and the cause of workingmen's cricket in general, but despite a fine fifty from Bill Gwynn, they lost in the final to Llandovery School.

The efforts of the Workingmen's Club were a showcase for the rising talent at junior level in the Swansea area, but success was also followed by a temporary slump, as Bill Gwynn was invited to play for the Swansea side. He accepted the offer, and turned out against his former team-mates in 1882. Without Gwynn, the workingmen failed to repeat their earlier feats and were unable to continue in the Challenge Cup.[24] Even so, they were still the most successful of the emerging workingmen's sides.

One of the first such sides to be formed was in Pontypool in 1858. Their Workingmen's Institute saw cricket as a form of beneficial entertainment in the summer months, but chiefly held games amongst Institute members.[25] During the 1860s a number of other clubs emerged, but they too only held fixtures amongst their subscribers, and the new phase in the game's evolution was not reached until the 1870s when games were held between teams from various workingmen's clubs and tradesmen's elevens against similar sides and teams from some of the smaller clubs. One of the earliest examples was in 1871 when the shipwrights of Mr Hill's boatbuilding company challenged an eleven from the Excelsior club in Cardiff.[26] Nevertheless, few games took place between the workingmen and the leading club sides who had their established and traditional fixture list with other gentlemen's teams, and gave no thought to matches with the workingmen. This was certainly the case in the early days of the Swansea Workingmen's side, who initially challenged sides such as the employees of Swansea Wagon Works,[27] or the workingmen of Neath, who like Swansea were able to secure games with the second elevens of the town clubs, but not initially the first teams.[28] The success of the workingmen's side, and the performances of Bill Gwynn in particular, led to a game with the Swansea first team in May 1880. It was a red-letter day for Gwynn's team, and in front of a crowd of several hundred, they secured a worthy victory by thirty-eight runs.[29] This encounter marked the coming of age for workingmen's cricket, with more of the leading clubs accepting their challenges in the 1880s.

The 1870s and 1880s therefore saw a proliferation of workingmen's and trades teams, and in Cardiff by 1885 there were sides of engineers, ironmongers, dockers and grocers (see Appendix C). The staff of the Electric Telegraph Company held fixtures with several of these sides, as well as an annual challenge with the workers from their Swansea office. The employees at the Theatre Royal in Cardiff organized a team which challenged sides drawn from visiting theatrical and operatic companies,[30] whilst there were regular games between the *Western Mail* and *South Wales Daily News*. In Brecon the clerks in the local banks held contests with the town club, whilst Bridgend challenged an XVIII from the local fire brigade.[31] Newport had a Commercial club, a Workingmen's eleven[32] and a team of employees from the various railway companies in the town, supplemented in 1873 by labourers and engineers working on the Crumlin viaduct.[33] Similarly, the employees on the new railway bridge over the Wye at Chepstow held games with local clubs, whilst in Barry matches were staged from 1885 by teams from the engineers and labourers constructing the new docks.[34]

In the coastal settlements the strongest workingmen's sides belonged to the numerous railway companies and, in Cardiff, a series of inter-company fixtures were staged, building on the foundations established by Charles Riches in the 1860s. An annual challenge between the employees of the Rhymney Railway and Taff Vale began in 1872 for which the Taff Vale side was able to hire a professional called Butler. In addition, in 1875 the leading players from the various company sides were assembled by Riches into a team called United Railways which played clubs including Cardiff, Newport and Rhymney.[35] Riches also persuaded his Cardiff colleagues to turn out as guests for the Taff Vale side when they travelled to play strong teams such as the GWR side at Swindon.[36] Railwaymen's teams were also formed in Monmouthshire, with the members of the locomotive, carriage and traffic department at the Pontypool Road station forming a side in 1876.[37] In 1882 a team called Severn Tunnel was formed by employees at the Caldicot junction, and by the late 1880s was sufficiently strong to challenge teams from Cardiff.

Several factors prompted this boom in workingmen's teams, not least the Early Closing Movement and the introduction of half-days into the working week. By the late nineteenth century, most people were working a 54-hour week, and with only a half-day at work on Saturdays, there was a chance for healthy recreation during the summer afternoons and evenings. This was especially true of the young clerks with sedentary jobs in the crowded offices or bustling businesses in the commercial centres. Many of them had played cricket at school and must have longed to put down their pens and pick up a bat or ball. As Richard Holt observed, these 'well-fed, relatively affluent young men with energy to spare needed games to play, especially when so much importance was attached to sport at school'.[38] Decent games could take place as the educational reforms had enabled them to gain a basic grounding in cricket, whilst the ethic of Muscular Christianity meant that they appreciated the benefits of recreation in an urban environment which, from a physical and mental point of view, was both unhealthy and overcrowded.

The workingmen were also able to play because of rising wages and a small weekly surplus which could be spent on cricket kit or equipment. A pair of flannels or a sweater would have been within their means, although a bat or pair of pads or gloves was still a prized luxury. Bats were often presented to club members on special occasions, and the fact that so many old bats have been discovered by their owners' descendants testifies to the cherished importance which working people then placed on these scarce items. Rising wages also made it possible for ordinary men to subscribe to clubs, but the fees of many sides were still beyond the means of the majority of workingmen, who probably had no wish to join in with the toffs and preferred matches amongst their own working friends. Even so, some clubs actually reduced their subscriptions in an attempt to lure some of the more talented and aspiring young players. In 1875 the Narberth club reduced its fees to half a crown in the hope that 'all the young men in the town will become members', whilst in April 1886 Swansea introduced a new rule whereby 'shop assistants who could play on the one evening in the week could enter the club at half the usual entrance fee'.[39]

These workingmen's teams swiftly grew in popularity, as testified by the following notice for Caerphilly in the *Western Mail* for 1874 – 'a few weeks ago a number of trades people of this place met together to establish a cricket club. When the fact became known to the public, it was taken up with great spirit and upwards of 50 people were quickly enrolled.'[40] This rapid growth was partly explained by the betterment factors associated with affiliation to a team playing regular fixtures. It gave the workingmen a chance to establish contacts that might enable them to escape from their humdrum existence, or rise up the ladder at their place of work. A series of good performances for the works team could only be beneficial and ultimately lead to promotion or better job prospects as the star batsman or bowler was seen as a decent chap by his boss, rather than just a name or number on the payroll. Holt has also shown that there were emotional rewards, as 'being in a team was to be "one of the lads"; it gave warmth, simple shared values and objectives, and an endless source of banter'.[41]

Participation in cricket, therefore, gave the workers a chance to establish a personal niche in the rapidly expanding and cosmopolitan urban societies. There were collective as well as individual advantages for the workingmen's teams, not least the opportunity of a victory over a local club patronized by the leaders of local society, thus proving that the workingmen were their sporting equals. This rising social consciousness of the working class, and the emergence of trade unions had important spin-offs for cricket, as the encouragement of sporting teams became an important facet of the union's activity. Inter-union rivalry led to annual challenges, such as the meeting of Cardiff's grocers and drapers each year at the Arms Park.[42]

In the coalfield areas, the mine-owners actively encouraged their workers' recreational activity and were able to organize their own sides despite the rigidity of the shift system. For example, the Powell Duffryn Company, which was the leading producer of steam coal in south Wales in the 1870s formed sides at Aberdare and Aberamman.[43] Similarly, H. A. Bruce, who later became First Baron Aberdare, created a side at Mountain Ash for the employees at the Navigation mine. Bruce was the club's president and even encouraged his young son William, who was educated at Harrow and Balliol College, Oxford, to play alongside the miners.[44]

The mine-owners also provided land for these new teams, with Peter Holmes, the owner of Van House, Caerphilly and the Black Vein Colliery, giving the local workingmen the use of a field near his house in 1874 so that they could establish a permanent venue for the games which became the sporting highlight of the summer for the miners. Contests with a neighbouring pit or rival company were eagerly awaited and in the case of Lanelay Colliery their annual contest with the Mwyndy Iron Ore Company was for a handsome silver cup costing five guineas.[45]

The ironmasters and owners of metal fabrication companies continued to support their worker's recreation and, like the mine-owners, enjoyed staging annual contests with rival establishments. In Port Talbot, challenges were held each year between Cwmavon Tinplate Company and the Ironworks,[46] whilst the owner of Caerleon Tin Works organized a forgemen's eleven for yearly games with the town side.[47] The success of these encounters led to the formation of clubs and a more extensive fixture list, such as at Ynyspenllwch Tin Plate Works near Clydach, where a club was established in the mid-1870s which, by the 1880s, had games against other workingmen's sides and small clubs in the Swansea Valley. Panteg CC also helped to forge good relations between the management and workers. The side was formed in 1876 by Sampson Copestake who founded the Panteg steelworks and, in the early years, the team included the labourers, plus W. H. Osborn-Taylor, the works manager and William Smith, the works director.[48]

These steel-making companies also provided land, with the Brown Lenox Company of Pontypridd acting as generous patrons to the town's cricket club during the late nineteenth century. The club had been formed in May 1870, and initially played in the grounds of Gelliwastad House. The wicket was poor, but without any other suitable venue, the club was grateful for use of this land. In 1873 the situation improved when Gordon Lenox moved to Pontypridd as resident director of the Brown Lenox Works. Lenox realized the shortage of suitable recreational facilities for his employees and other townspeople, so he gave the cricket club the use of farmland which he owned close to the River Taff where a decent wicket was laid out in one of the meadows.[49]

Close links with a factory or industrial philanthropist could also have its drawbacks as well as advantages, as some teams went out of existence following a slump in trade. This was the case at Ystalyfera where a side had been formed in 1866 and was composed of employees at the nearby tinplate works. The team flourished during the 1870s, but the club was hit by the depression in business during the 1880s. The drop in trade resulted in a shortage of money to pay for even the necessities of everyday life, never mind the cricket club's small subscriptions or equipment, whilst the workers' spare time, if any, was spent trying to support their families rather than relaxing on a cricket field. Many people left the area, and with a drop in both membership and playing strength, the club had drastically to reduce its fixture list. A few sporadic games with Morriston were held during the 1880s, before the club disbanded altogether.[50]

A change in relations with an industrial benefactor also forced clubs, such as Gowerton, to cut back on their activities. A side known as Gower Road had been created under the patronage of Col. J. Roper Wright, the owner of Elba Steelworks.[51] The colonel played in some of their matches, organized fund-raising events and provided a pavilion for the workers to change in. In 1884 he obtained a long lease from the landowner, J. T. D. Llewelyn, as well as improving access to the ground, and the club seemed to be going from strength to strength. Events however took a turn for the worse in March 1888 when a strike, described in the press as 'an unfortunate misunderstanding', began at the Elba Works. Ninety of the employees stayed out for most of the year, and the tension it created meant that few of the workers were willing to play, or even support the team, whose patron was the very person with whom they were in dispute. The consequence was that less games were held over the next few years, and the strike dampened the enthusiasm for cricket which the colonel's efforts had generated.[52]

In addition to sides organized by foundries, collieries, shops and trade unions, the 1870s and 1880s saw the emergence of pub teams. Their names added a touch of colour to the newspaper reports with names like Phoenix, Blue Anchor, Coronet, Imperial, Violet, Welcome, White Hart and White Rose. In some cases, the breweries took to the field themselves and in 1885 an eleven from Hancock's played local clubs in the Cardiff area.[53] The involvement of these public houses was not an entirely new trend; innkeepers had been patrons of recreation for many years and, moreover, there was a long established relationship between cricket and drinking. In the past, the Monmouthshire club had been based at the Beaufort Arms in Raglan, but this was a gentlemen's team, and what was new about the pub sides of the 1870s and 1880s was the nature of their participants.

The public house had become the focal point in the urban areas for those who lived and slept in the shadow of a factory or close to the docks, and they developed into community centres in these working-class neighbourhoods. Out of this developed a great desire to challenge a rival pub in an adjoining street or another part of town and establish a sporting supremacy over fellow workers. The recreational activities these public houses encouraged was not confined to cricket and, during the winter months, they ran rugby teams, with David Smith and Gareth Williams commenting that 'in default of any better facilities, teams invariably changed at a local arms, and clubs often had public houses as their headquarters'.[54] This was the case with the cricket team formed in 1875 by workingmen in the Amman Valley. The thirsty coal-miners and labourers gathered in the Cross Inn public house at Ammanford, and the pub became their changing room and pavilion. Naturally, the side took its name from the pub, before being changed to Ammanford in 1904.[55]

The involvement of pubs and breweries in sporting activity was also a reaction to the Temperance Movement, promoting the healthy advantages of frequenting pubs and confirming their benefits as centres for mass entertainment and recreation. The Temperance Movement also formed its own sides to counteract these claims, which helped to boost its membership and promote its cause. To prove the point that the demon drink was evil, the Temperance sides sought challenges with clubs not noted for their sobriety, with a keenly fought contest being held in July 1885 between Resolven and the local Temperance Club.[56]

Working-class recreation was therefore organized and promoted under middle- and upper-class control, although few of the landed gentry and leading cricketing figures actually got involved. Instead, patronage came from a wide number of entrepreneurs ranging from shopowners to businessmen, and colliery owners to ironmasters.[57] In some cases their involvement was altruistic, with the belief that by shaping working-class values and providing healthy and edifying recreation, it would prevent the workers from ruining their cultures. As Smith and Williams noted 'industrial society could degenerate into anarchy if it was not organised and whether interpreted in the literal sense that it re-created energies for the next day's work or the mythical sense of recreating associations with an idealised past, recreation, too needed to be organised'.[58]

Therefore, the intervention of these industrial patrons was out of a sense of moral guidance, fulfilling the same role as the clergymen in the

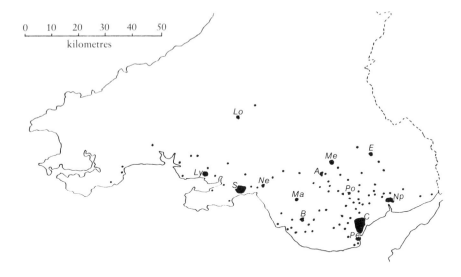

Figure 20. Location of clubs formed 1870–1885. Each dot represents one club, except for:

A – Aberdare (6)	*E* – Ebbw Vale (5)	*Ma* – Maesteg (2)	*Np* – Newport (16)
B – Bridgend (4)	*Lo* – Llandeilo (2)	*Me* – Merthyr (4)	*Pe* – Penarth (4)
C – Cardiff (91)	Ly – Llanelly (8)	*Ne* – Neath (3)	*Po* – Pontypridd (2)
			S – Swansea (43)

schools and more rural areas earlier in the nineteenth century. The religious leaders were finding it increasingly difficult in the anonymity of the expanding industrial settlements on the coastal plain to exert the influence they wielded in the countryside and the more tightly knit valley communities. So the lead had to come from the entrepreneurs who believed that cricket, and recreation in general, were the perfect vehicles for moral reform. It would benefit both the company and the workers, and suppress any feelings of discontent over working and living conditions. The geographical consequence of this trend was the widespread emergence during the 1870s and 1880s of cricket sides dominated by working people in the valley communities where previously Nonconformist opposition and a lack of spare time had prevented clubs being formed (see Appendix C). Figure 20 shows the location of new clubs during these two decades, ranging from Pontarddulais in the west to Abercarn in the Monmouthshire valleys, where even the local undertaker and his staff at the chapel of ease were able to field a side.[59] The notorious Georgetown area of Merthyr, renowned for its compact terraces of workingmen's homes, also had a cricket club and, once again, they were indebted to R. T. Crawshay for providing a field to use. They were holding fixtures by the mid-1870s with Thomastown, Abermorlais School and the Merthyr Vale club at Ynysowen. An indication of the native workingmen's involvement with the Georgetown club was the proliferation of Welsh surnames in the match reports, and the team for one match in 1875 included three Jones, two Lloyds, an Evans, a Thomas and a Rees.[60]

The spread of cricket in the valleys was just one part of a wider recreational revolution. Feelings against recreation gradually declined in the 1870s as rugby gained in popularity in these close mining- and steel-making communities. Clubs were formed in the late 1870s at Aberdare, Ammanford, Blaenavon, Ebbw Vale, Merthyr and Mountain Ash. They were followed in the 1880s by the growth of association football clubs, with the South Wales League including sides from Aberdare, Gelligaer, Maerdy and Porth,[61] whilst later on, boxing gained in popularity with Tom Thomas of the Rhondda becoming the first holder of the Lonsdale Belt in 1909. However, the most popular sport in the valleys was rugby, and the game which had previously been the pastime of young gentlemen at English public schools became a vehicle for communal pride in the working-class centres. As David Smith and Gareth Williams noted, 'with its urgency, excitement and physical commitment, it was particularly attuned to the rigours and privations of working-class life, itself so devoid of physical grace. It offered opportunities for an expression of group and community loyalties, for the achievement of personal recognition and the settling of grudges, for collective endeavour and common aspiration'.[62]

This participation in, and communal acceptance of, rugby boosted the spread of cricket in the valleys. Not least because of close links between the two games, as sports associations were created with their members playing cricket in the summer and rugby in the winter. As the Nonconformist opposition declined in the valleys, it allowed the promotion of rational recreation by a growing band of Muscular Christians. This encouragement began in the schools with more organized forms of the street ball games which the youngsters were playing. Many valley schools were able to stage fixtures from the 1870s onwards, often using the facilities of the local club and the fields donated by the industrialists. The standard of play steadily rose through the actions of the young schoolmasters who themselves were useful players. In fact, there were enough in Ebbw Vale by 1880 for a schoolmasters' eleven to be raised to play the town side.[63] The gospel of cricket was also spread in the Monmouthshire steel town by the Literary and Scientific Institution, which, in 1875, formed a side for the young workers to play Blaenavon, whom they beat by five runs.[64] Go-ahead young ministers played an active role in the valley communities, such as Revd C. E. T. Griffiths of Trevethin, near Pontypool. In 1876, he organized a side known as Trevethin Church CC and his young parishioners laid a wicket in a field near The Mason's Arms. Revd Griffiths ensured that the team was made up solely of regular churchgoers in order to advertise the benefits of rational recreation, and no doubt swell his congregation.[65] Even so, there were still a few protests by some religious leaders. In August 1874 the vicar of Tabor Welsh Independent Chapel at Maesycymmer preached a sermon entitled 'The Deadly Sin of Cricket', telling the congregation that 'workingmen ought not to join themselves with gentlemen, who had more money to spend, that it was a positive sin to go into a cricket field, that young men had no time to read their Bibles, all their time being taken up in cricketing'.[66] He finished by telling them that they were not to play cricket or else they would be excluded from the chapel!

His outburst was prompted by the Maesycymmer club renting premises from two of their farming members who were leading Calvinist Methodists. The younger members of the Tabor congregation enjoyed playing for the club, and probably thought nothing of associating out in the middle with the Methodists. But at a time of intense rivalry and friction between the denominations, the vicar of Tabor saw the cricket club as a symbol of another faith, and he did not want to lose anyone to a rival group. The Maesycymmer club was therefore the innocent victim of this religious in-fighting and, following the anti-cricket sermon, a smaller crowd than normal attended the fixture with Caerphilly. Many people were sad to see the cricket club caught up in this way, and to quote the reporter from the *Western Mail*, 'the greatest indignation is felt by the members of the club and all right-minded persons, that the pulpit should be made the means against this, the most harmless, most beneficial of outdoor recreations'.[67]

Religious support of the cricket boom was evident on the coastal plains even by some of the Nonconformist denominations, including the Congregationalists and Wesleyans, with Cardiff and Swansea each having their own Wesleyan teams by 1880, composed chiefly of young migrants from the West Country (see Appendix C). Many ministers, with an eye on the growing workingmen's involvement, saw no harm in encouraging their parishioners and choirboys to play, especially if it increased Sunday attendance and promoted moral and social reform. [68] This was the case in Cardiff with the Revd Joseph Waite, the Pastor of Charles Street Congregational church from 1862 until 1883. He was a man of great vision and energy, and served on the governing board of the new University and several schools. After seeing the way cricket improved the life of the young students, Revd Waite created a team for his parishioners.[69] There was also less friction between these religious groups on the coastal plain than those in the valleys and, during the 1880s, a regular round of games took place between teams from various churches. In many cases, the members of these sides were initially the choristers, with the St James Club of Cardiff originally being the St James's Choir CC, whilst the Dinas Powys team began in 1882 as St Andrew's Choir CC.[70] The playing membership gradually widened and the fixture lists extended so that, by 1885, almost every church and parish in the Cardiff area had a team, and the newspapers were full of the exploits of elevens representing St Catherine's, St German's, St John's, St Andrew's, St Columba, St Margaret's, St Mary's, and St Paul's, as well as Charles Street Congregational, Canton Wesleyans, Grange Wesleyans, Roath Wesleyans, Cardiff YMCA and Llandaff YMCA.[71]

Therefore, the involvement of workingmen and people of modest means saw the game enter a new phase in its development during the 1870s and 1880s. It was part of a wider recreational revolution that swept across the coastal plains and up the valleys from the pulpits, pubs and schoolrooms during the second half of the nineteenth century. These waves were not unique to south Wales, but occurred in the north as well, with J. B. Cowell, in his analysis of the growth of cricket in Anglesey, stating:

> The working classes were anxious to participate in organised sport during the summer months . . . Golf, tennis and cycling had become fashionable among late Victorian middle-classes, but these activities did not appeal to the working man. Besides, they were beyond the resources of ordinary folk, so their attention was turned to cricket, a game which they no longer regarded as socially above them.[72]

These trends also operated on a wider scale as British society as a whole came to place greater importance on athleticism, and cricket in particular during the summer months. As Keith Sandiford has observed, 'cricket was much more than just another game to the Victorians. They glorified it as a perfect system of ethics and morals which embodied all that was most noble in the Anglo-Saxon character'.[73] In earlier times, the inward-looking residents of the valley communities had resisted these trends and barriers existed against participation in sport. But the advent of rugby from the 1870s helped to sweep away these obstacles, much to cricket's benefit, and as Kenneth Morgan concluded 'new leisure activities emerged to quicken the pulses of Welsh workingmen and to provide their offspring with an alternative to the Sunday school outing'.[74]

10 / *The Growth of the Suburbs*

I F THE involvement of workingmen was an interesting social trend in the game's development, the most important geographical change during the 1870s and 1880s was the emergence of suburban teams. Figure 20 (on page 123) also shows the number of teams in the hinterland of the main settlements, with Cardiff having ninety-one sides being formed between 1870 and 1885, and Swansea forty-three. Newport had sixteen, whilst there were at least three in Neath, Aberdare, Bridgend, Penarth, Merthyr and Ebbw Vale (see Appendix C).

The timescale for the emergence of these sides varied across the region – in Cardiff the first appeared at Adamsdown and Roath in 1858, followed by Canton in 1866 and Whitchurch in 1869, whilst in Swansea they emerged a little later, with a side at Morriston in 1865, Oystermouth in 1869, Mumbles in 1871 and Sketty in 1878. Yet, despite the different timescale, they all resulted from the same process, namely a flight to the suburbs, as decent residential areas developed on the fringe of the built-up area, several kilometres away from the central area with its imposing town houses. The affluent residents of these expanding urban areas had previously lived in the inner locations, but the overcrowding, poor sanitation, pollution and high crime rates made these addresses increasingly unattractive. In contrast, the suburban locations were more peaceful, healthier and cleaner, and thereby more desirable for those wealthier people who could choose to live well away from the smoke, noise and evils of the Victorian city.

Many of the leading figures with the town cricket clubs therefore opted to move out to the rows of spacious suburban villas and lavish detached properties which were built along the roads, or close to the stations on the railway lines which ran out from the towns. In several cases, they moved to a quiet village in the hinterland of the urban centre, which gradually developed into a fledgling suburb as more town dwellers moved out. Such 'villages' became increasingly attractive to the in-migrants to south Wales who could not find a desirable residence in a more central location.

The 1870s and 1880s consequently saw the emergence of new communities, whose fairly wealthy residents were keen to establish their new collective identity and what better way than the formation of a cricket club to bring the people together in healthy and purposeful recreation. The emerging suburbs were also the destination of the *nouveaux riches*, whose first sign of a new social standing was a move out of the town to the green and leafy suburbs. The second was joining the new cricket club and rubbing shoulders for the first time with the leaders of local and civic society.

The scale of this suburban cricketing explosion can be gauged from calculating a per capita index in a sample of seven of the largest settlements between 1851 and 1881. This index is a simple statistical value obtained by dividing the male population by the number of teams in each of the seven places, using information from the cenus reports and the newspapers during that period.[1] The values for Cardiff, Llanelli and Swansea, shown in Table 2 steadily declined over the thirty-year period as the number of teams increased, illustrating both this suburban boom and the rise of workingmen's teams. In the case of Cardiff, this was an increase from two in 1851 to more than forty by 1881. The trend was less dramatic in the other two settlements – in Swansea the rise was from three to eighteen, whilst in Llanelli it was from one to eleven.

TABLE 2 PER CAPITA INDICES OF CRICKET TEAMS IN SEVEN SETTLEMENTS, 1851–1881

	1851	1861	1871	1881
Cardiff	6348	3484	1619	1207
Merthyr	8696	13582	14240	5301
Swansea	3748	3099	2438	1349
Newport	3512	6108	3014	3370
Llanelli	5633	1459	1528	1077
Neath	5000	2247	2160	3589
Bridgend	4721	2905	2207	7346

The index for Merthyr actually increased between 1851 and 1871, showing clearly that there were still barriers to the game's development in this iron and steel-making centre where Nonconformity still held sway. However, the index dropped dramatically from 14,240 in 1871 to 5,301 in 1881 as labourers took up the game in workingmen's suburbs such as Georgetown, and as some of the barriers were overcome. The trends are less clear in Newport, Neath and Bridgend where the index declined between 1851 and 1871 as suburban and workingmen's teams were formed, before rising again over the final decade.[2] The fluctuations in Newport reflected the problems some teams found in acquiring a permanent home. Yet, by the 1860s, suburban teams had emerged at Christchurch (1864) and at Llantarnam (1868), followed in the 1870s by teams at Maindy (1870), Malpas (1874) and Ponthir (1875). However, the latter combined with Caerleon and Llanfrechfa Lower in their early years and it was not until the 1880s that they established their own identity.[3]

During this period, suburban cricket reached its fullest extent in Cardiff, as the former market town was transformed into a 'coal metropolis' by the economic boom in the coalfield and steel-making centres in the valleys. By 1900 over eight million tons of coal and thousands of tons of iron ore were annually exported from the bustling docks which opened in Cardiff during the middle of the nineteenth century. The marketing of this 'black gold' and the majority of the administrative work of the colliery and shipping companies was performed in the town, and Cardiff's Coal Exchange became the focal point of the Welsh, and indeed the British, export coal trade.[7]

The consequence of this economic revolution was a dramatic rise in the town's population. In 1801 around 1,870 people lived in the pre-industrial centre, literally within the shadow of the historic castle. By 1851 the population had risen to 23,085 and to 94,666 in 1881. This demographic explosion resulted in the growth of the town's suburbs, as there were simply not enough properties in the old centre to house the influx of migrants. It also forced the subdivision of large houses and the construction of new terraces or courtyards on any spare plot of land. As the labourers flocked into these central locations, the more discerning townspeople sought a cleaner and quieter sanctuary away from the docks, offices and teeming streets of the inner area.

The rise in the industrial wealth of Cardiff, and the suburban development process which it set in motion, are clearly reflected in Figure 21 which shows the number of Cardiff-based teams mentioned in newspaper reports between 1851 and 1885.[5] In the 1850s there were only half-a-dozen active sides in the town, but as trade from the docks picked up, and more people poured into the town, the number of clubs rose to twenty by 1870, thirty-nine by 1880 and sixty-three by 1885. Behind this numerical growth are some highly interesting geographical patterns, as shown in Figures 22 to 25, which plot the location of clubs mentioned in press reports between 1870 and 1885.

In 1870 the majority of Cardiff clubs were to the east of the central business district, playing on moorland or farmland close to the workingmen's suburbs which were being created along the roads running out of the town towards Newport. Clubs also existed to the

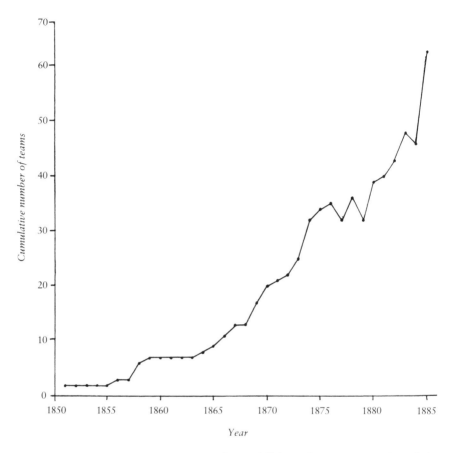

Figure 21. Cumulative number of Cardiff-based teams mentioned in newspapers 1851–1885

north at Whitchurch and Roath, and to the west in Canton, but none to the south-west where there was little housing anyway because of the marshy floodplain of the rivers Taff and Ely. By 1875 there was a significant increase in the number of sides in the more distant suburbs. There were two clubs in the middle-class suburb of Ely, close to the road running west to the market town of Cowbridge, whilst the affluent outer suburbs of Llandaff and Llanishen each boasted sides.

Figure 24 shows that by 1880 further growth had taken place in the inner suburbs, whereas few new sides emerged in the outer areas; Llandaff Workingmen's Club was the sole exception. In particular, the lower-middle-class suburb of Canton had five separate sides – Canton, Canton Wesleyans, Canton Rovers, Conway Road and Severn Road. This was part of a wider recreational boom in this workingmen's suburb

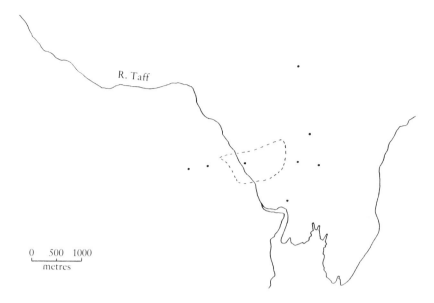

Figure 22. Known location of Cardiff-based clubs – 1870

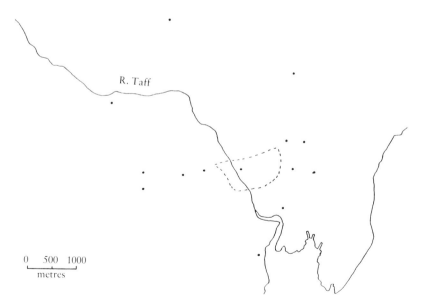

Figure 23. Known location of Cardiff-based clubs – 1875

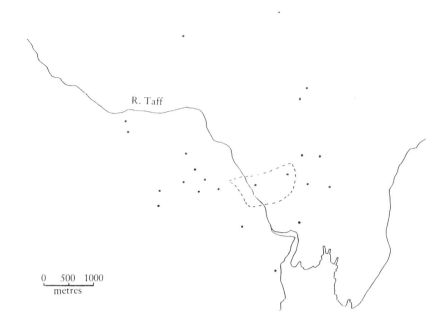

Figure 24. Known location of Cardiff-based clubs – 1880

and followed the formation, in the spring of 1878, of Canton Cricket and Athletic Club to provide honest recreation for local residents. The new club held its first cricket match in June against the Glamorgan Rifle Volunteers and in September a sports afternoon was held with running races.[6] The club's activities acted as a catalyst and led to the creation of four other sides within the space of two years, and enough interest was generated for the Canton club to be able to field a second eleven by April 1884.[7]

Figure 25 clearly shows that there was a further increase in the number of teams based in the inner suburbs and working-class areas by 1885. A side was formed to the north of the Central Business District at Cathays, close to the railway workshops, whilst in the east a new team represented Broadway. There were also new teams in the central areas such as Guildford Street, whilst others were established in the dockland areas at Loudoun Square and Roath Dock.

Therefore, the 1880s generally saw an infilling process, as there was an expansion in the number of clubs in the inner suburbs with a middle-and low-class population. This was at a time when workingmen were finding more time for recreation and a host of sides represented public houses, workingmen's clubs and churches. Many of the teams in these inner

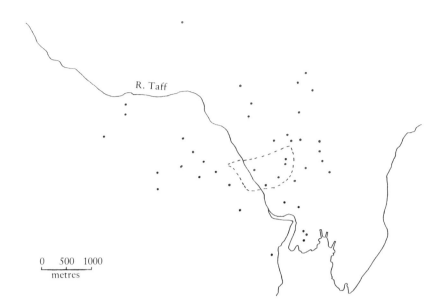

Figure 25. Known location of Cardiff-based clubs – 1885

suburbs also took the name of streets such as Severn Road and Guildford Street, and could easily have been formed as a result of the popularity of street sports, including street cricket. The creation of such teams also arose from the desire of the workingmen to show that bonds existed within their community and to reinforce their collective identity at a time when migrants were flooding in their hundreds into the town each month. Some of these newly arrived residents also formed their own teams in order to establish their little niche in a new and unfamiliar environment, whilst for others, especially the young, single migrants, membership of athletic or cricket clubs, meant comradeship, friendship and an identity in the melting-pot of life in the coal metropolis. A group of Yorkshiremen formed the White Rose CC, whilst some Scotsmen established the Caledonian CC.[8] A further motive was that many of the newcomers were shunned by the town club, and found it difficult to get a bat or bowl. As one letter to the *Western Mail* stated in May 1885 'if a fellow joins the Cardiff club, he will find the field so full on practice as to leave him, but small chance of securing an innings on most days of the week'.[9]

Whilst cricket was thriving in these inner urban areas, it was also taking root in the outer suburbs, and Figures 22 and 23 show the trend in the 1870s for an increase in the number of sides in these outer locations.

This was the time when rates of betterment migration were increasing, as leading townspeople left the overcrowded and insanitary areas and moved to the more pleasant and cleaner environments to the north and west of the town in suburbs such as Llanishen and St Fagan's.[10] The presence of wealthy businessmen and leading personalities from the social and political world of Cardiff in these fledgling outer suburbs influenced others of a similar, or rising, standing to follow their example during the 1880s. They 'leapfrogged' out to these outer suburbs and readily joined in with the recreational activities established by these innovators.

An example of this was in Llanishen where a side was created in 1873 by Walter Blessley and Thomas Ensor. Blessley was one of Cardiff's eminent architects and designed several of its new, imposing buildings, [11] whilst Ensor was a leading solicitor and Conservative councillor. Indeed, Ensor's obituary in March 1895 stated how he had been one of 'the first to build a villa residence at Llanishen and his example was soon followed by many others with the result that the district surrounding the pretty little village was quickly dotted with handsome mansions'.[12] Many of the occupants were fellow Conservatives and were only too happy to join in with their political colleagues. The end result was that Llanishen cricket club flourished and catered for the growing number of professional people from the town, as testified by the officers for 1894. The captain was H. G. P. Price, an insurance agent, William Puckridge was the vice-captain, and the secretary Ernest Prosser was an accountant, whilst the committee was made up of engineer J. M. Scott, land agent D. M. Jenkins and accountant Charles Clay.[13]

However, none of this expansion would have taken place without the co-operation of the landowners in the outer suburbs, and they are another group of individuals in this evolutionary process who merit close examination. Their property became increasingly attractive for housing developments, yet there were financial considerations which caused them to lease land willingly to cricket clubs. Firstly, it would make suburban living even more attractive if recreational facilities were available, and increase future demand for their land and more lucrative housing schemes. Secondly, at a time of declining profits from farming on the urban periphery, any money from a sports club was unlikely to be turned down, especially when cricket did no lasting damage to the land. Finally, with the prospect of the land soon changing from agricultural to urban use, the landowner could save money by leasing it on a short-term basis to the cricket club, rather than spending vast sums on improving the land, adding fertilizer or drains, and then seeing his efforts come to nothing as houses were erected on it.[14]

Cricket clubs often struck deals with a friendly local farmer, who was only too happy to see the young lads having a proper recreational area rather than using another, less suitable field and causing damage. The presence of a few prominent residents was also helpful in twisting a few arms or pulling strings so that land was secured. An example was the presence of Edgar David, the son of Revd William David of St Fagan's, on the committee of Fairwater CC. He used his influence for the club to acquire an area of farmland between Fairwater House and Llandaff Cathedral at a rent of just five pounds per annum. The enthusiastic members of the club soon levelled the land, enclosed it and erected a small pavilion at a cost of forty pounds.[15]

Not all suburban landowners were so willing to provide land to cricket clubs when large profits could be made by selling or leasing property for housing developments. This was the case in Llanishen where the club played on a number of fields around the suburban village. By the end of the century, the club needed a permanent base, as did the other recreational organizations serving Llanishen's growing population. An approach was made via a local farmer to the Bute estate in the hope of leasing six acres of land to the west of the village at Blue House Farm. However, the estate's land agent replied that 'he was unable to entertain on behalf of Lord Bute the application for a portion of the Bute property for recreational purposes'.[16]

The Bute estate had acquired a vast fortune by leasing large amounts of its extensive estate in Llanishen for building lavish properties in the emerging suburb, and they were aware that construction was likely to occur to the west of the village in the near future. Naturally, they did not want to lose out, especially when the demand for suburban housing was snowballing, yet they could have been more amenable to their residents' needs, temporarily leasing the land for recreation until it was required for housebuilding. It was even more surprising given the way the estate made the Arms Park available and helped the Cardiff club, but the question of hard cash made them change their tack in the suburbs.

The Llanishen residents turned instead to the smaller Lewis Murray–Threipland estate which, in contrast to the Bute estate, owned scattered plots in the suburbs. Some of their land lay close to an imposing railway embankment, along which the passenger trains and coal wagons travelled into the town and docks of Cardiff. This area was thus unsuitable for high-class housing and their agents were far more sympathetic to the approach from Llanishen CC to lease the land for a permanent recreation club. They realized they were unlikely to get an offer from a builder for this land in the near future when other more attractive plots were available and, in the case of the Bute estate, earmarked for imminent development. An agreement was soon reached with the Llanishen Parish Council to rent the land for eight pounds per annum and provide a home for the cricket and tennis teams.[17]

Assistance from the landowners was also needed, albeit in a rather roundabout way, in the inner areas as residential expansion from the 1850s reduced the number of open spaces where cricket could be played. Contrary to their actions in Llanishen, the Bute estate positively encouraged recreation by initially allowing the unrestricted use of eighteen acres of floodplain behind the Cardiff Arms Hotel. This area, which became known as the Arms Park, developed into the town's recreation ground and up until 1875 anyone was allowed into the Park and the nearby castle grounds without hindrance.[18] But many people disliked the somewhat chaotic situation on Saturday afternoons with a myriad of games taking place, often sharing boundaries, or overlapping. This was the case in June 1874 when the employees of the Rhymney Railway Company held their keenly fought annual encounter with the workers of the Taff Vale Company whilst, alongside, the staff of the *Western Mail* were engaged in a more social game between single and married workers.[19] In addition, an unruly element started to cause damage to the Park and articles in the *Cardiff Times* called attention to 'repeated acts of mischief and injury done to trees and fences'.[20]

To cure the situation, while maintaining a benevolent stance, the Bute estate restricted access to the Arms Park and castle grounds from April 1875 and limited the use of the Park to Cardiff CC and other bonafide clubs. The unorganized games of cricket ceased, but there were few other suitable areas of land in the expanding town where the cricketers of the inner suburbs could play. The simple answer was to form a proper club and obtain permission to use the Arms Park, so the tightening of regulations by the Bute estate added an extra incentive for the establishment of clubs in the inner suburbs.

With over sixty clubs in Cardiff by the mid 1880s, many of the gentlemen were able to hold subscriptions with the town club and a number of suburban teams. There were advantages to be gained by membership of a number of clubs, since playing for suburban teams such as Woodlands allowed the gentlemen to play several matches a week and keep their eyes in for the more serious and hard fought matches with the prestigious clubs on Cardiff's fixture list.[21] Indeed, the Woodlands club also extended invitations to members of the local gentry to guest in their eleven, alongside the leading cricketers from the town club, and as a result these games often had an air of country house cricket about them, and were a most pleasant diversion for the cricketers of Cardiff CC. Another advantage of joining a suburban club was that the gentlemen could also play in pleasant away matches or tours over the Bank Holiday period. This was the case for the members of Fairwater CC who in 1888 arranged fixtures at Yatton against the Somerset Cuckoos, at Lydney Park against Earl Bathurst's XI and at Penllergaer with

J. T. D. Llewelyn's XI.[22] A final advantage was that dual membership allowed the Cardiff players to run their eye over emerging talent, newcomers to the area, or any youngsters who could benefit by receiving coaching from Cardiff's professional. In fact, it was quite common for the town professional to visit the junior clubs in the area and late in the season an annual game was held between the Cardiff club and a XXII from the suburban clubs, during which a collection would be made to reward the professional for his efforts.[23]

The rising finances of these suburban clubs, both through subscriptions and the wealth of the Cardiff area in general, allowed them to become autonomous and hire their own professionals to look after their ground, prepare wickets and help coach the members. Once again, Fairwater led the way, and with a total income of around sixty pounds in the late 1880s, they were able to hire a groundsman/professional for twelve pounds. In 1894 they were also pleased to announce that they had 'engaged the services of John Barnes (late of Cardiff CC) as ground-man for three days in the week – viz. Tues, Fri and the day on which there is a match (if there is no match also Wed); on those days he will be able to bowl to members'.[24]

This pattern of suburban expansion was repeated in the other major settlements in south Wales and, by 1885, there were over thirty sides in each of the Swansea and Newport areas (see Appendix C). It was a geographical expression of the recreational boom that swept across the region, fuelled by the economic growth of the area, the emergence of workingmen's teams, the teachings of Muscular Christianity and the disappearance of Nonconformist barriers. This rise in the number of teams within relatively small and compact areas led to intense rivalries between clubs and quite often great importance was attached to the result of games. The extra competitive thrust surfaced in the new inter-club competition, the South Wales Cricket Challenge Cup, which took the game into the next stage in its evolution.

11 / *The South Wales Cricket Challenge Cup*

T HE SOUTH Wales Cricket Challenge Cup was inaugurated in 1879, and grew in popularity amongst the premier clubs in the early 1880s. But the Cup was a double-edged sword; on the one hand it helped to boost the game at the highest level and acted as a catalyst behind the formation of a proper county club, yet on the other it led to hostility and bad feeling between clubs, a rise in the number of professionals and claims that cricket was losing its image as a gentleman's recreation.

Nobody could have possibly imagined these negative consequences after the success of Cadoxton in the inaugural competition in 1879, and representatives of the leading sides looked forward to the cup matches of 1880. Public interest in the game was boosted by the new competition, and Cardiff CC decided to cash in on this greater awareness by arranging a three-day exhibition match at the Arms Park between the South of England XI and a XXII of Cardiff and District. The correspondent of the *Western Mail* applauded the decision, and wrote how 'we may hail the match which commences today as indicative of a revival in the interest felt in the noblest of outdoor games. The institution of a Challenge Cup for South Wales has, no doubt, helped in some degree to create the greater interest now felt in the game'.[1]

The rise in the number of suburban teams in the Cardiff area, and the influx of migrants meant that the town club could field a strong side against the English eleven, which included Test player G. F. Grace, his Gloucestershire colleague Walter Gilbert and Yorkshire professional Willie Bates. The visitors won on first innings by scoring sixty-nine to Cardiff's forty-nine, but the local players fought back in their second innings to secure a draw and the *Western Mail* was able to conclude that cricket is once more looking up in Cardiff – 'three years ago it would not have been possible to put such a good twenty-two in the field'.[2]

Confirmation of this healthy situation soon came as Cardiff won the cup competition for 1880 defeating Swansea in the quarter-final, Christ College, Brecon in the semi-final and Llandovery College by eighteen runs in the final.[3] Success, however, was short-lived as Cardiff were beaten by the Brecon scholars in the first round of the 1881 competition.[4] The honours were taken by Gifford and Rawson, and the Brecon team claimed another mighty scalp in its second-round encounter with Cadoxton. The initial contest ended in a tie, but Christ College won the replay by seventeen runs. However, they withdrew from the semi-final replay with their great rivals Llandovery, who in turn beat Swansea Workingmens Club by four wickets in the final thanks to a half-century from C. P. Lewis.

The format of the competition was changed to a regional knock-out competition in 1882. Two groups were formed using the River Neath as the boundary, with the winner of the western half meeting the winners from the east.[5] However, Cadoxton was included in the eastern region to balance the books,[6] and in the first round its bowlers Lewis Jenkins and Lewis Kempthorne inflicted a heavy defeat on Cardiff. They also defeated Newport, the other leading side in the east in the semi-final, and met Swansea in the final, who had only reached this stage after replaying the western semi-final with Llandovery College. The final was spread over two weekends at the end of September, but sadly conditions at St Helen's were far from ideal owing to bad weather. Cadoxton set Swansea a target of 153, but the wet wicket meant they were skittled out for just forty-nine by the bowling of Jenkins and Kempthorne.[8]

This change to a regional format proved popular, so the east and west divisions were kept in 1883. Swansea was victorious once again in the western group, defeating Morriston by sixty-nine runs after sixty-nine from Bill Gwynn and a return of 8–48 from Lewis Harrop.[9] Llanelly and Cadoxton had a closely fought game with the former defeating the cup-holders by just one run. But Llanelly found the Swansea bowlers far too strong in the next game, and Swansea progressed to the final to meet Cardiff who had defeated Newport and Penarth.[10]

The contest was held at the Arms Park, but neutral umpires were appointed to ensure no bias.[11] Heavy rain prevented a start on the first morning, and when play eventually got underway, Swansea scored 100, before Cardiff gained a first-innings lead with 126. Swansea were 85–5 in their second innings when rain intervened again, and the Cardiff team claimed a victory on the strength of the first-innings scores.[12] However, Swansea drew attention to the rules of the competition which stated that all innings must be played out and argued that the final could not be decided solely on first innings. With just five Swansea wickets left standing, Cardiff naturally felt they had the upper hand and, that a practical solution to overcome finding another suitable date or a sunny day, was to award them the cup. But Swansea insisted on the rules being adhered to, and as one reporter wrote 'much to the disgust of the home team, the game had to be abandoned'.[13]

The teams reassembled a fortnight later at the Arms Park to start a replay. This time Swansea fared much better, scoring eighty four runs in the first innings, and then Bill Gwynn took five wickets as Cardiff's disgruntled batsmen were dismissed for forty-six. Swansea extended their lead to ninety-five in the second innings and it seemed that the cup was destined to stay in the west. The very thought of this spurred on Cardiff's openers J. P. Jones and T. M. Barlow, and they laid a solid foundation as the run chase began. However, the introduction of Gwynn's spin once again confounded Cardiff's batsmen, and he took 5–20 to guide Swansea to a 22-run victory.[14]

Swansea's players were ecstatic at the result, especially after the high-handed way Cardiff had tried to bend the rules, and with so much rivalry between the two sides, they were even more delighted to deprive Cardiff of taking the cup away from the west. These feelings were shared by many others in Swansea, as testified by the following report from the *South Wales Daily News*:

> Placards were posted about the town announcing the result . . . Crowds of devotees of the game awaited the arrival of the team by the 8.20 train . . . A band played "See the Conquering Hero Comes" as the train entered the station, and F. Perkins [the captain], Gwynn and Addie were carried on the shoulders of some of their admirers . . . The band headed the impromptu procession which filled a good portion of High Street and loud cheers greeted the team on all sides.[15]

A huge celebration was held at the Mackworth Arms, and even neutral umpire George Rosser of Newport was invited to attend and accept the toasts to the officials. He was never one to miss out on a good party, so rather than returning home after play, he travelled west with the Swansea side, joined in the celebrations and just for good measure spent a couple of days relaxing in the Mumbles![16]

The above reports highlighted the depth of rivalry between east and west Glamorgan and, with the South Wales CC ever eager to find new ideas to boost interest and enthusiasm, a game between East Wales and West Wales was staged during the Cardiff Cricket Week in August 1883. All of the leading players turned out for this eagerly awaited contest. Honours on first innings went to the east, for whom Bridgend solicitor William Lewis hit eighty-three. However, C. P. Lewis responded with a half century for the west, helping his team to set a target of 146 to win.

It proved to be a tense final session, with no quarter asked or given, and the East Wales team 136–6 when stumps were drawn with honours even.[17]

The inauguration of the Challenge Cup therefore led to increased competition between the premier clubs, assisted the promotion of the game and heightened public awareness. Whilst these spin-offs were for the good of the game, the new competition also had a number of negative effects, which led to the end of both the cup and the South Wales CC itself. As the events in the 1883 final showed, the cup increased rivalry between the top clubs and this led to unnecessary friction between east and west. In fact, rather than bringing the clubs and players together, the Challenge Cup drove them even further apart. Disputes between teams were not a new feature of the game. In 1866 there was a dispute between the West Gloucestershire side, including both W. G. and E. M. Grace, and a XXII of Monmouth over the condition of the ball to be used for the match. Monmouth wanted to start with an old ball, but as the Doctor recollected: 'E.M. insisted upon the rules of the game being observed and would have none of it. There was no alternative but to send down to the town for another, and we had to wait patiently for over a quarter of an hour until the messenger returned. I was then bowled first ball, much to the delight of my opponents.'[18] In July 1872 a brawl occurred during a game between Pontypool and Abersychan, as several of the former side 'stripped themselves of vests and shirts, and set on the Abersychan men like so many tigers',[19] whilst in September 1880 the pages of the *South Wales Daily News* contained heated correspondence from the officials of the Penarth and Taff Vale clubs after the best Penarth batsman was given out l.b.w. in rather dubious circumstances by the Taff Vale umpire.[20] These three incidents were chiefly the result of weak or poor umpiring and sadly were nothing compared with the heated and prolonged controversies which the Challenge Cup set in motion. The competition aroused deep-rooted feelings and led to a series of smouldering disputes and rivalries, pitting club against club. In April 1884 Llanelly CC tried to defuse the build up in tension by suggesting another change in the format of the cup so that all of the clubs in each division played on a league basis, with the sides securing the most wins meeting in the final.[21]

However, these changes were thrown out and the South Wales CC bravely decided to keep the format the same for 1884. Just to rub salt in the wounds, Cardiff and Swansea met again in the final and the friction continued. Both clubs had enjoyed highly successful seasons, and the final was eagerly anticipated by the factions in the west and east. The Swansea team was delighted to win the toss to decide the location of the final, and Cardiff travelled to St Helen's at the end of August, determined to uphold the honour of the east and reverse the 1883 result. They put

Swansea in to bat and reduced them to 120–7 at lunch on the first day. However, during the afternoon session Swansea recovered to 220 and were greatly indebted to L. M. Richards, who interspersed safe drives with hearty slogs to leg in an unbeaten 103.[22] Cardiff ended the first day on 136–5 to leave honours even and everything to play for on the second day. But rain on the second morning delayed the start and then interrupted play again after lunch. Cardiff eventually reached 199–8 when another heavy storm swept in from Swansea Bay, preventing any more play. This time Swansea had finished up on top and, remembering Cardiff's attempts to have the 1883 final decided on first innings, they were upset at the thought of having to start afresh again. This time it was Cardiff who had to seek solace from the rule book, and Swansea reluctantly agreed to a replay at the Arms Park a fortnight later. But this was bad news for Swansea because, as the *South Wales Daily News* reported, 'unfortunately some of the most prominent players may not be able to take part. It will be a pity for one of the clubs to lose the match in consequence of not being able to put a representative team in the field'.[23]

The last thing Swansea wanted after the bad feelings between the clubs over the past few years was for Cardiff to gloat over an easy victory if Swansea sent a weak eleven to the Arms Park. So their officials decided that rather than send what virtually amounted to the second eleven for a thrashing at Cardiff, they would not send a side at all, and try and salvage some measure of pride out of the situation.[24] Cardiff were naturally delighted to claim the cup, but Swansea's actions rankled several of Cardiff's officials and the animosity continued between the two clubs, with a tit-for-tat action the following summer when Cardiff failed to send a side down to Swansea for their August fixture.[25]

The South Wales CC finally decided to change the format of the competition in 1885 into a league system rather than a straight knock-out, but neither Cardiff or Swansea entered the competition, feeling that they had nothing more to gain by taking part and would only have their reputations tarnished even more if further disputes arose. Other premier sides started to lose interest in the cup, with Cadoxton having their pride as one of the region's top sides dented by a comprehensive defeat at the hands of Pontardawe, one of the emerging sides in the Swansea area.[26] Cadoxton took umbrage and a couple of days later withdrew from their match with Llwynypia.[27]

Now that three of the big names had withdrawn, there was heightened interest in the cup matches by some of the smaller and emerging clubs. Unfortunately, so eager were some clubs to get their hands on the cup that they indulged in sharp practices. Several teams reverted to their bad old habits of relaxing membership criteria regarding residential eligibility in order to field a crack side for the cup, and the newspaper reports of the mid 1880s were riddled with comments over whether or not sides were truly representative.[28] These practices fuelled bad feelings between neighbouring sides, and matters came to a head in 1886 with an acrimonious dispute during the local derby between Swansea, who had re-entered the competition, and Morriston at St Helen's. The match was scheduled to start at 11 a.m., but the home side had difficulty in mustering a side and was not ready to start until noon. Such time-wasting annoyed the Morriston team, and a second difference of opinion occurred about the time for lunch. It was eventually resolved and play finally got underway with Swansea batting. As *The Cambrian* reported, all went well until after lunch at about 2.10 p.m. when:

> it was discovered that Edgar Reid, one of the not out batsmen, was not on the field, prepared to take his place at the wicket. The Morristonians now had a fixed idea that their opponents, having three of their good players absent, were determined to make an effort to obtain a drawn game, and play again with a better team . . . The crisis now came, and the visitors took their place in the field and without Reid being at the wickets. The ball was put in play, and the wicket-keeper removed the bails of Reid's wicket and he was given out by the umpire because he was not in his ground. The Morriston men claimed the wicket, but the home team strenuously objected, therefore, the wickets were pulled up and the match ceased amongst much excitement.[29]

The match was abandoned with Swansea on 48–5, but the arguments continued, with a letter in another newspaper putting forward Swansea's case:

> Anything more discreditable and uncricketlike than the conduct of the Morriston team and their supporters on Saturday, it would be difficult to conceive. The suggestion that the Swansea men were manoeuvering to bring about a drawn match is utterly without foundation . . . If an arrangement was made by the captains that lunch should not occupy more than half an hour, it was not generally so understood by the different members of the team, and certainly [not] by the not out batsman, [Reid was a Swansea doctor, and presumably quickly returned to his practice near the ground] who returned to the ground within 45 minutes, expecting to be in good time for the resumption of the game . . . under any circumstances one would imagine that no thorough sportsman would descend to such a pitiable trick to secure the downfall of an opponent's wicket.[30]

The writer of the letter then turned his attention to the Morriston spectators and their partisan behaviour at the St Helen's ground:

> Early in the game, the downfall of each Swansea wicket was greeted with yells of delight, while any good form shown by the batsmen was observed with

chilling silence. And then, when the dispute arose, and the game was stopped, they flocked to the pavilion in an excited crowd, gave vent to their feelings in language far more forcible than polite, applied the grossest epithets to individual members of the Swansea team, and finally demanded that their entrance money should be refunded.[31]

The following week a reply was published from a Morriston representative, which put the record straight as to Swansea's time-wasting tactics:

What are the facts? The Swansea men did not put in an appearance until 12 and some not until 1 o'clock. Play commenced about 12. The first two batsmen scarcely attempted to score, but did their best to keep their wickets intact – this in itself is nothing, but one of the batsmen afterwards remarked to a Morriston man, 'What are we to do, we haven't our best men here, we must keep up our wickets as long as possible.' Another member of the team tells his captain on Friday night that he shall not be able to play. 'Oh come down any time will do.' Now what is the inference?[32]

It was clear therefore that Swansea had initially been the guilty party and had yet again acted unfairly when missing their star players, but Morriston had also been too hasty in timing out one of the opposition. As the editor of the *Swansea Herald* wrote, 'Swansea are to be blamed for not turning up before they did and Morriston for being too hasty'.[33] Swansea withdrew from the competition for a second and final time, and Morriston went on to win the 1886 cup, defeating Llwynypia in the final. However, the 'timed out' fiasco drew an ugly veil over their success, and as one paper commented 'it was another nail in the coffin of these challenge cup competitions which have been successful only in arousing an undesirably strong and bitter partisan feeling'.[34]

The Challenge Cup had another impact, one which changed the character of these fixtures and the teams themselves. This was an increase in the number of professionals hired by the cricket clubs, so that cricket lost a certain amount of its amateur and Corinthian air. A talented professional, especially a fast bowler or cunning spinner, was highly sought after in the scramble for prestige and wider success during the 1870s and 1880s. Professionals had been part and parcel of the scene for many years, but by the 1860s they were being offered regular employment, rather than casual hiring for a local derby or prestigious fixture. The premier clubs initially established this trend, simply because they had the financial reserves to cover the cost of hiring the services of a professional. For example, in February 1867, the committee of Cardiff CC agreed 'that the secretary be empowered to engage a first-class professional bowler for an engagement of six weeks or longer, if the funds of the Club admit doing so'.[35]

Professionals also started to apprear in the valleys during the 1860s, as the growing wealth of the industrial settlements allowed many sides with rising aspirations to hire a paid player. An example was Treherbert, who secured a professional called Clarke in 1868,[36] but in the case of other sides it needed donations from patrons to hire a professional. This was the case with Ystalyfera which had been formed in 1866 and, in 1869, obtained the services of a bowler called Haine after help from J. P. Budd of Ynisdaren House. Budd also allowed the club to play in the grounds of his house, and Haine repaid his kindness by taking fourteen wickets against Cwmavon.[37]

There were enough professionals in south Wales by the late 1860s for Llewelyn and Homfray to be able to organize a Welsh version of the Gents and Players match which was a highlight of the English calendar. In July 1868 they arranged a two-day challenge between the Gentlemen and Professionals of south Wales, but it only showed the gulf between the amateurs and the paid players as the gentlemen were forced to follow on, before losing by six wickets.[38] J.T.D. was not too downhearted by this reverse and repeated the venture in 1869 at Neath. He was on top form for this re-match, and produced a matchwinning performance of forty runs and ten wickets as the Gentlemen won by 133 runs.[39]

However, the professional eleven was not as strong as it could have been for a variety of reasons, and the gentlemen had a rather facile victory. This happened again for the fixture in 1874 when invitations were sent to the professionals at the Cardiff, Cadoxton, Swansea, Llanelly and Bassaleg clubs. But some of them found it difficult to travel to the Arms Park, with their employers refusing to cover their travelling expenses for a match which did not involve the club. The upshot of these difficulties was that the Players found themselves three short on the morning of the game, and had to borrow three gentlemen members from the Cardiff club.[40]

One of the wealthiest cricket clubs during the closing years of the nineteenth century was Newport CC and an abundance of finance allowed them to hire both a number of top professionals, and at least one a year. During the 1870s they employed two professionals called Kelly and Murphy, before casting their net wider and hiring Herbert Beresford of Sheffield from 1878 to 1880, followed by Thomas Killick of Tunbridge Wells in 1881.[41] Having these well-respected English players helped Newport gain higher recognition, and they took part in the South Wales Cricket Challenge Cup. As Table 3 shows, by 1885 Newport was able to hire three professionals, and this practice became commonplace during the 1890s.[42]

TABLE 3 – PROFESSIONAL ENGAGEMENTS BY NEWPORT CRICKET CLUB 1880–1899

Year	Professional	Terms per week in shillings
1880	Beresford	$17\frac{1}{2}$ weeks @ 44s.
1880	Assistant	$11\frac{1}{2}$ weeks @ 25s.
1881	Killick	10 weeks @ 40s. and 7 weeks @ 30s.
1881	Assistant	7 weeks @ 30s.
1882	Richardson	20 weeks @ 40s.
1883	Beresford	17 weeks @ 45s.
1884	Beresford	16 weeks @ 45s.
1884	Jupp	8 weeks @ 60s.
1885	Jupp	$10\frac{1}{2}$ weeks @ 60s.
1885	Flowers	Total – £19. 14s. 6d.
1885	Moore	4 weeks @ 50s.
1886	Emmett	17 weeks @ 50s.
1887	Emmett	16 weeks @ 50s.
1887	Scott	Total – £17. 9s. 3d.
1888	Devey	16 weeks @ 63s.
1889	Devey	16 weeks @ 63s.
1890	Mee	18 weeks @ $52\frac{1}{2}$s.
1891	Mee	14 weeks @ 40s.
1891	Hucknall	19 weeks @ 33s.
1892	Silverlock	17 weeks @ 50s.
1892	Webb	8 weeks @ 25s. and 10 weeks @ 35s.
1893	Silverlock	18 weeks @ 55s. and 25 weeks @ 20s.
1893	Webb	18 weeks @ 40s.
1894	Silverlock	17 weeks @ 60s. and 31 weeks @ 20s.
1894	Barclay	17 weeks @ 42s.
1895	Silverlock	18 weeks @ 60s. and 30 weeks @ 20s.
1895	Barclay	18 weeks @ 42s.
1895	Jones	18 weeks @ 10s.
1896	Silverlock	19 weeks @ 60s. and 33 weeks @ 30s.
1896	Steeples	19 weeks @ 35s.
1896	Williams	13 weeks @ 10s.
1897	Silverlock	19 weeks @ 60s. and 33 weeks @ 30s.
1897	Steeples	19 weeks @ 35s.
1897	Williams	$16\frac{1}{2}$ weeks @ 10s.
1898	Silverlock	18 weeks @ 60s. and 34 weeks @ 30s.
1898	Steeples	18 weeks @ 50s.
1898	Hutchins	18 weeks @ 50s.
1899	Silverlock	18 weeks @ 60s. and 34 weeks @ 30s.
1899	Steeples	18 weeks @ 50s.
1899	Hutchins	18 weeks @ 50s.

The regular professional with Newport from 1892 was Arthur Silverlock, a fine batsman and spin bowler from the East End of London. Apart from a short break in 1909, he stayed with the club until 1914. In 1895 he scored 149,* 160,* 162 and 79* in successive innings and his efforts helped establish Newport as one of the top clubs in the region, besides making a name for himself as one of the best club cricketers outside south-east England.[43] As a result of its success, Newport was able to hire Dick Steeples, a former miner who had played as a fast bowler for Derbyshire, but this all meant a sizeable investment totalling almost £150 by 1899.

In return for this, the professionals had to be available to bowl in the nets at club members from noon until 1 p.m., 3 p.m. to 4 p.m. and 5.30 p.m. until 8 p.m., with each batsman having ten minutes at the crease. The club also helped to recoup their expenditure by having fines for poor conduct, and anyone found 'wantonly slogging the ball out of the field to be fined one shilling, to be paid before bowling be resumed'.[44] The Newport club was also innovative in the sense that it was the first club to introduce winter retainers to its professionals – a perk which county sides had only just introduced, with Surrey offering winter payments from 1894 so that its players did not move elsewhere. In fact, Silverlock's earnings of £3 a week were equivalent to what the established professionals at The Oval or Old Trafford could expect to earn.

Newport CC was fortunate enough to be part of a highly successful Athletic Club with other recreational sections, including rugby. The victories of the rugby side meant that pounds galore were pouring into the coffers of the Athletic Club each year. For example, in 1893, the gate receipts at 1st XV matches were £2,264. 5s., whilst a further £32. 17s. and 6d. was taken at 2nd XV games. Yet rarely did the gate receipts at cricket fixtures exceed even the 2nd XV takings. In 1881 just £3. 16s. was taken and this did not even cover the five guineas the club spent on kit and equipment from John Wisden.[45] In fact, the cricket section made a loss of £34. 3s. 9d. in 1887, and seventeen gentlemen, including George Homfray had to act as guarantors by making up the deficit.

By 1903 the gate money from cricket had risen to £28. 7s. 10d., but even so, the club's healthy financial state came paradoxically from rugby rather than cricket. Not that the cricketers were complaining, because this subsidy from the winter game allowed them to maintain annual subscriptions at just two guineas and have an ever rising investment in first-rate English talent. By 1898 the pot of gold from their rugby success allowed Newport to invest £144 in three professionals during the 18-week playing season, to say nothing of cash-in-hand bonuses for good performances, plus a winter retainer to Silverlock and the wages of a further eight people who looked after their Rodney Parade ground!

Swansea CC was also able to draw on financial reserves generated by the rugby club which shared its St Helen's home. From as early as 1874, the club had three professionals with William Bancroft junior being supported by Bennett and Underwood, although their fees were much lower than those paid by Newport. During the 1870s and 1880s Bancroft proved himself to be one of the most popular and successful professionals with his fast roundarm bowling and hard hitting. He was born in Bury St Edmunds, but brought up in Swansea when his father, William Bancroft senior, was appointed as groundsman and professional at St Helen's. In the mid-1860s, Bancroft junior took up an appointment with Rathway College, Oxford before playing in Yorkshire and Scotland during the 1870s.[46] However, he spent his winters in Swansea and was lured back home by two factors. Firstly, the more lucrative contracts being offered by Welsh clubs and, secondly, a friendship with J. T. D. Llewelyn who invited him to play regularly for the South Wales CC and Glamorganshire, as well as acting as private coach to the squire's sons. His presence helped Swansea win many games, but the increased expenditure on his services caused a rise in admission charges to 3d.[47]

In general, there were few cricket clubs who were so fortunate to be subsidized by rugby, and both Swansea and Newport were atypical in terms of their financial situation. But their decision to hire at least one professional on a regular basis during the 1880s and 1890s was true of countless other clubs throughout the region, as a host of players were hired in the scramble for success and, in the case of the leading sides, with the aim of winning the Challenge Cup. Many clubs were able to offset the expenditure by hiring out their professional to junior or suburban teams. From 1883 until 1895 Cardiff CC was served by the all-rounder Johnny Donovan, and to defray his costs he was hired out to smaller clubs such as Taff Vale, who were only too eager to improve their playing standard, as well as the Tynant colliery side at Garth, where Donovan worked in the winter months.[48]

The increasing wealth of the Valleys meant that the sides in these mining and steel-making communities could also afford top-class professionals from Northern England, who no doubt found life and winter work similar to what they were used to in their native counties. An example was the Rhymney club, who hired Riley of Yorkshire in 1880, whilst Llwynypia arranged for two of Yorkshire's top professionals, Emmett and Peate, to accompany them on their west Wales tour in 1888.[49]

The increase in the number of clubs wanting professionals meant that more appointments were available for ex-county players from England looking to see out their days in club cricket. Lucrative offers were drawn up to lure them and secure their services over several seasons, such as

Silverlock's winter retainer which, as Table 3 shows, was paid after he had had two successful seasons with the club. Legal contracts were also drawn up guaranteeing a professional's employment for an entire season, as it was not unknown for some aspiring clubs to dispense with players if their form dipped or if other, more talented, players became available. An example was the contract drawn up in February 1894 between John Barnes, the former Cardiff professional, and Edgar David, on behalf of the Fairwater club. Barnes was hired as 'groundsman and cricket professional', and his contract specified that Barnes would be available on Monday, Wednesday and Saturday (plus any other days that the committee decided) 'from 10 a.m. to 7 p.m. with an interval of a reasonable time for his meals and shall be lawful for the committee', who if they found him in an unfit or drunken state 'to dismiss the said John Barnes forthwith from the said service and employment and the said John Barnes shall thereupon forfeit all benefit and claim whatsoever under or by virtue of this agreement'.[50]

The rise in the number of professionals during the late nineteenth century was not, however, a trend unique to either cricket, or south Wales, as there was a wider rise in professionalism, with Gareth Williams stating that 'the last two decades of the nineteenth century were years of mounting anguish over the growth of professionalism in British sport'.[51] Indeed, Tony Mason showed how professionals were widespread in English football by the 1880s, with the officials of Preston North End being summoned before the Football Association and accused of making financial inducements to attract players both amateur and professional.[52] A similar, and rather shady, story began to emerge in rugby in south Wales, and the emergence of the game during the 1880s as a mass spectator sport saw it become smeared with the trail of finance.[53] During the next decade, the chiefly amateur game of rugby was hit by a wave of professionalism, fuelled by the formation of a Glamorgan League in 1894 and the availability of large amounts of money generated by large attendances.

The outcome was the formation of two distinct codes – one amateur (rugby union) and the other strictly professional (rugby league). Nevertheless, there was an element of shamateurism in the union code, as Welsh international W. M. McCutcheon claimed in 1905 that Swansea's rugby club had generously interpreted the phrase 'reasonable expenses' for the previous twenty years, and that it was only the downpayment from the rugby league clubs that tempted them to turn professional because their weekly salary from these clubs might not exceed that already 'paid' them in rugby union.[54] So if there were 'underhand' payments in rugby, it was only fair to assume that the same must have occurred in cricket. In fact, there was a fair amount of shamateurism in

English cricket; the 1878 issue of John Lillywhite's *Cricketers Companion* contained an article criticizing the 'gentlemen professionals', whilst in 1893 an article in *Cricket* drew attention to the 'highly paid professionals who pose as amateurs'.[55] In fact, it is quite hard to imagine that Henry Grace and Alfred Pocock travelled for nothing from the West Country to Swansea to play for the club against Cardiff in 1854, and there must have been sizeable payments to the Grace family for W.G.'s appearances for the South Wales CC during the 1860s.[56] The number of payments to amateurs was likely to have increased during the 1880s, as some clubs such as Cardiff, agreed to pay for its side's train fares,[57] and it is easy to imagine generous sums being quietly handed over in lieu of fares to a good amateur if he had just struck a century or taken a bag of wickets.

The increased competition aroused by the local derbies and the South Wales Cricket Challenge Cup in the 1870s and 1880s probably increased the number of shady deals with talented amateurs. But all of this remains pure speculation because unlike the bonafide arrangements with hired professionals in minute books or annual accounts, there are no documentary records in club archives of any special payments. In fact, it may not have been up to the treasurer to hand over these sums quietly, because a generous patron or benefactor may have willingly dipped into his pocket to pay for the services of a guest 'amateur' or reward a fine batting or bowling performance. What is abundantly clear, however, is that the 1870s and 1880s saw a rise in the number of professionals. By the 1890s, having up to three professionals was commonplace for the leading clubs, and there was a growing pool of money to pay, both above and below board, for the services of professionals and the expenses incurred by the amateurs.

Cricket thus became a rather different sort of game after the inauguration of the South Wales Cricket Challenge Cup. Some of the changes were for the better, but others such as the heated disputes which marred the cup matches and the local derbies were not, and prompted many of those amateurs with true Corinthian ideals to turn their backs on the club scene and look elsewhere for their cricket. In short, the Challenge Cup helped to open up a division that was to slow the pace of development.

12 / *Country House Cricket*

T HE 1870s and 1880s saw the spread of cricket to the masses, with an increase in working-class involvement, a rise in the number of teams, particularly in the urban areas, and more professionals being hired on a regular rather than a haphazard basis. These trends were not in fact unique to Welsh cricket, and as Gareth Williams observed 'the chief characteristic of the growth of organised sport in the late nineteenth century was its diffusion from the middle class downwards'.[1] So with cricket increasingly played by a broad cross-section of the population, the wealthier elements of the cricketing population in south Wales, like their counterparts in England, took action to preserve their identity and former importance. This situation towards the end of the century was rather different from earlier times when, as shown in Chapter 2, the leaders of society had been perfectly happy to play alongside professionals and other paid 'guests' as well as those less affluent individuals. But everything changed with trends operating on a wider scale causing increased social awareness and class consciousness. These changing social values as well as the rise of the workingmen caused the well-to-do and members of the gentry to distance themselves and disassociate from the paid ranks and lower classes in many aspects of life, including cricket.

Many of the gentlemen who had been brought up as Muscular Christians at public school in England or Wales abhorred the concept of money changing hands in sport, either officially to a professional or 'under the table' to an amateur. Many also did not like the way that their social distinction on the cricket field was being eroded by the more respectable status and image of some professionals, who now had better wages, more regular play and coaching positions with schools and colleges or, in the case of William Bancroft junior, as private coach to a wealthy benefactor and his family. This was part of the wider rise of the working class and Ric Sissons noted how the weekly earnings of professional cricketers in the late Victorian era exceeded those of skilled workers so that the professional became 'one of the more prosperous members of the working class'.[2]

In short, the professionals were no longer a second-class adjunct and, in some club sides, the gentlemen were not guaranteed a place at the top of the batting order, or even a place in the side, simply because of their name or social position. In addition, decent players were emerging from the lower ranks of society and, following the improvements in the education system and laws compelling children to attend school, no longer was it the case that the rich were the only ones to play cricket and be coached at school. Rising public involvement meant greater competition for places, and with victory at a premium in cup games or local derbies, clubs forgot any social niceties and selected elevens purely on cricketing merit.

All of these factors caused many of the gentlemen to look back fondly to the days when their fathers, or even grandfathers, played alongside other decent chaps at country mansions such as Cwrt-y-Gollen, Dolgarreg and Singleton House, and had the services of a somewhat subservient professional who did not mind batting low in the order and rolling up his sleeves to bowl after the gentlemen had turned their arms over. A handful of such games with a relaxed and dignified air continued to take place in the 1860s and 1870s, sometimes under the auspices of 'county games', such as those at Merthyr Mawr and by F.C. Morgan's Monmouthshire XI. But these annual challenges and one-off jollies were not the panacea, and the élite opted instead to rectify the position in the 1880s and 1890s by arranging more country house cricket and establishing nomadic elevens. Country house cricket also returned to the spotlight in England for the same reasons, having steadily grown in popularity since the 1840s. During the late nineteenth century, landowners laid wickets on their estates and staged their own festivals, which as George Plumptre noted were 'important status symbols for landowners who could still afford to regard their estates as places to provide social entertainment, which normally meant shooting in the winter and cricket in the summer. At a time when the upper classes had plenty of time for their leisure, when weekend parties were not interfered with by the modern phenomenon of the working week and were often more like week parties, lasting three or four days, cricket enjoyed its hey-day for social popularity'.[3]

These social aspects must not be discounted in south Wales in the revival of gentlemen's matches, as the cup games or inter-club matches often gave no opportunity for socializing or entertaining. In many cases, participation in these country house fixtures was the result of the lure of the ballroom and the champagne corks, rather than leather and willow. Indeed, Plumptre observed how in England these games by the turn of the century were 'the kind of ritual that the Edwardians loved, dressing up in the maximum finery, carriages drawn up alongside the boundary, huge picnics and promenading around the ground at the luncheon interval; a picture of dazzling, if self-conscious, social display'.[4]

Social reasons also influenced who was invited to take part in the cricketing jamborees, and R. L. Arrowsmith quoted the example of a player who failed to be invited to play at Wighill because, on an earlier occasion, he lit a cigar whilst Lord Hawke's port was being passed around![5] Several of these country house games in late Victorian England were entirely social fixtures, consisting of family, friends, estate workers or people from the neighbouring village, and umpired by the local vicar or the squire's butler or gamekeeper. Some matches involved top club sides or special elevens, including the leading players of the locality, leaving Arrowsmith to conclude that:

> the standard of country house cricket varied enormously. Some of it was little short of the standard of county or at least of Varsity cricket, some of it little better than village cricket. In its simplest form, the owner of a house collected his own side to play against a local side, a side raised by one of his neighbours or a wandering club.[6]

Many of the lords of the manor took these games very seriously and engaged a professional to prepare the wickets and take part in all of the fixtures during the summer season. Others wanted to maintain an air of dignity and exclusivity without paid players, and assembled the cream of amateur talent in the area and labelled their team a 'county' eleven. A host of these country house games occurred in the neighbouring counties of Herefordshire, Worcestershire, Gloucestershire and Somerset. In some cases, leading gentlemen from south Wales were invited to take part in these fixtures, with Basil Williams of Newport making 130 for a scratch eleven against Earl Bathurst's XI at Lydney Park.[7] The participation of these top players, plus the overall popularity of these matches, assisted their diffusion from the West Country into south Wales during the second half of the nineteenth century.

To an extent this was not an entirely new trend, because many of the country house teams were only an extension of gentlemen's clubs such as the Raglan club. From the 1860s many of the leading families in Monmouthshire, who had been members of the Raglan club, started to form their own sides for country house matches, including the Pelhams of Penallt, the Bosanquets of Dingestow Court[8] and the Walwyns of Croft-y-Bwlla. However, the two most active families were the Rolls of The Hendre and the Crompton-Roberts at Drybridge. J. E. W. Rolls was the son of the 7th Earl of Northesk and owned extensive areas of land in Kensington, south London and south-east Wales. John Rolls was also a benevolent figure to the county town of Monmouth and converted The Hendre from a modest house into an extensive country house, which by the turn of the twentieth century had no less than twenty-eight servants and 128 estate workers.[9]

John Rolls was a decent cricketer and appeared for Raglan, Monmouth and the county eleven assembled by F. C. Morgan. During the 1860s, his son J. A. Rolls formed his own side, partly for the entertainment of his father's staff, as well as for his friends and family. John Allan Rolls was an enthusiastic, if not highly talented cricketer, who first played whilst at Eton and Christ Church, Oxford and, on coming down, appeared for the Monmouth town side alongside local tradesmen and local dignitaries.[10] J. A. Rolls was also a prominent figure in Monmouthshire politics, standing as the county's Conservative MP from 1880 until 1885, and was created Lord Llangattock in 1892, before serving as mayor of Monmouth in 1896. It was therefore in keeping with his lofty social position to organize games on his family's estate, as the formation of a country house side was the way in which members of the gentry displayed their social position in mid-Victorian society. An indication of this was the composition of the side selected in 1862 to play an eleven raised by the Hon. Clifford Butler, who was a keen supporter of the Llantilio Crossenny club. Rolls's side included military friends, members of the local society and politics, and guests from the Newport club – in batting order they were 'E. Brewer, Capt Tyler, Capt Avery, Major Rolls, B. Davies, Capt. E. Tyler, Banniger, T. S. Wheeley, Sir S. Graham and Hon. F. C. Morgan'.[11]

The Rolls family often joined up with its friends, the Walwyns of Croft-y-Bwlla, but only sporadic games were held, rather than an extensive fixture list, and the Rolls found they could not compete with the top sides in the area. This was the case in 1873 when they challenged Ross. The *South Wales Daily News* reported how 'Major Rolls drove his four-in-hand to convey his team to the Ross ground, but the result proved that a team out of practice is not a match for an eleven who had played several matches'.[12] As well as games at The Hendre or Croft-y-Bwlla they also held an annual match at Abergavenny, followed by a grand dinner at the Angel Hotel. But the opponents often proved too strong for Rolls's team, and in 1861 his eleven mustered just forty-nine runs as the home team rattled up 267.[13]

Despite the defeats by Rolls's side, these games were a step in the right direction and, in the 1870s, the Drybridge club formed by Charles Crompton-Roberts became the leading gentlemen's team in the Monmouth area. Crompton-Roberts was another leading figure in the social world of Monmouthshire and was a Conservative county councillor. In 1870 he moved to Drybridge House at Overmonnow and, during the next couple of years, extended the house, laid out lavish gardens and opened a cricket ground.[14] Crompton-Roberts formed a more successful country house side than Rolls, and arranged regular fixtures during the 1870s and 1880s.

Drybridge staged its first fixtures during 1872 with games against Troy and Monmouth Grammar School. It also hosted Croft-y-Bwlla fixtures against Ross, with Crompton-Roberts providing a grand luncheon for the players and his friends.[15] Not surprisingly, the attendance at Drybridge's games read like a Who's Who of the local social world, with the report for one match in August 1872 noting how:

> there was a select and fashionable attendance amongst whom were her Grace the Duchess of Beaufort, Lady Blanche Somerset, Lord Henry Somerset MP, Lady Henry Somerset, Lord Fitzroy Somerset, the Countess of Westmoreland, Lady Grace Fane, Capt Curzon, Mr and Mrs Crompton-Roberts and sundry others, whilst the band of the Royal Monmouthshire Militia entertained the crowd.[16]

In 1874, Drybridge defeated a Combined Universities side by three runs,[17] and flushed by the success of these fixtures, Crompton-Roberts arranged for a cricket week at Drybridge in 1875. He secured two-day games with the Free Foresters, Combined Universities and Newport, and the week was a social and cricketing success.[18] In 1876, Drybridge included games with Ross, the Duke of Beaufort's Household XI, and the London Imperial Clown Cricketers.[19] As the rail network improved in the Monmouth area, Crompton-Roberts attracted other teams from further afield and, in 1883, the Drybridge Festival included a grand challenge between a Scratch Varsities XI and a team called 'The World'.[20]

The success of Rolls and Crompton-Roberts prompted a diversification of country house games in Monmouthshire. Other members of the local gentry followed their example, such as Godfrey Charles Morgan of Tredegar Park who held a cricket week, whilst his sister organized games for female members of the gentry.[21] W. E. C. Curre, an Old Harrovian who lived at Itton Court near Chepstow organized special matches, whilst the Walwyns of Croft-y-Bwlla held an annual cricket week.[22] These families had supported cricket for some time, so their involvement with country house matches was in a sense not new. Amongst the new names, and some of the most successful, were the Clays of Piercefield Park near Chepstow. In April 1861 Henry Clay, a banker and brewer from Burton-on-Trent purchased the Piercefield estate and he was succeeded in January 1874 by his son Henry Clay, who laid out a golf-course and cricket wicket in the grounds of his house.[23]

Henry Clay organized many 'private games' at Piercefield and acted as a kindly patron to Chepstow CC who used his ground for several of their fixtures during the 1880s. However, his most impressive cricketing act was to secure a three-day fixture at Piercefield Park in May 1882 between a Chepstow and District XXII captained by Clay and a United XI of All England, led by E. M. Grace, and remarkably Clay's side managed to win. Grace's team batted first and rattled up 268 with John Platts, the left-handed professional from Derbyshire, making 143, although he gave several chances and the fielding of Clay's side was initially rather poor. To compound matters, the local team was dismissed soon after lunch on the second day for 141 with W. E. C. Curre top scoring with thirty-one, before being bowled by Gloucestershire's Gilbert, who took 9–72, whilst E. M. Grace claimed 11–62.

Clay's men had to follow on, but they made a much better effort second time around, with four men getting into the twenties. Even so, the English team needed just sixty-seven runs to win on the final day, and so confident were they of achieving this comparatively easy task that Grace and W. J. Hughes returned home to the West Country. Yet much to the delight of the small, but partisan crowd, the Chepstow bowlers spearheaded by Alfred Mullins of Tidenham managed to bowl out their illustrious opponents for only forty-seven. The former Monmouth schoolboy took 4–24 and only Edward Pooley, the veteran Surrey wicket-keeper, got into double figures.[24]

It was not just in Monmouthshire that country house cricket was taking place during the 1870s and 1880s. This form of the game was also being staged in Cardiff through the auspices of the Bute Household XI. The Bute side was created in 1870 by the 23-year-old Third Marquess of Bute. The young aristocrat had been educated at Harrow and Christ Church, Oxford where, during his theological studies, he came to appreciate the importance of healthy recreation, and so on coming down he formed a side for his employees in Cardiff. Matches were staged in the grounds of Cardiff Castle, and on the Arms Park – the first in July 1870 against eleven gentlemen from the Cardiff club. A reasonable crowd was attracted and was entertained by the Band of the Royal Glamorgan Militia.[25] The following year they staged a match with Penarth on a half closing day in July and, with many people wanting to watch the game, the Marquess granted free admission to the contest.[26]

By 1873 enough interest was generated within the estate for two elevens to be fielded, and in August the second eleven challenged the St Fagan's club.[27] Later in September, two teams were selected from the Bute employees to play in a special match in the castle grounds to celebrate Lord Bute's twenty-sixth birthday. The marquess, his young wife and their many guests watched the game, and listened to the militia band, before retiring to the Angel Hotel in the evening for a grand dinner.[28]

The Bute Household club went from strength to strength in the mid-1870s, and adopted its own badge and colours – 'a dark blue cap, with the initials B.H.C.C. and a belt made of the Stuart plaid'.[29] The club's largest step forward came in June 1874 when the following notice appeared in the *Western Mail*:

> The Bute Household C.C. – which promises to be the leading cricket club of the Principality – has arranged for a three day match with the All England Eleven in the Cardiff Castle grounds on 3, 4 and 5 August. With commendable spirit, and enterprise, the Bute Household Club have undertaken to provide the whole of the expenses incident to the visit of the All England team. But with the view of benefiting certain local charities and at the same time affording the lovers of cricket in south Wales an opportunity of witnessing some first-class play, they have decided with Lord Bute's permission, to admit the public to the ground on payment of a small charge.[30]

It highlighted both the Butes benevolent atttitude to the townspeople and the grand hopes that the estate held for its club although, in the event, the fixture only took place over two days at the Arms Park. The admission charges were fixed at two shillings and sixpence for one-horse carriages and five shillings for two-horse carriages, and during the intervals musical entertainment was provided by the band of the Third Glamorgan Artillery and 103rd Bombay Fusiliers.[31] The Bute estate also took the innovative step of having a printing press from the local newspaper office stationed on the ground so that cards containing the scores could be issued to the spectators.[32] Despite the quite high admission fees, a fairly large crowd turned up and the *Western Mail* reported how:

> the beautiful grounds of the Castle, which have been the scene of many a vigorous contest by the Bute Household club presented a gay and animated picture as the afternoon drew on and people began to arrive . . . nature has hemmed in the cricket ground by a group of ornate trees and their umbrageous shade enabled hundreds of spectators to view the match unmolested by the dazzling light of the sun. A marquee erected for the accommodation of members and their friends, a long refreshment tent and two or three smaller ones used by the respective clubs, completed a scene of vivacity but seldom excelled, even in the grounds of Cardiff Castle.[32]

As well as paying close attention to the off-the-field arrangements, the Bute estate also ensured that it had a strong side for this fixture. Several of the town's leading players were given invitations, including J.P. Jones and Carlton Riches, as well as their professionals Randon and Selby, but the latter was indisposed after dislocating a thumb during a practice session. It was another guest, Lewis Jenkins of Cadoxton and the South Wales CC, who took the honours when the Bute side batted first and he top scored with seventeen as the Household XXII made eighty-nine runs. It seemed a modest score, but the All-England side collapsed to eighty all out with Riches taking seven wickets in between the showers. This spurred the English side on to greater things when rain allowed the Bute side to bat again, and they were reduced to 35–11 when stumps were drawn with honours even.[33]

The Cardiffians knew that they had acquitted themselves with honour and achieved a creditable first-innings lead, and if play had entered a third day, it would have made interesting cricket for the public who supported the Marquess's brave venture. However, not all of the supporters, despite the high entrance fee, were gentlemanly in their attitude, as a rather loud and unruly element was also present and intent on seeing the Englishmen beaten. Consequently, Major Bond of the Glamorgan Militia had to summon all of his night duty men from the docks to the Arms Park to prevent a fracas should the Bute team be bowled out and defeated on the second afternoon.[34]

The Bute estate was not deterred by these disturbances, and later in the season challenged the Tredegar Park side and an eleven raised by Col. Lindsay of Swansea.[35] The fixture list for 1875 expanded to include matches in June at St Helen's against Swansea and Cadoxton at the Gnoll.[36] In August they entertained the Swansea club to a return fixture in the castle grounds, which the *Western Mail* described as 'a match between the two strongest clubs in Glamorgan'.[37] The Swansea team included J. T. D. Llewelyn, C. C. Chambers and its professionals William Bancroft junior and senior, but the Bute side won on first innings, thanks to the bowling of Cardiff's professionals Walters and Lockwood.[38]

To an extent, the Bute Household side was more than just a country house side, but other leading houses in Glamorgan were staging more typical fixtures. Robert George Windsor-Clive, the Earl of Plymouth created a side for his workers at St Fagan's Castle, and actively supported the village side by providing land close to the castle. The earl was another Old Etonian, and a keen cricketer who played in several of the St Fagan's games.[39] His sons also took part in the country house games which the earl arranged, partly to entertain his children and relatives, when the family spent their summers in south Wales. Indeed, the earl's mother once wrote in her diary how 'Windsor and Oti played against the surrounding clergy, some of the reverend gentlemen being fat and mature'.[40]

The earl organized annual challenges between the Castle Household XI and both the St Fagan's club and Hewell Grange from Worcestershire, where he also owned land and spent some of his time. One of the staff in his estate office was H.A. Pettigrew, the Cardiff batsman, and he acted as coach to the earl's sides.[41] The success of their games led Robert Forrest, the earl's estate manager to extend support later in the nineteenth century, to other clubs including Barry Cricket and Athletic Club, for whom Forrest secured both a generous lease of land on Barry Island for a ground and cash to help finance the erection of a pavilion.[42]

Sir Julian Spearman also organized his own Lanelay XI which played leading sides in the Cardiff area,[43] but generally there was less country house cricket in its truest form in the Cardiff area compared with other parts of Glamorgan and Monmouthshire. This was partly caused by the accelerated rates of urban growth with land being swallowed up for building, compared with the more tranquil and rural atmosphere else-where in the county. Moreover, the proliferation of suburban sides such as Fairwater and Woodlands gave the gentlemen an opportunity to play in more relaxed games with their social equals. For example, Woodlands fixture list in 1876 included games against Nicholls' XI at Merthyr Mawr and the Tredegar Park side at Castleton,[44] whilst in the 1890s Fairwater played the Royal Monmouthshire Militia, The Bishop of Llandaff's XI and Earl Bathurst's Lydney Park side.[45]

More country house cricket took place as one moved west from Cardiff into the Vale of Glamorgan. The Earl of Dunraven continued to arrange matches in the grounds of Dunraven Castle, near Porthcawl, and in 1888 he helped establish Southerndown CC, before two years later leasing an area of his estate at St Brides Major to the club so that they could have a permanent home.[46] Country house games were also staged by E. H. Ebsworth of Llandough Castle, who in 1894 had a wicket laid in a field known as Cae Wyndham close to the market town of Cowbridge by the Kent professional Alex Hearne.[47] Ebsworth organized his own eleven to play at the ground and other sides in the Vale and Cardiff area. Bridgend were the opponents in the inaugural fixture, and quite fittingly Ebsworth, who was a decent player in his own right, scored the first run.[48] Further west, the Fox-Talbots organized games at Margam, whilst J. T. D. Llewelyn held special games in the grounds of Penllergaer House. To an extent, Llewelyn bucked the trend for exclusivity by inviting junior clubs from the area, such as Gowerton and Morriston, to challenge elevens selected by Llewelyn, containing some of the leading amateurs in the west.[49] He also organized unusual games in the grounds of his house, including a match at Christmas 1880, when two teams played a match on the frozen lake at Penllergaer. It was a fairly light-hearted encounter, and according to *The Cambrian*, 'was kept up with much animation until dark'.[50]

On the other side of the River Neath, the Earl of Jersey promoted games in the Baglan and Briton Ferry area. His estate agent, W. H. P. Jenkins, arranged annual fixtures between the Jersey Estate XI, which he led himself, and scratch elevens of gentlemen from Swansea, Margam and Porthcawl in the 1870s and 1880s next to Baglan House on Ty Isaf Farm. However, as David James has noted, the venue for these country house games had to be changed because:

> a small ripple had disturbed the friendship between Mr Jenkins and the farmer at Ty Isaf. The matter, however, was serious enough to cause the farmer to instruct his employees to scatter coal dust and ashes over the field. This had the effect of preventing the 'house' team from playing and the cows from eating, but in no way upsetting Mr Jenkins. He had the foresight to marry Lady Caroline, the sister of the Earl, and was able to purchase from his brother-in-law the field at Ynysmaerdy, where he continued to captain his eleven![51]

Some of the most popular, and grandest, country house games in the Swansea area took place from the late 1880s by a side known as the Public School Nondescripts, in the grounds of Killay House, which was the home of the Bransby Williams family.[52] The founder of this side was George Bransby Williams, the eldest son of Morgan Bransby Williams, who was educated at Clifton where he became an useful cricketer and rugby player. As he wrote in his memoirs:

> We started a holiday cricket club, and for more than twenty years about ten matches were played in August and September of every year . . . It was originally formed of our family and some friends from Rugby, Clifton, Malvern . . . From an orthodox cricketing point of view, the Killay ground suffered from some disadvantages. An area of about thirty or forty yards was level, but outside this the ground sloped rapidly upwards in one direction and downwards in the other. When fielding on the high side one's commanding position gave a good bird's eye view of the game, but rather interfered with efforts to take part in it. On the down side, a fielder in the 'sleepy hollow' was so far below the pitch that only occasional glimpses could be got of the bowlers and batsmen. However, it was all great fun: no-one took the games too seriously and everyone enjoyed them.[53]

The success of all of these country house games across south Wales also helped the South Wales CC find aspiring new talent from the amateur ranks who could join them on their London tours, which continued to be important aspects of the social calendar into the 1880s. In some cases, the scratch elevens which took the field in these house games took the name 'Gentlemen of South Wales' and included several of the leading players with the South Wales club. An example was the side, described as 'eleven gentlemen of south Wales who make their home at Maesllwch', assembled by the Green-Prices of Maesllwch Park for a match in September 1879 against a Herefordshire XI.[54]

These convivial meetings of gentlemen at palatial country retreats also led to the formation of wandering elevens, some of which took part in country house cricket in the West Country. An example was the team called 'The Cardiff Wanderers' or 'Y Crwydrwyr' which assembled in June 1884 for fixtures against Long Ashton, East Somerset and the Somerset Cuckoos. The touring party included several prominent Cardiff players including T. M. Barlow, W. W. F. Pullen, T. Robinson and H. M. Ingledew, plus someone with the nom-de-plume of 'A. Boozey', who presumably enjoyed the social aspects of the tour![55] In the early 1880s the Welsh Wanderers were resurrected by C. P. Lewis and in August 1881 they took part in two-day games against a Breconshire XI at Brecon and at Cardiff during the club's annual cricket week. Lewis invited many of the leading gentlemen cricketers to play for the Wanderers including Sir Joseph Spearman, William Morgan of Llwynypia, J. E. Moore of Cadoxton and Francis Dickinson, who played for Brecon and the Free Foresters and was director of the Crynant Colliery in Neath.[56] Around the same time, a wandering eleven was formed called the Monmouth-shire Butterflies. In September 1881 they played against Merthyr Mawr, Bassaleg and Newport, and their side contained several members of the local gentry including W. E. C. Curre of Itton Court and A. W. Redwood of Bassaleg.[57] These more social forms of cricket, given the descriptions and comments above, were highly popular amongst the higher echelons of the cricket-playing population. They were also in distinct contrast to the cut and thrust of local derbies or Challenge Cup games or the almost anarchic state of club cricket which was riddled with disputes and petty jealousies, and where professionals proliferated and money passed hands in return for putting in an appearance. In contrast, social recognition, a hearty lunch or dinner, plus plenty of wine, women and song were the benefits for the gentlemen taking part in these country house games.

Despite the more frivolous aspects, these country house games, and the amateur cricket which they spawned, were an important element in the game's evolution. They had a negative impact in the sense that the gentry, for so long the leaders in the innovatory process became detached from the game at grass roots and, as in so many other aspects of late Victorian life, away from their social inferiors.[58] But they had a positive role as well in that they helped to lay a foundation for the next stage in the development process, with the formation of proper county sides to represent south Wales.

13 / *The Formation of Glamorgan County Cricket Club*

CRICKET in south Wales moved into the next stage in its evolution with the creation in 1888 of Glamorgan CCC, the county club which has been the flagship of Welsh cricket during the twentieth century and the modern era of the game. For many years before 1888, individuals such as J. T. D. Llewelyn had tried to form a proper county eleven and the folding of the earlier Glamorganshire club in the late 1870s had fortunately failed to dampen his enthusiasm.

Ironically, J.T.D. 's dream eventually saw fruition at a time when the game, especially at the highest club levels, was in some turmoil following the disbanding of the South Wales CC in 1886, the end of the South Wales Challenge Cup and the preference for country house matches by the upper echelons of the cricketing hierarchy. The consequence was that many people felt that by the 1880s cricket in south Wales lagged way behind the game in England; the neighbouring English county of Gloucestershire had a recognized county side, and Somerset was on the fringe of first-class status. A letter to the *South Wales Daily News* in May 1881 summed up many people's feelings:

> The average play of the various clubs shows in particular a great inferiority in bowling and indeed it may be said that the ball is seldom handled in a thoroughly skilful style on Welsh grounds, excepting when a man trained in a university field makes his apperance amongst local players. The game of cricket is certainly in its infancy in south Wales, when the men produced by the several counties are compared with those which a single county in England turns out.[1]

Other letters and articles bemoaned the situation, and a few months later the following appeared in the same paper:

> It must be admitted that cricket in south Wales is in a backward state, and at

the present time there is very little chance of any marked improvement taking place, and the old adage 'that the nearer you get to London, the better the cricket' has recently been verified.[2]

There had been a noticeable drop in the number of games between the early county clubs formed back in the 1860s and 1870s. Their originators had all grown old together and their pursuit of exclusivity had been their downfall, with no new young talent to keep the sides going into the 1880s. Instead, the young emerging players showed a close affiliation to their clubs and those from the middle- or lower-class backgrounds no doubt found the local derbies more appealing than appearing with the toffs in county games at faraway country retreats. These feelings of attachment to a club increased after the addition of the Challenge Cup to the calendar and, together with an increase in the cricket-playing population as a result of education reforms and in-migration, there was greater competition for places in the club's 1st XI, whose officials were quite naturally unlikely to select somone who would pick and choose games, or disappear off for a nice 'jolly'.

The outcome of this rather parochial and insular swing in the games's development by the 1880s was a reduction in the amount of contact with top English players. It was now the responsibility of the leading clubs, rather than the gentry, to improve matters. Several organized exhibition matches, partly with an eye on boosting their membership levels, with the hope that fixtures with crack English sides would appeal to local emerging young players and those moving in from outside. Two examples were the games by an All-England XI and a XXII of Newport and District in September 1881 and a similar side from Cardiff in July 1882.[3]

Another solution was to organize cricket weeks, and in 1881 Cardiff organized five consecutive matches during the second week of August.[4] The centrepiece was the game between the South Wales CC and the MCC and the *Western Mail* hoped that 'the people of Cardiff, and especially the fair sex, will show by their attendance at the Park during the week an appreciation for the . . . game of cricket . . . and thus emulate the enthusiasm apparent at matches in neighbouring countries'.[5] In contrast, the Llanelly club decided to raise standards by inaugurating the Llanelly and District Challenge Cup, along the lines of the regional competition and, in an attempt to boost public interest, entry to the cricket ground at Stradey Park was free.[6]

The South Wales CC made a token attempt at improving matters by trying to extend its fixture list for 1882 by contacting the Australians and Wiltshire for matches.[7] Nothing came of the approach to the tourists, but the English side agreed to matches at Marlborough College and Cardiff.

In the match at the Arms Park, the South Wales side amassed 310 with J. P. Jones of Cardiff topscoring with sixty-one runs. C. P. Lewis took 5–29 to enforce the follow-on, but Wiltshire managed to hang on for a draw.[8] This was a rare highlight in a period of gloom for the South Wales club. During the 1880s they won just five of their thirty-one games and went through both 1880 and 1881 without a victory. Despite having many wealthy individuals as members, the finances of the South Wales CC were not in a healthy state at this time. The club began 1881 with a deficit of more than ten pounds[9] and this steadily rose causing the cancellation of the club's London tour in 1883.[10] The tour was replaced in early August by matches at Sydney Platt's private ground at Llanfairfechan against an eleven drawn from his Brynyneuadd club, plus a fixture at Shrewsbury against a Shropshire XII.[11] Both games ended in draws and, despite a victory over the MCC at Cardiff later in August, the South Wales club was clearly going through hard times.

The exclusive membership, like that of the county sides, proved to be at the root of the malaise. Despite reducing subscriptions from a guinea to half a guinea in 1879, the membership had only risen from 106 to 126 by 1883.[12] The annual general meeting saw the re-election of the same officers year after year, and as the same old faces kept appearing for the club, the press became increasingly critical of a selection policy apparently based on past reputations rather recent performances.[13] This parochial elitism was highlighted in a letter to the *Western Mail* in April 1886 which called for players to be:

> drafted out of the towns and not from the far corners of the counties as is at present the case simply because they may have been good players. I am afraid there is a savouring of cliquism in our midst in regard to the selection of teams, and so long as this state of things exists we shall never see a successful club in south Wales. The South Wales C.C. as now constituted has been a failure without doubt.[13]

This cliquism meant that many of the successful middle-class players felt that the South Wales club and the county sides preferred someone with a public school education, and many viewed their activities more as a form of social entertainment and a light-hearted meeting of Old Boys rather than serious sport. It left 'Old Stager' of the *South Wales Daily News* to ask:

> When, oh when, shall we be able to put in the field an eleven sufficiently strong to oppose, with some prospect of success, a really first-class team? Not I fancy until the miserable cliquism that at present marks the management of some of our leading clubs is swept away and men are played simply because they know how to play and not because their names are Jones, Brown, Robinson and so on.[14]

Just to compound matters, many of the leading clubs, and school or college teams, followed the earlier example of Cardiff and Swansea and pulled out of the Challenge Cup as the early euphoria over the new competition was replaced by antagonism and discontent. The 1886 competition attracted just six entries and the *Llanelly Guardian* stated that 'nobody apparently knows which team has won or is likely to win the South Wales Challenge Cup, and nobody seems to care very much'.[15] In an attempt to boost interest and participation, J. P. Jones of Cardiff suggested organizing a team called Cardiff United, composed of representatives of the junior clubs that used the Arms Park. But this upset the officials of bonafide clubs, and one wrote to the *Western Mail* that 'there is no doubt there is a lack of local interest in the competition, but, sir, it is most unfair that a team should be got together for the purpose of wresting a prize from properly-constituted clubs'.[16] These events were the death knell for the cup, for as in the words of the *South Wales Daily News*:

> What possible chance is there of any interest attaching to a competition in which no part is to be taken by our leading clubs as Cardiff, Newport, Cadoxton, Llandovery College, Lampeter College and Christ College, Brecon. It is no matter for regret that the Cup competition was not allowed to lapse altogether this season.[17]

The officials of the South Wales CC became increasingly embarrassed by these problems and at the AGM in April 1886 doubts were expressed over the future of the club. Consequently, they agreed to hold another meeting 'at the close of the season to consider the present unsatisfactory condition of the club and to decide as to the advisability or otherwise of dissolving it'.[18] The meeting was convened in December at the Angel Hotel in Cardiff, and the South Wales gentlemen realized that their club could not continue any longer. Three resolutions were thereupon unanimously decided – 'to discontinue the South Wales Cricket Club, to discontinue the South Wales Challenge Cup, and to present that cup to C. P. Lewis as a token of esteem and in recognition of the services rendered by him to south Wales cricket'.[19] But as David Smith observed: 'Only twenty months later, on 6 July 1888 J. T. D. Llewelyn convened a meeting at the same hotel in Cardiff and the present Glamorgan C.C.C. was founded'.[20] So after the demise of the South Wales CC and the turmoil in which the game found itself, what caused J.T.D to see so quickly the realization of his long-held dream?

The answer involves a number of factors and, no doubt, one of Llewelyn's prime motives was to unite the area, both from a geographical and a social point of view. The Challenge Cup had disintegrated into a series of disputes, and squabbles existed between both parties in the west and east, and also neighbouring clubs. There was also a social split with the gentry, who could have financed a county club, or at least provided the leadership and uniting bonds, becoming increasingly isolated form the club games. Their switch of allegiance meant that the town clubs, rather than being dominated by landed gentry or wealthy benefactors, were now being run by men of industry and commerce. Just as these men measured business success in terms of higher profits than rival companies, they equated cricketing success in terms of a win against neighbours or over a rival in another part of the county. In short, victories in local derbies or inter-regional contests meant more to them than the success of the region as a whole.

Llewelyn must have also been influenced by the healthy state of county clubs in the neighbouring parts of south-west England. Indeed, considerable interest was shown in the Cardiff area in the newly formed county championship and the performance of Gloucestershire, not least because there were so many English migrants in the area and up-to-date scores and reports were carried in the daily newspapers. So much interest was shown in Gloucestershire's match with Lancashire in June 1888 at Gloucester that the GWR agreed to run a special train from Cardiff with return tickets available at the cost of a single.[21] Monmouthshire also had a flourishing side, having gone from strength to strength with the support of gentry such as Charles Crompton-Roberts of Drybridge and the Hon. F. C. Morgan of Ruperra Castle. In 1882, Monmouthshire played the All-England Eleven, and for the rest of the decade their fixture list included annual encounters with Clifton, East Gloucestershire and Breconshire. Their elevens included members of the local gentry such as the Hon. A. L. Pelham of Penallt as well as leading club players such as Newport's Fred Phillips and George Rosser. They also included both professionals and amateurs, and one of the professionals to appear regularly in the mid 1880s was Henry Jupp of Newport, who had played for both Surrey and England, as well as twice touring Australia.[22]

An indication of Monmouthshire's rising, and united, prowess was a victory in August 1884 over East Gloucestershire in a low-scoring game. The English side was without several leading players, including W.G., who was playing for England against Australia, but nevertheless they were still quite formidable opposition. Monmouthshire scored 125 and 103, with East Gloucestershire replying with eighty-eight and forty-three. Jupp top scored with twenty-three in Monmouthshire's second innings, whilst just one Gloucestershire batsman got into double figures in their second innings.[23]

To the north, a flourishing side was emerging in Radnorshire, with a county club being formed in 1883 by Old Harrovian and Cambridge

Blue, Frank Cobden. He was able to build on the success of the Maesllwch club, established by the Green-Prices and, what had started out as basically a country house side, became a flourishing county side during the 1880s. An indication of Radnorshire's progress and desire to break away from the old restrictions was the club's letter in 1886 to J. E. Moore, the secretary of the South Wales CC noting that they were no longer interested in the South Wales club and its affairs.[24] The centrepiece of Radnorshire's activities was the annual Knighton cricket week, with fixtures against the MCC, Herefordshire, Free Foresters, Breconshire and the Ludlow Hunt.[25]

Another factor was the emerging talent at the Welsh public and grammar schools. The annual encounters between Christ College, Brecon and Llandovery College were keenly contested and drew good crowds, whilst some talented players such as George Rosser had graduated from Monmouth School. Indeed, the latter side was sufficiently strong to challenge and defeat Crompton-Roberts's Drybridge team, and hold annual fixtures with clubs of the pedigree of Newport, Chepstow and Abergavenny. However, there was a feeling that the young cricketers needed a greater stimulus, and something to aim for, such as a place in the county side. These feelings were expressed in *Lillywhite's Annual* for 1889, which stated that:

> The M.C.C. secretary and other enthusiasts who have ever been ready to give help whenever it has been sought, will not fail to foster rising talent, wherever it may be found, even if their kindness entails a journey into the somewhat remote regions of south Wales . . . There is some good material at Llandovery College and Christ College, Brecon, but the cricket generally wants stimulation and encouragement.[26]

Lastly and, by no means least, Llewelyn was also influenced by the sense of national identity which swept across the booming industrial region during the 1880s. As Kenneth Morgan noted, this decade in Wales 'proved to be, more than in any other region of Britain, a major turning point in a special sense. They provided the springboard for an age of national growth, dynamism and prosperity unknown since the union with England under the Tudors'.[27] Amongst the new bodies to be created was the University College of Wales at Aberystwyth in 1872, whilst in 1880 the National Eisteddfod Society was inaugurated to co-ordinate cultural and artistic affairs. These feelings spread to sport and on 12 March 1881, the Welsh Rugby Union was inaugurated at The Castle Hotel, Neath. This eventually became the ruling body of the amateur game and amongst its leading officials were several prominent personalities from the cricket world, including C. P. Lewis and C. C. Chambers of

Swansea, who was elected the Union's first president. However, the most influential figure was J.T.D. himself and, despite an earlier association with the rival South Wales Football Union, he served as president of the Welsh Rugby Union form 1885 until 1906, during which time he oversaw the healthy development of the game within south Wales and the success of the Welsh XV at international level.[28]

The combined success of the Welsh rugby team and the WRU in administering the game must have fuelled J.T.D.'s ambition to see a cricket team representing the economic and industrial heart of south Wales. Even so, the initial stimulus came from the premier clubs themselves and in particular, the emerging urban bourgeoise who, as Ric Sissons outlined, were actively involved in the formation of county sides in England.[29] Many in south Wales were not too upset at the demise of the Challenge Cup competition, but were sad that their leading players had nothing to aim for at a higher level, or lacked a chance of higher exposure which could benefit the club. One of the people who realized this was John Price Jones, the captain and secretary of Cardiff CC, who was also a playing member of the former South Wales club and on the Glamorgan-shire sub-committee. Jones became increasingly frustrated by the lack of support from the club's other sub-committees, as well as the old-fashioned and parochial nature of some of the leading members. He believed that the time was right to re-organize the club's structure and, at the 1886 AGM, he proposed dissolving the South Wales CC and forming a completely new Glamorgan side, selecting the best players within the area, regardless of their social aspirations. It was clear that the last thing that was needed was another version of the old club. Nevertheless, the officials deferred a vote on the proposal, but Jones proved that he and the Glamorganshire sub-committee meant business by announcing that they had already made provisional arrangements for fixtures between a Glamorgan side and the Rest of South Wales at Newport, the Arms Park and Llanelli.[30]

In the end, nothing came of the matches at Cardiff or Llanelli, whilst the match at Newport became a contest between an eleven captained by J. P. Jones and the next best XVIII of South Wales.[31] There were six Cardiff players in Jones's side but it could hardly be called a Glamorgan side, including as it did Gould and Purdon from Newport and Edward Davies of Crickhowell. Despite this unpromising start, Jones did not lose heart and during 1887 he continued to canvass the officials of other club sides for support of his idea. Some hesitated to give their support, especially in the west where some people were reluctant to show support for a leading figure from the east. It may have been no coincidence that no Swansea players appeared in his eleven in the match at Newport.[30] But Jones knew that no progress would be made if south Wales continued to be divided, and he made a determined effort to win support from the west. Towards the end of the 1887 season he gained the vital support of William Bryant, the Swansea secretary. This was just the incentive that Jones needed, and during the winter he approached J.T.D. for further support, knowing of the squire's desire to see a county club and of his good work for the WRU. The outcome was financial backing from Llewelyn and, now that he had the support of the west's premier club, other sides gave Jones their support in the early part of 1888. As a result, the squire of Penllergaer sent out the following letter in June to all the leading clubs in the region:

> I have much pleasure in convening a meeting at the Angel Hotel, Cardiff on Friday, 6 July at 6 o'clock in the evening to consider the advisability of forming a county cricket club. I need scarcely say that it is essential that the meeting should be thoroughly representative of cricket in the county, and shall be glad therefore if you will do your utmost to attend.[33]

J. P. Jones was delighted when over thirty representatives from south Wales clubs gathered at the Cardiff hotel, and although Llewelyn was delayed at the Midsummer Quarter Sessions court, it did not take long to decide umanimously 'that a county club for Glamorganshire be formed'.[34]

One of the people attending the meeting was M. S. Foulgar, a player with Cardiff and an employee with a local newspaper. He had been involved with the formation of Warwickshire CCC in 1882 when he had been living in Leamington Spa, and his experiences of how the English club had got off the ground were keenly sought. He told the meeting 'there was no reason why Glamorganshire, as a county side should not do as well as Warwickshire. The population was large, the material to work on better than existed in Warwickshire when that county club started, and there was more money'.[34] Foulgar added that the new club should consider having its own headquarters and home ground, but this added a note of discord to the hitherto harmonious proceedings, and Lewis Kempthorne of Cadoxton replied that the last thing the new club wanted was any more infighting. 'It would cost a great deal of money and then would come in the difficulty of deciding whether it should be at Cardiff or Swansea.'[35]

J.T.D. arrived at this point, took over the chair from J. P. Jones and oversaw the election of officers and a committee of fourteen. Llewelyn was unanimously appointed treasurer, whilst Jones was elected chairman. His Cardiff team mate William Yorath was appointed secretary, and the committee comprised many of the prominent and more active members of the now defunct South Wales club including J. E. Moore of

Cadoxton, Sir Julian Spearman of Lanelay, Edmund David of St Fagan's, William Morgan of Llwynypia, John Nicholl of Merthyr Mawr and both E. W. Jones and A. W. Morris of Cardiff, plus Bill Gwynn of Swansea, who had risen up from the grass roots of the game with the Swansea Workingmen's club.[37] All the leading personalities in south Wales cricket therefore supported the new club, and with such an impressive list of supporters it could hardly fail.

Llewelyn summed up these feelings of optimism in his closing address to the meeting:

> By good trial matches they would be enabled to unearth talent of very considerable merit, and that without going beyond the limits of the county. They had a good executive committee, and out of that would come a shrewd match committee who could take pains that next year Glamorgan would be represented by a strong team. Afterwards, they could play three or four, or even five of the various English counties not very far away and later on perhaps fly at a higher game.[38]

The new club was full of optimism, despite the failure of the earlier Glamorganshire side and the South Wales club. As Llewelyn's final sentence proved, the new club had its eye on more than matches in south Wales or the West of England, and was already thinking about joining the County Cricket Council which had been formed in England in the previous year. Consequently, the officials left the Angel Hotel with a great sense of adventure and with the air of confidence which was running through the region's society, boosted by its industrial and commercial prosperity.[39]

The committee of the newly inaugurated Glamorgan CCC had to face a few harsh realities and could not afford to get carried away on too much dreamy optimism. Firstly, there was the potentially thorny issue of securing a ground for Glamorgan's matches, and the committee had to discuss whether it should be in the west or east. Fortunately, the Swansea representatives realized that the Arms Park would be the most viable place from a geographical point of view if Glamorgan were going to start off by challenging an English county. The committee agreed to consider St Helen's once the club had got off the ground, and split matches equally between east and west, so J. P. Jones used his contacts with the Bute estate to use the Arms Park, and the marquess readily agreed for them to use the ground for their early fixtures. He also provided financial support to cover the cost of travel or hiring a professional, as well as agreeing to be the club's first president. The second issue was finance, so the committee canvassed the support of other leading figures in the social and business world, many of whom were only too keen to lend their support to J.T.D. and the new club. Lord Jersey, Lord Windsor, and Lord Aberdare all became vice-presidents, together with all the Welsh MPs and mayors,[40] as some of the Welsh gentry returned to support Welsh cricket after a few years absence. By the end of July 1888 enough financial support was obtained for fixtures to be arranged, and William Yorath contacted clubs in the area for the names of players who could form a viable county eleven.[41] He was inundated with replies, indicating both the level of support and the amount of talent now available in the region. Trials and net sessions were held and, during August, an eleven was chosen to play William Morgan's Llwynypia club. However, on the day of the match, Morgan and Yorath were let down by several of the amateurs who had been chosen, and three players had to be borrowed from the host club. Worse was to follow as Emmett and Peate, Llwynypia's guest professionals from Yorkshire, dismissed the county side for twenty runs and despite stubborn resistance from Morgan and Yorath, the county team was embarrasingly beaten by eight wickets.[42]

Yorath did not lose heart and contacted the MCC, Surrey, Herefordshire, Somerset, Worcestershire and Staffordshire for fixtures in 1889. Not surprisingly after the Llwynypia debacle, nothing came of his initial requests and the committee frustratingly spent the autumn of 1888 hoping that its earnest efforts would eventually see fruition with an inter-county game. The impasse was overcome when Foulgar used his contacts with Warwickshire and they agreed to play at the Arms Park in June 1889. It was another example of an English migrant playing a positive role in the game's development, but the Warwickshire club was worried about the expense of travelling to Cardiff and the as yet uncertain level of support, so they told Foulgar that they would only play if forty pounds was guaranteed.[43] Having come so far, J.T.D. was not going to let this request scupper his plans, so he, on behalf of the west area, and J. P. Jones, representing the east, dipped generously into their pockets and gave twenty pounds each to the Midlands county. Their kindness was soon rewarded with belated replies from the MCC and Surrey agreeing to fixtures in August, and this allowed the delighted officials to plan a short London tour along the lines of those undertaken by South Wales CC.

The long-awaited move forward by cricket in south Wales came on 21 and 22 June 1889, and in the spring and early summer careful preparations were made to the Arms Park wicket. Practice sessions were held during May, a trial game with a Colts XI was planned for early June, and the fixture was extensively publicized as the officials carefully ensured that no stone was left unturned in preparing for this important contest. Yet after their meticulous efforts, they were unable to raise their best eleven. William Llewelyn, the son of J.T.D. and one of the most promising young batsmen, was injured, whilst both William Morgan and Lewis Kempthorne were unavailable. To make matters worse, Warwickshire advised the Glamorgan officials that they would send down a powerful eleven, including Arthur Lilley, one of the best wicket-keepers in England and John Shilton, who was one of the most revered bowlers in the county. With such formidable opposition, the Glamorgan selectors were realistic enough to know that they could not rely on just amateur talent. Cardiff's James Lindley, who had been on the Nottinghamshire staff, and young Billy Bancroft of Swansea were the two professionals chosen to perform alongside some of the cream of amateur talent, including Lewis Jenkins of Cadoxton, William Lewis of Bridgend, Astley Samuel of Pontardawe, Daniel Thissen, the Morriston wicket-keeper, plus Cardiff's Daniel Jones, Alec Morris, Gowan Clarke and Theo Robinson.[44] The side was led by Edmund David of Cardiff and St Fagan's, and it seemed a fitting gesture after all the hard work which his family and all the other Muscular Christians had put into promoting cricket.

There were, however, a few sceptics who felt that Glamorgan was biting off more than it could chew by challenging one of the strongest sides in the Minor Counties to an eleven-a-side contest. A few wags, after seeing the name of the Glamorgan captain, claimed it was a case of 'David against Goliath',[45] but despite these claims, the Glamorgan side approached the game with confidence undimmed. David won the toss, elected to bat, but with the second ball of the match, Shilton dismissed Jenkins and soon the Welsh side had collapsed to 70–9. The sceptics looked like becoming 'I told you so's', but there was a spirited last-wicket partnership between Samuel and Thissen. The two west Walians tenaciously took the score to 136 and confused the opposition by calling to each other in Welsh, and as a result of their fight-back, the morale of the Glamorgan side was boosted. Lindley and Samuel then worked their way through the Warwickshire batting and, despite the presence of some illustrious names, the visitors were dismissed for 138. Glamorgan's batsmen knew that they needed a decent start in the second innings, but Shilton and Whitehead ripped through the top order to reduce Glamorgan to 42–7, and despite a stubborn twenty from Gowan Clarke, they were dismissed for a total of eighty runs. It left the visitors with a modest target of seventy-eight runs to win, and they comfortably reached it with only two wickets down, and batted on for exhibition purposes before time was called.[46]

More worrying than the eight-wicket defeat was the moderate support, especially after all the hype and pre-match publicity. Gate money on the first day was less than ten pounds, whilst on the second day receipts were just seventeen pounds,[47] and it meant that money earmarked for the London tour had to be used to cover the match expenses. This raised doubts as to whether Glamorgan could honour its fixtures up in town, but J.T.D. again came to the rescue agreeing to cover the expenses for the rest of the season. There was further good news when William Llewelyn and William Morgan became available for the London tour and a much stronger party was selected, including Cardiff's other professional William Wilkinson, and opener Hastings Watson. Their inclusion paid off as Glamorgan recorded its first ever victory, defeating Surrey Club and Ground by six wickets with Watson topscoring with fifty-eight, and Wilkinson returning match figures of 7–78.[48]

The victorious team returned to south Wales that night, but there was no chance of a celebration because the following day a return match was arranged with the MCC at the Arms Park. The victory over Surrey helped to boost the attendance, and hopes of another win were raised as the MCC struggled to raise an eleven, and had to borrow five substitutes from the Cardiff club. One of them, Alec Morris, dashed any hopes of an easy win, and topscored with forty-five of the MCC total of 140. Then the MCC's professional Alley took seven cheap wickets and Glamorgan slumped to 110, before on the second day rain interrupted proceedings and left the match drawn.[49] Despite the result and the bad weather, the gate receipts exceeded £100 and the club finished its first season with a profit of eleven pounds.[50] The officials were delighted by both this and the victory at The Oval, and the spirit of gay adventure was evident in an approach to the touring Parsees from India for a match in 1890. Nothing came of the request, but Somerset and Monmouthshire agreed to matches in 1890 and eight games were arranged, including a short London tour and a match on the return journey at Bath, plus a fixture at Swansea with the MCC. The season, however, proved to be very disappointing with six defeats, as Somerset recorded two victories by an innings and Glamorgan went down to a comprehensive defeat at Lord's. Surrey also won at The Oval by five wickets, and some of the amateurs enjoyed more of the social aspects of the London tour. Astley Samuel was one of these, but his excesses caught up with him during the match against Somerset on their way back home, and he was reported as being 'taken ill at Bath and unable to bowl with his customary effect'.[51]

The team's only victory during 1890 came against Monmouthshire at the Arms Park, and it also saw 19-year-old Herbie Morgan record the first century for Glamorgan. The young farmer from Penarth had only played because Daniel Jones dropped out the night before the game, and he celebrated his late call up by hitting four sixes and fifteen fours, before being run out for 147 as Glamorgan totalled 420 and Monmouthshire lost by an innings. It thrilled the correspondent of the *Western Mail* who wrote that 'lovers of the game are in hope that this is a good augury for local county cricket in the future'.[52] These optimistic words were confirmed as Glamorgan consolidated its first win as a minor county on Welsh soil, and went from strength to strength during the next decade.

14 / *The 'Brains' Behind Glamorgan*

LAMORGAN CCC may only have enjoyed two wins in its first twelve matches as a minor county, but everyone connected with the club remained optimistic for the future. With profits rising to ninety-seven pounds, the committee even considered a tour to north-east England to play Durham and Northumberland.[1] Devon was added to the fixture list to replace Warwickshire who wanted to play a stronger side, and the officials also introduced new colours, replacing the plain white caps and red badge, with a more striking and distinctive green cap with a dragon crest.[2] However, the most significant event of 1891 was the debut of Joseph Henry Brain, the former Oxford blue and Gloucestershire batsman. He was educated at Clifton College, and led the school XI in 1883. He also made his debut that season for Gloucestershire, before going up to Oxford where he won four Blues and led the university in 1887. As a freshman, he was in the Oxford side that defeated the 1884 Australians, and later in the summer he hit 108 for Gloucestershire against the tourists.[3]

His move to south Wales in 1890 followed his promotion within the family's brewing business. His father, J. B. Brain, was the chairman of the West of England Bank in Bristol and, together with his nephew Samuel Brain, had purchased the Old Brewery in the heart of Cardiff in 1882. Samuel Brain initially managed the day-to-day affairs of their new business venture, and it was only natural that his father wanted Joseph to join them after completing his studies. It was a great coup for cricket in south Wales to have such an illustrious cricketer as J. H. Brain based in Cardiff, and the Glamorgan committee was delighted when he agreed to take over the captaincy in 1891. He fulfilled this role until 1908, and also took on the secretary's duties from 1893, during which time the club expanded its fixture list and went from strength to strength. Whilst it would be wrong to say that Brain was another example of an English-born innovator, he quickly assumed the role of catalyst and oversaw the transformation of the Glamorgan team from a moderate eleven into a more successful minor county outfit.

His first positive act was to use his contacts to organize a match at the Arms Park in May 1891 between a Glamorgan XV and a Gloucestershire XII, including W. G. Grace, plus a return fixture at Bristol. The match at the Arms Park was chiefly a publicity stunt, as the Gloucestershire side played other first-class teams who provided far stronger opposition than the Welsh side. W.G. batted down the order at number eight, and made an unbeaten thirty-four as Gloucestershire declared at 140–7 before recording an innings victory. The Doctor batted at number nine in the return game and this time was dismissed for a duck by Robert Lewis, a left-arm spinner from Christ College, Brecon. But this came at the end of the first day after E. M. Grace had scored 135 as Gloucestershire amassed 351. On the second day the Glamorgan side was dismissed for ninety-three and forty-one, with Brain scoring just fourteen runs, whilst his younger brother William, the Oxford wicket-keeper, made a duck and one. It was a dismal performance and this time the *Western Mail* summed up the despondency by stating that 'even the most sanguine supporters of Glamorgan did not anticipate that they would be able to avert defeat, but few imagined they would make such a very poor batting display'.[4] Nevertheless, Brain and the committee still showed confidence, and the captain took a further step to raising standards by sending a letter to all of the clubs in the area asking for names of promising young players so that a trial match could be held over the Whitsun Bank Holiday.[5] So great was the response that a Colts XXII was raised and the experiment was repeated in 1892 and 1893. His efforts were rewarded with victories in five of the eight matches in 1892. Selwyn Biggs, the Welsh rugby international took nine wickets in the victory over the MCC at Cardiff, and then at Lord's William Morgan scored ninety-one and sixty-one, besides returning match figures of 13–143 as the Welsh side won by nine wickets at cricket's HQ.[6]

Brain also took steps to lure a top-class professional to south Wales to boost the Glamorgan attack and help coach the emerging youngsters. The only stumbling block was limited finance, and with professionals able to command substantial fees, it meant the club could not immediately consider such an outlay. J. P. Jones offered personally to subsidize some of the costs if a suitable candidate was found, as long as their choice joined Cardiff. There were, quite naturally, a few misgivings over Jones's motives and whether Cardiff would acquire a first-rate player at Glamorgan's expense. Nevertheless, the committee started to search for a suitable professional and George Porter, a 31-year-old fast bowler was interviewed. Porter was playing in the Lancashire Leagues and saw the Glamorgan offer as a way back into county cricket after a brief career with Derbyshire, but he demanded winter employment, preferably in a public house. Despite the close connections with Brain's Brewery, the officials were wary of agreeing to Porter's demands, knowing full well of the intemperate reputation of many northern professionals, and negotiations ended.[7]

What finally tipped the balance against Porter was the moderate financial situation. Just seventy-three pounds was raised in gate money during 1893, so rather than discussing terms for a professional and the romantic future of the club, the committee was forced to discuss the harsh realities of the deteriorating financial situation and a decline in attendance. They were brought back to earth with a tragic bump in August 1893 when William Llewelyn committed suicide in the grounds of Penllergaer House just a few weeks before his marriage to the daughter of Lord Dynevor.[8] His death cast a sombre shadow over the committee's discussions of how to boost both the finances and attendances. Indeed, some of the officials suggested disbanding the club because they could not always rely on the generous support of wealthy patrons such as J.T.D. or J. P. Jones. Other committee members took a more positive view, especially those who were successful businessmen and who had built up their fortunes through sheer hard work and cussedness. They had an air of confidence that things would look up, and argued that it would be hasty to wind up the club. They gained the support of the grief-stricken J.T.D., who knew that his son's dearest wish would have been for Glamorgan to continue. His touching words swayed the rest of the committee and a resolution was passed that 'Glamorgan CCC should continue to exist'.[9]

The major stumbling block for Glamorgan in the 1890s was lack of public support, so Brain decided to capture public interest by approaching the South Africans for a match at the Arms Park during their tour in 1894. Unfortunately, it proved to be an expensive flop with only a small crowd watching the Welsh team collapse to a crushing ten-wicket defeat. This was one of five defeats, and in his end of season review in the *Evening Express*,'Welsh Athlete' was left to conclude that Brain's 'efforts have met with practically no response and appearances all suggest that this will be the last season of the Glamorgan Cricket Club'.[10]

When the committee sat at the end of the season to review events, they had to face the fact that something had to be done if the club was going to continue. What made matters even worse was that Brain reported an increasing air of apathy and indifference in the team as testified by the away match with Wiltshire when two players failed to turn up at Cardiff to catch the train to Swindon. He also felt that there was a very casual air about the way that some of the local amateurs played, and he himself saw no place for this air of country house cricket when trying to challenge

English county sides or Test players. Brain was frustrated both by the lack of success and by being unable to raise a strong eleven, as the best amateurs were often unavailable. Some tried to mix business with pleasure, such as Swansea estate agent Astley Samuel, but these efforts often backfired. On the morning of the MCC game in 1890, Samuel had to make a business call, so after reporting for duty at St Helen's, and having a quick net, he left the ground, hoping to return in time to bat. However, Phillips, the MCC professional took 7–4 as Glamorgan were dismissed before lunch for fifty-seven runs. Samuel was recorded as being 'absent' and had more than a few apologies to make when he returned.[11]

It was clear that the club needed to raise standards by engaging at least one regular professional, and drafting in better players. Several names were discussed and the eventual choice was Swansea's Billy Bancroft who had already turned out for the club. He won the nod over several former English county and league professionals, as the committee, realizing how fickle its supporters were, believed that greater public interest would be generated through a Welshman's actions rather than an Englishman's. The 24-year-old from Swansea also had age on his side, as the other candidates were rather long in the tooth and were likely to give only brief service before seeing out their days in club cricket. A further factor in Bancroft's favour was his family's close friendship with J.T.D. Llewelyn and the hand of Sir John must have guided the committee towards choosing the Swansea professional at the sum of two pounds a week for twenty weeks.[12]

Bancroft's appointment led to a dramatic rise in the club's fortunes over the next couple of years. They went through 1895 without defeat, and in 1896 recorded comprehensive victories by an innings over both Herefordshire and the MCC. However, it was the match with Mon-mouthshire at Newport which epitomized the new spirit. Glamorgan were set 210 to win but lost five quick wickets and appeared to be in a hope-less position. But Bancroft got his head down and compiled a magnificent 119 to steer his team to a two-wicket victory.[13] They also managed to draw with the powerful Surrey side, with Swansea shipbroker Ernest Jones making a fine ninety-seven. The emergence of the 25-year-old former Wycliffe schoolboy and the regular presence of his clubmate Billy Bancroft were, however, just two small factors behind the improvements.

The main reason for the better performances was the presence in the side of several former English county players, both amateur and professional. William Brain, the former Gloucestershire wicket-keeper appeared regularly behind the stumps in 1895 and 1896,[14] whilst the batting was strengthened by the presence of William Pullen and Vernon Hill.[15] Pullen played for both Somerset and Gloucestershire during the 1880s and hit 161 for the latter when only eighteen years of age.

However, he failed to fulfil his schoolboy promise, and concentrated instead on an academic career. In 1892 he became a lecturer at Cardiff University, joined Cardiff CC and became friends with the Brains, who persuaded him to resurrect his county career with Glamorgan in 1895.

Vernon Hill was the son of Sir Edward Hill of Llandaff, the Conservative MP for Bristol. Hill had been in the Winchester XI before going up to Oxford where he also became friends with William Brain. Hill made his county debut for Somerset in 1891, and struck 114 in the 1892 Varsity match, but his business interests brought him to Cardiff in the mid-1890s and the presence of this bold striker of the ball was another coup for the Glamorgan side. Hill also helped boost public support by selecting an All-England XI for a special challenge at the Arms Park in 1895. His team included some of his former Somerset colleagues, plus C. B. Fry, one of England's most illustrious all-round sportsman. Hill also invited Ranjitsinjhi of Sussex and England to play, but the Indian 'prince' was late arriving and Hill had to borrow Hastings Watson as a substitute. A large crowd turned up, attracted by the better form of the Welsh side, just as much as by the presence of such well-known players and they saw Fry make a graceful seventy-one and Sammy Woods of Somerset a fine 106, before stumps were drawn with honours even.[16]

Greater public support gave the finances a further boost and allowed the bowling attack to become more potent through the selection of two professional fast bowlers from England, who were attached to local clubs. David Binch was a Lancastrian professional with the Penarth club, whilst Sam Lowe of Cardiff, who had appeared for his native Nottinghamshire in 1894, took thirty-five wickets at twelve runs apiece in 1896.[17] The presence of these various English cricketers was part of a process of Anglicization in the composition of the Glamorgan side during the 1890s. This is clearly shown in Table 4 which lists the percentage of Welsh-born players (natives) and those educated at public school.[18]

The table clearly highlights the rising number of English-born players from 12.50 per cent in 1889 to 29.17 per cent in 1892 and 54.17 per cent by 1896, so that the Glamorgan team steadily lost its native Welsh identity. In the first two seasons, the county was represented by just three Englishmen, with the remainder born in places such as Cardiff, Neath, Swansea, Aberystwyth, Bridgend, Chepstow, Pontypridd, Llanelli, Nantgarw and St Fagan's. It reflected the driving force for the formation of the club coming from inside south Wales and the desire to have a side, chiefly of local amateurs, representing the region. In these early years, it was deemed important for the side to have a clear native element in order to gain the support of both the general public and south Walian clubs. It was remembered that the early Glamorganshire and Carmarthenshire sides failed because of their reliance on imported talent.

TABLE 4 – BIRTH AND EDUCATIONAL BACKGROUND OF
GLAMORGAN PLAYERS, 1889–1896

	No. of players	% Welsh-born	% public-school educated	average age (stan. deviation)
1889	16	87.50	37.50	27.8 (+/−7.08)
1890	23	86.96	52.17	26.2 (+/−6.19)
1891	37	62.16	67.57	26.1 (+/−5.25)
1892	24	70.83	58.33	26.9 (+/−5.49)
1893	35	65.71	57.14	26.2 (+/−4.84)
1894	25	52.00	48.00	26.2 (+/−4.80)
1895	23	43.48	52.17	28.2 (+/−4.00)
1896	24	45.83	58.33	27.7 (+/−4.56)

Despite their native birthplace, several of the young gentlemen who
represented Glamorgan in 1889 and 1890 were educated at English public
schools. William Lewis and Jestyn Williams attended Charterhouse,
Ernest Jones and Bertie Letcher went to Wycliffe, whilst William Yorath
was at Bedford. The Welsh public and grammar schools were also
strongly represented with Alec Morris of Cowbridge Grammar, Alfred
Mullins of Monmouth and Robert Lewis of Christ College. Table 4
shows that the number of public school educated players fluctuated, as
some of the talented *nouveaux riches* and aspiring middle classes made
their county debuts, and the selection committee chose more English
professionals with northern, working-class backgrounds as opposed to
southern, public school backgrounds. Table 4 also shows that throughout these early years the average age remained roughly the same with
most players in their mid to late twenties. The standard deviation values
in brackets are a measure of variability around the average age, and show
that in the first few seasons some older amateurs were taking the field.
Indeed, in 1889 the county side regularly included 42-year-old Lewis
Jenkins and 44-year-old James Lindley. Yet by 1896 the oldest player was
36-year-old Edmund David, and during the season a further nine players
who were twenty-five or younger were selected. So whilst the average age
was fairly constant, there were generally fewer grey hairs in the side by
1896. This subtle trend partly reflected a desire to field more nimble and
competitive teams rather than portly and unathletic fielding teams. But it
was chiefly the result of young friends and former university acquaintances of the Brains being invited to turn out for the Glamorgan side.
Some had moved to south Wales or the West Country, but many had no
association with the area whatsoever and only played because they were
friends or business acquaintances of the Brains. One example was Victor
Hickley, a young brewer from Somerset, who helped Joseph Brain run

the Old Brewery in Cardiff. He made eight appearances from 1894 until 1898 when he moved to Yorkshire to run a brewery in Leeds.

Another example of the English players invited to appear for Glamorgan was the Revd Lyonel d'Arcy Hildyard, a Bury-born, Oxford graduate who had been in the varsity eleven with Joseph Brain. The presence of several other vicars such as Revds Arthur Batty and Cyril Kindersley also added to the cosmopolitan nature of the Glamorgan side, and owed as much to friendships with prominent players, as the rise of Muscular Christianity.[19] When added to the arrival of former Somerset and Gloucestershire players such as Vernon Hill and William Pullen, and the selection of more English professionals, it meant there was a strong English element in the Glamorgan side of the 1890s. Indeed by 1894 the Glamorgan side included players born in Staffordshire, Darlington, London, Southampton, Manchester, Nottingham and Leeds. The presence of a few migrants, who had moved to south Wales from overseas also added an international flavour to the team. These included John Courtis, an Australian-born businessman who owned a brickworks in Cardiff and Wallingford Mendelson, a half-Jewish and half-Maori postgraduate law student from New Zealand who spent his summers with relatives in south Wales whilst studying at Cambridge.[20]

This wide number of amateur and professional players with diverse backgrounds from outside Wales meant that there was only a little band of native cricketers in the side, including Billy Bancroft, Ernest Jones, Bertie Letcher and other leading players from the Swansea or Cardiff clubs. Some were Welsh rugby internationals, and the presence of Tom Barlow, Hugh Ingledew, and the Biggs brothers, Selwyn and Norman, helped to raise both the native element and boost attendances as people came to see their winter heroes perform on the cricket field.[21]

Despite the fact that their regular professional was Welsh, and their *éminence grise* was Sir John Llewelyn, it meant that the power in the club lay in the hands of Englishmen such as Brain and Hill. The club had struggled to compete in 1889 and 1890 with a strong native element, and the loss of this Welsh identity was the price Glamorgan had to pay for greater success in 1895 and 1896. This cultural split was not unique to cricket and, to a large extent, reflected trends within society in general. Indeed, Kenneth Morgan noted that within Welsh society by the turn of the century there was 'a massive and growing gulf between an anglicised, largely English-speaking and English-educated gentry class and the vast majority of the population, rural and industrial. Truly Wales now consisted of two nations'.[22] Out in the middle, Glamorgan also consisted of two groups, but there was a positive outcome as the abundance of English talent allowed the club to continue its development.

J. H. Brain was delighted by the better form shown by Glamorgan in 1896, especially since it vindicated his firm belief that the Welsh county would only improve if it raised its sights and attempted to play in a higher standard with English sides. The results showed that their playing resources had improved so that they could hold their own with the teams who had recently formed the Minor County Championship. Brain himself had been a leading figure behind the formation of the new competition, and served as chairman of the Minor County Cricket Association from 1896 until 1898. At the end of the 1896 season, he suggested to the club's committee that the club should join the new competition, especially now that finances were reasonably sound. The late Victorian air of confidence was still permeating the committee room, so it did not take long for the members to agree with the captain and contact Lord's. The MCC endorsed the application during the winter months and admitted Glamorgan to the Minor County Championship in 1897.

During the spring, a host of letters and articles appeared in the press praising Brain and the committee for their go-ahead approach[23] and there was a great sense of anticipation over their first championship fixture at The Oval against Surrey 2nd XI on 7 and 8 June. Glamorgan's officials took great care to try to field their strongest side, but they still had a few parochial barriers to overcome, especially the availability of some professionals, including William Russell of Cowbridge. The all-rounder was employed by E. H. Ebsworth of Llandough Castle, primarily to look after his private ground at Cowbridge, and the squire preferred that Russell devoted his time and energy to his job as groundsman. Ebsworth therefore told the county club that Russell was not available and, despite receiving a deputation from the selectors, he stood firm and the Glamorgan side left Cardiff General on the Paddington train without Russell.

The press pilloried Ebsworth for his narrow-minded and selfish attitude, with the correspondent of the *Western Mail* writing that Russell's inclusion 'would help the side to win a match in which the victory would do the Welsh county no end of good, for the winning or losing of this game may have much to do with the future of Glamorgan cricket'.[24] Despite Russell's absence, Glamorgan performed with much credit against a Surrey side which contained nine players with first-class experience. The Welsh bowlers restricted the English batsmen to 227 in their first innings, and although Henderson scored a century in their second innings, the game ended in a draw.[25] There were other signs of progress during the season, as William Brain hit 113 in just fifty-three minutes against Monmouthshire at Newport, and Sam Lowe took the first ever hat-trick for the Welsh county as Cornwall were dismissed for just twenty-five runs at Swansea.[26] The Cornishmen were chasing 259 in three and a quarter hours, but they were bowled out in just forty-five minutes to leave Glamorgan the winners by 233 runs. Glamorgan maintained this good form during August, beating Wiltshire by ten wickets and then Surrey 2nd XI were reduced to 142–9 with their last pair having to hang on in the final over to prevent a Glamorgan victory.[27] Brain was delighted when his team finished in second place of the competition, and there was further good news at the end of the season when the dispute with Ebsworth was settled, and Russell became available on a regular basis. Glamorgan maintained this impressive form by recording six victories in 1898. Edward Jones hit 101 against Cornwall, whilst Russell returned match figures of 10–50 against Wiltshire and 11–92 against Cornwall.[28] They did even better the following year by recording nine victories. Herbie Morgan hit 110 and William Brain 99 not out as Surrey 2nd XI were defeated by fifty-three runs,[29] and Billy Bancroft achieved the rare feat of a century and a hat-trick against the same opponents at Swansea.[30] His club-mate Harry Creber took fourteen wickets in both of the matches against Berkshire.[31] Yet, despite this good form, the team still faced a few financial worries. The increased travel costs and expenditure on English professionals meant that over £200 was owed to the bank, and the request for a fixture with the Springboks in 1900 had to be withdrawn.[32]

Whatever the dark financial clouds, 1900 saw Glamorgan become joint Minor County Champions, sharing the title with Durham and Northamptonshire. The Welsh side recorded six victories, with the bowling of William Russell being one of the key factors behind the county's success. He took 10–83 as Wiltshire were defeated by eight wickets, 9–86 in the innings victory over Surrey and 9–68 as Berkshire slipped to a seven-wicket defeat.[33] The batsmen also had their moments during 1900, highlighted by a massive 388 against Surrey 2nd XI at the Oval. Richard Lowe hit eighty and J. H. Brain eighty-eight, but the captain went one better in the return match at Cardiff by scoring 102 as Glamorgan recorded another innings victory.[34]

Although they failed to repeat this success in the early 1900s, the club continued to develop carefully under J. H. Brain's wise leadership. Improvements were also made to boost membership, with up-to-date scorecards made available from 1901, whilst in 1904 a new cricket pavilion was erected at the Arms Park.[35] J.T.D. also gave over £1,200 to Swansea Cricket and Football Club to allow new seating and terraces to be built at St Helen's,[36] and steadily more people turned up to watch the Welsh side. Public interest was also fired by the successful season of 1900 and by the attractive fixtures with touring teams which Brain was able to arrange now that the finances were healthier. In 1902 he secured a plum fixture with the Australians, although because of their previous record against touring sides, the 'Glamorgan' side included Silverlock of Newport and four guests from Wiltshire. Over 10,000 people turned up on the first day, and the *South Wales Daily News* gleefully reported how the crowd was 'ten times bigger than has ever assembled in Wales. Spectators seemed to so thoroughly appreciate it that the game may gain such encouragement as in a few seasons may make it as generally popular a pastime in Wales as it is truly national in England'.[37]

Herbie Morgan scored a fine half-century in Glamorgan's second innings, but Australia still recorded a six-wicket victory. Gate receipts exceeded £1,300 and at the end of the season Tom Barlow, the treasurer, was able to report a healthy profit of £273.[38] The club's finances were given another boost when the Aussies toured again in 1905. This time it was a combined Glamorgan and Monmouthshire side which played the tourists, but the game took place in damp conditions and Brain's XI were fortunate to escape from a heavy defeat when rain curtailed play on the final afternoon. Nevertheless, a crowd of 8,000 attended the first day and 10,000 on the second, and the sizeable gate receipts helped Glamorgan record another healthy profit.[39]

The improved financial situation allowed Brain to extend the fixture list to fourteen matches in 1905, whilst in 1906 Glamorgan travelled to Northumberland and Durham. It also allowed the selection of more English professionals, including Swansea's Harry Creber, who in 1905 became the first ever Glamorgan bowler to take 100 wickets in a season. The Birkenhead-born spinner had initially played in the Liverpool area, but the prospect of minor county cricket, and good professional contracts lured him to south Wales in the late 1890s.[40]

Following the hiring of these talented professionals, Brain was able to mould an even more competitive side by the mid 1900s. A few of the stalwart gentlemen had retired by this time, but there were some talented new amateur batsmen emerging including Cardiff's Norman Riches and Neath's 'Tal' Whittington. Both were second-generation cricketers, being sons of prominent players from the second half of the nineteenth century. Riches was the son of Carlton Riches, and Norman played minor county cricket whenever he could get time off from his family's dental practice.[41] He made his debut in 1900 as a seventeen year old and, in 1904, hit his maiden century for Glamorgan.[42] Riches established himself as a fine opening batsman, and showed particular liking for the Northumberland attack, hitting 109 against them in 1905 and 178* the following year.[43] Whittington was the son of T. P. Whittington, the former Glamorganshire and Cadoxton player. 'Tal' was educated at Weymouth College and Merchiston, before reading law at Oxford.[44] He too mixed business with pleasure and established himself as a bold and attractive batsman. At the end of 1907, he took over the captaincy from J. H. Brain and, together with Riches and the other professionals, he helped see Glamorgan to the most successful phase in their history. It followed a change in the format of the Minor County Championship, with the teams being divided into four regional groups, and the title being decided by an end of season knock-out competition between the divisional winners.

Glamorgan was in the western group, and some fine batting displays saw the team win all its zonal matches comfortably.[45] Glamorgan met Surrey 2nd XI in the semi-final at the Arms Park and, despite a first-innings deficit of fifty-two, Creber took 5–54 and Cardiff's Jack Nash claimed 4-31 to leave Glamorgan a target of 155. In the Glamorgan second innings Riches was dismissed for a duck and Brain made just three, but Glamorgan still managed a four-wicket victory with Billy Bancroft hitting eighty-six runs without losing his wicket.[46] Glamorgan secured home advantage for the final against Lancashire 2nd XI, but hopes of a first outright title were dashed as the visitors scored 243 and then bowled out Glamorgan for seventy-four. Despite a fighting eighty from Brain, Lancashire won by 108 runs to take the championship.[47] Glamorgan entered the knock-out stage again in 1908, and travelled to Chippenham to play Wiltshire in the semi-final.[48] Rain prevented any play until the third morning, and then Creber was almost unplayable as the home side batted on the drying wicket. He took 8–18 as the Wiltshire side was dismissed for forty-one, and Glamorgan then replied with 172 to earn a place in the final with Staffordshire at Stoke.[49] Staffordshire was one of the strongest minor county sides, with the legendary Sydney Barnes playing for them. Barnes, regarded by many as the greatest of all bowlers, was able to alter his bowling to suit all types of wickets, and he proved too much for the Glamorgan batsmen, taking 7–19 and 8–35 to leave Glamorgan in the runners-up spot for the second consecutive year.[50]

Glamorgan won the western Division again in 1909, thanks to some outstanding bowling from the professionals. Creber took 12–106 at Penzance,[51] whilst his Swansea colleague James Maxwell took 10–35 against Devon and 8–61 in the home match with Cornwall.[52] In the semi-final they faced Nottinghamshire 2nd XI at the Arms Park, and for the second year running there was rain interference. Glamorgan only made 136 in the first innings, but Nash exploited the wet conditions and took 6–30 as Glamorgan gained a victory on first innings.[53] The club was fortunate to secure home advantage for the 1909 final against Wiltshire and after their previous victory, the Welsh county was optimistic of a long-awaited Minor County title. Hopes were raised as Maxwell took 7–43 to dismiss Wiltshire for 122, but soon dashed as Glamorgan collapsed for just ninety-six runs. Wiltshire built up a strong lead as Glamorgan's bowlers wilted under the pressure. Glamorgan were set a target of 324 and, despite having Brain, Riches and Whittington, it proved way beyond them, and they were finally dismissed for 159, to give Wiltshire the title.[54] The Glamorgan players left the Arms Park mortified by having lost their third successive final, but their gloom soon disappeared and, like the committee, they were able to reflect that Glamorgan had gone from strength to strength during the 1900s. This success had several positive spin-offs at the top of the cricketing hierarchy, in particular a boost to other county sides in south Wales, with both Monmouthshire and Carmarthenshire becoming members of the Minor County Championship. The former side was able to build on the good foundation laid by the earlier 'county' elevens raised by country landowners such as Charles Crompton-Roberts. This was evident in the victory by a Monmouthshire XI over Glamorgan, with Newport captain Fred Phillips taking six wickets and top scoring with forty-eight to see Monmouthshire to a two-wicket win.[55] There was also a lot of rivalry between Newport and Cardiff, in business as well as sport, with a feeling that anything Glamorgan could do, Monmouthshire would do better. The result was the creation of the Monmouthshire County Cricket Association in 1892 by Fred Phillips, a member of the well-known Newport brewing family.[56]

Monmouthshire was fortunate to be able to call upon the services of Arthur Silverlock, and the all-rounder more than anyone else helped establish Monmouthshire as a minor county side. In 1894 he helped the county to record its first victory over Glamorgan since the creation of a properly constituted county club, taking 8–78 as Glamorgan slumped to a six-wicket defeat.[57] In 1895 he scored 120 and took sixteen wickets against Herefordshire, whilst ten years later he hit a career best 206* against Berkshire.[58] Another factor in Monmouthshire's favour was the presence of other talented professionals attached to the Newport club, such as Dick Steeples and Edwin Diver, the former Surrey and Warwickshire wicket-keeper.

The growth of Newport docks meant that, as at Cardiff, some cricket-playing businessmen were attracted to the port. Amongst the people who migrated to Newport in the early 1890s was Foster Stedman, who played for his native Lincolnshire before moving to south Wales where he acted as Lord Tredegar's agent. His estate duties also included organizing country house games at Tredegar House for the staff, plus friends and family of the Morgan family. Many of the leading gentlemen cricketers in Monmouthshire were also invited, giving Stedman a chance to judge if they merited inclusion in the county side. The presence of talented amateurs such as Stedman, plus professionals of the calibre of Silverlock and the sound financial base at Newport, allowed Monmouthshire to diversify its fixture list and contemplate joining the Minor Counties. It received a further boost in 1900 when Glamorgan, who were then minor county champions, slumped to a three-wicket defeat at Newport, as Silverlock hit a century and Steeples claimed eight wickets.[59]

After this victory the Monmouthshire officials approached the MCC and they were admitted to the Minor County Championship in 1901. However, the county suffered a rather unfortunate start to its new career with two innings defeats to rivals Glamorgan. In the match at the Arms Park, Herbie Morgan hit a mammoth 254 as Glamorgan scored 538, but there were mitigating circumstances as Monmouthshire started the match without four team members who had been travelling to Cardiff by train and were delayed by an accident in the Newport tunnel.[60] Matters improved in 1902 and the two Welsh minor counties held a closely fought match at Swansea. Silverlock took 11–85, but Glamorgan eventually won by the slender margin of one wicket, thanks to an unbeaten fifty-seven runs from William Brain.[61]

During the mid 1900s, Monmouthshire achieved greater success, finishing second in 1905, after some fine batting displays from Edward Stone Phillips, who had won a Blue at Cambridge the previous year. Phillips was educated at Marlborough and Pembroke College and, although becoming a director of Phillips Brewery, he found plenty of time to play cricket for Newport and Monmouthshire. In 1905 the 22-year-old hit an unbeaten 133 against Glamorgan, whilst Silverlock struck 155* and Steeples took 9–45 in their second innings as Monmouthshire won by an innings and sixteen runs.[62] The following year Phillips hit 150 against Glamorgan at Swansea, whilst Steeples took 12–69, but both matches ended in draws.[63]

The success of Glamorgan and Monmouthshire also resulted in the resurrection of a Carmarthenshire side which took part in the Minor County Championship during the 1900s. There had been talk back in the 1880s about re-forming the Carmarthenshire team. In 1883 a Carmarthenshire team was assembled to play Herefordshire, but it included several professionals from outside the area, and was not a truly representative side.[64] In 1889 representatives for Llanelly discussed the topic at their AGM and asked C. P. Lewis to look into the matter.[65] He felt that it was not financially viable and nothing happened, but the issue rose again in the early 1900s, and this time the Llanelly officials took action and organized a match with Breconshire in 1902. Silverlock acted as their guest professional, and Carmarthenshire won by five wickets after Llanelly's Fred Rees had taken 8–56. The Llanelly club also tried to arrange a fun-raising game with Nottinghamshire, but the English side wanted a guarantee of fifty pounds and Carmarthenshire's limited finances meant that discussions were terminated.

Indeed, limited financial support prevented Carmarthenshire from organizing other games in the early 1900s, but the committee was confident that Carmarthenshire could become a minor county. The county committee, chaired by C. P. Lewis, found an ally in Sir John Llewelyn, who was always willing to give support to emerging sportsmen. In 1906 Sir John persuaded the WRU to loan the west Wales county £100 to help fund matches. Fixtures were consequently arranged with Breconshire, Glamorgan and the Gentlemen of Essex. The contest with the latter drew a sizeable crowd, but the visitors proved far too strong for the aspiring Carmarthenshire side. 'Cheerful' Charlie McGahey hit an unbeaten 305 as Essex declared on 540–8, before bowling out the Welsh side for 177 and 87.[66] A few weeks later Glamorgan inflicted another innings defeat on the Carmarthenshire side,[67] but these heavy reverses failed to dampen the enthusiasm of C. P. Lewis and the Carmarthenshire committee, and they approached the MCC with an application to join the Minor County Championship.

The county was admitted in 1908 but had a torrid time, failing to secure a win in its first two seasons.[68] The abysmal run continued into 1910, as Glamorgan rattled up 531–9 at Swansea, with Whittington scoring 133 and Charles Elers of Bridgend 151, as Carmarthenshire lost by an innings and 327 runs.[69] Later in the season, they finally managed three overdue victories, defeating Dorset home and away as well as Cornwall.

These victories boosted the morale of the Carmarthenshire club, especially since their lack of capital meant that they had to rely on amateur talent. Hopes were high for 1911, but it only saw Carmarthenshire suffer further heavy defeats.[70] These pitiful performances and overwhelming defeats did little to generate support from the clubs or public of west Wales, and the club's finances remained in an unsatisfactory state. Hiring decent professionals was out of the question, and Carmarthenshire were considered by some to be a third-class county – in fact, to save undue embarrassment Glamorgan often rested its leading players when playing the west Wales side. In 1912 C. P. Lewis and the Carmarthenshire committee realized that they could not continue and pulled out of the competition. Carmarthenshire's brief career as a minor county was therefore an expensive failure, but it also highlighted the huge gulf between the standard of amateur and the increasingly professional cricket being played by Glamorgan and Monmouthshire.

The early twentieth century therefore saw a long-awaited improvement at minor county level, and by the time that the First World War broke out, Glamorgan and Monmouthshire were established as successful sides. Much of this was due to the actions of generous benefactors and English migrants, but head and shoulders above all of these stood J. H. Brain, the captain and secretary of Glamorgan CCC. When hostilities ceased, his team-mates were able to join the ranks of the first-class game, but sadly the Cardiff brewer was not alive to witness the final act in the development process and the fruition of his efforts. His health had deteriorated from 1910 and he died in June 1914 after a heart attack. The *Western Mail* fittingly summed up his immense contribution to the evolution of the game, both on and off the field by saying that 'his prowess at the wicket won him celebrity; his sportsmanship won him friendship; his generous patronage of the game won him gratitude'.[71]

15 / *The Golden Age*

D ESPITE the attractions of success and fame in the world of minor county cricket with Glamorgan or Monmouthshire, the more amateur forms of the game still retained their popularity in the late Victorian and early Edwardian era. The Corinthian and traditional spirit of country house fixtures and games with wandering elevens still appealed to many of the gentlemen, who did not want to play in the minor county games with their worldly wise and cunning professionals. Many of the amateurs could not take many days leave and play in the umpteen championship fixtures, never mind the time taken up with travelling all over England. Consequently, there were fewer oppor-tunities with Glamorgan, or even Monmouthshire, for those amateurs who wanted to mix business with pleasure and, as a result, they turned to the more relaxed and casual cricket offered by suburban sides or country house teams. There were also trends operating in late Victorian society as a whole towards glorifying the actions of an amateur. As Patrick Scott found in England, the amateur was:

> a personification of good social standing – presumably well-off, if at public school or university, or if able to give his days to cricket, and presumably a chivalrous player – the great amateur players were the idols of the schoolboys, but they were parentally-approved idols in an age of social mobility and disturbed social values.[1]

Archer Windsor-Clive was one of the archetypal amateurs who turned his back on the cut and thrust of minor county games and played instead for St Fagan's. The Old Etonian and Cambridge tennis Blue made his Glamorgan debut in 1908, but he only played twice again in 1909 and once in 1912, preferring instead during his university vacations to play in the more relaxed atmosphere of the St Fagan's club and its sumptuous hospitality. The highlight of the St Fagan's season was the match with Hewell Grange in Worcestershire and, as one participant remembered, these fixtures were highly enjoyable for other reasons apart from cricket:

> We were transported by special train to Hewell. Food and drink were lavishly provided en route and the team camped in tents on the field. The next morning there might be a trip to Redditch, and after the match, more merriment which often included singing and dancing on the square in the light of hurricane lamps.[2]

In 1894 a gentlemen's side was formed called the Water Rats. It included many of the amateur sportsmen such as Hugh Ingledew and Ralph Sweet-Escott, who excelled at rugby during the winter. By the early 1900s, the fixture list included games with suburban sides such as Llanishen and Fairwater, crack sides such as Newport and an annual tour to the West Country. But despite these commitments the club was entirely self-financing with no entrance fees or subscriptions, and all of the players paid their own expenses.[3]

In 1904 a wandering side called the Glamorgan Gypsies was formed following on from the success of E. H. Ebsworth's XI and they played several annual matches in the Cardiff area and the Vale of Glamorgan. Many of their games took place at Ebsworth's ground in Cowbridge, and included old boys of the nearby grammar school, as well as some of the county stars. Indeed, in 1906, they held a two-day match against the Free Foresters, and included in their side the Brain brothers, V. T. Hill and H. G. Moore-Gwyn.[4]

Further west, the Public School Nondescripts continued to stage popular games at Killay House with the gentlemen cricketers in the Swansea area. Many good university players also appeared as guests having been invited to Killay by Morgan Williams's sons who were up at Cambridge. Several Glamorgan players including Edward Jones and Dr Alec Cameron also took part, and in 1908 James Maxwell received an invitation to appear against a side called Swansea Wednesdays. However, the former Somerset professional proved to be far too good, and scored 188 including 12 fours and 15 sixes![5]

However, the relaxed atmosphere and hearty lunches were two of the attractions of playing for the Nondescripts, as remembered by J. H. Morgan who wrote:

> there is no better way of enjoying the game . . . green trees and white tents formed a joyful background – and the lunch. Oh, the delightful lazy loaf after lunch! Which reminds me of the old timer who was moved to write:

> I'm not a good cover, I freely admit
> And I'm not very handy at point,
> I'm growing inert and no longer exert
> The nimble gymnastical joint;
> I cannot rejoice when a hurricane cut
> Contuses my chin with its crunch.
> When fielding to hitters, my heart pitter-patters,
> But trust me to sparkle at lunch,
> I radiate freely at lunch.[6]

In 1901 the Nondescripts even challenged the full county side to a contest at St Helen's, but like Maxwell's hurricane hitting, it only showed the huge gulf between amateur and professional cricket. Harry Creber took 5–19 as the Nondescripts were dismissed for eighty-seven runs before Glamorgan ran up 443–8 with Joseph Brain scoring 116 and William Russell ninety. Billy Bancroft guested for the Killay side and hit fifty in the second innings, but he could not prevent an innings victory for the county side.[7] The game proved that, despite being jolly good fun, the standard of games held by amateur sides such as the Nondescripts was well below that of a county, or sometimes even a decent club side. The result was that many of the talented amateurs were left wanting to try something more competitive, yet still with an air of country house cricket and good social credibility. The outcome was the creation in 1905 of a side called The Gentlemen of Glamorgan by 'Tal' Whittington of Neath.

The 24-year-old solicitor had yet to establish a regular place in the Glamorgan side, and also wanted to give cricket in the west a boost, so he suggested forming an all-amateur eleven which would play exhibition matches at The Gnoll. He gained the support of W. B. Trick, the mayor of Neath, who contacted his brother, who was mayor of Stoke Newington, and the outcome was a fixture with eleven gentlemen from the Essex county club in July 1905. Whittington led the Glamorgan side, which was composed of his amateur friends from Swansea, Llanelly and Neath, plus Harry Creber who agreed to turn out after Whittington agreed to pay his travel expenses from Swansea. Essex brought a powerful eleven, including several of their first-team regulars after their previous county engagement with Warwickshire, and not surprisingly they were comfortable winners by five wickets, with Bert Tremlin taking 12–61.[8] Despite the adverse result, the game was a social success for the Welsh amateurs, as a lavish banquet was held on the first evening at the Castle Hotel.[9] Essex agreed to a return encounter in 1906 and this time Whittington assembled a stronger Glamorgan eleven. It included Walter Brearley, the volatile England fast bowler, who had fallen out with the Lancashire authorities and refused to play for the county. Whittington approached the amateur who was playing Lancashire League cricket, and he readily agreed, possibly with an eye on a future career in south Wales. Whittington also secured the services of Riches, Arthur Gibson and John Cadogan of Cardiff, but several amateurs from Swansea and Newport declined invitations for a variety of reasons.

The Newport amateurs felt it was too far to travel to Neath at their own expense, especially when they had to face the fiery Essex attack, whilst the Swansea players were wary of Whittington's intentions, especially when Brearley had no residential qualifications. There was still a lot of intense rivalry between Neath and Swansea, and some felt that the Neath batsman was just trying to promote his own club and ground in order to make The Gnoll rather than St Helen's the major venue in the west. Indeed, their reluctance to support Whittington was mentioned in the speeches at another banquet at The Castle Hotel on the first evening of the 1906 match. Alderman Trick condemned their actions by saying 'I am glad to find there is still one club of sportsmen in Glamorgan. That club is Cardiff, who have generously placed any of their amateurs at the disposal of the game's promoters here in Neath. It is a pity that others have been unable to follow their actions.'[10]

The absence of the Swansea batsmen left the Glamorgan batting rather fragile and despite Riches's presence, Essex recorded another comfortable ten-wicket victory. A decent crowd supported the game, and with around seventy pounds taken in gate receipts, Whittington persuaded Essex to return in 1907. Once again, he looked outside the county's boundaries to secure the services of a guest amateur and contacted Archie MacLaren, the Lancashire and England batsman. The presence of the former Test captain would have been a huge draw, but sadly he was unable to play. Fortunately, Brearley was still at loggerheads with the Lancashire committee and Whittington secured his services, along with Cardiff's professionals Joe Hirst and Trevor Preece, plus Billy Bancroft and Harry Creber from Swansea, with Whittington once again covering their travelling expenses.

The Gentlemen of Essex were not as strong in 1907 as in previous years and Brearley took eight wickets as they were bowled out for 166. Bancroft scored ninety-seven as the Glamorgan side gained a healthy first innings lead, but just as Whittington's side seemed poised to register a famous victory for amateur cricket in south Wales, the heavens opened and the match ended in a watery draw.[11] It also turned out to be the final game for this chiefly amateur side, as the following year Whittington was elevated to the captaincy of the Glamorgan club. This meant that he devoted all of his time and organizational energies into affairs in the minor county world and had no time to set up any 'rival' contests or counter-attractions. However, they had for a few seasons been a pleasant and sociable diversion from the worries of playing for a top club or the full county eleven.

Whilst these events took place at the top of the cricket hierarchy, the emergence of Glamorgan and Monmouthshire in the minor county world also prompted a number of other positive, and long-awaited developments at club level during the late nineteenth and early twentieth century. In particular, there was the formation of new cup competitions and leagues to replace the inter-club friendlies. These changes helped further to raise the standard, and the number of people playing good cricket, but more importantly it meant that the game at grass roots level made rapid headway after a period of relative stagnation, and once again, it was the middle class and leaders of urban cricketing society who were responsible for these important changes.

By the mid 1880s, the plethora of suburban sides in the Cardiff area allowed J. P. Jones, the Cardiff captain, to select a Cardiff United side in 1886 to challange Taff Vale and the second eleven of the town club.[12] The top players from the junior and workingmen's clubs were selected and following their decent performance, Jones considered other ways of boosting the game. He did not have to look very far, as the rugby clubs in the area had flourished following the introduction of the Cardiff and District Football Challenge Cup in 1886. It was organized by T. Page Wood, a Cardiff sports shop owner for all clubs within a six-mile radius of the town, with competing sides paying an entrance fee of five shillings and playing members of Cardiff RFC barred from taking part.[13]

The new competition proved to be an instant success and, during 1887, letters appeared in the press suggesting a similar cup for the cricket clubs. In April one stated how 'there are in Cardiff now over fifteen clubs which no doubt would avail themselves of the opportunity of contesting for a local cup were one offered for competition'.[14] Once again, Page Wood took the initiative and inaugurated a Cardiff and District Cricket Union to oversee the organization of a cup competition. Sir Morgan Morgan agreed to act as president, whilst the town's MP Sir Edward Read served as vice-president. Page Wood agreed to sponsor a cup and rules were drawn up similar to the rugby competition. The first games in the Cardiff and District Challenge Cup took place in June and July 1988, and later in the season the final took place between Taff Vale and St Paul's.[15]

Improvements also took place in the west, where there were a host of smaller clubs in the Swansea suburbs and hinterland. Their members decided to form a league and, in April 1893, a meeting was held in Swansea at which the Swansea and District Cricket League came into being.[16] Subscriptions of two shillings were levied, allowing a large shield to be presented to the winners. Amongst the clubs that took part in the early 1890s were Sketty, Gowerton, Sunnybank, Clydach, Penllergaer, Singleton, Ynysygerwyn, St Judes, Neath YMCA, Swansea Church and Pontarddulais.[17] The cream of the league talent was also assembled into an XVIII to challenge the full Swansea side, and a touring party was selected for an annual five-day tour of Devon.[18]

Like the South Wales Challenge Cup, the new leagues also caused a few problems, and disputes arose over the registration of decent players. In 1895 Gowerton withdrew from the Swansea and District League after a dispute with officials over the late registration of players and dissatisfaction over the way some people turned out for more than one side. Other sides also withdrew or disbanded, but their places were taken by stronger sides such as Briton Ferry Steelworks, Resolven and Llanelli Steelworks. Their participation helped to raise the standard and prompted a tightening up of the regulations, so that all players had to be registered by 11 May and were unable to play for any other league side. These changes pleased Gowerton, so they rejoined the league in 1899, and the following year won the Challenge Shield after a play-off with Clydach, with whom they had tied with the same number of points.[19]

The success of these leagues led to the creation of other similar competitions, such as the Glamorgan League in 1897, which involved clubs in the Taff and Rhondda valleys, including Treherbert, Aberamman, Treorchy, Hill's Plymouth, Ynysybwl, Pontypridd, Ferndale and Mountain Ash. The boom in local leagues in south Wales also led to the idea of a regional competition, similar to those in Lancashire and Yorkshire, and including top West Country sides such as Thornbury, Lansdown, Gloucester and Bedminster. During the autumn of 1894 the officials of Cardiff, Newport and Swansea were contacted about a Western Counties and South Wales Cricket League, but nothing came about.[20] Cup competitions were also introduced and, in 1890, a Monmouthshire Challenge Cup was inaugurated. The knock-out contest excluded Newport and involved instead smaller clubs on either side of the River Usk, and a play-off between the winners from the West and the East.[21] Abertillery and Chepstow were two of the more successful sides, but the latter annoyed the competition's officials by including Gloucestershire's Edward Peake for the 1890 final against Abercarn. Regulations were tightened up to prevent a repetition, but even so, Chepstow maintained its success in the cup by winning the Monmouthshire competition four times in the 1890s. Another significant development around the turn of the century was the attraction of top-class English professionals to south Wales. These were lured by several factors, not least the better standard of club cricket, the prospect of playing for a minor county and lucrative offers from the wealthy clubs on a par with terms offered by English counties.

Previously, it was only the premier sides such as Newport, Cardiff or Swansea who had been able to afford big name professionals with their capital backing from rugby clubs, but by the early 1900s many other sides were in a position to sign well-known players. Llanelly pulled off perhaps the biggest coup by signing Ernie Vogler, the South African googly bowler who was described in 1907 by the England Test captain as 'the best bowler in the world'. In all, Vogler took over 400 first-class wickets and on his Llanelly debut in 1913 he took 8–41 against Briton Ferry, and later in the season scored 121 in the match with Hill's Plymouth.[22]

Other clubs were able to spend money on more than one professional for the first time, such as Neath (or the Gnoll Park Club as it was known at the time) by opening up a subscription fund and gaining the backing of wealthy industrialists. The club had previously only been able to afford one professional, but by 1906 it hired three at a cost of £109. These included Jim Briggs, the brother of Lancashire's Johnny Briggs, and Bert Tremlin, the Essex fast bowler, using their contacts with the mayor of Stoke Newington.[23] Briton Ferry Steelworks CC also attracted a number of well-known players, including Derbyshire all-rounder Henry Bagshaw, Arthur Webb, the former Hampshire batsman, and in the years before the Great War, Billy Bates, the former Yorkshire batsman and left-arm spinner.[24] As David James noted, their presence had a dramatic effect on the young cricketers in the Briton Ferry area:

> They were men who had played with the very great of England . . . they conducted themselves about the wicket and its environs as if they owned the turf, and it rubbed off on the eager hosts of young men who came from the grime of the steelworks . . . Furnacemen, rollermen, labourers, apprentices, strove to emulate the skills and deportment of men like Arthur Webb . . . and the professionals in their turn were quick to spot the untutored talent that thronged the practice nets and to nurture it.[25]

The presence of these top names, plus the various league and cup competitions gave a further boost to public interest in the game at club level. Vogler's presence in the Llanelly side naturally drew large crowds to Stradey Park, rivalling those that watched the town's famous rugby club. As the local paper noted 'long before the advertised time for pitching the wickets, people were wending their way Stradeywards in some unusally large numbers. One would have thought there was a football match on'.[26] In 1910 the benefit match for the club's Ceylonese professional Alfred Holsinger drew a crowd of 2,000, whilst fifteen pounds was donated by subscribers together with a further £4. 16s. 9d. when a collection was made on his behalf. Large crowds were also attracted to encounters between the leading sides from the west and the east, with £18. 16s. taken in 1903 in gate receipts for the match between Llanelly and Cardiff.[27] This was more than Neath took during the whole of 1904,[28] although the crowd was swollen by a large contingent of people from the Rhondda who had travelled to see the Wild West show in Sophia Gardens and mistook the Arms Park for the showground![29] Local derbies sometimes provoked violence, although such recurrences were not as frequent as in the late nineteenth century. The chief exception was the uproar after the match in 1909 at the Gnoll between Llanelly and Neath, following some dubious decisions by the Llanelly umpire and his rejection of an appeal so that Llanelly could level the scores for a draw:

> An angry crowd surrounded the Llanelly players at the conclusion of the match, but unavailing efforts were made to get at the Llanelly umpire, against whom the wrath of the crowd was apparently concentrated. Free fights were fought and the Llanelly players were struck . . . The only policeman present, together with several of the Neath officials, attempted to disperse the crowd, but they refused to leave . . . Meanwhile, another policemen had arrived and together with the police succeeded in getting the players out of the ground . . . Mr Percy Rees, the Llanelly captain, said the Neath crowd were the worst he had ever seen. He had not seen anything like it, even at a football match.[30]

A final development at club level was that teams from more distant parts of England also started to tour south Wales following improvements in communications and in the standard of play. In 1886 Brentford from London visited the Newport area, whilst in 1894 Swansea undertook a tour to south Devon, and Swanland Manor of Yorkshire travelled to Swansea.[31] Even the smaller teams in south Wales were able to travel over greater distances around the turn of the century, as cheaper fares became available and clubs could afford to pay travel bills. In 1902 Treorchy arranged fixtures at Whitland,[32] whilst Neath YMCA had annual tours to west Wales with matches at Pembroke, Tenby and St David's.[33] Some were even venturing further afield, and in 1894 a team was assembled which travelled over to France to play various clubs in the Paris area.[34]

Therefore, there were changes at all levels of the game in south Wales during the years leading up to the Great War. The same happened in England during the second half of the nineteenth century, and cricket historians view the late Victorian and early Edwardian period as 'The Golden Age'.[35] A host of books have been devoted to the exploits of this period's heroes, such as W. G. Grace, Archie MacLaren and Prince Ranjitsinhji,[36] but the improvements ran deeper than just county level. This was a vintage period lower down the English cricketing hierarchy as the sprawling Edwardian cities had a plethora of clubs ranging across the social spectrum, catering for young and old, and in some cases women as well as men. Smaller towns and villages also had their range of sides, and as John Arlott wrote 'churches, institutions, schools, factories, collieries and the most fortuitous groupings of young men had their teams. Never, before or since, were there so many active cricketers in England'.[37]

The same could equally be said about south Wales and its Golden Age saw the establishment of a healthy framework from county through club to workingmen's and school level. Never before had there been so many cricketers in south Wales as there were in 1914, but at the end of the season they had to swap cap, bat and ball for gas-mask, helmet and rifle, and the cricketers trooped off to fight in the Great War. Thousands failed to return, including Glamorgan's William Edwards, Charles Davies and Archer Windsor-Clive who was tragically killed in the Battle of Mons in August 1914 just a fortnight after leaving Cardiff with the Coldstream Guards.[38]

Those who were fortunate enough to return found life in general, and cricket in particular, very different after the War. Indeed, as George Plumptre noted, the hostilities 'brought to an abrupt end a way of life which, in retrospect, could not have gone on anyway, but the manner in which it was extinguished left it with an aura of glamour which a natural, slower death might have tarnished'.[39] The major change was the elevation of Glamorgan from the Minor County Championship to the first-class world of the County Championship, yet the seeds for promotion were sown before war broke out. Worcestershire and Northamptonshire were promoted to the championship in 1899 and 1905, so in 1909 the Glamorgan committee discussed the question of their elevation. The requirement was sixteen fixtures with other first-class sides, but Glamorgan's moderate capital reserves meant that hard-headed realism held sway over romantic dreams. Nevertheless, Whittington contacted clubs and businesses throughout the region asking for subscriptions and donations.[40] Some exhibition matches were also staged in 1910, but the depression in industry hit the attendances and at the end of the season the treasurer reported that the overdraft had risen to £574. With expenses exceeding £1,000, the committee gloomily had to postpone the campaign for first-class status, and consider instead whether they could remain as even a minor county. Another circular was issued in an attempt to avert the unthinkable step of withdrawing from the Minor County Championship and even packing up altogether.

> There are many gentlemen in the County who are interested in the well-being of our national game, and who would deplore any circumstances which would lead to the winding up of the county cricket club owing to want of support. On the other hand, it is manifest that unless some steps can be taken to relieve the Club of their present burden of debt, and at the same time broaden the area of support by largely increasing the members' subscriptions, the county cricket club cannot hope to justify its existence.[41]

Fund-raising events were held, and fewer professionals were hired, and as a result the deficit was reduced to forty-two pounds by the end of the 1913 season. The campaign restarted, but the outbreak of war imposed another halt. By the time that cricket resumed in 1920, the committee, reflecting society as a whole, looked forward with great optimism and determined to set aside the earlier disappointments. Their vigour was epitomized by Whittington, the secretary, who travelled the length and breadth of England, convincing other counties that Glamorgan could join the championship, as well as canvassing businessmen for further financial help. Sidney Byass loaned £1,000 on a ten-year basis, and eight counties agreed to fixtures.[42] The MCC endorsed Glamorgan's application and admitted the Welsh county to the first-class ranks for the start of the 1921 season. There was plenty of backslapping, and dear old Sir John Llewelyn, one of the few remaining stalwarts from the good old days of south Wales cricket, had a smile on his face. It broadened as Glamorgan made a fairytale start to life as a fully fledged county side, defeating Sussex at the Arms Park in their opening championship match,[43] and although they ended at the bottom end of the table for the next few years, J.T.D. was content in the knowledge that his long-held dream had finally been achieved.

Another change took place at the top of the hierarchy in 1923 as a Welsh Cricket Union was formed with players from Glamorgan combining with those from Monmouthshire and north Wales in annual first-class matches against the MCC, Ireland, Scotland and the touring sides. But it was not all progress in the 1920s as Monmouthshire had an unhappy time as a minor county after the Great War and languished at the bottom of the championship table. Tenth place in 1927 was their highest position, and the lack of success was converted into major financial worries. By 1929 the club's overdraft exceeded £400, and forced drastic cost-cutting measures, with fewer professionals being hired and even the amateurs paying their own hotel bills.[44] Things got even worse during the depression of the 1930s, and the committee realized that the club could not continue. In July 1934 Monmouthshire amalgamated with Glamorgan, thereby extending the first-class county's Welsh identity and allowing it to be more representative of south Wales.[45]

The years after the Great War also saw huge changes at club level, with the creation in 1926 of the South Wales and Monmouthshire Cricket Association, although once again, the stimulus came from the top of the hierarchy. Glamorgan found life extremely difficult in the county championship during the 1920s, and the first five seasons saw them finish no higher than thirteenth place. The side badly needed strengthening, but the limited finances meant that hiring more professionals was impossible. The answer was to produce more local talent, but a stumbling block existed in a general lack of competitiveness at club level, and despite the presence of small, local leagues and cup competitions, many clubs still preferred their traditional friendlies established back in the nineteenth century.

In 1921 the leading clubs in the west established the Glamorgan County Cricket League, whilst across the Lougher, a Carmarthenshire League was also created, including Ammanford, Hendy and Pontyberem.[46] In 1922 an attempt was made to establish a South Wales League, but Cardiff was reluctant to join and forsake its popular fixtures with English clubs. Swansea, Newport and Neath also withdrew support, and the scheme was shelved. However, Glamorgan's continued failure caused the idea to resurface in 1925 and through the persistence and faith of leading club officials such as Hugh Baxter of Swansea and J. D. D. Davis of Neath, nine clubs – Barry, Briton Ferry Steel, Briton Ferry Town, Cardiff, Gowerton, Llanelly, Neath, Newport and Swansea – agreed to form a new league competition.[47] The first fixtures in the new South Wales and Monmouthshire Cricket Association took place on 4 May 1926, and by means of celebration, Norman Riches scored 194 for Cardiff against Llanelly, and Newport's Ken Raikes took 6–9 at Briton Ferry Steel.

Despite the General Strike that summer and the hardship it produced in the valley communities, a further thirty clubs applied to join the Association and a second division with western, northern and eastern sections was organized, thereby reducing travel costs. Cardiff shipowner Daniel Radcliffe donated a handsome trophy for the winners of Division One and it ended up at Neath at the close of the first season. The new league transformed the top of the club structure, and ultimately led to more successful Glamorgan sides in the 1930s. Alan Meredith noted that it also proved 'an immediate hit with the public, and crowds of a thousand plus were the order of the day. In the First Division, Neath and Briton Ferry Town would play regularly in front of crowds of up to four thousand . . . This public support was the main source of income for most clubs, but it also meant that clubs had to provide entertaining cricket in return'.[48]

The 1920s also saw the emergence of wealthy industrial sides, with the Hill's Plymouth club of Merthyr regularly fielding an all-professional side, utilizing the company's extensive finances and ability to offer jobs in the steelworks to promising players. In the west, the steel-making company of Richard Thomas and Baldwins supported four clubs – Elba, Baldwins, Morewoods and Panteg – and ensured that they had a crop of decent professionals. In addition, the 1920s witnessed the disappearance of country house cricket. In some cases it was due to estates being sold off for house-building, or as in the case of the games at Killay House, the death of their leading proponents.[49] Similarly, Viscount Evan Morgan, who succeeded to the Tredegar Park Estate in 1934 had no interest in hunting or cricket, so the Tredegar Park Club, established by Foster Stedman, declined.[50] But the chief factor behind the demise of this more social form of the game was the War itself. As Arrowsmith noted:

> The First World War was responsible for the gradual disappearance of many things, but there are few things which it destroyed so suddenly and so completely as country-house cricket. In 1914 there was still plenty to be played, since 1919 there has hardly been any . . . men had to work harder than they had done in earlier years, there were more counter-attractions such as golf and the great increase in the amount of first-class cricket made it hard for good amateurs to find time for other matches.[51]

The 1920s, therefore, saw the final stages in the development process and the emergence of the modern form, and structure, of cricket in south Wales. It wiped away many of the earlier characteristics, such as country house matches and Glamorgan's career as a minor county. Yet at the same time, it built on the strengths of the existing club structure and significant improvements took place through the creation of the South Wales and Monmouthshire Cricket Association. Cricket in the 1920s was thus very different from that in the Golden Age before the Great War, and remarkably J. T. D. Llewelyn, the Grand Old Man of South Walian cricket, was still alive to witness these final developments. When he died in July 1927 he was able to go to his cricketing heaven safe in the knowledge that all of his efforts, plus the countless pounds and hours he had invested in promoting the game, had paid off.

16 / *Conclusion*

T HIS DETAILED analysis of the history of cricket in south Wales has shown that the game's evolution was neither haphazard or chaotic. Behind the individual feats of batsmen or bowlers and the affairs of clubs or county sides, there was order and a structure similar to those patterns identified by academics such as Hagerstrand and other sports' historians and geographers. The game underwent an evolutionary process and the success of Wilf Wooller's team in 1948 by winning the County Championship was the culmination of a process which had developed since the first recorded game at Cwmgwili in 1783. In between these two dates, the game of cricket in south Wales passed through the six distinctive stages, similar to the sequential pattern identified in England by Christopher Brookes:

1. *Pre-1760*: an unorganized folk-game, staged in churchyards or on common land.

2. *1760–1830s*: a more formalized, though still quite primitive version, with games being staged in rural centres or market towns.

3. *1830s–late 1850s*: the creation of clubs in the industrial centres and the establishment of formal rules and standard regulations. Inter-club fixtures replaced the former friendlies and practice sessions, although the participants were chiefly still the wealthy and landed gentry.

4. *Late 1850s–late 1880s*: an inter-club competition was held, whilst representative 'county' elevens were formed to promote both the game and the region. Improvements occurred at school level and cricket spread down the hierarchy to the working classes and became a popular mass recreation during the summer months.

5. *Late 1880s–1914*: new Minor County sides were formed, whilst localized leagues and cup competitions were inaugurated. English-born migrants emerged at the top of the decision-making hierarchy, whilst many of the wealthy and the gentry retreated to country house matches.

Professionals became more numerous and a major force at club and 'county' level, whilst suburban sides emerged in the hinterlands of the largest settlements.

6. *Post–1914*: the emergence of the modern format of the game. Glamorgan joined the first-class County Championship, and amalgamated with Monmouthshire, whilst at club level, the game was strengthened by the creation of regional leagues and associations.

This historical evolution of the game was not, however, just a mirror image of the English pattern. There were fundamental differences in terms of the time scale and, whereas in England, the aristocracy and gentry were dominant from the mid seventeenth until the early nineteenth century, their counterparts in south Wales only assumed importance from the late eighteenth century but retained that importance until the late nineteenth century. County teams emerged in England in the mid nineteenth century, with a County Championship established in 1890, but the Welsh counties only entered the Minor County Championship around the turn of the century, and it was not until 1921 that Glamorgan became the seventeenth and youngest member of the County Championship.

As well as these interesting historical and social changes, there were some subtle alterations to the geographical nature of the game. These are highlighted in Figure 26, which uses the same time scale as above.[1] Stage One saw the establishment of teams at culture hearths in Carmarthenshire and Monmouthshire, but their activities were extremely localized, with practices amongst members. Games against neighbours emerged in Stage Two, which also saw the formation of new teams in the industrial centres on the coastal plain. Even so, inter-club fixtures still existed alongside the short-distance, inter-club matches. Stage Three saw a continuation of this mix, and a further rise in the actual number and distribution of clubs, with a growth in the valleys, as well as on the coastal plain. Inter-club fixtures disappeared in Stage Four, as transport improvements allowed long-distance, inter-club fixtures within the region, and in the case of the South Wales CC outside the area as far away as London and the South Coast. The growing number of clubs also meant a rise in the actual total of fixtures. This increase continued in Stage Five, when the new trend was the formation of district and minor county sides, staging fixtures inside as well as outside south Wales, sometimes as far away as north-east England. However, inside the region some of the internal cohesion present in Stage Four was lost and the area was split east-west. The final stage witnessed the success of Glamorgan, the regional side, taking part in a national competition all over England, plus an inter-club structure based on leagues and cups which helped to bring back internal cohesion and unite the area.

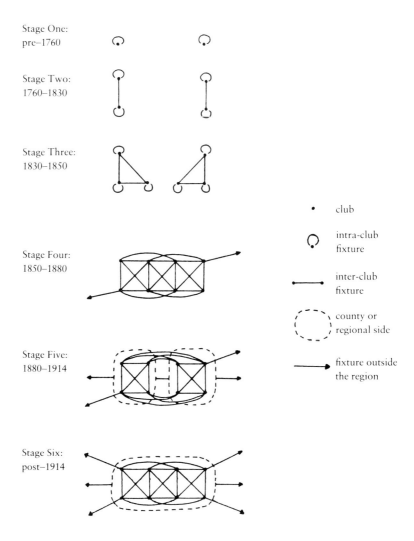

Stage One:
pre–1760

Stage Two:
1760–1830

Stage Three:
1830–1850

Stage Four:
1850–1880

Stage Five:
1880–1914

Stage Six:
post–1914

• club

intra-club fixture

inter-club fixture

county or regional side

fixture outside the region

Figure 26. A Model of the Changing Geographical Characteristics of Cricket in south Wales

Whilst these historical and geographical changes were taking place, the game was diffusing through the region in a similar way to that hypothesized by Torsten Hagerstrand's diffusion theory. Figures 4, 14, 15 and 21 all show the classic sigmoid curve (see Figure 2) which the Scandinavian geographer believed was the characteristic feature of innovation diffusion. The game started at specific culture hearths in the late eighteenth and early nineteenth century, and then developed during the rest of the century through the actions of a number of innovators, including the landed gentry, religious leaders and affluent industrialists. But, as in Hagerstrand's theory, several barriers also existed, including the geographical confines of the valleys, the poor transport infrastructure, the limited amount of spare time and opposition from Nonconformists. Gradually, these barriers were overcome as people and railway lines moved into the previously isolated communities, and religious leaders preached the virtues of Muscular Christianity and encouraged their congregations to take part. Healthy recreation was also encouraged at school and this led to more cricket being played during the growing amount of spare time with which working people found themselves following the introduction of a shorter working week. The removal of these barriers meant that cricket's diffusion eventually reached a ceiling level in the early twentieth century.

The cricket clubs too acted as innovators on a wider recreational scale and several rugby clubs owe their origin to the formation and success of cricket elevens during the summer months, and the wish to extend sporting comradeship into the winter. The same is also true of Cardiff City Football Club, which originated in 1899 when members of Riverside CC, who included several migrants from the West Country, decided to form an association football club in order to keep fit during the winter.[2] During the nineteenth century, many cricket clubs held annual sports days when their members took part in a variety of athletic pursuits. For example, in May 1870 the Swansea CC Athletic Sports included a 250-yard running race, a 120-yard hurdle race, sack races, bicycle competitions and a hammer-throwing event. These sports days were highly popular amongst the members and drew large crowds. Over 4,000 people attended Cadoxton's Athletic Sports on Easter Monday 1881, and these annual events proved to be excellent money spinners as testified by the £200 which the club raised in entrance fees and attendance at their 1876 Sports Day.[3] Such events helped clubs expand their fixture list and subsidize their playing costs, as well as fostering the development and promotion of other games.

The facts also reflect considerable support for Hagerstrand's concept of neighbourhood effects and contagious spread, in addition to abundant evidence of diffusion curves and barrier effect. This leads to an investigation of the personalities involved, which neatly avoids falling into the trap of viewing space and distance as mechanisms which assisted the diffusion process on their own. Cricket first emerged at a few selected points, and its early growth was concentrated in these poles because of the advantages they possessed in terms of good wickets, transport infrastructure and patronage by the landed gentry. In the pre-railway era, cricket spread to adjacent areas rather than more distant ones and was a function of a lack of long distance transport by either private or public means. Geographical interaction only developed when the public transport network improved and barriers, both physical and spiritual, were overcome.

Hagerstrand also suggested that ideas trickled down the hierarchy, and in the case of cricket in south Wales, there is evidence for hierarchical diffusion in terms of both settlements and society. Taking first of all the way in which the game spread to, or from, settlements, there was not a perfect top to bottom spread. This was because the game began in rural areas and went up the hierarchy from the countryside to the small towns and market centres of the early nineteenth century. Everything changed as the economic boom generated rapid rates of urban growth and the emergence of enormous industrial centres and booming ports in the second half of the nineteenth century. This resulted in a different pattern, as the game now spread down the settlement hierarchy from the towns and cities to their surrounding suburbs and dormitory villages, as the leading personalities of the town clubs and urban society sought to establish a new collective identity in the hinterland.

Hierarchical diffusion was more clearly evident from the point of view of society. The gentry, such as J. G. Philipps of the late eighteenth century, J. H. Vivian in the early nineteenth and J. T. D. Llewelyn and J. D. Nicholl in the mid nineteenth century, acted as innovatory leaders, forming elevens, giving cash to support teams, or providing the land on which fixtures could take place. The Welsh landed gentry were leaders in geographical terms within south Wales although, on a wider scale, they were not innovators since they were only introducing, or spreading, ideas from England. As Tony Lewis observed, they 'looked to England for education, business, social and political contact, constantly mimicking the habits and pleasures of the corresponding classes over the border'.[4]

During the second half of the nineteenth century, organizations such as the South Wales CC and the early 'county' teams tried to reinforce the gentry's position by seeking exclusivity rather than fostering the growth of the game lower down the hierarchy. Consequently, the role of diffusion leader was taken over by religious leaders such as the Revd William David of St Fagan's, and the Revd Hugo Harper of Cowbridge Grammar. From their pulpits and schoolrooms, these clerics helped the game spread down the social ladder to the aspiring middle-classes and the perspiring workingmen.

This channel of hierarchical diffusion was clearly defined in Monmouthshire, and Figure 27 shows the spider-like web which existed during the nineteenth century. The process started at Level One in the early nineteenth century through the actions of the landed gentry such as the Duke of Beaufort and the members of the Monmouthshire club at

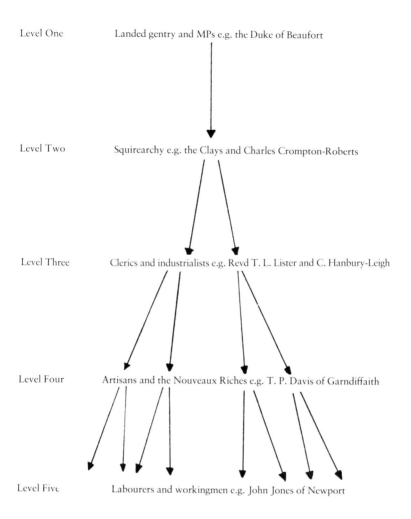

Figure 27. Hierarchical diffusion – the channels in nineteenth-century Monmouthshire

Raglan. The squirearchy at Level Two and the clerics and industrialists at Level Three became involved in the the mid and late nineteenth century. Through the actions of people such as John Rolls of Monmouth and Capel Hanbury-Leigh at Pontypool, it spread down the social ladder to the *nouveaux riches* such as T. P. Davis, the postmaster of Garndiffaith at Level Four and finally to the average workingman – John Jones of Newport – at Level Five.

Whilst the hierarchical structure, as shown in Figure 27, was the strength of the diffusion process during the early and mid nineteenth century, it also became a major weakness during the late nineteenth century and early twentieth century. The individuals at the top of the social and cricketing ladder in south Wales became increasingly detached from the game at grass roots level lower down the hierarchy, and rather than fostering the growth of the game and the participation of people beneath them, they preferred to play their cricket in almost splendid isolation at faraway country mansions in the company of equals. This was, in fact, a trend not peculiar to cricket, as Philip Jenkins concluded that over time the 'Glamorgan gentlemen came to be increasingly divided from their social inferiors'.[5]

Such isolated activity left a vacuum and, despite the inauguration of the South Wales Challenge Cup, cricket drifted without direction for some time. Fortunately, wealthy industrialists and those leaders of premier clubs, such as J. P. Jones of Cardiff, who occupied Level Three, helped to direct the game's development in the late Victorian and Edwardian era, whilst those at Levels One and Two continued to dabble in 'county' matches or country house cricket. By the turn of the century, even the *nouveaux riches* at Level Four were helping to guide the game forward. Indeed, at this stage, the stimulus for the formation of clubs and leagues often came from those lower levels in the social hierarchy and not from the top as in the past.

This detachment by Levels One and Two in the hieararchy helps to explain the deceleration of the evolutionary process during the late nineteenth century. In the 1830s, there had been a successful county side at Raglan and, as outlined above, there were well-defined diffusion channels, but it was well over a hundred years before a successful regional side emerged, and the modern form of the game evolved. One of the reasons for this slowing down was certainly the parochial and insular attitude of exclusive clubs such as the South Wales CC and the early 'county' clubs. They ignored the rapid progress both at club level and at grammar or ordinary schools, as well as the claims of workingmen lower down the social ladder, preferring instead to see the preservation of their cosy little social world of cricket. The resurrection of the South Wales CC in 1874 and the creation of county sub-committees brought the opportunity of forming a representative county team, but it only led to the perpetuation of old amateur ideals and the game at the higher levels rather stagnated during the 1870s and 1880s.

It was not until the late nineteenth century saw the arrival of former English county players, both amateur and professional, that the game finally moved forward. Indeed, the success of Glamorgan and Monmouthshire at minor county level was largely based on talent either born or educated in England. In contrast, Carmarthenshire and, to an extent, the South Wales CC failed due to their reliance on local amateurs. It was only when people like J. H. Brain, with both a wider vision and deeper experience, were at the helm of south Wales cricket that the game moved out of the stagnation into which it had fallen and progressed towards Stage Six.

Yet it would be wrong to attach all of the blame to people like C. P. Lewis or J. C. Nicholl. In the late nineteenth century, cricket somewhat ironically faced increasing competition from rugby, and although many rugby clubs had started as winter offshoots of cricketing activities there was now evidence of 'the tail wagging the dog' with the creation of cricket leagues and cups as a result of their success in the world of rugby. In terms of the diffusion structure in Figure 27, the detachment of the upper levels of the hierarchy and the rivalry with rugby therefore allowed ideas to filter in from outside the cricket hierarchy.

Cricket could easily have taken off in the late nineteenth century, given the firm foundations and clear channels of diffusion which had evolved. Nevertheless, it was rugby which caught the general public's interest, developing rapidly in the 1880s and 1890s. As Gareth Williams has noted, its explosive growth was fuelled by two important factors. Firstly, the continued economic boom, which generated capital and attracted an ever growing stream of migrants and, secondly, the support of a cluster of upwardly mobile young professional men. Cricket competed unsatis-factorily with rugby for the backing of this class of young solicitors, architects and small entrepreneurs. Indeed, as Williams observed, the winter game had a central appeal for both participants and spectators, through 'its theatricality, its opportunity for self-expression as well as entertainment, its affirmation of life after work, and a sense of wholeness denied elsewhere'.[6]

On a wider scale, the growth of rugby symbolized the emergence of Wales as a nation, and the fervour at club and international matches epitomized the feelings of national pride which swelled into a crescendo inside Wales. According to Williams, it was 'not merely a prominent constituent of Welsh popular culture, but a pre-eminent expression of Welsh consciousness, a signifier of Welsh nationhood'.[7] Clear proof that rugby, and the country as a whole, had come of age arose in 1905 when Wales defeated the mighty New Zealanders at the Arms Park. This first-ever victory over the All Blacks was in stark contrast to events in the cricket world, and that same summer, Glamorgan were dismissed for just twenty runs by Wiltshire at Chippenham,[8] whilst even the combined might of south Walian talent was dismissed for a meagre eighty-four and seventy-eight as Yorkshire won by seventy runs.[9]

This sharp contrast between the state of the summer and winter games first received attention in the press during the mid 1880s. A letter to the

Western Mail in April 1886 bemoaned the fact that 'whereas we get 2,000 to 3,000 persons to see a [rugby] football match, we see 100 to 200 to witness a cricket match. Cricket, compared with [rugby] football here is at a very low ebb'.[10] A few months later another correspondent called 'Forward' suggested three reasons why rugby was more popular:

1. They have good matches and advertise them well.
2. They are played upon the most convenient day i.e. Saturday.
3. Because no time is wasted at a football match, and as a rule, punctuality is observed in starting.[11]

Many saw the formation of a county club as the panacea, and a letter in the *Western Mail* in July 1886 stated that this 'is the only method to stir up the interest in the doings of cricketers in South Wales'.[12] Yet the gulf between rugby and cricket continued after the formation of Glamorgan in 1888 and Monmouthshire a few years later. One reason behind the continuation of this gap was the fact that cricket at both club and county level had distinctive social barriers and as shown in Figure 27 was part of a hierarchical structure. This was in contrast to rugby which never excluded the workingman and helped to bond together communities and provide a 'focus for local and communal identity, a prized commodity in the ribbon-developed valleys which lacked appropriate civic foci'.[13] As Gareth Williams stated the winter game had 'a symbolic, unifying role because it was socially inclusive'.[14]

At the root of the problem was that cricket increasingly became synonymous with England at a time when the national spirit was strong within Wales. The game had spread from the London area and, by the late nineteenth century, its leading personalities were educated in, or had migrated from, the other side of Offa's Dyke. Many press reports frequently made reference to cricket as the 'olde English game', whilst a notice in the *Western Mail* promoting the Cardiff cricket week of 1881 hoped that the locals would 'show an appreciation for the real English game of cricket, equal to that they bestow on the game of [rugby] football'.[15] Yet the Welsh now held new aspirations and ambitions and had a deep desire to be autonomous from England. They wanted to support things which were Welsh, especially the actions of Welsh sportsmen, rather than Englishmen such as the Brain brothers, Vernon Hill or Harry Creber. Despite the presence of Billy Bancroft, and a few stars from the rugby world, the two games became polarized in the minds of the general public, with rugby being seen as a Welsh sport and cricket as an Englishman's recreation.

Therefore, it was for reasons of differing values within society and culture that rugby took off and cricket continued its slow development around the turn of the century. The fact that the power in south Walian cricket lay in the hands of Englishmen, rather than natives, did however have one blessing, because it needed people with the vision and popularity of J. H. Brain and Vernon Hill to get the game out of the rut in which it found itself by the 1880s and 1890s. Without their help, the game could have withered, and not reached Stage Six until much later in the twentieth century, with another name instead of Glamorgan's being etched into county cricket's history as champions for 1948 and 1969. Nevertheless, it is impossible to escape from the overall conclusion that the snowball of development which the game of cricket had built up, started to melt in the golden summer sun of the late Victorian and early Edwardian era. As a result, during the final two phases of its development, the following three-fold split, rather than a productive unity, acted as a retarding influence on the game's evolution:

1. In terms of the hierarchical structure, the gentlemen at the top preferred the company of their social equals in country house matches or games with wandering elevens, and thus became isolated from those lower down the ladder.

2. There was a clear division between the world of amateur and professional cricket, in terms of the format of the game and the playing standards. More professionals were hired by the clubs, and many of the inter-club matches were notable for their cut and thrust rather than for a friendly and amiable air.

3. There was also a cultural split, with the power both on and off the pitch in the hands of the English-born or English-educated, rather than any native personalities.

In contrast, the amateur game of rugby lacked these restrictive divisions and was, more importantly, dominated by Welsh-born and often Welsh-speaking people. It thus made rapid progress during this period. Given their seasonal differences, the summer game of cricket and the winter game of rugby could have existed and flourished side-by-side, but the end result was rather different, and as one contemporary writer stated in 1914, 'in the sense that nationality is a community of memories, so is rugby football the national game. The names of the giants are on the lips of the people'.[16] If the three factors above had not divided the game of cricket and slowed down its development, how different it might have all been. Who knows, the population of south Wales could have been toasting a historic success in 1905 on the cricket square, rather than on the rugby pitch at Cardiff Arms Park!

Appendices

A: Data Sources

Newspapers were used as the main source of information for this study. For the pre-1850 period the following were used: *The Cambrian Daily Leader, Monmouthshire Merlin, Hereford Journal, Cardiff and Merthyr Guardian, The Welshman, Carmarthen Journal, Swansea Journal, Bristol Gazette,* and *South Wales Press.* From 1850 onwards the following were used: *The Cambrian Daily Leader, Cardiff Times, Cardiff and Merthyr Guardian, Evening Express, Monmouthshire Merlin, Western Mail, South Wales Daily News, The Welshman, Carmarthen Journal, Western Telegraph, South Wales Daily Post, Llanelly Guardian, Monmouth Beacon, Brecon Reporter, Swansea and Glamorgan Herald, Pontypool Free Press, Star of Gwent, Hereford Times, Central Glamorgan Gazette, Wrexham Advertiser, Western Daily Press* and *Monmouthshire Mercury.*

Their chief advantage is that the reports and news items which they contain provide a fascinating contemporary insight into both cricket and society as a whole in the eighteenth and nineteenth centuries. However, a few problems occur when using them, the main one being that not all of the games that took place were actually included either as line scores or match reports. Those that were printed represent only the tip of the iceberg and, even today, many hundreds of games take place without even the bare details being recorded in the press. Instead, only major matches at a club or county level are covered by the local and national newspapers, and one must assume that the same principles applied in the past. Many factors explain the exclusion of games by the newspapers listed above:

1. Matches between village or pub teams only had a local importance and did not warrant inclusion in papers such as the *Cambrian, Western Mail* or *South Wales Daily News,* which had more of a national or regional coverage;

2. Club secretaries may not have submitted scores or wanted reports to be published if their team suffered a heavy defeat or lost to an inferior team;

3. Sports news, especially line scores of minor cricket matches, was likely to

be omitted by newspaper editors during a local election, an outbreak of cholera, during civil unrest or at the time of another major news item.

4. There was a change in editorial policy with less coverage given to cricket or sport in general. This may well explain the absence of any reports or line scores in the *Monmouthshire Merlin* for 1847.

5. Matches in the early nineteenth century were only among members of town clubs so therefore did not warrant news space, unless a remarkable feat occurred or a prominent member of local society was involved. This explains why theatre records in Carmarthen for 1828 mention the town cricket club, but none of the local or national newspapers mention the club's activities until much later.

6. The inclusion of scores or reports depended on where the newspapers were sold. The *South Wales Daily News* was distributed chiefly in the coastal plain of Glamorgan and Monmouthshire, and the valleys in the south-east, so it concentrated on games in these areas rather than those further west.

There are added complications because some of the newspapers lacked a consistent policy in their coverage of matches. For example, the *Cardiff and Merthyr Guardian* included accounts of Monmouthshire's matches in 1834 and 1836, but not those in 1835 or 1837. Such gaps might indicate that no matches took place, but from time to time indications were given in the published reports that games had been missed. For example, the account of the fixture in August 1836 in the *Cardiff and Merthyr Guardian* between Newport and Pontypool described it as 'the fourth match between the two sides'. However, only the two games in 1836 were covered by the paper, and none of the earlier fixtures. To compound matters in the pre-1850 period, there was no geographical logic in the way newspapers selected match reports or cricket news. One of the earliest references to a game taking place (in Carmarthen in 1783) cropped up in the *Hereford Journal* whilst the 1815 encounter between Usk and Pontypool appears in the *Bristol Gazette*. Matches in the Neath area were covered by newspapers based in Haverfordwest, whilst the news that a club had been formed in Cardiff in 1819 was given in the *Carmarthen Journal*.

There were also subtle differences in the way teams were named in the reports. In some cases, they were not given their correct description in match reports and rather than bearing their club's name, the eleven carried the surname of their captain. This was the case in August 1843 on Crumlin Burrows with a match reported in *The Cambrian* as Swansea against the 73rd/75th Regiment, yet the *Monmouthsire Merlin* called it a match between Mr. Starling Benson's XI and Capt. Napier's XI. Benson was Swansea's captain/wicket-keeper, whilst Capt. Napier was the leader of the two regiments, and one of Swansea's earliest fixtures could have been missed had research been based solely on the *Monmouthshire Merlin*.

The standard of coverage improved after 1850 as the quality of the newspapers got better. However, there still remained differences in terms of the number of games covered. Seventy-seven fixtures were included in the *Western Mail* in 1869, yet the *Cambrian* had a mere twelve. In the 1870s the coverage in the *Western Mail* declined from seventy-four in 1870 to just thirty-nine in 1871. It rose again to 117 in 1885, but in this year, the *South Wales Daily News* covered no less than 336 matches. Yet despite this large number of reports, even the *South Wales Daily News* could not be considered as a thorough source, because it excluded the South Wales CC's games in London against the MCC and Surrey Club and Ground, and overall a quarter of the games in the *Western Mail* were not included in the *South Wales Daily News*.

Given these problems and inconsistencies, an attempt was made to quantify the number of matches which were excluded. This was possible by using the excellent *Lillywhite's Guides* for the period from 1852 until 1868. (I am most grateful to David Smith for access to his collection of these *Guides*.) Club secretaries sent details of their playing record to the compilers of these *Guides*, so a definitive total of matches played by some of the leading clubs can be gained. Table 5 compares the number of matches mentioned in these seasonal reports with the actual number of match reports in the newspapers for each club. It was found that a third of the matches were not included in the newspapers (145 out of 218). It would have probably been a lot higher had more of the smaller or junior sides been included in *Lillywhite's Guides*.

TABLE 5 – A COMPARISON OF MATCHES INCLUDED IN LILLYWHITE'S GUIDES AND NEWSPAPERS, 1852–1868

Season	Team/club	Lillywhite	Newspaper	Newspaper +/−
1852	Cardiff	3	4	+1
	Llanelly	7	7	−
1853	Llanelly	8	8	−
1854	Llanelly	6	6	−
1855	Llanelly	7	8	+1
	Neath	6	3	−3
1856	Chepstow	4	0	−4
	Lampeter	11	3	−8
	Llanelly	7	6	−1
1857	Chepstow	4	2	−2
	Haverfordwest	7	4	−3
	Llanelly	3	3	−
1858	Haverfordwest	5	3	−2
	Llanelly	4	4	−1
	Newport	6	6	−
1859	Breconshire	7	5	−2
	Carmarthenshire	6	2	−4
	Haverfordwest	6	0	−6
	South Wales CC	1	1	−
1860	Breconshire	6	5	−1
	Haverfordwest	8	8	−
	Newport	6	4	−2
	South Wales CC	5	5	−

Season	Team/club	Lillywhite	Newspaper	Newspaper +/−
1861	South Wales CC	6	6	−
1862	Breconshire	4	2	− 2
	South Wales CC	4	4	−
1864	Welsh Wanderers	5	3	− 2
	Llandovery College	5	2	− 3
	Blaina	9	4	− 5
	Newport	12	7	− 5
	Usk	4	1	− 3
1865	Llandovery College	6	2	− 4
1866	Llandovery College	3	1	− 2
1868	Llandovery College	6	1	− 5
	Haverfordwest	6	5	− 1
	Pontymoile	8	5	− 3

Therefore, the newspapers were not a highly accurate data source, omitting at least 33 per cent of matches which took place in the mid nineteenth century. It would have been nice to have had a higher level of accuracy, say 85 or 90 per cent, but this would be impossible because few scorebooks survive in libraries or record offices. However, if one accepts this 66 per cent accuracy level as being too low and turns instead to other sources, an even more fragmented and distorted picture emerges by using other secondary sources. Club histories or centenary brochures often skimp on events in the past, through lack of source material or sheer ignorance. J. H. Rees's centenary book on Gowerton, David James's books on the Briton Ferry clubs, and Bob Harragan's recent history of the Llanelly club are notable exceptions in this minefield of cricketing literature. Another problem is that many clubs mentioned in the newspapers from the nineteenth century are now extinct, and their records have either been destroyed or have disappeared over time. Indeed, the author was shocked, but delighted to stumble across the Burry Port CC scorebook for 1909 in a secondhand bookshop in Swansea in 1991. Other teams such as the Catch 'Em Alive Oh's who played in 1885 were formed for a handful of games, and were not a properly constituted club. No records exist about them today, apart from the names of the eleven in the *Western Mail* or *South Wales Daily News*.

In short, other reliable sources do not exist and these problems of newspapers excluding at least 33 per cent of the matches and haphazard coverage must be accepted as a necessary and, at times, quite intriguing hindrance rather than an impossible barrier. In any case, the pursuit of a 100 per cent or even 90 per cent accurate data source is impossible when undertaking sports history because of the very nature of the topic under study. As Rowland Bowen concluded in his book *Cricket: A History of its Growth and Development* (1970), one is left 'to exhibit the various pieces of evidence and speculate ideas and see what they amount to'.

B: Terminology

A second hindrance exists with the terminology the newspapers and other written records used, because some of the terms had different meanings from what they mean today. At times, others were somewhat ambiguous and, unless great care was taken, the wrong impression could quite easily have been gained.

1. *County team.* In the early nineteenth century some teams were referred to as county sides, in the sense that they were composed of people from the hinterland as opposed to townsfolk. An example of the use of this 'town and county' definition was the mention by the *Monmouthshire Merlin* for 28 August 1830 that 'our county gentlemen were the winners of the match and not the Clifton club'. However, the term county eleven was increasingly used later in the century for sides representing the entire county, although it was still used for teams representing the more rural areas of a district.

2. *Professional/amateur.* These terms were used in the mid and late nineteenth century to denote the difference between a professional, whose services had to be paid for by cash, and someone who was playing solely as an amateur and was not making any financial gain from cricket. However, in the early part of the century, the terms were used in rather different contexts. A report in the *Monmouthshire Merlin* for July 1836 mentioned 'the amateurs of the noble game of cricket' in its report of a match between Raglan and Hereford. In this case, the term amateur was used in the context of those who love the game, and presumably derived from the French 'amour'.

The terms were also used to describe the proficiency and ability of team members. For example, the *Cardiff and Merthyr Guardian* for 30 September 1837 referred to a dinner in Merthyr held by the town's cricket club and stated 'they mustered professors and amateurs to the number of 40'. This could have been a vague and incorrect reference to the club hiring professionals, which could have been possible given the wealth in Merthyr in the 1830s. However, the cricket club's major activity was practices amongst members, and without fixtures there was no need for professionals in the modern sense. One plausible explanation was that they had a coach to help improve standards, but another quite simple one was that some members were very good players whilst others were less able but loved the game. A similar interpretation can be made of the reference in the *Monmouthshire Merlin* for 13 August 1840 that 'the non-professional gentlemen of Monmouth have beaten the professionals of that town'. It would admittedly have needed the talented players to have been over confident and the less talented to have excelled for once, or had a stroke or two of luck. Even so, it was quite an unlikely result and, for that reason alone, merited inclusion in the newspapers at a time when not all of the games were included.

3. *Gentlemen's team.* This sort of description was ambiguous as it could have meant that no professionals were playing and it was an all amateur eleven with no money changing hands for taking part. However, it was also used to describe the spirit in which the game was played by this particular team. In this context, its participants could have been both amateur and professional and played in a respectable way, never seeking to gain any unfair or illegal advantage over the

opposition. In other cases, a reference to a side as 'The Gentlemen of . . . ' meant a side composed of the members of a particular club.

4. *Promoter*. The advertisements in *The Cambrian* for the match in 1855 between the All-England XI and a South Wales team refer to the Bute Estate and Lord Jersey as being the promoters of the game. At first sight, this could be taken to mean that the two estates were dynamically active and taking steps to boost the game by going out of their way to tout for exhibition fixtures. However, these two landed estates played a far less active role, as the itinerant elevens such as the All-England Eleven, merely came to an agreement with the owners of the ground, either a club or individual so that a match could take place. Therefore the people described as 'promoters' were not actively promoting the game, as in the modern sense with boxing, but were undertaking a more passive role, merely agreeing for games to take place on their land.

C: Dates of Formation

The chronological list below for the period from 1785 until 1890 contains dates of when clubs or teams (excluding the county sides) were either formed, known to be in existence or had their matches recorded for the first time in the newspapers listed in Appendix A. For the reasons already mentioned in Appendix A, clubs may have been in existence before the date shown below or other clubs may have been formed, but in both cases they were excluded from the newspapers used. Brackets are used when clubs have been re-formed after going out of existence after their initial creation. [S], [C], [N] and [L] indicate sides that were based in Swansea, Cardiff, Newport and Llanelli.

1785	Swansea
1815	Pontypool, Usk
1819	Cardiff
1820	Newport
1824	Raglan/Monmouthshire
1826	Maesteg
1828	Carmarthen
1830	Cardigan, Lampeter, Tenby
1831	Merthyr
1834	Abergavenny, (Newport), (Pontypool)
1837	Pontypool Tradesmen, Ross
1838	Chepstow, Haverfordwest, Monmouth Town, Pembroke
1839	Llanelly
1840	Bridgend, Cowbridge, Dowlais, Kilvey, (Swansea)
1842	Tredegar
1843	Rhymney, Taibach
1844	Llandeilo
1845	Brecon, (Cardiff), Llandovery, Neath
1846	(Maesteg), Ynysygerwn
1848	Merthyr Early Risers, Pembroke Garrison, Cambrian [S], Taff Vale [C], (Abergavenny)

1849   Newport Tradesmen [N], Ogmore Valley, Crickhowell
1850   Ferryside, (Cowbridge)
1851   Aberdare, (Crickhowell), Nantyglo, Uskside
1852   Blaina, Cwmavon, Cwmamman, Ebbw Vale, Swansea Union [S], (Llanelly)
1853   Neath Early Risers, Neath Tradesmen, St. Woolo's [N], (Llandovery), (Lampeter)
1854   Aberamman, Cross Inn
1855   Abercarn, Crumlin
1856   Brynmawr, Neath Abbey, Pontymoile, St Mary's [C], Tivyside
1857   Blaenavon, Penllergaer, Newport/Abergavenny/Hereford Railway, (Usk), (Merthyr), Milford Haven, Cefncethin, Merthyr Mawr
1858   Adamsdown [C], Briton Ferry, Primrose Hill, Roath [C], Caerphilly, Cardiff YMCA [C], Pontypridd, Cowbridge Morning Club, Brecon United Morning Club, Llandeilo Juveniles, Llandovery Juveniles
1859   Bute Docks [C], Newport Commercials [N], Prince of Wales [S], Llanelly Juveniles [L], Machen, GWR Newport [N], Varteg
1860   Newport West End [N], Risca, Milford Juniors, Haverfordwest Juniors, Usk Juveniles, Pontymoile Juveniles, Dafen, Hafod, Ystrad Meurig, Manorowen, Fishguard, Burton
1861   Pembrey, Llantilio Crossenny, Mountain Ash, (Pontypool), Newport United [N], Newbridge, Penarth
1862   St Fagan's, Oxford Street [S], Priskilly, Haverfordwest United
1863   Cadoxton, Caerleon, Panteg, Welsh Wanderers, Newcastle Emlyn, Penmark
1864   Afan, Beaufort [C], Magor, Newport Atheneum, Tenby, Christchurch, Newport Engineers [N], Narberth
1865   Garndiffaith, Glynneath, Morriston [S], Ravenhill [S], Vale of Neath Railway, Blue Cap [C], Golden Mile
1866   Llandyssul, Pontardawe, Canton [C], Ystalyfera, Llantwit Major, Windsor [C], Prince of Wales [C], Dunraven, Brecon Knickerbockers, Usk Rifle Volunteers, (Raglan), Abersychan, Abergavenny Commercials, Haverfordwest Early Closing Association, Commerce House [C], (Crumlin) The Oaks [N], Blackwood, New Tredegar
1867   Albion, Bassaleg, (Cardiff YMCA), Penmaen, Loughor, St Briavels, Pentrechwyth, Drapers [C], Ironmongers [C], Yniscedwyn, Monmouth Agincourt, Hirwaun, (Pontypridd), Danygraig, Llanwenarth, Llanvachos/Penhow, Prince of Wales [L], Drybridge, Croft-y-Bwlla
1868   Schoolmasters [C], Treherbert, Brecon Morning Star, Llanfrechfa, Llantarnam, Victoria [L], Llanharan, Pontneathvaughan, (Swansea), Gorseinon
1869   Excelsior [C], Gower, Garth, Llandough, Llanstephan, Neath Juniors, Penhow, Tondu, Whitchurch [C], Caldicot, Llwynhendy, (Dafen), Oystermouth [S], Wauntreoda [C]
1870   Bute Household [C], Clydach, Maindy [C], Pentre, Red Cap [C], Stuart [C], Trecynon, Tredegar Park [N], Treorchy, Newport Victoria [N],

Phoenix [N], Aberdare United, Maerdy, Pontardulais, Lower Machen, Newcastle, Electric Telegraph [C]

1871   Mumbles [S], Hearts of Oak [C], Hope [C], Phoenix [C], Science and Art [C], St Brides and Southerndown

1872   Ely Paper Works [C], Greenhill [S], Llanelly Wanderers [L], St Fagan's Castle Household, Taffs Well, Tydee [N], Westbourne [C], White Star [N], Welsh Etceteras, Cogan Pill, Rhymney Railway

1873   Abertillery, Caerleon Tin Works, Cardiff Commercials [C], Caldicot Works, Abercarn Chapel of Ease, Colwinstone, (Ely), Gilwern, Lisworney, Llanishen, [C] Llandow Wanderers, Pentwynmawr, Pontymister, Saundersfoot, Neath Workingmen, Star of Hope [N], Porth

1874   Abercarn Good Templars, Aberdare Crown, Belle Vue [C], Bridgend Wanderers, Ystrad, Burry Port, (Caerphilly), Coronet [C], Castlemartin, Cremorne [C], East Grove [C], Ebbw Vale Excelsior, Merthyr Evening Star, Garth Works, Kidwelly, Llandaff [C], Llangadock, Llanvair, Malpas [N], Maesycymmer, Maesteg Good Templars, Penarth Windsor, Rhondda Valley, Sennybridge, Standard [C], South Wales Daily News [C], Tongwynlais, Aberdare Welsh Harp, Western Mail [C], Maesglas, Felinfoel, Brynhyfryd [S], Glanmor [S], Pontyates, Ponthenri, Pyle, Cardiff Grocers [C], Highmead Wanderers, Llantwit and Black Vein

1875   Cross Inn (Ammanford), Brynamman, Cardiff Law School [C], Cardiff Wanderers [C], Cardiff Wesleyans [C], Cwmpennar, Fleur-de-Lys, Good Templars [C], Georgetown, Llangunnor, Llantrisant, Resolven, Swansea Steelworks, Thomastown, Troedyrhiw, United Railways [C], Wick, Ebbw Vale Literary and Scientific Institution, Oxford [C], Maesyderwen, Ponthir, Pontypridd Victoria, Treforest

1876   Alexandria [N], Rudry, Maesllwch Park, Llynfi, Atheneum [L], Excelsior [N], Cardiff Banks [C], Canton Wesleyans[C], Conway Road [C], Gelligaer, Islwyn, Lanelay, Llansawel, Monmouthshire Butterflies, Pontllanfraith, Pontypool Road Railway, Llandeilo Royal Welshmen, Swansea G.W.R. [S], Swansea Workingmen [S], Woodlands [C], Llangrwyney, Trevethin Church

1877   Cwmbwrla [S], Gellygroes, Heath [C], Star of Tredegar, St Helen's [S], Southerndown, Bridgend Juniors

1878   Carlton [C], Carlton [S], Cymmer Convivials, Essex [S], Gabalfa, [C] Llansamlet [S], Llanrumney [C], Llwynypia, Newport Banks, Richmond [C], Swansea Telegraphists [S], St Thomas [S], St Margarets [C], Roath Rovers [C], Yellow Star, Porthcawl, Swansea Schoolmasters [S], Sketty [S]

1879   Gower Road, Aberdulais, Kensington [S], Melbourne [S], Llandeilo Literary Institution, Melincrythan, Portskewett, Roath Lillywhites [C], Skewen, Tythegstone, Glanafon, Llanelly Workingmen [L], Star [L], Aberdare Crusaders, Clytha, Chepstow Workingmen, Duke Street [C], Star [S], Nelson/Llancaiach, (Oystermouth), Aberdare Star, Aberdare Cambrian, Swansea Good Templars [S]

1880   Manorbier, Charles St Wesleyan [C], Duffryn, Ebbw Vale Star, Fochriw, Govilon, Gowerton, Grangetown [C], Grange Wesleyan [C], Penarth Star, St John's (C], Springfield [S], Swansea Rovers [S], Swansea Wesleyan [S], Swansea YMCA [S], Colorado Beetles [C], Llandaff Workingmen's Club [C], Canton Star [C], Jolly Grangers [C], St Bride's Major, Highfield [N], United Press [C], Lanherne [S], Newport Drapers [N], Neath Star of Hope, Severn Road [C]

1881   South Wales University College [C], Llangennech, True Britons [L], Penclawdd, Belville [C], Bonvilston, Pickwick [C], Star [C], St Nicholas, Anchor [C], Cathays Barracks [C], Brynymor [S], Crynant, Merthyr Cambrian

1882   Dinas Powis, Llannon, Llanelly Rovers, Bridgend Wyndham Street, Pontyberem, Bedwas, Cambrian [C], Crusaders [C], Glossop Terrace [C], Newport Workingmen [N], St James [C], St Paul's [C], Herne Brothers [C], Severn Tunnel

1883   St Clears, Blue Ribbon [C], Dumfries Place [C], Fern Rangers [C], Llanelly Cambrian, Royal Oak [C], St German's [C], Aberamman St Elvan's, Woodville [C], Windsor [S], Llandaff Young Workingmen's Friendly Society [C], St Columba [C], Welcome [C]

1884   Cathays Lillywhites [C], Merthyr YMCA, St Catharine's [C], St Andrews, Ferndale, Guildford Street [C], Penarth Institute of Good Templars, Roath Dock [C], Treboeth [S], Ystrad Mynach, Westley [S], Forrest [S], Bridgend Young Mens Friendly Society, Treshenkin, Glyncorrwg, Pwllywrach, Laugharne

1885   Barry Dock, Blue Anchor [C], Broadway Wesleyans [C], Caledonian [C], Cardiff Solicitors [C], Dockers [C], Engineers [C], Cathays Works [C], Charles St Congregational [C], Cork [S], Cross Keys, Hanbury [C], Hancock's [C], Imperial [C], Longcross [C], Loudoun Square [C], Llwydarth, Melrose [C], Newport Travellers [N], Pwllypant, Riverside [C], Roath Wesleyans [C], Rookwood Rangers [C], Ruperra, Treharris, Violet [C], Waunifor, White Rose [C], White Hart [C], Lampeter Young Mens Friendly Society, Pendine Rovers

1886   Fairwater [C], Crusaders [S], Kidwelly Long Vacation Club, Carmarthen Drapers

1887   Barry Cadoxton, Llanelly Starlight [L], Cresselly, Bryncaerau, Ogmore Rovers, St Hilary, Bryncethin

1888   Bridgend Wesleyans, Hope [S], Manselton [S], St Judes [S]

1889   Hayes [C], Llanelly Tuesdays [L], St Martins [C]

1890   Radyr, Barry Athletic, Sketty Church [S], St Saviours [C], Marlborough Road [C], Cathays Wesleyans [C]

D: The Level of Support and the size of Crowds

As well as investigating the rise in the number of clubs and inter-county matches, it would have been nice to study the increase in public support and attendances at matches. The chapters on the games held in the late nineteenth and early twentieth centuries include a few statistics on money raised and estimated attendances, but this is all that can be achieved at the present, owing to the paltry and somewhat dubious evidence available for the earlier part of the nineteenth century. Some mid-nineteenth-century newspaper reports allude to the level of support, but it was often the estimate made by the correspondent rather than an official, accurate total. Many might therefore have been wildly inaccurate and part of the hype which the individual clubs, whose officials submitted the report, wanted to generate, In the absence of reliable figures, it was decided to leave this topic to one side. The quality of data is far better for the late nineteenth century, with attendance figures occasionally mentioned in annual reports or financial statements which included gate receipts. However, even the latter are not perfect indications of the attendances, because they only included money paid at the public entrance and excluded the members of the host club who were allowed free entry to their ground and pavilion. In addition, there was often a line of people outside the Arms Park peering over, or sitting on the wall lining the ground. Great care therefore needs to be taken with these figures, but it could be an avenue for future research, making comparisons with levels of spectator interest for rugby in south Wales, as well as cricket in England.

Notes

Chapter 1

[1] Cwmgwili 131, Dyfed Record Office.

[2] C. Box, *The English Game of Cricket* (London, 1877), 72.

[3] J. Williams, 'Cricket' in A. Mason (ed.), *Sport in Britain* (Cambridge, Cambridge University Press, 1989), 127.

[4] A. R. Lewis, 'Cricket in Wales' in E. W. Swanton (ed.), *Barclay's World of Cricket*, (Collins, 1980), 513.

[5] G. Williams, 'Sport and Society in Glamorgan 1750–1980', in *Glamorgan County History, Volume Six* (Cardiff, University of Wales Press, 1988), 381–400.

[6] W. F. Mandle, 'The Professional Cricketer in England in the Nineteenth Century', *Labour History*, 23 (November 1972), 8.

[7] C. Brookes, *English Cricket: The Game and its Players throughout the Ages* (Weidenfield and Nicholson, 1978), 6–7.

[8] J. Bale, *Sport and Place: A Geography of Sport in England, Scotland and Wales* (Hurst, 1982); see also J. Bale, 'Geographical Diffusion of Professionalism in Football in England and Wales', *Geography* (1978), 188–97, and 'Geography, Sport and Geographical Education', *Geography* (1981), 104–15.

[9] J. Rooney, 'Sports from a Geographic Perspective', in D. W. Ball and J. Loy (eds.), *Sport and Social Order: Contributions to the Sociology of Sport* (Reading, Addison-Wesley, 1975); see also J. Rooney, *A Geography of American Sport* (Reading, Addison-Wesley, 1974).

[10] See M. G. Bradford and W. A. Kent, *Human Geography: Theories and their Application* (Oxford University Press, 1977). Hagerstrand's work was first published in Swedish in 1953 and was translated into English by Allan Pred in 1967 in *Innovation Diffusion as a Spatial Process* (University of Chicago Press).

[11] J. Bale, op. cit., 75.

[12] C. Brookes, op. cit., 7.

[13] H. D. Morgan, *A Short History of Morriston C.C.* (the club, 1990), 1.

[14] E. D. R. Eagar, 'History of the Game in England', in E. W. Swanton (ed.), *Barclay's World of Cricket* (Collins, 1982), 1.

[15] H. S. Altham and E. W. Swanton, *A History of Cricket* (Allen and Unwin, 1947), 17.

[16] F. S. Ashley-Cooper, *The Cricket Field* (London, 1922). A manuscript in the

Bodleian Library dated 1344 (no. 264) refers to a game of club-ball, which the 1985 Wisden believed was a primitive form of single-wicket cricket, although many cricket historians doubt whether or not the participants were involved in an actual form of the game – see *The Cricket Statistician* (Winter, 1985).

[17] R. Bowen, *Cricket: A History of its Growth and Development throughout the World* (Eyre and Spottiswoode, 1970), 32.

[18] See H. T. Waghorn, *The Dawn of Cricket*, quoted in R. Bowen, ibid.

[19] *The Cricket Statistician*, (Spring 1987), 13.

[20] E. Midwinter, 'The ABC of Cricket Mythology', *The Journal of the Cricket Society*, 15 (1991), 3.

[21] H. S. Altham, *A History of Cricket* (Allen and Unwin, 1926), 21. This is the first edition of H. S. Altham and E. W. Swanton, op. cit.

[22] C. J. Robb quotes a reference whereby Cromwell's Commissioners were asked to destroy sticks which Robb believed were bats – see *The Cricketer Magazine*, 18 August 1956.

[23] R. Bowen (1970), op. cit., *The Cricket Statistician*, Summer 1986, 29.

[24] *The Post Man*, June 1709.

[25] See J. Arlott's introduction in J. Nyren, *The Young Cricketers Tutor* (Davis-Poynter, 1974).

[26] G. Williams, op. cit., 383–4.

[27] H. M. Waddington, 'Games and Athletics in Bygone Wales', *Transactions of the Honourable Society of Cymmrodorion*, (1954), 84–100.

[28] I am very grateful to Bob Harragan for providing information on John Taylor's travels.

[29] H. M. Waddington, op. cit., 93–5.

[30] Badminton Manorial Records for Brecknockshire, NLW, MS 224.

[31] See *Bygones relating to Wales and the Border Counties*, 1891–92, 273–4.

[32] H. M. Waddington, op. cit., 94.

[33] *South Wales Press*, April 1882.

[34] T. J. McCann and P. M. Wilkinson, *Sussex Archaeological Collections*, 110, 118–22.

[35] G. M. D. Howat, *Village Cricket* (Newton Abbot, David and Charles, 1978), 11.

[36] G. Williams, op. cit., 381–2.

[37] *Wisden Cricketers Almanack* for 1985 (John Wisden), 253 refers to a match in 1763 at Pembroke as being the first in Wales. Subsequent research has failed to confirm this, or discover the source of the reference, based on the work of H. S. Altham and E. W. Swanton (1947), op. cit. It could well be a confusion with a match at Pembroke College, Oxford referred to in the diary of Revd James Woodforde see *The Cricketer*, Winter Annual, 1929/30.

Chapter 2

[1] C. Brookes, *English Cricket: The Game and its Players throughout the Ages* (Weidenfeld and Nicholson, 1978).

[2] *Hereford Journal*, 31 July 1783. The quote mentions an 'ordinary' which was a light lunch, rather than a grand banquet for the teams.

[3] See D. Williams, *The Rebecca Riots* (Cardiff, University of Wales Press, 1955), especially Chapter 1; F. Jones, 'The Vaughans of Golden Grove', *Transactions of the Honourable Society of Cymmrodorion*, (1963), 96–145, 223–50; A. G. Prys-Jones, *The*

Story of Carmarthenshire – Volume Two (Merlin Press, 1972); F. Jones, 'Cwmgwili and its families', *Carmarthenshire Historian*, (1976), 20–66.

⁴ Cwmgwili 131, Dyfed Record Office, Carmarthen.

⁵ D. Williams, op. cit., 23.

⁶ Cwmgwili 131, op. cit.

⁷ P. Jenkins, *The Making of a Ruling Class – The Glamorgan Gentry 1640–1710* (Cambridge University Press, 1983), especially Chapter 7.

⁸ *Hereford Journal*, 5 May 1785.

⁹ D. T. M. Jones MS no. 1213, NLW.

¹⁰ 'The History of Monmouth C.C.', *The South Wales Cricketer's Magazine* (August 1949), Vol. 2, no. 4.

¹¹ There are few records as well about other games in which the Monmouth side may have taken part. Instead, there are indirect clues, such as the reference in E. Anthony's *Herefordshire Cricket* (Hereford, Anthony Brothers, 1903) to a match in 1837 between Abergavenny and Pontypool as 'the first match played in the neighbourhood for nearly half a century'.

¹² *Carmarthen Journal*, 30 July 1819.

¹³ *Bristol Gazette*, 21 September 1815; *The Cambrian*, 5 August 1820.

¹⁴ *The Cambrian*, 4 August 1819.

¹⁵ A. R. Hawkins, *Cwrt-y-Gollen and its Families* (Brecknock Museum, 1967).

¹⁶ The Raglan Tithe Apportionment, D/Pa 36–17, Gwent Record Office.

¹⁷ *The Cambrian* for 9 September 1836 reported how around 100 club members gathered at the Beaufort Arms for their end of season ball.

¹⁸ *The Cambrian*, 25 August 1825; *Hereford Journal*, 2 September 1829. The formation of the club at Raglan may have also been an offshoot of the gatherings at Cwrt-y-Gollen.

¹⁹ *The Cambrian*, 29 August 1829. Indeed, one of the reasons why the Raglan club achieved so much early publicity in the press was through the involvement with the club of Reginald Blewitt of Llantarnam Abbey, who in 1829 established the *Monmouthshire Merlin* and served as its editor until 1832.

²⁰ T. Bevan, 'Glamorgan Communications – Number One: The Story of the Roads', *Glamorgan Historian*, 1 (1963) 146–57.

²¹ *The Cambrian*, 29 June 1831.

²² *Monmouthshire Merlin*, 29 August 1835.

²³ The *Cardiff and Merthyr Guardian* for 23 May 1845 reported how 'Cardiff C.C. have met upon three occasions since our last edition and have engaged with great ardour and spirit in the delightful exercise.'

²⁴ *Cardiff and Merthyr Guardian*, 13 June 1845.

²⁵ G. B. Buckley, *Fresh Light on Pre-Victorian Cricket* (Birmingham, Cotterell, 1935); *Monmouthshire Merlin*, 5 May 1832.

²⁶ *Monmouthshire Merlin*, 21 June 1838.

²⁷ *Monmouthshire Merlin*, 28 July 1833, 31 May 1838 and 24 August 1838.

²⁸ *Monmouthshire Merlin*, 15 July 1834; 21 June 1838.

²⁹ *The Cambrian*, 4 September 1830; *Monmouthshire Merlin*, 20 August 1832.

³⁰ E. Anthony, op. cit., 11. For a report on the match see *Monmouthshire Merlin*, 13 July 1836.

³¹ *Carmarthen Journal*, 27 August 1830.

³² *Bell's Life*, 9 September 1837.

³³ *The Cambrian*, 9 and 31 July 1831.

[34] The Vivian Collection, Letters to H. H. Vivian, C3, NLW. A similar 'Holiday Club' was formed by young gentlemen in Cardiff during the 1850s.

[35] *The Cambrian*, 10 September 1841, 6 September 1844 and 9 September 1846.

[36] *The Cambrian*, 28 September 1840.

[37] *Cardiff and Merthyr Guardian*, 3 July 1847.

[38] *Cardiff and Merthyr Guardian*, 3 August 1848.

[39] *Cardiff and Merthyr Guardian*, 1 September 1848.

[40] *Cardiff and Merthyr Guardian*, 16 and 30 July 1849.

[41] *The Cambrian*, 10 October 1840.

[42] *Monmouthshire Merlin*, 25 August 1835; 23 May 1840.

[43] For a more detailed description, see D. H. James, *History of Briton Ferry Cricket Club* (the club, 1981), 10–11.

[44] Newport played their games on the Marshes near the River Usk, whilst Cardiff's earliest matches were at Splott Farm and at Longcross, close to the road to Newport, before moving to a field behind the Cardiff Arms close to the River Taff – see *Cardiff and Merthyr Guardian*, 14 August, 12 September 1846.

[45] For other differences see G. D. West, *The Elevens of England* (Darf, 1988).

[46] Sanders was also guilty of not paying attention, with a letter in the *Monmouthshire Merlin* for 12 June 1858 saying that 'he was not attending to the game; if he had been doing so, he would have seen the ball and could easily caught it or got out of its way, as it was by no means a swift ball'.

[47] E. Anthony, op. cit., 61; *The Cambrian*, 3 August 1853. It was not just Welsh cricket with these features as G. D. West, op. cit. showed how George Parr, considered to be the premier batsman in England, took six hours to score twenty-five runs in a rain-affected match in 1848.

[48] *Monmouthshire Merlin*, 5 May 1832.

[49] *Monmouthshire Merlin*, 31 July 1836.

[50] *Monmouthshire Merlin*, 9 August 1844.

[51] See *The Cambrian*'s report of Swansea's games in 1848.

[52] *Cardiff and Merthyr Guardian*, 14 August 1846.

[53] *Carmarthen Journal*, 31 July 1846.

[54] *Cardiff and Merthyr Guardian*, 23 September 1854.

[55] *The Cambrian*, 24 August 1855.

[56] G. Howat, *Village Cricket* (Newton Abbot, David and Charles, 1979).

[57] *The Cambrian*, 20 August 1841.

[58] *Monmouthshire Merlin*, 4 July 1840.

[59] *Looking Back – A History of Abergavenny C.C. 1834–1984* (Abergavenny, Dover and Co., 1985), 6.

[60] *Carmarthen Journal*, 22 September 1843.

[61] *Monmouthshire Merlin*, 25 August 1837.

[62] *Monmouthshire Merlin*, 5 June 1838.

[63] The Diary of Lewis Weston Dillwyn, 31 July 1845, NLW Manuscript Collection.

[64] *Monmouthshire Merlin*, 6 August 1836; see also the report on the conviviality after the match between Neath and Swansea in *The Cambrian*, 21 July 1848.

[65] *The Cambrian*, 29 September 1854.

[66] *Monmouthshire Merlin*, 2 June 1838.

[67] *Monmouthshire Merlin*, 23 May 1840.

[68] *Cardiff and Merthyr Guardian*, 11 July 1840.

[69] *Cardiff and Merthyr Guardian*, 8 August, 26 September 1840.

[70] *Cardiff and Merthyr Guardian*, 27 July 1839.

[71] *Cardiff and Merthyr Guardian*, 20 August 1842.

[72] *Cardiff and Merthyr Guardian*, 28 September 1849.

[73] *The Cambrian*, 3 August 1855.

[74] *Monmouthshire Merlin*, 15 August 1846.

[75] *Cardiff and Merthyr Guardian*, 2 May 1846.

[76] *Monmouthshire Merlin*, 27 September 1834.

[77] *Monmouthshire Merlin*, 20 June 1845.

[78] *Monmouthshire Merlin*, 8 August 1851.

[79] *Monmouthshire Merlin*, 30 July 1852; 7 July 1855.

[80] *The Cambrian*, 4 July 1845.

[81] *The Cambrian*, 7 May 1852.

[82] *The Cambrian*, 6 August 1852.

[83] *Cardiff and Merthyr Guardian*, 8 June, 14 September 1850.

[84] *Cardiff and Merthyr Guardian*, 11 August 1854.

[85] C. Brookes, *English Cricket: The Game and its Players throughout the Ages* (Weidenfield and Nicholson, 1978).

[86] *Monmouthshire Merlin*, 14 July 1834.

[87] *Monmouthshire Merlin*, 8 August 1832.

[88] *Cardiff and Merthyr Guardian*, 27 July 1833.

[89] *Carmarthen Journal*, 5 August 1836.

[90] *Monmouthshire Merlin*, 4 August 1837.

[91] *The Cambrian*, 23 August 1850. In 1864 Pascoe St Leger Grenfell formed Kilvey CC and acted as its president in its formative years – see *The Cambrian*, 7 July 1865. The family also provided housing and schools for its workers, and financed the erection of churches. The business was once described as 'one of the soundest and most lasting commercial organisations in the district' – M. E. Chamberlain, 'The Grenfells of Kilvey', *Glamorgan History*, 9 (1972), 123–42.

[92] A. Stewart, *Family Tapestry* (Swansea, 1961).

[93] *The Cambrian*, 27 August 1847. In 1854 he also made a generous donation to boost cricket in Neath, as reported in *The Cambrian*, 5 May 1854.

[94] *The Cambrian*, 27 August 1852.

[95] Vivian's brother-in-law was closely connected with the Prince Regent and Vivian himself knew leading political figures such as Frederick Engels and had even travelled to Elba to visit Napoleon. His son H. H. Vivian, later Lord Swansea, entertained Gladstone, as well as the Prince and Princess of Wales (later to be King Edward VII and Queen Alexandria) when they visited Swansea – see R. A. Griffiths, *The Vivians and Singleton House* (Llandysul, Gomer Press, 1988).

[96] A. Stewart, op. cit., 119.

[97] Vivian offered £1,000 to anyone who could devise a remedy to solve smoke pollution from his works, and during the 1830s, he ensured the town had an adequate mail service, helped open a branch of the Bank of England in Swansea, provided houses and schools for his workers at Hafod, and supplemented their wages with free coal and a rudimentary pension. He was also a leading figure behind schemes to develop Swansea Harbour, and oversaw the construction of many churches, schools and hospitals – see R. A. Griffiths, op. cit.; S. Jones, 'The Vivian Family', *Transactions of the Port Talbot Historical Society*, (1974), 5–18.

[98] *Cardiff and Merthyr Guardian*, 19 July 1834, 22 August 1835.

[99] This game took place on Crumlin Burrows and could have been an added stimulus

for providing Swansea with a decent wicket at Singleton – *The Cambrian*, 27 August 1847.

[100] Brecon's membership lists are held in Brecknock Library.

[101] *Looking Back*, op. cit.

[102] R. J. Harragan, *The History of Llanelli C.C.* (Llanelli Borough Council 1990), 10–11.

[103] *Monmouthshire Merlin*, 25 August 1837.

[104] *The Cambrian*, 3 August 1838.

[105] Chepstow C.C. Rules and Regulations for 1838, Gwent Record Office.

[106] *Monmouthshire Merlin*, 22 May 1841; 18 May 1849.

[107] *Carmarthen Journal*, 7 July 1845.

[108] *The Cambrian*, 23 June 1848.

[109] *The Cambrian*, 24 June, 12 August 1853.

[110] *The Cambrian*, 2 July 1852.

[111] *The Cambrian*, 9 July 1852.

[112] *The Cambrian*, 16 June 1854.

[113] *The Cambrian*, 15 July 1853.

[114] C. Brookes, op. cit., 33.

[115] He must have liked the Raglan area a lot because he named his third son Raglan George Henry.

[116] Benjamin Hall became Commissioner of Works and Public Buildings in 1855 and in this capacity oversaw the construction of the great clock of Westminster, which through his links with the project became known as Big Ben.

Chapter 3

[1] The newspapers used were the *Bristol Gazette*, *The Cambrian*, *Carmarthen Journal*, *Monmouthshire Merlin*, *Cardiff and Merthyr Guardian*, *Hereford Times*, and *The Welshman*.

[2] *The Cambrian*, 9 July 1831.

[3] *Monmouthshire Merlin*, 30 August 1834.

[4] D. Egan, *People, Protests and Politics*, (Llandysul, Gomer Press, 1987).

[5] D. J. V. Jones, *Before Rebecca* (Merthyr, 1973); G. O. Pierce, 'Nonconformity and Politics', in A. J. Roderick (ed.), *Wales Through the Ages: Volume Two* (Llandybïe, Christopher Davies, 1960), 168–76.

[6] H. Carter and S. Wheatley, *Merthyr Tydfil in 1851*, University of Wales Social Science Monograph, Number 7.

[7] K. O. Morgan, *Rebirth of a Nation* (Oxford University Press, 1981), 71.

[8] D. Egan, op. cit., 13. The pubs and unlicensed beerhouses provided the solace the workers needed from the rigours of work and G. A. Williams has recounted tales of how nobody worked in Risca for two days after heavy drinking sessions on pay day – see G. A. Williams, 'The Emergence of a Working-class Movement', in A. J. Roderick, op. cit.

[9] J. B. Hilling, 'The Buildings of Cardiff', *Glamorgan Historian*, 6, 28–82; see also M. J. Daunton, *Coal Metropolis, Cardiff 1870–1914* (Leicester University Press, 1977).

[10] *Cardiff and Merthyr Guardian*, 12 May 1849.

[11] *Cardiff and Merthyr Guardian*, 4 August 1849.

[12] *Swansea Journal*, 23 August 1843. Illegal beerhouses abounded in the industrial centres and G. A. Williams, op. cit., 141, estimated that there were 200 in Dowlais in 1836.

[13] *The Cambrian*, 21 July 1854.

[14] D. J. V. Jones, *The Last Rising* (Merthyr, 1985).

[15] R. Sissons, *The Players: A Social History of the Professional Cricketer* (Kingswood Press, 1988).

[16] D. Williams, *The Rebecca Riots* (Cardiff, University of Wales Press, 1955), 156.

[17] *Monmouthshire Merlin*, 27 August 1840.

[18] *Monmouthshire Merlin*, 5 and 12 June, and 7 August 1841.

[19] *Monmouthshire Merlin*, 21 August 1841.

[20] Napier was beaten up whilst trying to arrest four men at Cwm Cille Fach Farm near Llangyfelach, but he soon recovered from his injuries and three days later was playing cricket in Swansea – see E. R. Baker, *The History of the Glamorgan Constabulary*, Part 9, 8–15.

[21] *Monmouthshire Merlin*, 11 June, 11 July 1841. Napier learnt his cricket whilst at the Royal Military Academy, Woolwich and he served with the Rifle Brigade in Monmouthshire from 1838.

[22] *Monmouthshire Merlin*, 18 August 1843.

[23] E. R. Baker, op. cit., Part 37, 5–9 and *Glamorgan Police Magazine*, vol. 7, no. 4, 1559–1561.

[24] *Cardiff and Merthyr Guardian*, 1 June 1839.

[25] *Monmouthshire Merlin*, 30 June 1840.

[26] *Hereford Journal*, 9 June 1840.

[27] R. J. Harragan, *History of Llanelli C.C.* (Llanelli Borough Council, 1990), 1.

[28] *South Wales Press*, quoted in R. J. Harragan, op. cit., 4.

[29] *Monmouthshire Merlin*, 14 May 1842.

[30] *The Cambrian*, 28 August 1841.

[31] *Monmouthshire Merlin*, 26 July 1844.

[32] *Monmouthshire Merlin*, 27 June 1845.

[33] There were hidden dangers in using this method of transport and then tethering horses for a long time in the heat of a summer's day. The *Monmouthshire Merlin* for 31 August 1839 reported how four of the Raglan players were injured leaving the Forest of Dean ground because one of their horses which had become restless during the sunny afternoon, bolted and tipped over their carriage.

[34] A. Jacks (ed.), *Chepstow C.C. The First 150 Years, 1838–1988* (the club, 1988).

[35] The flow lines and distances are given in terms of travel in a straight line.

[36] *Cardiff and Merthyr Guardian*, 11 September 1847.

[37] *The Cambrian*, 10 September 1841; 28 September 1843.

[38] R. J. Harragan, op. cit., 15.

[39] *The Cambrian*, 16 September 1853.

[40] D. G. West, *The Elevens of England* (Darf, 1988).

[41] K. E. Kissack, *Victorian Monmouth* (Ledbury, Bosbury Press, 1986), 184.

Chapter 4

[1] A. A. Thomson, 'Lords and the Early Champions, 1787–1865', in E. W. Swanton (ed.), *Barclay's World of Cricket* (Collins, 1980), 12.

[2] E. Anthony, *Herefordshire Cricket* (Hereford, Anthony Brothers, 1903).

[3] *Carmarthen Journal*, 19 August 1850.

[4] He was the town's mayor in 1851/2 and 1861/2 – see the *Cardiff and Merthyr Guardian*, 8 July 1864. Several of Cuthbertson's gentlemen friends, including J. H. Vivian, contributed to the fund – *The Cambrian*, 5 May 1854.

[5] *The Cambrian*, 8 June 1855.

[6] *Cardiff and Merthyr Guardian*, 9 June 1855.

[7] He also joined in with their practice and helped coach them – *Cardiff and Merthyr Guardian*, 16 June 1855.

[8] *Cardiff and Merthyr Guardian*, 11 August 1855.

[9] *The Cambrian*, 16 and 30 May 1856.

[10] *The Cambrian*, 6 June 1856.

[11] Grace and Pocock did not appear in this match, possibly because the financial inducements were not attractive enough for them to travel over from Thornbury.

[12] *Monmouthshire Merlin*, 21 July 1849.

[13] The *Monmouthshire Merlin* for 1 August 1851 does not give their real names, but instead 'Monmouthshire Lillywhite' versus 'Gloucestershire Pet', which could have been Homfray against an 18-year-old Henry Grace. The same paper reported on 25 June 1852 that Homfray also ran a foot race over 150 yards after a match to raise funds and there was betting of one sovereign a side on the outcome.

[14] *Cardiff and Merthyr Guardian*, 18 September 1858.

[15] *Monmouthshire Merlin*, 19 August 1858.

[16] *Monmouthshire Merlin*, 25 June 1859.

[17] *Cardiff and Merthyr Guardian*, 15 August 1857.

[18] Homfray was also a playing member of Clifton – see the *Western Mail*, 19 June 1869. For a history of the South Wales CC see D. T. Smith, *The South Wales Cricket Club 1859–1886* (privately published, 1986).

[19] D. T. Smith, op. cit., 23.

[20] A return fixture was arranged against Surrey at Newport in 1861, but it was 'postponed for an indefinite period' – ibid., 8.

[21] Ibid.

[22] W. G. Grace, *Cricket* (Bristol, Arrowsmith, 1891), 52.

[23] These performances helped E. M. Grace establish his reputation in English cricket, and won him a place in George Parr's team to tour Australia in 1863.

[24] Wisden described Grace as the most dangerous batsman in England during the early 1860s, and a testament to his abilities was that he amassed over 3,000 runs in 1863. He adopted what was a revolutionary style by hitting across the line, and it is said that he terrified so many bowlers in the West Country that it was seriously suggested that E. M. should not be allowed to play.

[25] The *Monmouthshire Merlin* for 7 July 1860 includes a reference to Homfray's XI playing William Lloyd's XI at Newport, whilst *The Cambrian* for 31 August 1860 included a report on his team's visit to Swansea.

[26] J. D. Coldham, 'Notes on Early South Wales Cricket', *South Wales Cricketer's Magazine* (July 1949), 5.

[27] The *Western Telegraph* of 9 July 1863 even described Homfray's side as 'a band of wandering Welshmen'.

[28] *The Cambrian*, 21 August 1863.

[29] *The Cambrian*, 24 August 1866.

[30] *The Cambrian*, 21 August 1863.

[31] Lloyd also became involved with many of the social issues and problems in Breconshire, including stopping flooding, providing a water supply and the provision of a public library and mental hospital, whilst his two brothers Penry and Thomas Conway Lloyd became Chief Constable of Brecon and a colonel in the South Wales Borderers respectively.

[32] W. G. Grace, op. cit., 87–8.

[33] Ibid., 88.

[34] *J. D. Llewelyn: the first photographer in Wales* (Welsh Arts Council, 1980). Some of his early shots include a young J.T.D.

[35] *South Wales Daily Post*, 7 July 1927.

[36] It was a common practice to guest for several clubs, allowing the gentlemen to play on a regular basis. J.T.D. followed suit by guesting for sides in west Wales, including Llanelly – see *The Cambrian*, 2 September 1859.

[37] R. W. Thomas of Saundersfoot, quoted in R. J. Harragan, *A History of Llanelli C.C.* (Llanelli Borough Council, 1990), 21–2.

[38] *The Cambrian*, 6 May 1864.

[39] *Cardiff and Merthyr Guardian*, 6 October 1865 – his talents as a bowler were more frequently reported in the press, such as his feat in 1870 of dismissing W. G. Grace. In 1881 he took all ten wickets against Llanelly, and in 1865 took eight wickets for the South Wales CC against the Gentlemen of Kent.

[40] *The Cambrian*, 3 May 1861.

[41] *Cardiff and Merthyr Guardian*, 27 September 1862.

[42] The new name also helped to defeat the creditors of the old club. See W. I. Davies, *Neath C.C. – A Short History* in The Borough of Neath's pamphlet to celebrate the 1951 Festival of Britain. They held the name Cadoxton until 25 March 1898 when they became Neath Athletic Association – Cricket Section, then Gnoll Park CC and finally Neath CC in 1905.

[43] *The Cambrian*, 15 May 1863.

[44] *The Cambrian*, 17 and 24 July 1863.

[45] *Cardiff and Merthyr Guardian*, 27 May 1864.

[46] *The Cambrian*, 9 and 16 September 1864.

[47] *The Cambrian*, 13 October 1865.

[48] The Mackworths were the MPs for Cardiff between 1739 and 1790, whilst Sir Herbert Mackworth was a partner in a banking business in London. It was when Sir Herbert lived at The Gnoll that the house and grounds were extended.

[49] See W. I. Davies, op. cit., 27. For further history on the Gnoll ground see A. K. Hignell, *The Grounds of Glamorgan* (A.C.S., Nottingham, 1985).

[50] In 1865 they also played the GWR at Swindon – see *Cardiff and Merthyr Guardian*, 18 August 1865.

[51] *The Cambrian*, 29 June; 6, 13 and 20 July; 10 August 1866.

[52] Some sources claim it was Lovering who bagged Grace's wicket – see W. I. Davies, op. cit. George Howitt was also hired by clubs in Derbyshire for matches against the All-England XI between 1865 and 1870, and was presumably based in the north of England.

[53] R. J. Harragan, 'The First Touring Team in Wales', *The Cricket Statistician*, 44, 27–8.

[54] *The Cambrian*, 17 July 1868.

[55] J. Mulvaney and R. Harcourt, *Cricket Walkabout* (Melbourne, Melbourne University Press, 1967).

[56] *Western Mail*, 19 June 1869.

[57] At the time, Lovering was a painter in Neath, and despite professional status, this was his debut at Lord's. As a result of his performance, and J.T.D.'s contacts, Lovering secured an engagement at Eton College the following year.

Chapter 5

[1] For general background information on the evolution of county cricket in Wales, see the two articles by R. Bowen in *The Cricketer*, 2 September 1961, and the Winter Annual.

See also R. J. Harragan, 'Cricket in Wales 1763–1900: Some notes', *Journal of the Cricket Society*, 10 (1985) 1, 37–41; 2, 67–8; 3, 38–9 and R. J. Harragan, 'Early Welsh County Cricket', *The Cricket Statistician*, 70 (1990), 35–8.

² *Cardiff and Merthyr Guardian*, 8 and 15 June 1850; 28 May, 8 July and 6 August 1853.

³ *Lillywhite's Scores and Biographies* for 1855.

⁴ *Carmarthen Journal*, 24 August 1846.

⁵ *The Welshman*, 17 August 1852.

⁶ *The Welshman*, 10 September 1853.

⁷ *Western Telegraph*, 7 July 1854.

⁸ *The Welshman*, 8 September 1854.

⁹ K. O Morgan, *Rebirth of a Nation* (Oxford University Press, 1981), 90.

¹⁰ *Carmarthen Journal*, 26 September 1859.

¹¹ *Carmarthen Journal*, 21 July 1860.

¹² *The Welshman*, July 1860 – indeed the correspondent of the *Western Telegraph* described it as Carmarthenshire against Haverfordwest.

¹³ *The Cambrian*, 16 August 1861.

¹⁴ For instance, the 1863 contest at Swansea saw gentlemen from Llanelli, Llandovery, Carmarthen and Haverfordwest facing a Glamorgan side drawn from Cardiff, Swansea and Cadoxton, including J.T.D. – *The Cambrian*, 19 June 1863.

¹⁵ *Lillywhite's Scores and Biographies for 1864*.

¹⁶ *Llanelly Guardian*, 23 June 1864.

¹⁷ Carmarthenshire Record Office, A19, Vol. 37, 79.

¹⁸ Ibid.

¹⁹ *Cardiff and Merthyr Guardian*, 15 June 1866.

²⁰ Tredegar Park Deposition, Letter no. 71/637 to Hon. F. C. Morgan, dated 30 October 1868, NLW Manuscript Collection. F. C. Morgan was a keen huntsman and saw cricket as a means of keeping in touch, and taking part in recreation, with his gentlemen friends during the summer. See R. Phillips, *Tredegar: The History of an Agricultural Estate* (Newport, Tredegar Memorial Trust, 1990).

²¹ K. E. Kissack, *Victorian Monmouth* (Ledbury, Bosbury Press, 1986), 184–6.

²² A scorebook in Brecknock Museum states on its cover 'Breconshire C.C. 1848–1860.'

²³ The involvement of J. J. de Winton provided yet another link between the nineteenth-century county games and the Cwmgwili gatherings of the eighteenth century, because he married Miss Emma Philipps, the grand-daughter of J. G. Philipps – see F. Jones, 'Cwmgwili and its Families', *Carmarthenshire Historian*, (1976), 20–66.

²⁴ He stood in 1836 as a Liberal in the Borough of Brecon Parliamentary Elections and switched in 1859 to a Tory candidate, but he lost on both occasions.

²⁵ *The Cambrian*, 21 August 1863, and the match scores in the Breconshire scorebook in Brecknock Museum.

²⁶ *Brecon Reporter*, June 1864.

²⁷ *Western Telegraph*, 28 September 1855.

²⁸ *Cardiff and Merthyr Guardian*, 9 August 1862. For information on the Nicholl's Estate, see H. M. Thomas, *Merthyr Mawr House* (Glamorgan Archive Service, 1976).

²⁹ *Cardiff and Merthyr Guardian*, 11 August, 6 October 1865.

³⁰ *Monmouthshire Merlin*, 12 October 1859.

³¹ *The Cambrian*, 24 August 1866.

³² *Cardiff and Merthyr Guardian*, 20 July 1866.

[33] R. J. Harragan (ed.), *Bridgend C.C. 1840–1990: 150th Anniversary Souvenir* (the club, 1990).

[34] *Cardiff and Merthyr Guardian*, 15 June 1866.

[35] *The Cambrian*, 26 June 1868.

[36] A. Trollope (ed.), 'British Sports and Pastimes', *Saint Paul's Magazine*, (1868), 302.

[37] *The Cambrian*, 5 March 1869.

[38] *Swansea and Glamorgan Herald*, 19 May 1869.

[39] The *Monmouthshire Merlin* for 16 June 1869 described it as 'the match of the season'.

[40] *Western Mail*, 16 June 1869.

Chapter 6

[1] Cardiff: Cardiff, St Mary's, Adamsdown, Roath YMCA, Bute Docks, Beaufort, Blue Cap, Canton, Windsor, Prince of Wales, Albion, Drapers, Ironmongers, Schoolmasters, Excelsior, Whitchurch, Taff Vale.

Newport: Newport, Commercials, Great Western Railway, West End, United Atheneum, Christchurch, Engineers, Oaks, St Woolo's, Uskside, Tradesmen.

Neath: Neath, Railways, Neath Abbey, Cadoxton, Penllergaer, Neath Juniors, Early Risers, Tradesmen.

Swansea: Swansea, Union, Cambrian, Prince of Wales, Hafod, Oxford Street, Ravenhill.

Llanelli: Llanelly, Cross Inn, Juveniles, Prince of Wales, Victoria.

[2] *Cardiff and Merthyr Guardian*, 4 July 1868.

[3] *Carmarthen Journal*, 9 June 1867.

[4] *The Cambrian*, 28 May 1866.

[5] *Cardiff and Merthyr Guardian*, 23 August 1867.

[6] *Pontypool Free Press*, 30 June 1860.

[7] *Brecon Reporter*, 20 September 1858; *Monmouthshire Merlin*, 12 September 1861.

[8] *The Cambrian*, 21 August 1867; 10 July 1868. The census for 1861 gives Llantilio Crossenny as having 748 residents and 740 for Magor, whilst the 1871 census for Penmaen records 161 inhabitants.

[9] *Monmouthshire Merlin*, 26 August 1865.

[10] *The Cambrian*, 20 September 1861.

[11] *Cardiff and Merthyr Guardian*, 16 August 1862; *The Welshman* for September 1859 also mentions a heated dispute between Carmarthen and the town's Training College.

[12] The *Llanelly Guardian* for 23 June 1860 mentions that the Llanelly 2nd XI travelled to play the new Dafen club.

[13] The *Monmouthshire Merlin* for 23 June 1866 reported on a match between Ebbw Vale Seconds and Beaufort Seconds.

[14] *The Cambrian*, 3 May 1861.

[15] *Carmarthen Journal*, 2 August 1861.

[16] *The Cambrian*, 3 August 1855.

[17] *The Cambrian*, 24 June 1853; 24 June and 18 September 1857.

[18] *Cardiff and Merthyr Guardian*, 10 July 1863; *Monmouthshire Merlin*, 22 June 1860.

[19] *Carmarthen Journal*, 3 August 1867.

[20] D. Williams, *A History of Modern Wales* (Murray, 1950), 255.

[21] Charles Kingsley quoted in R. J. Holt, *Sport and the British* (Oxford University Press, 1989), 93.

[22] R. J. Holt, ibid, 83–4.

[23] C. Brookes, *English Cricket: The Game and its Players throughout the Ages* (Weidenfield and Nicholson, 1978), 91; 'Cricket at Lord's', *Belgravia*, (September 1871), 219.

[24] 1864 Clarendon Commission's Report on the Public Schools, quoted in W. F. Mandle, 'Games People Played', *Historical Studies*, (April 1972), 523.

[25] This had been an earlier stumbling block, as *The Cambrian* for 10 June 1837 included a letter from a Swansea school which stated that they were 'ready with the assistance of two or three old schoolfellows to play at cricket any eleven gentlemen residing in or about Swansea'.

[26] *The Cambrian*, 12 September 1856.

[27] *The Cambrian*, 6 September 1850.

[28] *Llanelly Guardian*, 11 July 1863; One of the earliest inter-school games in the valleys was between Mr Kernick's school and Mr Fuller's establishment – see *Cardiff and Merthyr Guardian*, 4 October 1856.

[29] It was established as the Cowbridge Free School in 1648 by the Stradling family of St Donat's Castle – see I. Davies, *A Certaine Schoole* (Cowbridge, Brown and Son, 1967).

[30] Manuscript 6516A at the NLW Aberystwyth. See also the Appendices in I. Davies, op. cit.

[31] Ibid. especially the entries for 10 May, 19 and 20 August.

[32] Ibid. especially 15 and 16 October.

[33] Lessons took place during the morning and evening.

[34] I. Davies, op. cit., 64 stated that Harper, a graduate of Jesus College, only accepted the Cowbridge post on the condition that the Oxford college paid for the rebuilding of the grammar school.

[35] He later wrote 'I became Headmaster of the school and was keenly anxious for its interests, and I venture to hope not unsuccessful in promoting them.' See H. D. Harper, 'Jesus College and Cowbridge School: a letter to H. H. Vivian', Manuscript LB41: 373.51 at Cardiff Central Library.

[36] *Cardiff and Merthyr Guardian*, 28 September 1849.

[37] He transformed the Dorset school into one of the leading English public schools, and provided it with its own cricket field – see D. F. Gibbs, *A History of Cricket at Sherborne School*. He later returned to Oxford to become Principal of Jesus College.

[38] *Cardiff and Merthyr Guardian*, 6 September 1856.

[39] *The Cambrian*, 4 September 1857; *Cardiff and Merthyr Guardian*, 19 September 1857.

[40] *Cardiff and Merthyr Guardian*, 24 August 1861; *The Cambrian*, 4 September 1857.

[41] *The Cambrian*, 2 June 1865.

[42] *Cardiff and Merthyr Guardian*, 8 September 1860; *The Cambrian*, 29 May 1863.

[43] *The Star of Gwent*, 14 September 1867 recorded a game between the Revd T. L. Lister's XI and the Albion club of Bassaleg.

[44] Whittington's family hailed from the Neath area, and his brother William played for Cadoxton. W. P. Whittington also attended Fettes in Scotland.

[45] W. G. Evans, *A History of Llandovery College* (Trustees of Llandovery College, 1981).

[46] Ibid., 36.

[47] *Llanelly Guardian*, 29 May 1863; see also the entry for 20 May 1863 in the diary of William Rees, Manuscript 2.647 in Cardiff Central Library.

[48] *The Cambrian*, 16 September 1864.

[49] Quote by David Samuel of W. G. Evans, op. cit., 73.

[50] In 1874 Whittington left Llandovery to become head of Ruthin School.

[51] E. G. Parry, *Christ College, Brecon, 1541–1991: An Illustrated History* (the school, 1991).

[52] In other schools it was the practice for the Headmaster's House to challenge the rest of the pupils, so this was further evidence of the prominent role that Farrar played in the sporting life of the school. I am most grateful to David Smith of Corsham for all this information on Christ College.

[53] J. Lewis, *Swansea Guide for 1851* (reprinted in 1990 by West Glamorgan County Council), 48.

[54] *The Cambrian*, 12 September 1856.

[55] *Swansea Grammar School 1682–1932*, Special Issue of the Swansea Grammar School Magazine, issued on the occasion of the celebration of the 250th Anniversary of the foundation of the school. Swansea Library SW 3.192.

[56] Ibid.

[57] *The Cambrian*,18 September 1863.

[58] *The Cambrian*, 5 October 1866; 23 May 1868.

[59] *Swansea Grammar School 1682–1932*, op. cit.

[60] *The Welshman*, 3 October 1857.

[61] *The Cambrian*, 31 August 1866.

[62] The *Western Telegraph* for 30 August 1862 recorded the Philipps of Picton Castle playing against the Grammar School.

[63] *Hereford Times*, 27 May 1860.

[64] *Pontypool Free Press*, 13 July 1861.

[65] Quoted in D. T. W. Price, *A History of St David's University College, Lampeter*, Vol. One, Chapter 7 (Cardiff, University of Wales Press, 1977).

[66] *The Welshman*, 11 June 1852.

[67] I am indebted to Gareth Hughes, a lecturer at Trinity College and their Principal Clive Jones-Davies for this information and access to Edmunds's diary.

[68] As a result of their success an annual series of games with the town club was staged – *The Welshman*, 8 September 1856.

[69] *Carmarthen Journal*, 13 June 1867.

[70] W. David, *The Pedigrees of the David family of Fairwater* (Cardiff, Lewis, 1894).

[71] *Cardiff and Merthyr Guardian*, 8 September 1860; 22 August 1868.

Chapter 7

[1] H. M. Waddington, 'Games and Athletics in Bygone Wales', *Transactions of the Honourable Society of Cymmrodorion*, (1954), 84–100.

[2] I. Davies, *A Certaine Schoole* (Cowbridge, Brown and Son, 1967), 89–90.

[3] *Carmarthen Journal*, 19 June 1845.

[4] Williams quoted in D. Smith and G. Williams, *Fields of Praise* (Cardiff, University of Wales Press, 1981), 22.

[5] *Western Telegraph*, 29 June 1855.

[6] *Llanelly Guardian*, 30 May 1863.

[7] *The Cambrian*, 13 October 1865.

[8] Other sides were also formed by Muscular Christians around this time, with the *Hereford Times* for 19 May 1866 reporting on how the Revds James Horrox and Arthur

Wyatt established a side at Raglan. Similarly, *The Cambrian* for 16 August 1867 stated that the Revd William St. G. Lowther of Nicholaston parish on the Gower Peninsula had formed a team to play annual contests against sides from Swansea. Lowther was previously a vicar in Wiltshire, Devon and Yorkshire, and served at the Gower parish from 1865 until 1873, during which he actively encouraged his parishioners to play cricket. I am grateful to Matthew Pinsent and the staff at Church House for all their help in tracing the careers of these clergymen.

[9] I am grateful to Richard Baxter of Cardiff YMCA for this information.

[10] *Central Glamorgan Gazette*, 16 August 1867; 6 August 1869.

[11] *Swansea and Glamorgan Herald*, 18 August 1866.

[12] *Carmarthen Journal*, 19 October 1866.

[13] *Western Mail*, 20 July 1869.

[14] *The Cambrian*, 17 August 1866.

[15] *Star of Gwent*, 13 July 1867.

[16] The contact may well have been Captain Fyfe, the ex-Newport player who was now stationed in north Wales and playing for Wrexham.

[17] *Wrexham Advertiser*, 6 July 1867; *Western Telegraph*, 29 May 1867.

[18] *Western Mail*, 7 July 1869.

[19] Even the chief engineer, Joseph Tomlinson, played for the club – *Monmouthshire Merlin*, 13 July 1859.

[20] J. Davies, *Cardiff and the Marquesses of Bute* (Cardiff, University of Wales Press, 1981), 279–85. Tom Riches was foreman and works manager to the Bute Dock Trustees, 1869–1872.

[21] *Cardiff and Merthyr Guardian*, 3 September 1859.

[22] *Cardiff and Merthyr Guardian*, 22 July 1864.

[23] *Cardiff and Merthyr Guardian*, 15 August 1864. Railway workers were also responsible for the encouragement of cricket in north Wales, with Bangor CC being formed in 1856 by 'a number of respectable young men connected with the railway'. J. B. Cowell, *A History of Bangor C.C. 1856–1964* (the club, 1965).

[24] B. Thomas, 'The Migration of Labour into the Glamorganshire Coalfield, 1861–1911', *Economica*, 30, 275–94.

[25] *The Cambrian*, 19 August 1859.

[26] T. E. H. Onslow played for Hampshire between 1846 and 1849, whilst C. W. Onslow appeared for Kent in 1841 – see ACS Guides to County Cricketers – *Hampshire Cricketers 1800–1982* (ACS, Nottingham, 1983) and *Kent Cricketers 1834–1983* (ACS, Nottingham, 1984).

[27] Five were from Jesus College, Cambridge, whilst two were vicars from Hereford and Worcester – *The Cambrian*, 31 July 1855.

[28] *Carmarthen Journal*, 28 July 1856; 20 August 1858.

[29] *Western Telegraph*, 24 August 1860.

[30] *Western Mail*, 31 August 1871.

[31] *Cardiff and Merthyr Guardian*, 13 and 27 July 1866; see also *Southerndown CC 1888–1988: Centenary Season Handbook*.

[32] F. S. Ashley-Cooper (1924) in 'Gloucestershire County Cricket', page 12 refers to the first match in August 1858.

[33] *Monmouthshire Merlin*, 31 August 1861.

[34] *Hereford Times*, 4 August 1860.

[35] *Western Telegraph*, 7 September 1861.

[36] *Monmouthshire Merlin*, 18 July 1862.

[37] *Cardiff and Merthyr Guardian*, 24 July 1852. This was just one of a number of philanthropic actions which Lady Guest made for her workers, because in 1855 she financed the erection of Dowlais Central School, and in 1863 covered the cost of opening a Memorial Library. See J. B. Hilling, *Cardiff and the Valleys* (Lund Humphries, 1973), 110.

[38] *Western Telegraph*, 13 May 1857.

[39] *Swansea and Glamorgan Herald*, 18 August 1866.

[40] *Swansea and Glamorgan Herald*, 23 August 1866.

[41] *Swansea and Glamorgan Herald*, 15 September 1866.

[42] *Swansea and Glamorgan Herald*, 23 August 1866.

[43] A. C. Clark, *The Story of Monmouthshire* (Monmouth, Monnow Press, 1972), Volume 2, 32.

[44] An indication of his wealth was that when he died in 1861 his will included property whose value was in excess of £100,000.

[45] *Monmouthshire Merlin*, 28 June 1856.

[46] *Pontypool Free Press*, 30 September 1865.

[47] In 1859 there was a meeting at the Hanbury Arms to discuss the amalgamation of the Pontypool and Pontymoile sides. A merger never took place, probably because the ironworkers wanted their own club and separate identity.

[48] James was appointed in 1853 from a strong panel of candidates, including Hugo Harper, but his appointment was controversial because of his lack of teaching experience, and he resigned after only a short time at the school.

[49] E. Donovan *et al.*, *Pontypool's Pride – The Official History of Pontypool R.F.C. 1868–1988* (Abertillery, Old Bakehouse Publications, 1989).

[50] The new rugby club flourished in the 1870s and benefited from its close connections to the cricket club, with Charles Toye, the honorary secretary of the cricket team, using his contacts during the summer to gain fixtures with the prestigious Newport rugby club.

[51] Kenneth Morgan analysed their emergence and concluded that during the second half of the nineteenth century 'there was emerging a more integrated middle class in the valley towns and villages, also a new group of small businessmen, shopkeepers, solicitors, journalists and sometimes more affluent workmen.' See K. O. Morgan, *Rebirth of a Nation* (Oxford University Press, 1981).

[52] *Pontypool Free Press*, 6 May 1865.

[53] *Monmouthshire Merlin*, 3 June 1865.

Chapter 8

[1] See Breconshire scorebook in Brecknock Museum; *Lillywhite's Scores and Biographies for 1870*; *Western Mail*, 20 and 25 June 1870.

[2] *Lillywhite's*, op. cit.; *Western Mail*, 16 July 1870.

[3] *Western Daily Press*, 16 May 1870.

[4] In the second innings, Grace was bowled by Llewelyn for thirty-two, much to the Doctor's annoyance.

[5] *Lillywhite's*, op. cit.

[6] D. M. Green, *The History of Gloucestershire C.C.C.* (Christopher Helm, 1990), especially Chapter 2.

[7] Glamorganshire easily won by seven wickets in 1871 at Hereford, and recorded their highest ever score of 309–8 in the return match at Cardiff. *Hereford Times*, 24 June 1871, *Lillywhite's Scores and Biographies for 1871*.

[8] *Western Mail*, 6 September 1872.

[9] *Western Mail*, 25 June 1870.

[10] *Western Mail*, 6 July 1871.

[11] One indignant member of the Science and Art club wrote to the *Western Mail* claiming that he did not believe that 'Lord Bute would, if he was aware of it, permit one club to monopolise whenever they chose the whole of the Park field' – *Western Mail*, 8 July 1871.

[12] *Western Mail*, 10 July 1871.

[13] *Western Mail*, 11 July 1871.

[14] *Western Mail*, 19 July 1871.

[15] The former Rugby schoolboy was a JP for Monmouthshire and by playing for both Bassaleg and Cardiff, he was able to play for Monmouthshire and Glamorganshire – see *Western Mail*, 30 May 1873. T. Nicholas, *History and Antiquities of Glamorgan* (Longman, 1874 – reprinted by Stewart Williams Publishers, 1970).

[16] The Welsh Wanderers held annual fixtures against Cheltenham College.

[17] E. W. Swanton, 'The County Championship', in *Barclay's World of Cricket* (Collins, 1980); R. W. Brooke, *A History of the County Cricket Championship* (Guinness Publishing, 1988).

[18] *Western Mail*, 6 July 1874.

[19] *Western Mail*, 10 August 1874.

[20] Ibid.

[21] Ibid.

[22] *Western Mail*, 14 August 1874.

[23] *South Wales Daily News*, 14 August 1875.

[24] *Western Mail*, 21 August, 3 September 1875.

[25] D. T. Smith, *The South Wales Cricket Club, 1859–1886* (privately published, 1986).

[26] Later known as The Kings School, Gloucester.

[27] Some records show he was a triple Blue, gaining Blues for cricket, rugby, and athletics (the hammer and the hurdles), but official records do not confirm his athletics Blue.

[28] In the 1867 encounter, Jones took thirteen wickets to give Christ College its first victory in the annual series.

[29] He was also a talented fielder and a report in *John Lillywhite's Cricketers Companion* for 1875 on the 1874 Varsity match observed how Jones 'fielded marvellously well at mid-off'.

[30] *Western Mail*, 29 May 1876.

[31] *Western Mail*, 28 June 1876.

[32] *Western Mail*, 6 July 1876.

[33] *Western Mail*, 4 July 1876.

[34] *Western Mail*, 16 May 1877.

[35] *Western Mail*, 30 May 1877.

[36] They originally agreed to a three-day game on 8, 9 and 10 July, but when the itinerary was finalized 10 July was dropped from the plans – *Western Mail*, 12 June 1878.

[37] *Western Mail*, 15 June 1878.

[38] *Western Mail*, 22 June 1878.

[39] *Western Mail*, 24 June 1878.

[40] *Western Mail*, 30 June, 2 July 1878.

[41] *Western Mail*, 5 July 1878.

[42] R. J. Harragan, 'The Australians come to Swansea', *Journal of the Cricket Society*, 14 (1989), 2, 30–5.

[43] *Western Mail*, 23 July 1879.

[44] Ibid.

[45] D. Smith and G. Williams, *Fields of Praise* (Cardiff, University of Wales Press, 1981), 31.

[46] Ibid, 3.

[47] Ibid, 5.

[48] *Frederick Lillywhite's Guide* 1880.

[49] Carmarthen subsequently withdrew from their match with Cardiff. For a full set of scores for the competition see D. T. Smith, op. cit., 43.

[50] *Llanelly Guardian* for June 1879, quoted in R. J. Harragan, *The History of Llanelli C.C.* (Llanelli Borough Council, 1990), 42.

[51] *South Wales Daily News*, 30 August 1879.

[52] The *Western Mail* for 23 April 1880 reported how the club had a balance of £41 in arrears, but expected this to be more than wiped out by the entrance fees to the competition.

Chapter 9

[1] W. G. Evans, *A History of Llandovery College* (Trustees of Llandovery College, 1981), 87.

[2] From C. P. Lewis's obituary in the *Llandovery School Magazine* for 1923. Evans, op. cit. also stated on p.71 that 'the school's rugby tradition really dates from his arrival'.

[3] *South Wales Daily News*, 18 June 1879.

[4] *South Wales Daily News*, 24 June 1880.

[5] *Western Mail*, 12 July 1880.

[6] *South Wales Daily News*, 15 July 1880.

[7] *Western Mail*, 1 August 1880.

[8] *Western Mail*, 3 June and 3 July 1881.

[9] *Western Mail*, 3 and 4 August 1881.

[10] C. P. Lewis's obituary in the *Carmarthen Journal* for 29 May 1923 ends with the remark 'he was picked to represent the English cricket eleven to play against Australia, but was unable to undertake the journey'. This was presumably Lord Harris's tour but there is no confirmation of this invitation. If he did receive an invitation, his duties at Trafalgar House, the school's boarding house, would have prevented him from obtaining leave to go on the lengthy winter tour. See D. T. Smith, *The South Wales C.C. 1859–1886* (privately published, 1986), 16.

[11] Lewis could be quite outspoken when he did not agree with matters, and it could have been the fact that he was not afraid to speak his mind which brought him into conflict with the warden. In 1881 he turned down a place in Wales's first rugby international with England, claiming that the Welsh team was not representative. He later became a member of Llandovery's town council and was mayor of the town in 1894/5 and 1904/5.

[12] Chapman was at the school between 1886 and 1896, and was the father of A. P. F. Chapman, who captained England seventeen times, first in 1926.

[13] *South Wales Daily News*, 1 July 1876.

[14] *Western Mail*, 7 June 1873. Morson also introduced rugby to the school.

[15] *South Wales Daily News*, 26 June 1875.

[16] D. T. W. Price, *A History of St. David's University College, Lampeter*, Vol. 1 (Cardiff, University of Wales Press, 1977).

[17] *Western Mail*, 25 July 1880.

[18] D. T. Smith, *First-class Cricketers from Christ College, Brecon* (privately published, 1979), 21–3. In 1897 and 1898 Gifford appeared in first-class cricket for the MCC, but he spent much of his time in Argentina and whilst out in South America helped to improve the standard of cricket in the region.

[19] Rawson can also claim an unusual soccer double, having played for Oxford University in the 1873/4 and 1876/7 FA cup finals, and refereeing the 1875/6 final.

[20] *Western Mail*, 27 June, 11 July 1881.

[21] J. M. Jenkins, D. Pierce and T. Auty, *Who's Who of Welsh International Rugby Players* (Wrexham, Bridge Books, 1991).

[22] *South Wales Daily News*, 1 August 1879.

[23] *South Wales Daily News*, 16 and 31 May 1881.

[24] *South Wales Daily News*, 31 July 1882.

[25] *Monmouthshire Merlin*, 3 July 1858.

[26] *Western Mail*, 27 July 1871.

[27] *Western Mail*, 27 June 1876.

[28] *Western Mail*, 19 June 1878.

[29] *Western Mail*, 10 May 1880.

[30] The *Evening Express* for 19 May 1888 recorded a match between the members of the 'Human Nature' Theatrical Company from the Theatre Royal and the 'Punch Bowl' Opera Company who were appearing at the Grand Theatre.

[31] *Western Mail*, 18 July 1873; *Central Glamorgan Gazette*, 9 August, 4 September 1878.

[32] *Monmouthshire Merlin*, 8 May 1873.

[33] *South Wales Daily News*, 28 July 1879.

[34] D. Moore (ed.), *Barry Centenary Book* (Barry, Centenary Book Committee, 1984), 309.

[35] *Western Mail*, 15 June 1874; *Western Mail*, 1, 15 and 28 June 1875.

[36] For example, in 1885 Riches persuaded William Pullen, the ex-Somerset and Gloucestershire batsman, now living in Cardiff to guest for the Taff Vale side against GWR Swindon. He topscored with eighty-seven, but Taff Vale lost by nine runs – *Western Mail*, 23 May 1885.

[37] *Western Mail*, 14 June 1876.

[38] R. J. Holt, *Sport and the British* (Oxford University Press, 1989), 87.

[39] *South Wales Daily News*, 11 June 1875; *Western Mail*, 21 April 1886.

[40] *Western Mail*, 11 May 1874.

[41] R. J. Holt, op. cit, 153.

[42] *Western Mail*, 19 June 1874.

[43] *Western Mail*, 16 September 1875.

[44] *South Wales Daily News*, 31 July 1875.

[45] *Western Mail*, 16 September 1875.

[46] *Western Mail*, 2 June 1881.

[47] *Western Mail*, 18 June 1873.

[48] R. Purday, *One Hundred Years of the Phoenix: the story of Panteg C.C. 1876–1976* (the club, 1977).

[49] The Brown Lenox Company was based at Millwall, and its works at Pontypridd manufactured anchors, chains and cables for the Admiralty. They also supplied chain cables for Brunel's *Great Eastern* steamship, liners such as the *Lusitania*, *Queen Elizabeth* and *Queen Mary*, plus warships *Rodney*, *Nelson* and *Hood*. The Pontypridd CC

Centenary Brochure (the club, 1970) also mentions that Brown Lenox provided money for cricket teas and equipment.

[50] B. Hughes, *The History of the Ystalyfera C.C.* (the club, 1980). There are no records of any games between 1890 and 1905. The same happened at Panteg where production at the steelworks ceased in the late 1870s and the side disbanded between 1880 and 1882 – see Purday, op. cit., 12.

[51] Gower Road took the name Gowerton in 1886, whilst the Elba Works began operations in 1872 and were purchased by Col. Wright in 1876.

[52] J. H. Rees, *One Hundred Years of Cricket in Gowerton, 1880–1980* (the club, 1980), 9. This was only a temporary lapse and after the grievances were settled Col. Wright's generosity and patronage allowed Gowerton to become one of the leading clubs in west Glamorgan.

[53] *South Wales Daily News*, 4 May 1885.

[54] D. Smith and G. Williams, *Fields of Praise* (Cardiff, University of Wales Press, 1981), 6.

[55] L. Senchal, 'The History and the Development of the South Wales Cricket Association, with reference to Ammanford Cricket Club', unpublished BA dissertation, University of Wales, 1987.

[56] *South Wales Daily News*, 28 May 1885.

[57] Rigauer believed that their involvement was simply because a worker's cricket team, or any other type of sports club, was good for business and could help boost profits. He noted how recreation shares many of the characteristics inherent in industrial production, namely discipline, authority, competition, achievement, rationalization and bureaucracy, so the encouragement of a workingmen's club would help the industrialist boost production as well as improving the health of his staff – B. Rigauer, *Sport and Work* (New York, Columbia University Press, 1981). See also N. L. Tranter, 'The Social and Occupational Structure of Organised Sport in Central Scotland during the nineteenth century', *International Journal of the History of Sport*, 4 (1987), 301–14; C. Lamoureux, 'Factory, Sport and Local Life', *International Journal of the History of Sport*, 7 (1990), 414–31, and R. J. Holt (ed.), *Sport and the Working Class in Modern Britain*, (Manchester, Manchester University Press, 1990).

[58] D. Smith and G. Williams, op. cit., 29.

[59] *Western Mail*, 30 July, 2 September 1873.

[60] *Western Mail*, 27 June 1876, 24 August 1878.

[61] Mountain Ash RFC was founded in 1875, Merthyr and Aberdare in 1876, Ammanford and Blaenavon in 1877, and Ebbw Vale in 1879. I am grateful to John Jenkins of Aberystwyth for details on the formation of these early clubs. For information on early soccer see B. Lile and D. Farmer, 'The Early Development of Association Football in South Wales 1890–1906', *Transactions of the Honourable Society of Cymmrodorion* (1984), 193–215.

[62] D. Smith and G. Williams, op. cit., 30.

[63] *South Wales Daily News*, 1 and 8 June 1880.

[64] The *South Wales Daily News* for 5 June 1875 noted how it soon 'became very popular with the young members of the Institution for whose recreative benefit and pleasure it was primarily established'. The youngsters won their first match watched by several influential inhabitants of the valley, with a number of prominent members of the Institution committee.

[65] A. Crane, B. Derrick and E. Donovan, *Pontypool's Heritage* (Newport, Starling Press, 1990).

[66] *Western Mail*, 29 August 1874.

[67] Ibid.

[68] This was similar to the situation in the industrial towns of Lancashire where there was equally strong church presence in workingmen's cricket. See J. Williams, 'Churches, Clogs and Cricket', *Journal of the Cricket Society*, 14, 3, 49–52.

[69] J. A. Jenkins and R. E. James, *The History of Nonconformity in Cardiff* (Cardiff, William Lewis, 1901).

[70] *South Wales Daily News*, 30 August 1881; *Dinas Powis Centenary Brochure 1882–1982* (the club, 1982).

[71] It was assisted by the continued growth of the YMCA movement and the popularity of Sunday Schools, who held games on outings or arranged special matches with junior clubs. The Charles Street Wesleyan Church had fixtures with the Cardiff Drapers and Engineers, plus an annual outing to Llandaff by their Sunday School boys during which they challenged a side raised by the Bishop of Llandaff. *Western Mail* and *South Wales Daily News*, 16 July 1880.

[72] J. B. Cowell, 'Anglesey Cricket in the Nineteenth Century', *Transactions of the Anglesey Antiquarian Society and Field Club*, (1976), 84–94.

[73] K. A. Sandiford, 'Cricket and the Victorian Society', *Journal of Social History* (Winter, 1983), 303–17.

[74] K. O. Morgan, *Rebirth of a Nation* (Oxford University Press, 1981).

Chapter 10

[1] This is similar to the per capita index used by J. Bale in *Sport and Place: A Geography of Sport in England, Scotland and Wales* (Hurst, 1982), but in this case just the male population value, rather than the total population for each registration sub-district, was used.

[2] In part these are statistical quirks caused by the small number of clubs, with never more than six in Neath nor three in Bridgend during any one season.

[3] R. T. Mole, *The History of Ponthir C.C.* (Cwmbran, Village Publishing, 1983).

[4] For further information on the growth of Cardiff see M. J. Daunton, *Coal Metropolis: Cardiff 1870–1914* (Leicester University Press, 1977); H. Carter, 'Cardiff' in G. Gordon (ed.), *Regional Cities in the U.K. 1890–1980* (Macmillan, 1981), 171–90; E. L. Chappell, *History of the Port of Cardiff* (Cardiff, Priory Press, 1939); W. Rees, *Cardiff: A History of the City* (Cardiff Corporation, 1962).

[5] The *Cambrian Daily Leader* 1851–85; *Cardiff and Merthyr Guardian* 1851–85; *Western Mail* 1869–85; *South Wales Daily News* 1872–85.

[6] *Western Mail*, 14 June, 19 September 1878.

[7] *South Wales Daily News*, 21 April 1884.

[8] *South Wales Daily News*, 14 July 1885.

[9] *Western Mail*, 12 May 1885.

[10] For further information on the process of suburban development in Cardiff see A. K. Hignell, 'Patterns and Processes of Suburban Development in North Cardiff, 1850–1919', (unpublished Ph.D. thesis, University of Wales, 1987).

[11] Amongst the buildings he designed were Pierhead Chambers, the Great Western Hotel, and the Prince of Wales Theatre.

[12] *Western Mail*, 7 March 1895; see A. K. Hignell, op. cit.

[13] *Evening Express*, 23 November 1894.

[14] This latter factor explains why many sides both in the suburbs and elsewhere failed

to find a permanent home of their own in the early days and were forced to lead a gypsy-like existence, until a regular venue was obtained.

[15] Letter dated April 1886 in Fairwater CC minute book, GRO CL/MS 4.975, 4.976.

[16] Entry dated 5 May 1903 in Llanishen Parish Council minute book, GRO P/55/3.

[17] A. K. Hignell, op. cit.

[18] For further information on the history of the Arms Park see D. Parry-Jones, *Taff's Acre: A History and Celebration of Cardiff Arms Park* (Collins Willow, 1984).

[19] *Western Mail*, 15 June 1874.

[20] Quoted in A. K. Hignell, *The Cricket Grounds of Glamorgan* (Nottingham, Association of Cricket Statisticians, 1985), 5.

[21] The same happened in Newport where George Rosser played in 1881 for Pontymister, Malpas, Rudry, North Risca, Machen and Bassaleg, as well as the town club. Rosser Diaries, Newport Reference Library, 74.40 1–9.

[22] Fairwater CC minute book op. cit.

[23] *The Cambrian*, 23 September 1864; *Western Mail*, 18 September 1871. Swansea's professional William Bancroft junior also coached at Kilvey, Gorseinon and the Swansea Grammar School.

[24] Fairwater CC Annual Report for 1894 in Fairwater CC minute book, op. cit.

Chapter 11

[1] *Western Mail*, 17 June 1880.

[2] *Western Mail*, 21 June 1880.

[3] For a full breakdown of the scores and the activities of the club see D. T. Smith, *The South Wales Cricket Club 1859–1886* (privately published, 1986).

[4] It was held on the neutral ground of Widemarsh Common, Hereford.

[5] *Western Mail*, 21 April 1882.

[6] D. T. Smith, op. cit., 46.

[7] *Western Mail*, 20 July 1882.

[8] *Western Mail*, 30 September 1882.

[9] D. T. Smith, op. cit., 47.

[10] Ibid.

[11] One of them was George Rosser the leading all-rounder with Newport. Rosser Diaries for 14 September 1883. Newport Reference Library, 74.40 1–9.

[12] *Western Mail*, 2 September 1883.

[13] *Llanelly Guardian*, 2 September 1883.

[14] *Western Mail*, 17 September 1883.

[15] *South Wales Daily News*, 17 September 1883.

[16] *Rosser Diaries*, op. cit.

[17] *Western Mail*, 25 August 1883.

[18] W. G. Grace, *Cricket* (Bristol, Arrowsmith, 1891), 79.

[19] *Pontypool Free Press*, 27 July 1872.

[20] *South Wales Daily News*, 21, 23 and 28 September 1880.

[21] *Western Mail*, 4 April 1884.

[22] *Western Mail*, 30 August 1884.

[23] *South Wales Daily News*, 1 September 1874.

[24] *Western Mail*, 15 September 1884.

[25] *Western Mail*, 10 August 1885.

[26] *Western Mail* and *South Wales Daily News*, 17 August 1885.

[27] *South Wales Daily News*, 20 August 1885. Cadoxton 'wired to say they cannot get a team and consequently they have retired from the contest'.

[28] *The Cambrian*, 1 June 1883; *Western Mail*, 28 May 1883.

[29] *The Cambrian*, 20 August 1886.

[30] *Swansea Herald*, 18 August 1886.

[31] Ibid.

[32] *Swansea Herald*, 25 August 1886.

[33] Ibid.

[34] *Swansea Herald*, 18 August 1886.

[35] *Cardiff C.C. 1867–1967* (the club, 1967), 17.

[36] *The Cambrian*, 9 October 1868.

[37] *Western Mail*, 19 May 1869.

[38] *The Cambrian*, 29 July 1868.

[39] *Western Mail*, 10 August 1869.

[40] *Western Mail*, 11 August 1874.

[41] 'Cricket', in W. J. T. Collins (ed.), *Newport Athletic Club: the record of half a century, 1875–1925* (the club, 1925). See also the update by the club in 1975 to celebrate the club's centenary, especially the section on cricket by J. F. Burrell and W. E. Davies.

[42] Newport CC minute books and accounts 1880–99. I am very grateful to Duncan Pierce of Heytesbury for this information.

[43] J. F. Burrell, 'The Story of Arthur Silverlock', *Cricket Statistician*, 15 (1976), 19–22.

[44] Newport CC Special Rules for 1900.

[45] Newport CC Annual Reports 1880-1899.

[46] His obituary in *The Cambrian* for 27 April 1906 listed the Settle clubs, Dunfermline and Merchiston Castle.

[47] *The Cambrian*, 2 June 1893.

[48] During this time he was assisted by other professionals called Harrison and Henry Street, an aggressive batsman who played county cricket for Derbyshire in 1887.

[49] Rosser Diaries for 24 September 1880, op. cit.; *Western Mail,* 7 August 1888.

[50] Fairwater CC minute books, GRO CL/MS 4.975.

[51] G. Williams, 'How Amateur was My Valley: Professional Sport and National Identity in Wales, 1890–1914', *British Journal of Sports History*, 2 (1985) 248–69.

[52] A. Mason, *Association Football and English Society* (Brighton, 1980), 70–8.

[53] G. Williams, op. cit.

[54] *South Wales Daily News*, 8 November 1905.

[55] Quoted in R. Sissons, *The Players: A Social History of the Professional Cricketer* (Kingswood Press, 1988).

[56] Midwinter outlined how Grace was paid £1,500 for the 1873/4 tour to Australia, and he estimated that the Doctor grossed £120,000 from cricket – see E. A. Midwinter, *W. G. Grace: His Life and Times* (Collins, 1981).

[57] *Cardiff C.C. 1867–1967*, op. cit., 27.

Chapter 12

[1] G. Williams, 'How Amateur was My Valley: Professional Sport and National Identity in Wales, 1890–1914', *British Journal of Sports History*, 2 (1985) 248–69.

[2] R. Sissons, *The Players: A Social History of the Professional Cricketer* (Kingswood Press, 1988).

[3] G. Plumptre, *The Golden Age of Cricket* (Macdonald Queen Anne, 1990), 157.

⁴ Ibid., 167.

⁵ R. L. Arrowsmith, 'Country House Cricket', in E. W. Swanton (ed.), *Barclay's World of Cricket* (Collins, 1980), 560.

⁶ Ibid.

⁷ *Star of Gwent*, 27 July 1867.

⁸ One descendant of the Bosanquet family was B. J. T. Bosanquet, who played for Oxford University and Middlesex, and Test cricket for England and is reputed to have 'invented' the googly on the billiard table at Dingestow Court.

⁹ K. E. Kissack, *Victorian Monmouth* (Ledbury, Bosbury Press, 1986).

¹⁰ *Monmouthshire Mercury*, June 1857. His son, the Hon. Charles Rolls, went on to establish the successful motoring partnership with Henry Royce, and created Rolls-Royce, before being killed in a flying accident in 1910. See J. W. Axten, *Hon. Charles Stewart Rolls 1877–1910* (Monmouthshire Historical and Educational Trust, 1977).

¹¹ *Monmouthshire Merlin*, 9 August 1862.

¹² *South Wales Daily News*, 5 July 1873.

¹³ *Monmouthshire Merlin*, 24 August 1861.

¹⁴ *Monmouth Beacon*, 28 October 1871.

¹⁵ *Western Mail*, 26 August, 3 and 17 September 1872.

¹⁶ Ibid.

¹⁷ *Monmouth Beacon*, 29 August 1874.

¹⁸ *Monmouth Beacon*, 28 August 1875; *Western Mail*, 26 August 1875.

¹⁹ *Western Mail*, 14 July, 10 and 25 August 1876.

²⁰ *Monmouth Beacon*, 7 July 1883.

²¹ *Western Mail*, 8 and 10 September 1874; *Evening Express*, 4 and 19 September 1888. See also R. Phillips, *Tredegar: The History of an Agricultural Estate* (Tredegar Memorial Trust, 1990).

²² *Evening Express*, 9 July 1888; *Western Mail*, 25 August 1871.

²³ I. Waters, *Piercefield* (Chepstow, Comber Press, 1975), 27–8.

²⁴ *Chepstow Weekly Advertiser*, May 1882.

²⁵ *Western Mail*, 7 July, 25 August 1870.

²⁶ *Western Mail*, 19 July 1871. The marquess was not always so generous, and for later matches by the Household XI, and Glamorgan, he charged an entrance fee to the Arms Park. See 'South Wales Gossip', in *Amateur Sport*, 12 June 1889.

²⁷ *Western Mail*, 12 August 1873.

²⁸ *Western Mail*, 12 September 1873.

²⁹ *Cardiff C.C. 1867–1967* (the club, 1967), 18.

³⁰ *Western Mail*, 20 June 1874.

³¹ *Western Mail*, 4 August 1874.

³² *Western Mail*, ibid.

³³ *Lillywhite's Scores and Biographies for 1874*.

³⁴ *Western Mail*, 10 August 1874.

³⁵ *Western Mail*, 8 and 10 September 1874.

³⁶ *Western Mail*, 14 and 21 June 1875.

³⁷ One letter to the pro-Bute newspaper questioned this description, and asked 'How is it that these clubs have become so designated?' *Western Mail*, 20 August 1875.

³⁸ *Western Mail*, 19 August 1875.

³⁹ The earl appeared against Cogan Pill in 1872. *Western Mail*, 26 August 1872. For background information on Lord Windsor, see W. P. Williams, 'A Monograph of the Windsor Family' (Cardiff, Daniel Owen, 1879).

[40] C. Despres (ed.), *St Fagan's C.C. 1862–1987: 125 Not Out* (the club, 1988), 4.

[41] *Western Mail*, 28 September 1872.

[42] D. Moore (ed.), *Barry Centenary Book* (Barry, Centenary Book Committee, 1984).

[43] *Western Mail*, 28 July 1881.

[44] *Western Mail*, 16 September 1876.

[45] Fairwater C.C. minute book, GRO CL/MS 4.975, 4.976.

[46] *Southerndown C.C. Centenary Season Handbook* (the club, 1988), 7.

[47] B. L. James and D. J. Francis, *Cowbridge and Llanblethian – Past and Present* (Barry, Stewart Williams, 1979), Part IV, 171–6.

[48] *Western Mail*, 18 June 1897. Ebsworth enjoyed all country sports and was a fine shot – his splendid home was decorated with tokens of his prowess, and in the hall was a huge stuffed brown bear which Ebsworth shot on a business trip to St Petersburg. He also promoted croquet and hockey on his private ground and employed a groundsman to look after the wicket.

[49] J. H. Rees, *One Hundred Years of Cricket in Gowerton, 1880–1980* (the club, 1980); H. D. Morgan, *A Short History of Morriston C.C.* (the club, 1990).

[50] *The Cambrian*, 29 December 1880.

[51] D. H. James, *The Briton Ferry Steelworks C.C. 1896–1974* (the club, 1975). The Jersey estate games proved so popular that in 1881 the earl decided to lay a permanent wicket for the less affluent cricketers of the Briton Ferry area, from which Briton Ferry Town CC came into being, followed in 1890 by the granting of land for a wicket for the employees at the town's steelworks, which developed into the Briton Ferry Steelworks club in 1896.

[52] B. Lile, 'The Lost Domain: The Williamses of Killay House and their relatives. Part Two', *Gower*, 40, (1989) 65–75; see also Part One, *Gower*, 39, 30–43, and Part Three, *Gower*, 41, 70–8.

[53] G. B. Williams, 'A Family Budget', 146–7 quoted in B. Lile, op. cit. George's younger brothers Aubrey, Milbourne and Dyson were regular participants in these games and Dyson went on to secure a place in the Glamorgan side of the early 1900s. He also served as their treasurer from 1913, but committed suicide in 1922. See R. J. Harragan, 'The Tragic Dyson Williams', *The Cricket Statistician* (Autumn, 1985), 9–10.

[54] *Western Mail*, 1 September 1879. The side included South Wales members Penry Lloyd and A. J. de Winton.

[55] *South Wales Daily News*, 9 June 1884.

[56] *South Wales Daily News* and *Western Mail*, 11 August 1881.

[57] *South Wales Daily News*, 26 September 1881.

[58] P. Jenkins, *The Making of a Ruling Class – The Glamorgan Gentry 1640–1790* (Cambridge University, 1983), 196–216.

Chapter 13

[1] *South Wales Daily News*, 16 May 1881.

[2] *South Wales Daily News*, 29 August 1881.

[3] *Western Mail*, 9 July, 9, 10 and 11 September 1881; both W. G. and E. M. Grace appeared at Newport for the English side which won on first innings by scoring ninety-six runs as opposed to Newport's seventy-two.

[4] The week began with a game between Mr Berkeley's XI and the Welsh Wanderers, followed by a two-day match between the South Wales CC and the MCC, and Cardiff against William Morgan's XI. Then there was another two-day match between Cardiff

and Sir Julian Spearman's XI, before the final match of the week involving Cardiff and Malpas – *Western Mail*, 4 August 1881.

⁵ *Western Mail*, 9 August 1881.

⁶ Seven local sides plus Llanelly's second eleven, entered the competition in its first year, each paying an entrance fee of 3d. In a bid to foster local talent all of Llanelly's first team was banned from appearing. At the end of the competition, a Llanelly and District XVIII was selected to play an eleven assembled by C. P. Lewis – *South Wales Daily News*, 8 September 1881; R. J. Harragan, *The History of Llanelli C.C.* (Llanelli Borough Council, 1990), Chapter 6.

⁷ *Western Mail*, 21 April 1882.

⁸ *Western Mail*, 12 August 1882.

⁹ *Western Mail*, 22 April 1881.

¹⁰ *South Wales Daily News*, 10 July 1883.

¹¹ It was described in some papers as a North Wales XII.

¹² James Lillywhite's *Cricketers' Annual* for 1879 and 1883.

¹³ *Western Mail*, 19 April 1886.

¹⁴ *South Wales Daily News*, 5 April 1886.

¹⁵ *Llanelly Guardian*, 26 August 1886.

¹⁶ *Western Mail*, 7, 8 and 10 May 1886.

¹⁷ *South Wales Daily News*, 3 May 1886.

¹⁸ *Western Mail*, 10 April 1886.

¹⁹ *Western Mail*, 6 December 1886; D. T. Smith, *The South Wales C.C. 1859–1886* (privately published, 1986), 15.

²⁰ D. T. Smith, ibid., 15.

²¹ *Evening Express*, 4 June 1888.

²² K. E. Kissack, *Victorian Monmouth* (Ledbury, Bosbury Press, 1986), 183–7. Jupp toured Australia with Grace's XI in 1873/4 and Lillywhite's team in 1876/7.

²³ *Western Mail*, 13 August 1884.

²⁴ *Western Mail*, 19 April 1886.

²⁵ *South Wales Daily News*, 3 August, 11 August 1885. Cobden also secured games with Shropshire, I Zingari, Derbyshire Friars, Christ Church Cardinals and the Heythrop Hunt, and they were sufficiently strong to defeat Herefordshire. He was also able to arrange a challenge with the powerful Worcestershire side, but it ended in a heavy innings defeat for his team.

²⁶ James Lillywhite's *Cricketers' Annual* for 1890.

²⁷ K. O. Morgan, *Rebirth of a Nation* (Oxford University Press, 1981), 25.

²⁸ D. Smith and G. Williams, *Fields of Praise* (Cardiff, University of Wales Press, 1981).

²⁹ R. Sissons, *The Players: A Social History of the Professional Cricketer* (Kingswood Press, 1988).

³⁰ *South Wales Daily News*, 13 April 1886.

³¹ *South Wales Daily News*, 21 June 1886.

³² Regional rivalries also retarded the formation of county clubs in England. Disputes between Canterbury, Gravesend and Maidstone prevented the formation of Kent CCC until 1870, whilst friction between Liverpool and Manchester hampered the formation of Lancashire CCC.

³³ A. K. Hignell, *The History of Glamorgan C.C.C.* (Christopher Helm, 1988), 18.

³⁴ Ibid., 18–19. It was proposed by Edward Jones of Cardiff and seconded by Mr Johns of Llwynypia.

³⁵ *South Wales Daily News*, 9 July 1888.

[36] Ibid.

[37] Glamorgan CCC minute books 1888–1910. I am most grateful to the club for allowing me access to these, which are held at the club's office at Sophia Gardens.

[38] *South Wales Daily News*, 9 July 1888.

[39] Morrah observed how there was great confidence throughout much of late Victorian society – 'this era was one of solidity, the building up of British prosperity and security after the desperate struggle of the Napoleonic Wars. As the age progressed its paramount characteristic became self-confidence'. P. Morrah, *The Golden Age of Cricket* (Eyre and Spottiswoode, 1967).

[40] Glamorgan CCC minute books, op. cit.

[41] J. H. Brain's private records. I am grateful to Chris Brain for access to these records which his family keep at The Old Brewery.

[42] *Evening Express*, 9 August 1888.

[43] J. H. Brain's private records, op. cit.

[44] For details on all of these Glamorgan players see A. K. Hignell, *A Who's Who of Glamorgan C.C.C.* (Derby, Breedon Books, 1992).

[45] See the *South Wales Daily News* and *Western Mail* for mid-June 1889.

[46] *South Wales Daily News* and *Western Mail*, 22 and 23 June 1889. For general comments on the 1889 season, see also 'South Wales Gossip', *Amateur Sport*, No. 1, 24 April to No. 26, 16 October.

[47] Glamorgan CCC minute books, op. cit.

[48] *Western Mail*, 20 and 21 August 1889.

[49] *Western Mail*, 22 and 23 August 1889.

[50] Glamorgan CCC minute books, ibid.

[51] *Western Mail*, 30 August 1890.

[52] *Western Mail*, 27 May 1890.

Chapter 14

[1] Glamorgan CCC minute book 1888–1910.

[2] The side kept these colours until introducing blue and gold with a different motif in the early 1930s.

[3] A. K. Hignell, *A Who's Who of Glamorgan C.C.C.* (Derby, Breedon Books 1992). Brain scored over 2,300 runs for the English county including a career best 143 against Surrey.

[4] *Western Mail*, 16 May 1891.

[5] Glamorgan CCC minute book, op. cit.

[6] *Western Mail*, 24 and 25 August 1892.

[7] Glamorgan CCC minute book, op. cit. With hindsight, Glamorgan made the right decision about Porter as a few years later he broke down with a severe back injury and was forced into retirement. He later went into umpiring, but died in 1908 after getting sunstroke at his Derbyshire home.

[8] D. Frith, *By His Own Hand* (Stanley Paul, 1991).

[9] Glamorgan CCC minute book, op. cit.

[10] *Evening Express*, 30 August 1894.

[11] *South Wales Daily News*, 21 June 1890.

[12] Glamorgan CCC minute book, op. cit. The offer may have also prevented the Welsh rugby international from going north to rugby league.

[13] *Western Mail*, 28 and 29 July 1896.

[14] In 1893 William Brain achieved a unique feat by recording a hat-trick of stumpings

off three consecutive balls in a match against Somerset.

[15] A. K. Hignell op. cit., 102, 170–1.

[16] *Western Mail*, 3 and 4 August 1895.

[17] Ibid. Lowe was offered a lucrative contract with a South African club in 1902, but he opted to stay with Cardiff, for whom he played until retiring in 1906.

[18] Those whose birth details are unknown have been omitted. See A. K. Hignell, op. cit.

[19] Hillyard played county cricket for Somerset in 1882/3 and Lancashire in 1884/5, before leaving Oxford and entering the church. Despite the fact that he was a vicar in Windsor and East Rowley, he remained a close acquaintance of Joseph Brain and made his Glamorgan debut against Gloucestershire in 1891. Revd Arthur Batty was a vicar from Yorkshire and Durham who had been up at Oxford with William Brain, whilst Revd Cyril Kindersley, was an Old Harrovian who had been up at Cambridge with Ralph Sweet-Escott.

[20] Courtis became lord mayor of Cardiff in 1911, but sadly Mendelson committed suicide in South Africa in 1902 after moving there from his native New Zealand to seek new opportunities; A. K. Hignell, 'Overtures on Mendelson', *Journal of the Cricket Society*, (Spring 1992), 24–7.

[21] J. M. Jenkins, D. Pierce and T. Auty, *A Who's Who of Welsh International Rugby Players* (Wrexham, Bridge Books, 1991). Barlow and Ingledew both had the right social credentials to play alongside the English gentlemen as they were solicitors in Cardiff. Norman Biggs was a policeman, but he met with a decidedly sticky fate in 1908 when he joined the Nigerian Police and was killed by a poisoned arrow during a native uprising.

[22] K. O. Morgan, *Rebirth of a Nation* (Oxford University Press, 1981), 113.

[23] A. K. Hignell, *The History of Glamorgan C.C.C.* (Christopher Helm, 1988).

[24] *Western Mail*, 5 June 1897.

[25] *Western Mail*, 9 June 1897.

[26] *Western Mail*, 20 June 1897; *South Wales Daily News*, 25 July 1897.

[27] *Western Mail*, 4 August 1897.

[28] *Western Mail*, 18 June, 31 July, 21 August 1898.

[29] *Western Mail*, 14 June 1899.

[30] *Western Mail*, 28 June 1899.

[31] *Western Mail*, 30 June, 11 and 20 August 1899.

[32] In their Annual Report for 1899, the officials expressed their sadness at the 'unsatisfactory balance sheet and call upon members to do all they can to improve the finances by introducing new members or procuring further donations'.

[33] *Western Mail*, 6 and 30 June, 1 August 1900.

[34] *Western Mail*, 20 July 1900.

[35] A. K. Hignell, *The Cricket Grounds of Glamorgan* (Nottingham, A.C.S. 1985), 6.

[36] Ibid., 12.

[37] *South Wales Daily News*, 5 August 1902.

[38] Glamorgan CCC minute book, op. cit.

[39] *South Wales Daily News*, 8 and 9 August 1905.

[40] Creber bowled over 500 overs in 1905, and took 100 wickets at fifteen apiece and, despite all the hard work, the left-arm spinner repeated the feat the following year with 112 wickets at an average of 13.81. He also found a useful partner in another English professional, Kent-born Jack Nash who joined Cardiff in 1900, and the off-spinner took 10–93 against the MCC in 1903 and 8–31 against Devon in 1904.

[41] A. K. Hignell, *A Who's Who of Glamorgan C.C.C.* (Derby, Breedon Books, 1992).

[42] He scored 183 in Glamorgan's first innings against Monmouthshire as they totalled

429–9 dec. and won by an innings and 252 runs – *Western Mail*, 18 and 19 June 1904.

[43] *Western Mail*, 1 July 1905; 27 June 1906.

[44] A. K. Hignell, op. cit., 217–18.

[45] Their total of 540 against Devon, at the time, was a record total by a minor county, and it still remains the third highest. Riches made 171 and J. H. Brain 117 – *Western Mail*, 18 and 19 July 1907. The following day at Blandford Forum, Riches hit 217 against Dorset, with his Cardiff colleague Edward Sweet-Escott scoring 104.

[46] *Western Mail*, 31 August, 1 September 1907.

[47] *Western Mail*, 12 September 1907.

[48] They tied with Monmouthshire for first place in the Western group, and proceeded to the semi-final stage after Sir Francis Lacey, the MCC secretary, decided in their favour on the somewhat dubious grounds that they had been runners-up the year before.

[49] *Western Mail*, 5 and 6 September 1908.

[50] *Western Mail*, 8 and 9 September 1908 – Barnes became a publican in north Wales after the Great War and, despite being into his fifties, appeared for Wales in their first-class matches in the 1920s.

[51] *Western Mail*, 2 July 1909.

[52] *Western Mail*, 23 and 30 July, 12 August 1909.

[53] *Western Mail*, 24 and 25 August 1909.

[54] *Western Mail*, 1 and 2 September 1909.

[55] *Western Mail*, 24 August 1890.

[56] J. F. Burrell and W. E. Davies, 'Cricket', in *The Centenary History of Newport Athletic Club 1875–1975* (Cwmbran, Starling Press, 1974), 91–101.

[57] *Western Mail*, 19 August 1894.

[58] J. F. Burrell, 'The Story of Arthur Silverlock', *Cricket Statistician*, 15 (1976), 19–22.

[59] *Western Mail*, 24 June 1900.

[60] *Western Mail*, 20 July 1901.

[61] *Western Mail*, 17 August 1902.

[62] *Western Mail*, 4 June 1905.

[63] His cousin Gordon Phillips was also a fiery fast bowler, and the former Repton schoolboy took 8–114 as Monmouthshire recorded an innings victory over Glamorgan in 1908.

[64] E. Anthony, *Herefordshire Cricket* (Hereford, Anthony Brothers, 1903), 126.

[65] R. J. Harragan, *The History of Llanelli C.C.* (Llanelli Borough Council, 1990), Chapter 8.

[66] *South Wales Daily News*, 8 July 1906.

[67] *Western Mail*, 25 July 1906.

[68] In 1908 Whittington scored 188 as Glamorgan won by an innings and 259 runs at Llanelli, whilst at Newport, Silverlock scored 142 as Monmouthshire also recorded an innings victory. Things went from bad to worse in 1909 as Silverlock scored 246 not out at Newport, and Creber took 13–67 at Llanelli and 10–93 at Swansea as Carmarthenshire slumped to further heavy defeats. *Western Mail*, 23 July, 18 August 1908; 18 June, 11 July 1909.

[69] *Western Mail*, 17 June 1910 – this remains Glamorgan's largest margin of victory.

[70] *Western Mail*, 12 July 1911.

[71] *Western Mail*, 27 June 1914.

Chapter 15

[1] P. Scott, 'Cricket and the Religious World in the Victorian Period', *Church Quarterly*, 3, (1970), 134–44.

[2] C. Despres (ed.), *St Fagan's C.C. 1862–1987: 125 Not Out* (the club, 1988), 5.

[3] *Western Mail*, 24 October 1984.

[4] *The Cricketer*, 6 September 1906.

[5] *The Cambrian*, 20 August 1908.

[6] J. H. Morgan, *Glamorgan County Cricket* (Convoy Press, 1952).

[7] *Western Mail*, 23 and 24 July 1901.

[8] *The Cambrian*, 14 July 1905. The Essex side then travelled to Llanelli to play the Carmarthenshire side.

[9] I am grateful to Gwyn Gratton of Briton Ferry for access to Neath CC's archives which contain reports, scorecards and accounts of these games.

[10] Ibid.

[11] Ibid.

[12] *Western Mail*, 14 June 1886.

[13] *South Wales Daily News*, 8, 20 and 22 September 1886.

[14] *South Wales Daily News*, 27 April 1887.

[15] The new Union also co-ordinated fixtures in order to maximize the use of the Arms Park, and selected an XVIII which challenged Cardiff. *Evening Express*, 26 May 1888; *Western Mail*, 9 July, 18 August 1888.

[16] J. H. Rees, *One Hundred Years of Cricket in Gowerton 1880–1980* (the club, 1980), 11. In 1893 the league was known as the Swansea and District Cricket Union, before the name changed the following year.

[17] Ibid., 12.

[18] *Western Mail*, 27 August 1894.

[19] J. H. Rees, op. cit., 15–16.

[20] *Western Mail Cricket Annual* for 1902 – GRO D/D x 294/4/13. *Evening Express*, 21 November 1894.

[21] A. Jacks (ed.), *Chepstow C.C. 1838–1988: The First 150 Years* (the club, 1989), 16.

[22] Vogler also appeared for Middlesex and the MCC. See R. J. Harragan, *History of Llanelli C.C.* (Llanelli Borough Council, 1990), 85.

[23] Neath CC records, op. cit.

[24] After retiring from club cricket, Bagshaw became a first-class umpire and when he died in 1927 he was buried in his umpire's coat. For details on Bates and Webb, see A. K. Hignell, *A Who's Who of Glamorgan C.C.C.* (Derby, Breedon Books, 1992), 42–3, 213–14.

[25] D. H. James, *Briton Ferry Steelworks C.C. 1896–1974* (the club, 1975), 8.

[26] R. J. Harragan, op. cit., 82.

[27] *Cardiff C.C. 1867–1967* (the club, 1967), 35.

[28] Neath CC records, op cit. A total of £13 2s 8d was taken in 1904.

[29] *Cardiff C.C. 1867–1967*, op. cit. – 'They had not been on the ground for many minutes before they complained that there were no horses and demanded their money back: they were unfortunate, of course.'

[30] R. J. Harragan, op. cit., 78–9.

[31] *Western Mail*, 4 September 1894; *South Wales Daily News*, 3 September 1886; *Evening Express*, 14 August 1894.

[32] *Western Mail Cricket Annual* for 1902, op. cit.

[33] Neath CC records, op. cit.

[34] *The Cambrian*, 11 June 1894.

[35] D. Frith, *The Golden Age of Cricket 1890–1914* (Lutterworth Press, 1978); P. Morrah, *The Golden Age of Cricket* (Eyre and Spottiswoode, 1967).

[36] B. Darwin *W. G. Grace* (1934); E. A. Midwinter, *W. G. Grace. His Life and Times* (Collins, 1981); M. Down, *Archie: A Biography of A. C. MacLaren* (Allen and Unwin, 1981); S. Wilde, *Ranji – a Genius Rich and Strange* (London, Kingswood Press, 1990).

[37] J. Arlott, in S. Nowell-Smith (ed.), *Edwardian England 1901–1910* (1964).

[38] A. K. Hignell, op. cit., 220–1.

[39] G. Plumptre, *The Golden Age of Cricket* (Macdonald, Queen Anne, 1990), 7.

[40] A. K. Hignell,*The History of Glamorgan C.C.C.* (Christopher Helm, 1988), 53–4.

[41] Glamorgan CCC minute book for 1911.

[42] A. K. Hignell, (1988), op. cit., 63–4.

[43] Ibid., 66–9.

[44] Monmouthshire CCC Annual Report for 1929.

[45] A. K. Hignell, (1988), op. cit., 105–6.

[46] G. Evans, *Pontardulais Cricket Club Centenary, 1876-1976* (the club)

[47] *Western Mail*, 29 April 1926. A tenth club, Pontypridd, was also invited to take part, but they opted for friendlies instead – see A. Meredith, *A Hard Slog: The History of the South Wales Cricket Association 1926–1986* (Llandeilo, Towy Press, 1987).

[48] Meredith, op. cit., 10.

[49] R. J. Harragan, 'The Tragic Dyson Williams', *The Cricket Statistician*, (Autumn, 1985), 9–10.

[50] R. Phillips, *Tredegar: The History of an Agricultural Estate* (Tredegar Memorial Trust, 1990).

[51] R. L. Arrowsmith, 'Country House Cricket', in E. W. Swanton (ed.), *Barclay's World of Cricket* (Collins, 1980), 560.

Chapter 16

[1] This is similar to the model produced for South Australia in C. Forster, 'Cricket and Community', in R. L. Heathcote, *The Australian Experience: Essays in Land Settlement and Resource Management* (Sydney, Longman, 1988). See also C. Forster, 'Sport, Society and Space: The Changing Geography of Country Cricket in South Australia', *Sporting Traditions*, 2, (1986), 23–47.

[2] P. Jackson, *The Cardiff City Story* (S. A. Brain, Cardiff, 1974); J. Crooks, *Cardiff City Chronology 1920–1988* (Pontypool, Sargeant Brothers, 1986).

[3] *Western Mail*, 28 May 1870; *South Wales Daily News*, 19 April for both 1876 and 1881.

[4] A. R. Lewis in E. W. Swanton (ed.), *Barclays World of Cricket* (Collins,1980), 513.

[5] P. Jenkins, *The Making of a Ruling Class – The Glamorgan Gentry 1640–1790* (Cambridge University Press, 1983), 213.

[6] G. Williams, 'Rugby Union', in A. Mason (ed.), *Sport in Britain: A Social History* (Collins, 1989), 308–43.

[7] G. Williams, 'From Popular Culture to Public Cliché: Image and Identity in Wales 1890–1914', in J. A. Mangen (ed.), *Pleasure, Profit, Proselytism: British Culture and Sport at Home and Abroad 1700–1914* (Frank Cass, 1988), 128–49.

[8] *Western Mail*, 13 and 14 June 1905. This remains their lowest ever total.

[9] *Western Mail*, 3 and 4 May 1905.

[10] *Western Mail*, 19 April 1886.

[11] *South Wales Daily News*, 10 September 1886.

[12] *Western Mail*, 20 July 1886. The letter begins 'despite the fact that there are a number of clubs in south Wales, no one can deny that the summer game is not as popular

as the winter one . . . When one looks for a reason, it is not far to seek one. Local cricketers have nothing to aspire to. They are confined to one or two clubs, and the captaincy of these is about the highest place they can attain. It would naturally be supposed that the town clubs would be open to aspirants, but these clubs are practically closed to many excellent cricketers. The town [rugby] football clubs do not afford a parallel. Merit is there more recognised and until that is the case with cricket, its present sluggish state will continue'.

[13] G. Williams, (1989), op. cit., 308.

[14] G. Williams, 'How Professional was my Valley. Professional Sport and National Identity in Wales, 1890–1914', *British Journal of Sports History*, 2 (1985), 248–69.

[15] *Western Mail*, 9 August 1881.

[16] *Welsh Outlook*, February 1914, 18–19.

Index